Carrie Holba

E86$2345   I

D0915881

Building Library Collections

by Arthur Curley and Dorothy Broderick

Sixth Edition

The Scarecrow Press, Inc.

Metuchen, N.J., and London

1985

Library of Congress Cataloging in Publication Data

Curley, Arthur.
   Building library collections.

    Rev. ed. of: Building library collections / by Wallace
John Bonk and Rose Mary Magrill. 5th ed. 1979.
   Bibliography: p.
   Includes index.
    1. Collection development (Libraries) 2. Book
selection. I. Broderick, Dorothy M. II. Bonk, Wallace
John, 1923-   . Building library collections.
III. Title.
Z687.C87 1985   025.2'1   84-23665
ISBN 0-8108-1776-4

Copyright © 1985 by Arthur Curley and Dorothy Broderick

Manufactured in the United States of America

Table of Contents

INTRODUCTION

When Mary Duncan Carter and Wallace J. Bonk produced the first edition of *Building Library Collections*, more than a quarter-century ago, they stressed their desire to present a variety of opinions on principles of selection and described their efforts as "a general introduction to book selection and acquisition," particularly in the public library.

The authors of the sixth edition have attempted to preserve that preference for description rather than prescription, acknowledging the issue-oriented nature of collection development; but, they have also sought to serve the needs of both students of collection development and practitioners in all types of libraries. And, most especially, the sixth edition has been restructured and revised to reflect the major changes in collection development theory and practice which recent years have wrought. Significantly, the title chosen by Professors Carter and Bonk anticipated some of these changes, to which the authors of the sixth edition have paid particular attention, such as the evolution of emphasis from book selection to collection development, the latter implying a broader policy framework within which selection (in a multitude of formats) occurs.

The entirely new chapters on "Why Libraries Exist" and "The Philosophy and Framework of Collection Development" are placed deliberately at the outset, as is the expanded and updated chapter on "Studying the Library's Community," in order to stress the importance to effective collection development programs of prior definition of institutional mission, analysis of community needs, formulation of written selection policies, and establishment of goals and objectives for collection development as an outgrowth of relating the library's purposes to the community's informational, educational, and cultural needs and aspirations.

As the practicing librarian will wish to address that framework of purpose and policy as prelude to selection activities, so also (the authors hope) will the library school course in collection development or book selection wish to proceed—as does the organization of this text—from theory to practice, from general to specific.

Other changes which the authors have sought to reflect in the
revisions and expansions of this edition include the growth of
cooperative collection development in resource-sharing networks, significant increase in the importance of non-book formats in all types of libraries, the greater complexity of censorship challenges in an age of easy access to a wide range of
communications media (as well as shift of battleground from
public to school libraries), and a most challenging expansion of
the library's potential informational role in an Information Society. To foster discovery and variety as supplements to selection
from familiar sources, the range of book and non-book review
sources has been broadened. Material formerly found in a separate chapter on selection by subject has been integrated into the
basic selection chapters, to reflect the interdisciplinary nature of
collection development in most libraries (and to avoid the suggestion that very different principles of selection apply to fiction
and non-fiction). And, while the most fundamental intellectual
freedom statements are still included in the appendices, the
many interpretive and supplemental statements are not, since
they are now conveniently available in the American Library
Association's *Intellectual Freedom Manual*.

The challenge implicit in the title that has identified this text
for over a quarter century continues to inspire the authors of the
present edition: that library collections of excellence and effectiveness are not merely selected; they are *built*.

Building
Library
Collections

CHAPTER 1

WHY LIBRARIES EXIST

Introduction

Libraries exist to facilitate communication whether that be between persons in the present or from someone in the past to someone in the present or from someone in the present to some future person. This view of librarianship is fundamental to the building of adequate library collections.

We collect current materials so that those of us alive at this moment may communicate with each other; the living author/film producer creates his or her particular view of our society and we are allowed to accept or reject that view, but always we have the right to be exposed to it. Some current authors and other media producers look at our past and some look to the future, but their audience is we, the alive-now people.

We collect materials from the past—we often term these classics—so that today's readers and viewers may gain insight into the views of those who came before us. We do not have to like those views, we do not have to accept them as accurate; but we do need to know what those who came before us thought of their world.

We collect materials from the past and present so that those who come after us will have the materials necessary for them to understand their heritage.

What distinguishes types of libraries is the emphasis placed on each of these goals. Large research libraries, for example, place great emphasis on building a collection for future scholars, and pride themselves on being able to serve today's scholars because they had the same goal in the past. Small public libraries and school libraries are more concerned with collecting materials from the present for today's users, while large public libraries combine a major concern with the present with minor concerns for past materials and those of potential interest to future generations. Special libraries come in many variations: some are private libraries devoted to particular subjects such as art or a period of history; some are found within universities and support a particular discipline such as law or medicine; some are in business and industry and support the research and development needs of the employees and management. Regardless of their setting, the one characteristic special libraries have in common is a narrow, clearly defined role in collection development. The nature of the library's collection is directly related to user needs in combination with the library's stated purposes for existing. Users of a major research library may wish they could borrow current bestsellers as well as find the weighty tomes necessary to produce scholarly publications, but they understand that the library's resources must be used to purchase research materials and not be spent on the ephemeral works of the present.

The best libraries are those with clearly stated goals and clearly defined clienteles whose needs match those of the libraries' stated goals. Dissatisfaction by users, or a large percentage of non-use by the community, can be kept to a minimum when libraries take the time to match their goals with their potential users' needs. This approach helps keep the librarian's personal value system from interfering unduly with the provision of library materials, a situation devoutly to be desired.

These are the general principles of building a library collection. There are specifics which differ by type of library, and we begin by looking at the purposes of the public library.

Purposes of the Public Library

The public library's purposes are numerous, primarily because of all the types of libraries—academic, public, school, special—it has the broadest range of clientele. To seek to meet the needs of preschool children through the elderly, the educated and illiterate, the rich and the poor, all races, all ethnic groups, *et al.*, is a formidable task. It is the range of clientele to be served, and not lack of intellectual rigor on the part of public librarians, that makes defining the purposes of *the* public library so difficult.

Traditionally, public libraries are seen as being civilizing agencies within society. This view sees the library as attempting to provide people with information and knowledge which it is hoped will lead to wisdom and understanding. The Reverend Thomas Bray felt that collections of books, spread about through a country, would "ennoble [people's] minds with principles of virtue and true honor, and file off that roughness, ferocity and barbarity, which are the never failing fruits of ignorance and illiterature." This view of the library sees it as an "open door," through which people can participate in all the accumulated wisdom of the race. Underlying this aim of the library is the faith accepted by our society that reading is a good thing, that it leads to desirable ends, and that it has the power to alter people for the better. This educational aim has been advanced by leaders of the public library movement in the United States since its inception.

Critics of the above view of the library point out that it has several undesirable assumptions. First, in Bray's use of the words "ferocity and barbarity" is an assumption that people are not innately good, but need controlling forces in their lives. Second, it assumes the existence of "truth" that is not only universal, but mirrors that of the governing class of society. It does not encourage pluralism, but rather is seen as an advocate of a particularly pernicious elitism.

Another purpose of the library in a democratic society might be called the civic aim. The public library offers citizens of a democracy the means by which they may become informed and intelligent citizens. The emphasis here lies not so much on their improvement as "liberally educated" human beings as on their improvement as functioning parts of a free society. Thomas Jefferson believed that the people of a country would never consent to the destruction of their liberties if they were informed and that nothing could do more good toward making them informed than the establishment of a small circulating library in every county. Where the people have the responsibility for electing public officials, and in our era, of voting on numerous referenda, it becomes imperative that they do their voting from knowledge, not from ignorance. Furthermore, individual citizens may be called upon to take some part in community affairs—even though it may be only as a member of some local committee—and it is certainly desirable that they be informed in order that they may act their part intelligently.

Inherent in accepting the civic aim of the public library is a commitment to provide as many points of view as possible on current issues. It is not the library's aim to tell people how to vote, or what opinions to hold on current issues, but rather to provide the range of views on these issues so that people may make up their own minds about where they stand on the issues.

The civilizing and civic aims of the public library are abstract goals, and rarely measurable. Meeting the utilitarian needs of people is a more concrete goal. As Gerald Johnson wrote: "Its sole reason for being [in the minds of some] is to help people get along in the world, to help school children get better grades, to help business men make more money, to help preachers write sermons that will keep the congregation awake."

This view requires librarians to buy books on how to make a killing on the stock exchange, how to improve our work skills, and the self-help books that teach us how to be our own best friend. It requires the library to have an up-to-date Information and Referral file that allows people to locate the person within local government who can help them solve a problem, locate the nearest Planned Parenthood Clinic, or find the local Alcoholics Anonymous group's meeting schedule.

As with the other aims of the public library, this is subject to abuse if the library staff insists on making value judgments about what type of information will be available. In our current environment, listing the local Gay Rights group or the Abortion Clinic can be a source of controversy. Here again, librarians must decide whether they are going to provide all information sources or only those approved of by the vocal segment of the community.

No aim of the public library provides more entertaining historical reading than a discussion of providing "recreational" reading. No doubt the Calvinist underpinnings of American society that reject the idea of pleasure have much to do with the antipathy expressed toward pleasurable media experiences. A film or a book that does nothing more than delight the soul of its viewers/readers is somehow deemed less worthy than that which raises lofty questions for discussion.

Unlike the first three aims discussed, which focused on words such as information and knowledge, the recreational aim of public libraries is confused by focusing on the genres of materials rather than the content. Novels are lumped together, ignoring the differences between Tolstoy and Tarzan. All novels, regardless of their quality, are seen as less important than the trashiest of nonfiction—at least this appears true as library annual reports brag about the increase of nonfiction circulation, denigrating their fiction circulation.

Judging the importance of content by the medium/genre in which it is found is one of the sillier library decisions. This is a point we will return to in later chapters. For now, let it be noted.

The question to be addressed at this point is whether members of the public have a right to find what they want to read in their tax-supported libraries. If librarians accept the idea that people have a right to know how their contemporaries view society, it seems inevitable that popular expressions of those views as demonstrated by appearances on bestseller lists and popular television talk show appearances by the authors, make provision of the materials appropriate and necessary.

Purposes of Academic Libraries

College and university libraries, like public libraries, have a range of clienteles, but their various clienteles have a common concern: a search for knowledge. Recreational interests play no part in these libraries unless they establish dormitory collections, in which case they do acknowledge that some students will want to relax on occasion.

For the purposes of our discussion, the difference between a college and a university is a matter of degrees offered: colleges offer only undergraduate degrees, universities offer graduate degrees. Both must serve the student body, the faculty, and the administrators.

Academic librarians have an easier task when it comes to defining their clientele than do public librarians. They know, or can find out, what courses are offered, at what level (it makes a difference whether a course of study is undergraduate, masters, or doctoral level). They know, or can find out, the research interests of the faculty. And they had better know what the administration will need to know.

Support of the teaching program is essential if an academic library is to be successful. This aim requires constant monitoring of course enrollments. As society changes, so does emphasis on what course of study will lead to success. When we were faced with the famous "baby boom" becoming a teacher was a good idea and Schools of Education experienced large student bodies; as the birth rate declines, wanting to be a teacher is not such a good idea, and enrollment falls. Acquiring this information is essential for academic librarians who must redistribute the budget according to current emphases. Books about computer programming may well replace books about pedagogy.

Faculty interests are also given high priority in academic libraries. Large university libraries pride themselves on being able to support the research interests of their faculty members. College libraries may fulfill this goal by providing free or inexpensive interloans and/or database searches.

The area in which academic libraries most often fall short in meeting the needs of their clientele is in extra-curricular interests of both students and faculty. One has only to look at the meetings scheduled in the typical Student Union Building today to see that college students and faculty have interests that surpass those taught in formal courses. If no formal course taught on the campus addresses the question of a nuclear weapon freeze, or the development of nuclear power as a viable alternative, is the academic library justified in ignoring these areas of public concern when members of its community care deeply?

The question that needs addressing by academic librarians is the systematic exclusion of materials not deemed "scholarly" but which may prove vital to future social scientists. There is little question that some future social historian is going to do a thesis or write a book on the subject of the Moral Majority, yet the primary source writings by leaders of the Moral Majority are unlikely to turn up in the average university library's acquisitions profile.

Purposes of Junior College and School Libraries

While Junior Colleges (or Community Colleges, as they are often called) may resent being placed in the same category as school libraries, the fact is that they share more in common than they have differences. Both fall somewhere between the diversity of public libraries and the total intellectual focus of academic libraries. Both must serve students and faculty, but neither can meet all the needs of either group.

They also share a commitment to providing the most appropriate materials, regardless of format. This commonality is their most important distinction from public and academic libraries, both of which, with notable exceptions in the case of public libraries, have been seriously remiss in providing diversity of formats of information.

In striving to meet the needs of their clientele, Junior Colleges and school libraries have accepted the fact that information comes in many forms, and buy accordingly. The difference is not so much in their purposes as opposed to academic libraries, as it is in how they perceive meeting the needs of their clientele. They are less reluctant to allow a videocassette, a filmstrip, slides, and 16mm films into the library proper.

Both Junior College and school libraries provide their faculty members with the best current materials about teaching. They do not attempt to meet the needs of faculty research, but they do strive to make faculty aware of what is being written about "education" and current problems related to education.

Purposes of the Special Library

Of all the types of libraries, the special library has the easiest task in defining its purposes. It exists to meet the needs of the organization within which it finds its home. While the same statement can be made about all other types of libraries, each of the others has a higher level of flexibility in broadening the mission of the library than does the special library. The Folger Shakespeare Library cannot suddenly decide to expand its coverage to include the works of Ernest Hemingway, nor can a library specializing in art decide to add astronomy to its mission. Having said that, it should not be presumed that the special librarian has an easy task; only that the mission is defined in more narrow terms and generally is more clearly defined.

If the special library exists within a medical setting and is to serve only the medical personnel, the librarian knows that technical materials are what are needed, not popularized books for the lay public. If the library is housed within a pharmaceutical firm, it probably has as its major goal support of the research of scientists working on developing new products.

Special libraries differ from other libraries in that much of the collection may consist of unpublished reports and locating such items may prove to be the special librarian's biggest challenge. Finally, it should be noted that special libraries may differ more from each other than any other of the types of libraries. Some will be collecting only first editions and primary source materials; others will be emphasizing the periodical literature of the discipline; still others may have a heavy emphasis on audiovisual materials.

Conclusion

While all libraries exist to facilitate communication, they differ in who they want to put in communication with whom. How these purposes affect the selection process will be explored in Chapters Four and Five. But first we must look at how libraries can identify the clienteles to be served.

Bibliography

Books

Bobinski, George S. *Carnegie Libraries: Their History and Impact on American Public Library Development.* Chicago, American Library Association, 1969. 257p. Anecdotal, readable.

Boston Athenaeum. *The Athenaeum Centenary.* Boston, Gregg Press, 1972. 236p. The first two chapters focus on the Athenaeum's influence on literature and its own history. Remainder consists of lists and synoposes of collection strength.

Ditzion, Sidney H. *Arsenals of a Democratic Culture; A Social History of the American Public Library in New England and the Middle States from 1850 to 1900.* Chicago, American Library Association, 1947. 263p.

Eastman, Linda A. *Portrait of a Librarian: William Howard Brett.* Chicago, American Library Association, 1940. 104p. Major figure in the development of the Cleveland Public Library.

Garrison, Dee. *Apostles of Culture: The Public Librarian and American Society, 1876–1920.* New York, The Free Press, 1979. 319p.

Hadley, Chalmers. *John Cotton Dana; A Sketch.* Chicago, American Library Association, 1943. 105p. Makes the reader want to know more about a leader who was ahead of the field in so many ways.

Kruzas, Anthony Thomas. *Business and Industrial Libraries in the United States, 1820–1940.* New York, Special Libraries Association, 1965. 133p.

Lydenberg, Harry Miller. *History of the New York Public Library.* New York, The New York Public Library, 1923. 643p. Fascinating look at the early beginnings.

Melvil Dewey, His Enduring Presence in Librarianship. Edited by Sarah K. Vann. Littleton, Colo., Libraries Unlimited, 1978. 278p.

Miska, Francis. "The Interpretation of American Public Library History." In *Public Librarianship: A Reader* edited by Jane Robbins-Carter. Libraries Unlimited, 1982. pp. 73–90. Critical evaluation of the strengths and flaws of U.S. library history with an emphasis on Shera and Harris.

Rider, Fremont. *Melville Dewey.* Chicago, American Library Association, 1944. 151p.

Shera, Jesse. *Foundations of the Public Library.* Chicago, University of Chicago Press, 1949. Emphasis is on the founding of the Boston Public Library.

Shiflett, Orvin Lee. *Origins of American Academic Librarianship.* Norwood, N.J., Ablex Publishing, 1981. 308p. Readable and fascinating.

Tauber, Maurice F. *Louis Round Wilson: Librarian and Administrator.* New York, Columbia University Press, 1967. 291p.

Thompson, James. *A History of the Principles of Librarianship.* Hamden, Conn., Linnet Books, 1977. 236p. From ancient times onward. British.

U.S. Commissioner of Education. *Public Libraries in the United States of America: Their History, Condition & Management.* Washington, D.C., Department of Interior, Bureau of Education, Government Printing Office, 1876. 1187p. Reprinted, Totowa, N.J., Rowman and Littlefield, 1971. 2 vols. The classic study, rich in historical foundations.

U.S. National Commission on Libraries and Information Science. *Toward a National Program for Library and Information Services: Goals for Action.* Washington, D.C., U.S. Government Printing Office, 1975. 106p.

Whitehill, Walter Muir. *Boston Public Library, A Centennial History.* Cambridge, Mass., Harvard University Press, 1956. 274p.

Williamson, William Landram. *William Frederick Poole and the Modern Library Movement.* New York, Columbia University Press, 1963. 203p.

Wright, Louis, B. *The Folger Library Two Decades of Growth: An Informal Account.* Charlottesville, VA, University Press of Virginia, 1968. 300p. A special view of a very special library.

Journals

See issues of *Journal of Library History, Philosophy, and Comparative Librarianship.*

Harris, Michael. "The Purpose of the American Public Library: A Revisionist Interpretation of History," *Library Journal*, 98:2509–2514, September 15, 1973. An attack on the "founding fathers" praised in Shera's work.

CHAPTER 2

STUDYING THE LIBRARY'S COMMUNITY

All libraries have similarities; none are identical. Because that is true, it is essential that librarians understand their communities as they work to build effective library collections.

There is no task in librarianship that requires more time, effort, and intelligence than sound collection development. While anyone with reasonable intelligence can do an adequate job of selecting individual titles for all general libraries, only a dedicated selection librarian can build a library collection. A "library collection" in the sense of the title of this book means more than a group of print and nonprint materials housed in a building called a library. A library collection has coherence and if there are gaps they are there by design and not because of oversight or disinterest on the part of the librarian.

In order to assure coherence a Collection Development Policy must be written. It is a road map telling the selector which portions of the collection are to be treated as interstate highways, i.e., are of major importance, and which are unpaved country roads to be treated as interesting side trips if circumstances, i.e., money, permit. A collection development policy also provides continuity, assuring that the map is followed even when the drivers change.

All libraries, even the smallest—one might say especially the smallest—need a collection development policy. It can be an elaborate document or a few concise pages; its size is less important than its clarity. Essentially, the policy describes the community the library hopes to serve (not all libraries strive to serve all segments of their community, and none serve all segments of their clientele equally); the purposes the library will serve in the lives of its patrons; and the methods to be used in achieving the established goals.

While it is tempting to give priority to a discussion of the purposes of libraries, the truth is that the potential clientele to be served defines the library's purposes *de facto*. This reality makes it essential that the community be analyzed before collection building decisions are made.

Some Examples

• A hospital library serving only the professional staff has a different focus than one that is expected to serve patients.

• The decision of a school or public library to buy materials in Spanish is determined more by the presence of Spanish speaking members within the community than by curriculum.

• An academic library buys at a different depth level in subjects taught only in the undergraduate departments than for those subjects in which a doctorate is offered.

• The large research library whose real mission is to collect the materials needed by scholars of the future has a different view of a collection than one whose focus is on the scholars of today. In this case preservation has as high, if not a higher, priority than current use.

This last example is crucial to decision-making in all types of libraries. There are too many librarians in all types of libraries who manage to convey to their publics that usage is close to sacrilege. Those are the librarians described by Walter M. Miller in *A Canticle for Leibowitz:*

> Brother Librarian groaned as yet another lead-sealed cask was rolled out of storage for unsealing. Armbruster was not impressed by the fact that the secular scholar, in two days, had unraveled a bit of a puzzle that had been lying around, a complete enigma, for a dozen centuries. To the custodian of the Memorabilia, each unsealing represented another decrease in the probable lifetime of the contents of the cask, and he made no attempt to conceal his disapproval of the entire proceeding. To Brother Librarian, whose task in life was the preservation of books, the principal reason for the existence of books was that they might be preserved perpetually. Usage was secondary, and to be avoided if it threatened longevity.[1]

How the Principle Works in Practice

A Public Library Example

If the survey of a community of 75,000 shows that 10% of the adult populace is functionally illiterate, the public library will have to decide whether it will seek to play an educational role in the community and buy materials that will aid new adult learners to read, or whether it will seek to serve only that portion of the community which will use its resources immediately. Should the library decide that serving new adult learners shall have a high priority, the collection development policy will state that fact. But such a decision must then impact on all aspects of the library's service program or it will be useless.

For example: the person or staff responsible for selecting materials will have to become familiar with the characteristics of effective materials in this area and forego concern with literary excellence. Staff time will be allocated for attendance at conferences and workshops dealing with adult illiteracy. At least one staff member may be assigned to take the course offered by the Literacy Volunteers of America—not so the staff member will become a teacher (although he or she may decide to become a volunteer as a free-time activity)—but because the library will then have someone trained to evaluate materials suitable for new readers.

The library's in-service training program will alert all staff members to the type of help they must be willing to give new readers and the attitude they must display to minimize the intimidating atmosphere a library has for those new to its use. All signs and directions within the library will be looked at in a new way to assure they are stated as simply as possible. As many signs as possible will be accompanied by drawings or symbols that can be "read" by people who cannot read the actual words.

If the library has a community meeting room, it may actively volunteer its use as a meeting place for formal classes for adults learning to read. If it has small rooms, it may provide the space for one-on-one learning situations. And finally, the commitment to new readers will be reflected in library-sponsored programs that address the concerns of new learners, and programs that will help explicate the problems for the fluent readers of the community.

On the other hand, if the library perceives the clientele to be served as those self-motivated people who walk through the doors on their own, then an internal survey of the demands, needs, and interests of the current users will determine the materials that will be given high priority. Library programs will focus on this group's concerns and will not place much emphasis on luring new users to the library.

A School Library Example

A familiar complaint of high school librarians is that the only teachers whose students use the library with any regularity are those in the English and social sciences departments. When this is the case, the chances are high that the library's collection is heavily weighted toward serving these groups. In most cases, the librarian's background is in one of those disciplines, with a strong component of the other present. Without malicious intent, the librarian is doing what is comfortable and easy.

By analyzing the school's total community of students, the librarian may find it fairly simple to expand library usage. Does the school have woodworking and mechanical arts classes? If so, how up-to-date and useful are the library's materials in these fields? Is there too much emphasis on hardcover books to the detriment of the workbook format so popular in these fields? Do library displays focus on literary and historical topics, ignoring the artifacts created in shop classes?

Similar questions can be asked about the science courses. Many concepts in biology and physics are best learned through audiovisual materials rather than from print sources. Does the librarian recognize this fact and buy accordingly? Are science fair projects given the limelight in the library's display areas?

Because there is such a strong relationship between the clientele to be served and the total library service program, we begin with a discussion of analyzing the library's community.

Surveying the Community

The primary reason for undertaking a systematic analysis of the community is to avoid thinking that one's friends, neighbors, and the current library patrons are the sum total of the community. All people, including librarians, have a very narrow circle of acquaintances and the temptation to believe that one's circle is representative of the entire community is very strong. Rarely does the membership of governing boards reflect the entire community either, so care must be taken to identify the true nature of the community's populace. Only after a community analysis is done can we begin to assign priorities. As with the collection itself, if a particular group is to receive minimal service it should be by design and not through ignorance of its existence.

There are four major categories of libraries: special, school, academic, and public. Of these, the public library has the most diverse community. This is true regardless of the surface appearance of homogeneity of similar education and social class within a community. People, regardless of the characteristics assigned them by social scientists, are not intellectual clones. And however individual libraries may differ in defining their mission, it is people's minds with which we concern ourselves.

A look at how a public library might survey its community, with appropriate comments peculiar to other types of libraries, will provide some idea of the scope of a community survey. In 1980 the American Library Association published *A Planning Process for Public Libraries*. It is currently the most elaborate and detailed guide available for identifying the information needed to develop a full library service program. It is also expensive to implement both in terms of time and actual money. It requires an expert statistician if it is to be done well and used wisely.

Although many libraries will not have the resources necessary to follow all the steps outlined in *A Planning Process*, all librarians can benefit from studying it and excerpting those portions that are feasible for their situation.

Whatever type of study is undertaken, it should be accepted that many hours of staff and volunteer time will be necessary and that there will be actual financial costs involved over and above staff time. If at all possible, the Friends of the Library membership should be recruited for participation in the study, school libraries can involve the Parent-Teacher Association, and academic libraries can use any one or more of the service organizations found on any campus. While membership in these groups is also non-representative of the total community, these people represent a vast reservoir of talent that can be used more wisely than is generally the case.

All too many librarians undertaking a community survey believe they must originate the compilation of data. Actually, a wealth of data already exists and must merely be located and analyzed. Census data will provide information about total population size, racial groups, age of the populace, income level, occupations, and educational levels. Good school systems have their own data on current school-aged inhabitants as well as a census of preschoolers. Colleges and universities do know how many students they have, at what level of study, and what course enrollments are. Declining enrollment in education classes and over-crowding in computer science classes should tell the librarian something important about allocation of book funds.

The library's Information and Referral file can be a gold mine of information. Many, if not all, of the agencies represented in the I&R file will have done some kind of community analysis and will have data on the population they seek to serve. A volunteer can be assigned to each agency, arrange for a personal interview with the director of the agency and, working with a standardized interview form, bring back to the library information about the agency's clientele and the information needs of the clientele as perceived by the agency personnel. Formal studies by agencies, where they exist, can be added to the data collection file. This procedure carries an additional benefit beyond the collection of information: there is a very good chance that the agency will obtain a new view of the library and become a source for referral of its clientele to the library as well as a possible co-sponsor of library-based programs.

One agency that deserves special attention in economic hard times is the local unemployment agency. The library should know what jobs are available in the community, the skills they require, and how the unemployed match or mismatch the skills. If, as is all too often the case presently, the skills needed do not match the skills of the people looking for work, the library has a golden opportunity to build a collection of materials that allow people to re-educate themselves. Library programs on how to write résumés, how to conduct oneself at an interview, etc., are also possibilities.

It is essential that public librarians obtain detailed data from the educational institutions within their communities. The public and independent schools, from kindergarten through postgraduate study, impact on library use by creating demands through curriculum assignments, and also through their library collection policies that may assume certain areas are best provided by the public library. If that is the case, the public library should be aware of it and give appropriate weight to this information when assigning its own priorities. For example, colleges and universities often offer courses in Popular Culture, but their libraries consider it their sole responsibility to collect materials *about* popular culture, not the examples of popular culture. Thus, a public library in the area may need to discuss with the Popular Culture professors the actual books they would like their students to read. If the university library is not going to buy science fiction titles, or current romances, this may be the opportunity the public library needs to inform college students that the public library has something for them. After all, college students are most apt to be the future users of public libraries, whether in the city of their undergraduate days or elsewhere.

In requesting such data from schools and institutions of higher learning, the public librarian may discover that the librarians within these institutions do not possess a comprehensive view of their own specialized communities. This, in turn, may stimulate these institutions to undertake their own study and the end result will be an analysis of the total information resources within the community. It may stimulate cooperation among various types of libraries and result in better library service for all.

One often overlooked area in data collection is the compilation of a definitive list of media resources within the community. The library should know what sources dispense information to which members of the population. The daily or weekly newspaper, the local radio stations, the local television stations are obvious. Less obvious are the newsletters or bulletins published by churches and such local organizations as the League of Women Voters and the Chamber of Commerce. Even a cursory analysis of the content of these newsletters can provide much insight into the interests of the members which can be capitalized on in building the library's collection and increasing its use. If, for example, a church runs a series of programs on parenting, the library can provide a list of parenting materials. Of even greater importance is the identification of subjects that carry a high level of emotional commitment for the group's members. In some parts of the country the building of a nuclear power plant is much more controversial than abortion; gun control more controversial than equal rights for women, and so on.

Schools often ignore such youth groups as the Scouts, Camp Fire, 4-H, and the Boys and Girls Clubs in their areas. All of these are dispensing information as well as creating the need for it among their members. A school community survey must move outside the school's walls to where the students spend their non-school time. Academic libraries should want to know how many of their potential patrons are members of the local microcomputer club or are active in service organizations.

The opportunities libraries have to discover the multi-levels of their communities are practically endless. Nothing but good can come from beginning the process, regardless of how limited it must be initially.

Using the Data

The biggest danger in using data is in letting numbers alone dominate the subsequent decisions. The largest group identified may not be the group that most needs good library service. In a college town, for example, there may be a high educational level among the adults, but it may be the group less in need of good public library service because it has access to other sources of information, e.g., the college or university library, and its members may be the largest purchasers of their own recreational reading materials. In a high-tech community, the professionals may have their work-related information needs met by a good special library within their companies, and may expect the public library to meet only their recreational reading needs and to serve their children well. The library needs to know the expectations of people as well as their socioeconomic descriptors.

Similarly, the school library's largest group of patrons may be those expected to go to college. The temptation to give this group most of the service, most of the materials, is strong. But the group that will end its formal education with graduation from the school system may be the group that most needs reaching.

On the other hand, a community dominated by blue collar industry, where most students go to work upon high school graduation, or drop out, provides a different challenge for its school and public libraries. For schools, the challenge is to stimulate reading beyond that offered in the classroom, which is often two or more levels below that offered to the college bound, and to help students understand that lifelong learning will be essential in an ever-changing world. For the public library, the data analysis may indicate that a small van or bookmobile scheduled to stop at factories during lunch hours and stocked solely with paperbacks and videocassette recordings is what is needed. Special needs can be met through delivery of requested subjects or materials.

User studies show that there is a large dropping off of library use with each "graduation" level. Fewer high school students use the library than elementary school students; fewer adults use a library than young people. If the library is developing a long-range plan by which it hopes to reach a majority of adults (no public library does at the moment), it is vital that public libraries actively seek to serve the youth of the community, not just with school assignments, but with their personal needs and interests being met.

The trap here is that public libraries decide, on occasion, that their children's and young adult services will be solely recreational, while school libraries decide that their sole responsibility is for classroom assignments. Neither is making a wise decision. Young people need to know that all libraries are sources of information and pleasure. Only when that message is imparted can we expect young people to consider the library a place of importance after they have left school, and to understand that their information needs will not stop when they have finally escaped from teachers' assignments.

Finally, it must be noted that data become obsolete quickly and a library must be on constant alert to update and revise its community analysis. The opening of a new industry, or sadly, the closing of an old one, brings change. The influx of a new group of immigrants with special language needs can occur; the development of a shopping mall can change the traffic patterns of a community and isolate the library. All these facts and more must be fed into the library's decision making process. Change is the norm in American society and it must be the norm for libraries seeking to serve their communities well.

Reference

1. Miller, Walter M. Jr. *A Canticle for Leibowitz*. Philadelphia, Lippincott, 1959. Paging is for Bantam Edition, 1961, p. 161.

Bibliography

Achleitner, Herbert K. and E. W. Neroda. *Methods of Community Analysis with an Emphasis on Libraries*. Chicago, Council of Planning Librarians, 1980. 13 p. (CPL Bibliography No. 22) Unannotated, alphabetical arrangement of books and articles from 1924 through 1978.

Adams, J. Emily. "Developing Data Collection Instruments for the Planning Process." *Public Libraries*, 21:60–61, Summer 1982.

Albright, John B. "A Bibliography of Community Analyses for Libraries." *Library Trends*, 24:619–643, January 1976. Annotates 81 studies.

American Library Association. Young Adult Services Division. Committee on Outreach Programs for Young Adults. *Look, Listen, Explain; Developing Community Library Services for Young Adults*. Chicago, American Library Association, 1975. 24p. Presents techniques for investigating a community in order to learn about information needs of young adults. Aimed at the beginning librarian.

Association of Research Libraries. Office of University Library Management Studies. *SPEC Kit on User Statistics and Studies*. Washington, D.C., 1976. Examples of statistical data collection on level and type of library user in large research libraries.

Association of Research Libraries. Office of University Library Management Studies. *SPEC Kit on User Surveys*. Washington, D.C., 1976. Compilation of user assessment techniques used in large research libraries.

Atkin, Pauline. "Bibliography of Use Surveys of Public and Academic Libraries, 1950—Nov. 1970." *Library and Information Bulletin*, 14:1–82, 1971.

Bachus, Edward J. "Studying a Branch Library Service Area." *Library Journal*, 103:144–145, January 15, 1978.

Beasley, Kenneth E. "Librarians' Continued Efforts to Understand and Adapt to Community Politics." *Library Trends*, 24:569–581, January 1976. Brief historical review.

Berelson, Bernard. *The Library's Public*. New York, Columbia University Press, 1949. 174p. Classic review of research on public library use.

Blasingame, Ralph and Mary Jo Lynch. "Design for Diversity: Alternatives to Standards for Public Libraries." In *Studies in Library Management*, vol. 3, edited by Gileon Holroyd, pp. 11–35. London, Linnet Books, 1976. Discusses the differences between "place communities" and "interest communities" and the implications of these differences for library planning.

Bloss, Meredith. "Standards for Public Library Service—Quo Vadis?" *Library Journal*, 101:1259–1262, June 1, 1976. Describes efforts of Public Library Association to develop new standards.

Bolton, W. Theodore. "Life Style Research; An Aid to Promoting Public Libraries." *Library Journal*, 107:963–968, May 15, 1982.

Broadus, Robert Newton. "Use Studies of Library Collections." *Library Resources and Technical Services*, 24:317–324, Fall 1980.

Burns, Robert W., Jr. "Library Use as a Performance Measure: Its Background and Rationale." *Journal of Academic Librarianship*, 4:4–11, March 1978. Discusses assumptions, basic steps, and methodology of user studies.

Burns, Robert W., Jr. and Ron W. Hasty. *A Survey of User Attitudes Toward Selected Services Offered by the Colorado State University Libraries*. Urbana, University of Illinois Graduate School of Library Science, 1975. 51p. (Occasional Paper No. 121)

Casey, Ann D. *General Reference Sources for Accessing Census Bureau Data; An Annotated Bibliography*. Rev. Washington, D.C., U.S. Department of Commerce, Bureau of the Census, 1978. 13p.

Childers, Thomas. *The Information-Poor in America*. Metuchen, N.J., Scarecrow Press, 1975. 182p. Comprehensive review of research.

"Community Analysis and Libraries." Issue edited by Larry Earl Bone. *Library Trends*, 24:429–643, January 1976. Contains fourteen articles, most of which are also cited individually in this bibliography.

Croneberger, Robert and Carolyn Luck. "Analyzing Community Human Information Needs: A Case Study." *Library Trends*, 24:515–525, January 1976. Describes a Detroit Public Library project.

Cronin, Blaise. "Assessing User Needs." *Aslib Proceedings*, 33:37–47, February 1981.

Daniel, Evelyn H. "Performance Measures for School Libraries: Complexities and Potential." In *Advances in Librarianship*. Vol. 6, pp. 2–51. New York, Academic Press, 1976. State-of-the-art review; useful for any type of library.

D'Elia, George P. M. "Procedure for Developing a Typology of Adult Users of the Public Library." *Library Resources*, 3:123–140, Summer 1981.

D'Elia, George P. M. and S. Walsh. "User Satisfaction with Library Service—A Measure of Public Library Performance?" *Library Quarterly*, 53:109–133, April 1983.

DeProspo, Ernest R. "The Use of Community Analysis in the Measurement Process." *Library Trends*, 24:557–567, January 1976. Suggests how decision-makers may use study results.

DeProspo, Ernest R. and others. *Performance Measures for Public Libraries.* Chicago, American Library Association, 1973. 71p. Results of a study sponsored by the Public Library Association.

Dewdney, Pat. "Citizen Participation, an Experiment in London, Ontario." *Canadian Library Journal,* 34:157–163, June 1977. How citizens helped study the community.

Du Mont, Rosemary Ruhig and Paul F. Du Mont. *Assessing the Effectiveness of Library Service.* Urbana, University of Illinois Graduate School of Library and Information Science, 1982. 23p.

Durrance, Joan Coachman. "Model for the Selection of Factors Which Affect the Public Policy Information Needs of Citizen Groups." *Library Resources*, 4:23–49, Spring 1982.

Eisner, Joseph. "Finding Out What They Think of Us." *Wilson Library Bulletin*, 51:400; 428–429, January 1977. How the Plainedge (N.Y.) Public Library used direct-mail techniques to survey citizens.

Evans, Charles. "A History of Community Analysis in American Librarianship." *Library Trends*, 24:441–457, January 1976. Reviews earlier studies.

Fasick, Adele M. and Claire England. *Children Using Media; Reading and Viewing Preferences Among the Users and Non-Users of the Regina Public Library.* Toronto, University of Toronto, Faculty of Library Science, Centre for Research in Librarianship, 1977. 79p. Findings from interview survey of 540 children, conducted in 1976.

Fuller, Muriel L. "Looking at Your Community." *Illinois Libraries*, 57:76–82, February 1975. Basic review of why and how to study a community.

Gallup Organization, Inc. *Book Reading and Library Usage: A Study of Habits and Perceptions.* Princeton, N.J., 1978. 48, 72p. Report prepared as background for the 1979 White House Conference on libraries. Excerpted in *Public Librarianship: A Reader,* edited by Jane Robbins-Carter, pp. 205–210. Littleton, Colo., Libraries Unlimited, 1982.

Gotsick, Priscilla. *Assessing Community Information and Service Needs.* Morehead, Ky., Morehead State University, Appalachian Adult Education Center, 1974. 23p. (Library Service Guide No. 2) Guide to collecting and interpreting information.

Govan, James F. "Community Analysis in an Academic Environment." *Library Trends*, 24:541–556, January 1976. Brief state-of-the-art review.

Hays, Timothy and others. "The Patron Is Not the Public." *Library Journal*, 102:1813–1818, September 15, 1977. Report of a survey in the Piedmont area of North Carolina.

Hodowanec, George V. "Library User Behavior." *Collection Management*, 3:215–232, Summer–Fall, 1979.

Howard, Edward N. and D. M. Norman. "Measuring Public Library Performance." *Library Journal*, 106:305–308, February 1, 1981.

Javelin, Muriel C. "Analyzing Information Needs of Local Community Organizations: A Case Study." *Library Trends*, 24:527–539, January 1976. Report on Nassau (N.Y.) Library System project.

Kunz, Arthur H. "The Use of Data Gathering Instruments in Library Planning." *Library Trends*, 24:459–472, January 1976. Examples drawn from experiences of the Nassau-Suffolk (N.Y.) Regional Planning Board.

Liesener, James W. *Instruments for Planning & Evaluating Library Media Programs.* Rev. ed. 1980. College Park, University of Maryland Library Services.

Liesener, James W. *A Systematic Process for Planning Media Programs.* Chicago, American Library Association, 1976. 166p. Techniques for determining needs and priorities in a school.

Lyman, Helen H. *Literacy and the Nation's Libraries.* Chicago, American Library Association, 1977. 212p. Contains section on community assessment.

Lyman, Helen H. *Reading and the Adult New Reader.* Chicago, American Library Association, 1976. 259p. Characteristics and reading interests of new readers; building collections for such readers.

McMurdo, George. "User Satisfaction." *New Library World*, 81:83–85, April 1980. Discussion. 81:122, June 1980.

Madden, Michael. "Library User/Nonuser Lifestyles." *American Libraries*, 10:78–81, February 1979. Also in *Public Librarianship: A Reader*, edited by Jane Robbins-Carter, pp. 211–218. Littleton, Colo., Libraries Unlimited, 1982.

Martin, Allie Beth. "Studying the Community: An Overview." *Library Trends*, 24:433–440, January 1976. Emphasizes the values of community assessment.

Martin, Lowell A. "User Studies and Library Planning." *Library Trends*, 24:483–496, January 1976. Brief comments on the variety of studies which have been done and their value.

Martyn, John. "Information Needs and Users." In *Annual Review of Information Science and Technology*, Vol. 9, pp. 3–23. Washington, D.C., American Society for Information Science, 1974. Bibliographic review.

Massey, Morris E. "Market Analysis and Audience Research for Libraries." *Library Trends*, 24:473–481, January 1976. Marketing expert shares techniques from that field.

Measuring the Quality of Library Service: A Handbook. Compiled by M. G. Fancher Beeler and others. Metuchen, N.J., Scarecrow Press, 1974. 208p. Reprints selections from 21 articles and reports on library use. Includes bibliography of 17 items.

Mick, Colin K. and others. "Toward Usable User Studies." *American Society of Information Science Journal*, 31:347–356, September 1980.

Monat, William R. "The Role of the Social and Behavioral Sciences in Determining Library Operations and Impact." *Library Trends*, 24:583–596, January 1976. Application of social and behavioral science methods to library community analysis.

Monroe, Margaret E. "Community Development as a Mode of Community Analysis." *Library Trends*, 24:497–514, January 1976.

Pacey, Philip K. R. "How Art Students Use Libraries—If They Do." *Art Library Journal*, 7:33–38, Spring 1982.

Palmer, E. Susan. "Effect of Distance on Public Library Use; A Literature Survey." *Library Resources*, 3:315–354, Winter 1981.

Palmour, Vernon E. "Planning in Public Libraries: Role of Citizens and Library Staff." *Drexel Library Quarterly*, 13:33–43, July 1977. Entire issue is on various aspects of library measurement.

Palmour, Vernon E. and others. *A Planning Process for Public Libraries.* Chicago, American Library Association, 1980. 304p. The basic current document and approach.

Rike, Galen. *Statewide Library Surveys and Development Plans; An Annotated Bibliography 1956–1967.* Springfield, Illinois State Library, 1968. 105p. (Research Series No. 14)

Schrader, Alvin M. "Performance Measures for Public Libraries: Refinements in Methodology and Reporting." *Library Resources,* 2:129–155, Summer 1980.

Strain, Paula M. "Engineering Libraries: A User Survey." *Library Journal,* 98:1446–1448, May 1, 1973. Example of community analysis in a special library.

Tauber, Maurice F. and Irlene R. Stephens. *Library Surveys.* New York, Columbia University Press, 1967. 286p. Includes chapters on surveys on various types of libraries and library functions.

Tobin, Jayne C. "Study of Library 'Use Studies'." *Information Storage and Retrieval,* 10:101–113, March–April 1974. Analysis of the kinds of studies which have been reported in the literature.

Toronto Public Libraries. *Goals, Objectives, and Priorities.* Toronto, 1975–76. Several documents from the "Goals, Objectives, and Priorities Studies" of the TPL. Includes comments from staff members, consultants, and citizens. Covers both adult and juvenile service.

Townley, Charles T. *Identification of Information Needs of the American Indian Community That Can Be Met by Library Services.* Minneapolis, Minn., National Indian Educational Association, Library Project, 1975. 330p. Final report on a project funded by U.S. Department of Health, Education, and Welfare.

Vainstein, Rose. "Teaching the Elements of Community Analysis: Problems and Opportunities." *Library Trends,* 24:597–618, January 1976. State-of-the-art in library education.

Warncke, Ruth. "Analyzing Your Community: Basis for Building Library Service." *Illinois Libraries,* 57:64–76, February 1975. Basic article on why and how to conduct a study.

Warren, Donald I. "Six Kinds of Neighborhoods: Parochial, Diffuse or Stepping Stone? Different Strokes for Different Neighborhoods, a Community Leader's Handbook." *Psychology Today,* 9:74–78; 80, June 1975.

Warren, Roland L. *The Community in America.* 3rd ed. Chicago, Rand McNally, 1978. 448p. Emphasizes the types of relationships which develop between people and social organizations existing in the same location.

Warren, Roland L. *Studying Your Community.* New York, Free Press, 1965. 385p. Practical manual for interested citizens.

Webb, Kenneth and Harry P. Hatry. *Obtaining Citizen Feedback: The Application of Citizen Surveys to Local Government.* Washington, D.C., The Urban Institute, 1973. 105p. Discusses use of citizen surveys, potential disadvantages and possible procedures.

Wilson, Pauline. *A Community Elite and the Public Library; The Uses of Information in Leadership.* Westport, Conn., Greenwood Press, 1977. 172p. Where and how the elite seek information.

Zweizig, Douglas. "With Our Eye on the User: Needed Research for Information and Referral in the Public Library." *Drexel Library Quarterly,* 12:48–58, January–April 1976.

Zweizig, Douglas and Brenda Dervin. "Public Library Use, Users, Uses: Advances in Knowledge of the Characteristics and Needs of the Adult Clientele of American Public Libraries." In *Advances in Librarianship*, Vol. 7, pp. 231–255. New York, Academic Press, 1977. Reviews findings of those studies which concentrated on people (as opposed to circulation studies).

Zweizig, Douglas and E. J. Rodger. *Output Measures for Public Libraries: A Manual of Standardized Procedures*. Chicago, American Library Association, 1982. 92p.

CHAPTER 3

PHILOSOPHY AND FRAMEWORK OF COLLECTION DEVELOPMENT

The purposes for which libraries exist, the nature of the community and its needs, and the social philosophy which underlies prevailing principles of selection are interactive elements which contribute to the framework of collection development in any particular library. Whether this framework has taken on the form of a written collection development policy, or not, it exists. To insure that the balance of elements in the framework reflects and supports the institution's mission is a major reason for codification of collection development policy.

Book Selection vs. Collection Development

The terms book selection and collection development may sometimes seem to be encountered interchangeably in casual use, as though they were synonymous. This is by no means the case, of course, as even brief reflection will confirm; the distinction, moreover, far from being merely semantic, is central to a library's very definition of purpose.

When Charles Coffin Jewett convened, in 1853, the first national conference of librarians in the United States, he welcomed the delegates with the following statement of purpose: "We meet to provide for the diffusion of a knowledge of good books and for enlarging the means of public access to them."[1] A century later, this statement was still to be found featured as the introductory cornerstone of one of the most influential "collection development" texts, *Living with Books: the Art of Book Selection* by Helen Haines.[2] From the Jewett manifesto, implying as it does a whole philosophy of library service as well as collection development, Haines proceeds to the building blocks of selection: testing book values, judging an author's credentials, and other techniques for separating the "good books" from the rest.

Throughout much of the history of librarianship, particularly as practiced in public and school libraries, selection of books was seen as virtually the whole of collection development. Book selection can and should be one of the most challenging, imaginative, and professional functions of the librarian; in this text, of all places, there is certainly no intent to deprecate its importance. On the other hand, the extent to which the term "collection development" has supplanted "book selection" in library school curricula, professional literature, and library policy documents is much more than a matter of changing lexicographical fashion. Traditional interpretations of the latter term have exerted profound influence on definitions of the library's appropriate societal role, and at the narrower end of the interpretive spectrum the connotations have at times been: a) judgmental, b) restrictive, c) passive.

These are strong, pejorative adjectives, and no suggestion is made here that they fairly characterize any specific time or place in the history of librarianship; it is to impart some sense of the duality of values which has underlain the evolution of collection development philosophy that they are invoked—and for which some elaboration seems in order.

a) Surely Mr. Jewett's exhortation, cited above, that libraries "provide for the diffusion of a knowledge of good books. . . ," was both intended and understood as a dynamic, humanistic statement of mission. The zeal and idealism which emanate from his statement were forceful factors in the American library movement. (Remember: in 1853, the seminal Boston Public Library was but aborning and the New York Public Library was nearly a half century shy of conception.) Yet, the seeds of subjectivism can be seen. The 1850's marked the onset of the most massive wave of immigration in United States history, and perceptions of the library's ameliorative social role in the volatile melting pot have been well documented. Sadly, in certain social circumstances, selectors of "good" books too easily become judges of goodness, defenders of traditional values or the established order, and unwitting champions of mediocrity and censorship. Book selection procedures in some major American libraries had, by the mid-twentieth century, become elaborate judgmental constructs for the apparent (though seldom baldly stated) purpose of keeping the "bad" books out. Ironically, Mr. Jewett's statement includes another term, "access," which has taken on a far greater-than-he-intended breadth of scope for latter-day collection developers, and which signifies a major shift of focus in the definition of a library's mission: from "selecting" what will be made available, to providing "access" to the widest range of ideas, opinions, and informational resources—as determined by the user's need, not just the librarian's judgment.

b) The historical prevalence of the term book selection reflects, also, the extent to which insistence on the primacy of one format has exerted a restrictive influence on the range of library resources. The introduction of audiovisual resources into American libraries involved a long and hard-fought struggle against strong resistance, both overt and subtle, from defenders of the book as the very *raison d'être* of the library. Even paperbacks were slow to gain acceptance in many libraries, encountering in part a bias against even minor deviation from the traditional book format. Certainly, format is a matter of some practical importance to an institution which must process, store, and provide access; but of greater interest to the student of collection development philosophy is the degree to which resistance to new formats has masked deeper resistance to changing social values and to expanding definitions of the library's appropriate role in a complex, multi-cultural, changing society. The very convenience and accessibility of the paperback or audiovisual medium, which seem such assets to the library seeking to reach out to broader segments of its community, have seemed quite the reverse to the library whose collection philosophy rested on assumptions rooted in McGuffeyesque pedagogy, knowledge as the product of hard work, or cultural chauvinism. More recently, the nontraditional, ephemeral, and even evasive nature of its format has been among the factors fomenting resistance to development of information and referral resources, but again not infrequently as euphemism for more philosophical bases of opposition.

c) The very title of this text suggests an assumption that collection development is no passive process. In many libraries, of course, it never has been. Keyes Metcalf's depiction, in his *Random Reflections of an Anachronism*,[3] of the intensive search strategies which the great Harry Miller Lydenberg contributed to the practices of collection development in the early years of this century, is a model example of "building" library collections. Nonetheless, from the comfort of historical perspective, the term book selection may be deemed to reflect a more reactive process—and one which prevailed in both the theory and practice of collection development for much of the library profession's history. The act of "selection," practiced knowledgeably and conscientiously, may produce a collection of interest and even excellence. In its narrowest sense, however, the term selection suggests known entities among which choices are made, entailing most often the limitations of reliance on reviews in a few popular publications, acquiring only what one's regular jobber can supply, or subscribing to only "indexed" periodicals. An analogy might be that of selecting a vacation package from those advertised in the newspaper travel section as opposed to exploring off the beaten path. Just some elements of a dynamic program of collection development might be: a wide and diverse range of review sources, active acquisition of small and alternative press publications, collection analysis and evaluation, regular retrospective purchases, alternative sources for "out-of-print" and "out-of-stock" items, multi-media resources, studies of nonuser as well as user needs, community information files, database access, cooperative collection development, and collection goals which acknowledge intangible (not just utilitarian) aspects of the library's mission.

While it is not possible, or perhaps even desirable, to exclude entirely any hint of authorial value judgment from a presentation on the philosophy of collection development, the purpose here in contrasting different approaches has been precisely to indicate the issue-oriented nature of the subject and the extent to which values derived from personal and larger social contexts do influence the development of library collection philosophy. Clearly, a library's collection policies should grow out of the library's sense of its institutional and social mission. It is a tribute to the extraordinary range and diversity of its potential that there is, and can be, no single or completely non-controversial definition of that mission.

Policy Guidelines

Among the reasons for formulating a written collection development policy, not the least is the opportunity presented by the formulation process itself to address the issues in a constructive framework and to clarify aspects of institutional mission and their implications for goals and objectives of collection development. Viewed from this perspective, the need should be apparent for careful consideration as to appropriate involvement in the process of administration, staff, faculty and other community representatives, trustees, governing board, and parent-institution officials.

The form of the collection policy framework is rather more readily determined than is its substance. Especially helpful to this process are the concise *Guidelines for Collection Development*[4] produced by the Resources and Technical Services Division of the American Library Association.

Major elements to be included in most collection development policy documents are:

Institutional mission, goals and objectives
Analysis of community and user needs to be served
Intellectual freedom and access statements
Designation of responsibility for materials selection
General subject boundaries
Levels of collection strengths and collecting intensity
    (Minimal, basic, instructional, research, comprehensive)
Limitations (language, geography, form)
Detailed policies by subject
Detailed policies by form
Gift, deaccession, retention, and duplication policies
Cooperative relationships

The relative degree of importance accorded each of these elements will vary according to the functions which the document is intended to serve. These may include: clarification of collection development goals and objectives; communication (or justification) of purpose; documentation of rights of access and intellectual freedom; differentiation of policy and implementational responsibility; guidance to materials selectors; basis for budgetary allocations; framework to facilitate cooperative collection development.

Formal codification of collection development policies has become a relatively widespread practice only in the past decade or so, as a sampling of the professional literature will indicate. As library education has expanded its research orientation, as specialization and analytical activity have intensified within the profession, and as greater accountability for expenditures has been demanded in libraries of all types, librarians have been forced to abandon formerly haphazard and leisurely patterns in favor of more professional, analytical, even scientific approaches to collection development. The growth of regional and cooperative networks has also forced libraries into a comparative framework and into viewing combined library collections in a more comprehensive perspective. Especially important is the recognition that any collection exists to further the goals and objectives of a particular institution and to serve the informational needs of a particular clientele. This may seem terribly obvious, but it requires clarification of goals and more than just good intentions to translate those goals into a planned program of collection development. Analysis must precede collection development, and that analysis must be directed not just at the collection in a vacuum but to user needs, nonuser needs, societal need, the numerous intangibles which characterize a target community and the humanistic potential of libraries.

The framework of collection development has probably never been apolitical. It is not without significance that two political leaders, Thomas Jefferson and Benjamin Franklin, were instrumental in the establishment of libraries. But while Jefferson saw libraries as vehicles for education and enlightenment, Franklin saw them as a means of pooling resources for economic benefit. Idealism and pragmatism have remained twin constellations in the framework. The application of analytical techniques to the process of collection development represents an increasingly important instrument for insuring the quality and adequacy of library resources (citation analysis, performance measures, quantitative use studies, etc., are discussed in Chapter 13); in a period (such as the present) of diminishing support and demands for more stringent accountability, the popularity of quantitative analysis may also be seen as a pragmatic response to economic realities. This matter would merit little mention here, but that what is being altered may be more than mere methodology of collection analysis; focus on the tangible—that which can be quantified and measured—renders more difficult to defend those less tangible elements in the framework of collection development. Some illustrations follow.

A study of acquisition and circulation records undertaken at the University of Pittsburgh Libraries, and released in 1977, determined from an analysis of books purchased in one particular year that over a five-year period only 56% of those materials actually circulated. And so, since the focus of the study was "the cost-benefit implications of book and journal use,"[5] the study team contended that "academic libraries are spending too much money on books and periodicals that are little used or not used at all. . . . And if a minimum of two uses were to be applied as an *ex post facto* criterion of the wisdom of the book selection, it would show that 58% of Pitt's collection should not have been bought."[6]

A harsh conclusion, indeed. One critic responded that "Pitt could cut its book budget in half and then buy the wrong half of the books."[7] For our purposes in examining this illustration, the crucial question is not whether the selectors at Pitt spent their money wisely, but whether inclusion of such a rigid use-related criterion in the collection development policy of a major university would truly reflect and enhance the mission of the institution. Some research libraries, after all, do not circulate materials at all. Nor does circulation take into account books consulted/read in the library, but not borrowed. Collection development policy cannot properly be planned in a vacuum, nor in a "cost-benefit" context unless the term "benefit" is provided a thorough and sophisticated definition derived directly from the institution's definition of its purpose.

Another conclusion of the study just cited, in response to what was deemed an unfavorable ratio of use to collection size, was: "It is evident that resource-sharing alternatives to local purchases must be explored."[8] The implications of this statement, mirrored in many a financially strained institution, are very serious. The potential of resource sharing as a means of increasing access to a broad spectrum of resources is one of the most positive elements in the framework of collection development; its misuse as merely a budget-cutting excuse threatens the very viability of the concept. The research and information needs of our society represent a challenge so complex and so extensive that cooperative approaches must be based upon interconnecting strengths, not on sharing poverty. If a library's collection policy mandates the acquisition of only high-use materials, what is there left over to share? What will be the effect on journal prices, and journal survival, as subscriptions to specialized publications are cancelled by libraries expecting simply to "share" someone else's? What library which accepts the responsibility of acquiring expensive but little-used materials to support possible future research or to serve as a library of record will then be willing to share such resources with libraries whose missions have been reduced to *circulation*? And, besides the obvious example of research, the precise nature of which can hardly be predicted, nor regularly replicated or it would not meet the definition of research, are there no subtler informational and cultural needs which escape the use-analysis net but which the very essence of a library's *raison d'être* requires that it address? At almost any point in the first half of this century, use-analysis tests would have suggested mere waste in the New York Public Library's regular acquisition of town and city directories and other such compendia from places one never heard of in Poland, or Germany, or Czechoslovakia; by mid-century, as streams of refugees from war-torn Europe arrived in that city, those resources in their public library became for thousands, whose very records of existence had been obliterated, a vital link to proof of identity and claims for reparation. Should not a library's collection development policies make allowance for obligations to future users? One might even argue that providing a bridge to connect past and future is a major reason for having libraries. But if our statements of purpose and our collection development policies do not say so, and allow the predominance of short-term utilitarian goals, then those analytical tools which collection developers must learn to use in furthering an institution's mission may become instead the means of its dismantling.

The Baltimore County Public Library has made extensive use of statistical analysis and market studies in shaping its collection development policies, and its widely publicized experiments have become a significant point of reference in the evolving collection development framework of the 1980s. "Give 'em what they want" is the Library's own description of its basically utilitarian collection development policy, the result of "some hard-nosed cost analysis" which "raised the question of whether each title was earning its keep."[9] The rule of thumb at Baltimore County for "earning its keep" is considered to be seven circulations, and the Library has undertaken a vigorous program of weeding out titles which do not meet such standards and duplicating very heavily in anticipation of popular demand.[10] "A book of outstanding quality is not worth its price if no one will read it," says the Head of Materials Selection, and so the Library "operates by responding to requests and predicting demand. Many of the commercial merchandising techniques of bookstores have been reproduced in BCPL branches."[11] As is the case with other instances cited above, what may appear at first to be a matter of selection principles or simply use analysis penetrates, in fact, to the philosophy of collection development and its relationship to a library's most fundamental purposes. As an opponent of the demand-based philosophy responded: "A strong case can be made that the most useful books are likely to be not those that circulate the most, but those that make the most difference in our lives. . . . Studies have shown again and again that patrons select their books primarily by browsing. What is available is what they take out. If we restrict the range of what is available, we do a disservice to the free circulation of ideas, information, materials. Nor does the possibility of interlibrary loan remedy this. To think so would be to equate possibility with actuality. . . . Libraries have a responsibility to ideas, to nurturing, sustaining, preserving, and making readily available the intellectual capital of our society to anyone who may want or need it, now or in the future. Collections are built to last over time."[12]

The case against passive selection practices, and for *building* library collections, is implied in this plea from a library administrator: "Because it is easier to select materials for known, static interests, we neglect the challenges for creative collection development. . . . The middle-brow scope of our collections has predetermined our audience, and the vocal preferences of that audience continue the narrowing process. We must try to represent our entire community by making the library a vehicle for access to the widest possible range of literary, artistic, and intellectual expression. It is the rough edges of literature—the experimental, the exotic, the potentially influential or controversial—which can lend richness and excitement to our collections. Let all people find what they want at the library, but let them also be surprised to find things they didn't know existed. Let us reflect the known interests of the community, but also represent the writer in search of an audience, the idea whose time has not yet come, and the new literature in process of creation."[13]

Although our profession has prized objectivity, we have probably seldom attained it. In hindsight, one sees with ease the rather patronizing bias in earlier efforts to improve the masses with "good" books; and the evolution of collection development philosophy over the past century has involved considerable reaction against a presumed elitist past. Defense of the public's right of access to popular materials of essentially entertainment value has been part of a larger pattern of evolution toward a more democratic philosophy of service. Yet, not a small amount of latter-day bias of an anti-intellectual nature can be detected in the process. The framework of collection development is a framework of values. Our long commitment to principles of intellectual freedom (a crucial factor in the framework under consideration here, but one accorded an entire chapter on its own) is very much a matter of adherence to a particular set of values, and like so many of the elements that appropriately constitute the framework of collection development, derived in turn from a broader framework of social and cultural values—as is that most humanistic and progressive concept itself: the library.

References

1. Haines, Helen E. *Living With Books: the Art of Book Selection.* 2nd ed. N.Y., Columbia University Press, 1950. p. 15.

2. Ibid.

3. Metcalf, Keyes DeWitt. *Random Reflections of an Anachronism.* N.Y., Readex Books, 1980. 401p.

4. *Guidelines for Collection Development.* Chicago, American Library Association, 1979. pp. 1–8.

5. *Library Journal,* 102:1438, July 1977.

6. Ibid.

7. *Collection Building: Studies in the Development and Effective Use of Library Resources.* (N.Y., Neal-Schuman Publishers). 1:22, 1978.

8. *Library Journal, loc. cit.*

9. Rawlinson, Nora. "Give 'em what they want!" *Library Journal,* 106:2188–90, Nov. 15, 1981.

10. Davis, Ken. "The selling of the library." *Publishers Weekly,* 216:26–28, August 13, 1979.

11. Rawlinson, *loc. cit.*

12. Bob, Murray C. "The case for quality book selection." *Library Journal,* 107:1707–10, Sept. 15, 1982.

13. "Viewpoint: Rough edges." *Library Journal,* 97:2817, Sept. 15, 1972.

Bibliography

Boyer, Calvin J. and Nancy L. Eaton. *Book Selection Policies in American Libraries.* Austin, Texas, Armadillo Press, 1971. 222p.

Broadus, Robert N. *Selecting Materials for Libraries.* 2nd ed. New York, H. W. Wilson, 1981. 464p.

Drury, Francis K. W. *Book Selection.* Chicago, American Library Association, 1930. 369p.

Futas, Elizabeth. *Library Acquisition Policies and Procedures.* 2nd ed. Phoenix, Arizona, Oryx Press, 1984. 400p.

Katz, William A. *Collection Development.* New York, Holt, 1980. 352p.

Kujoth, Jean S. *Libraries, Readers, and Book Selection.* Metuchen, N.J., Scarecrow Press, 1969. 470p.

McClennon, Archibald W. *The Reader, the Library and the Book.* London, Bingley, 1973.

McColvin, Lionel Roy. *The Theory of Book Selection for Public Libraries*. London, Grafton, 1925.

Merritt, LeRoy C. *Book Selection and Intellectual Freedom*. New York, H. W. Wilson, 1970. 100p.

Spiller, David. *Book Selection: An Introduction to Principles and Practice*. 2nd ed. London, Bingley, 1974. 142p.

CHAPTER 4

PRINCIPLES OF SELECTION FOR PUBLIC LIBRARIES

Once a library has adopted a Collection Development policy, the challenging work of actually selecting individual titles begins. One may draw the analogy between the adoption of the Constitution of the United States and all the subsequent legislation and judicial review that followed to make the Constitution a living document. Lofty statements must be implemented by concrete actions that do as little violence to the principles of the governing document as possible.

Since librarians are human, with all the foibles that encompasses, and each brings to the work situation values and personal principles that have been acquired over many years of living, disagreement about what materials *ought* to go into libraries is inevitable. As we explore the diversity of opinions on this subject, it is important to keep in mind that differences of opinion are vital to continuing intellectual growth for the staff as well as the public using the library. Good administrators try to build a staff that contains a wide range of views on major issues, thus assuring that neither the staff nor the library collection reflects a single, dominant point of view.

Some Traditional Principles of Selection

1) *Select the Right Materials for the Library's Users.* The first question is, who are the library's patrons? Is the library to serve only those who actually come to it today? Or should the librarian attempt to provide for all those who may come some day? Should the librarian, to put it another way, select for present clientele only, or also for some potential clientele (however that potential group may be defined)?

One of the underlying principles of the free public library is that it is open to all. This statement implies that the librarian has the responsibility for selecting for all the members of the community—even though they may not come to the library at the moment—since they are all welcome to come. Some librarians believe that this ideal is a central tenet to be observed in determining the library's selection policies. They do not interpret this first principle—the right materials for the library's users—as requiring that the librarian serve only those who come to the library. Rather they feel that it imposes on the librarian the responsibility for reflecting in the library collection all the manifold interests of this potential community-wide clientele.

Even if the librarian agrees with this view, there are still two approaches to carrying it out which could be taken. One is the passive approach: let those who come, come; the library will have a good collection to serve them so that future readers will find the materials they want. The other is the active approach: buy through the whole range of subjects, but proselytize to increase the use of the library by those not now using it.

The problem here is not in buying a wide range of subjects—most libraries do that automatically. What is at issue is whether all materials bought are at the same or similar cultural taste level. In the early 1950s there was much discussion about adding phonodiscs to the library collection, and the argument advanced was that adding a new format would bring in new users. When an evaluation of the new service took place, it was often found that all adding phonodiscs had done was to enrich the experience of those already using the library. It was then concluded that new formats did not bring in new users.

The majority of users of public libraries are at what Herbert Gans defines as middle, or upper middle cultural taste levels. The phonodiscs bought were of classical music at the middle, or upper middle, cultural taste levels. Had the phonodiscs focused on popular music, country and western, rock, and folk, the result might well have been different. It is not enough to assume that non-users have different subject interests from users. We must also recognize that their taste levels are different.

As libraries add videocassettes and videodiscs to their collections, they must recognize that buying Shakespeare's plays is not the sole answer; the collection must also contain *The Godfather, Raiders of the Lost Ark,* and whatever else of lower middle cultural taste level is available. At the same time, most libraries are going to want to acknowledge that there is a level below which they do not fall, and that members of the community whose taste level is "low culture" will never find in the library the materials they want most. These people will have to continue to buy *Hustler* and the daily racing form and the tabloids found at the check-out counters of supermarkets. The question is not whether this is fair or unfair to this segment of the population; it is a fact of life that most libraries could not withstand the outrage they would find expressed by the majority of their patrons who are at higher cultural taste levels.

With that caveat in mind, we move to another traditional statement of principle which reflects this conviction that the library should serve the whole community—and not merely the group of present users: 2) *See to it that No Race, Nationality, Profession, Trade, Religion, School of Thought, or Local Custom Is Overlooked.* Again, if one accepts this principle, it is argued that one buys in these areas even though members of these particular groups may not be active present users of the library. They are all potential users, and their possible future interests should be anticipated.

There is an additional argument that may be made here that has nothing to do with whether the materials will be used by the people they are about: many library users have a range of interests and are eager to read about people different from themselves as well as to find people like themselves in the books they select. If libraries applied the "Cookbook Theory of Book Selection" to other areas of the collection, they would find themselves building a diverse collection automatically. In the "Cookbook Theory" the reasoning goes like this: this is a book about Chinese cooking; we do not have any Chinese in our community, but we do have people who are interested in experimenting with recipes from all over the world, therefore, this book belongs in our library. The opposite of the Cookbook Theory is the "We Don't Have Any of Them Theory" of selection, in which the librarian argues that because there are no Chinese, Blacks, Mormons (name your group), in the community, books about these people are not needed, wanted, and if bought, will remain unread. If the library is to fulfill its civic aim as discussed in Chapter One, it becomes essential that it view its umbrella community as the nation, not just its immediate environs.

The above discussion presumes the materials under discussion are positive in tone, favorable to the groups identified. A major complication occurs when one analyzes such phrases as "School of Thought" and "Local Custom." There are schools of thought and local customs built on hatred of some groups within society. Does a library buy materials that preach the inherent inferiority of non-whites? Does it buy the writings by avowed Ku Klux Klan leaders? Does it buy materials offensive to a particular religious group within its community? These are not idle questions and librarians must work through for themselves where they stand on this explosive issue.

To move to an even broader, albeit less controversial, principle: 3) *Every Library Collection Should Be Built up According to a Definite Plan on a Broad General Foundation.* The librarians who advocate this approach have advanced the view that the library collection has its own needs, apart from the needs of the community which it serves. These librarians feel that the selector has a responsibility to the collection itself and should attempt to round it out. Such a collection would have material on all subjects, whether or not there were any groups in the community interested in the various subjects, either as active or potential users.

There are some very practical problems involved in the acceptance of this principle, which have led many librarians to abandon any attempt to carry it out, even though in theory they consider it good. If the library is limited in funds, as most libraries are, if it is not one of the behemoth collections, the librarian may well have cause to hesitate before attempting to build the well-rounded collection. If item "A" is purchased because it has intrinsic worth, expounds its subject brilliantly, is highly authoritative, but does not represent a present reading interest in the community, then item "B," which is of interest to the community, cannot be purchased. The librarian may then ask: Can one justify the use of limited funds to buy materials which *may* be used some day? Can one justify spending limited funds to build the ideal, the well-proportioned, the balanced collection, when there is not enough money available to buy all the materials present readers want?

Librarians who accept the principle of building a broad collection reject the above arguments as spurious. They maintain that one can build a well-rounded collection in any size library; all that differs is the depth of the collection, not its scope. They further argue that no really good book is without a readership. They do acknowledge that the issue comes down to whether materials bought must satisfy many readers, or whether individuals with tastes different from the majority have a right to find their special interests reflected in the collection.

Some librarians prefer to concentrate on the majority, the patrons whose tastes they can easily identify. For those librarians, the following principle is primary: 4) *Demand Is the Governing Factor in Selection.* Librarians who object to the idea of letting user demand govern selection operate on the unspoken assumption that the populace using libraries have worse taste than the librarians doing the selecting. These librarians assume that accepting this principle means they must abandon the effort to build a well-rounded collection, abandon the idea of buying for potential rather than actual users. There is no evidence that buying to meet the demands of current users in any way changes the nature of the collection being developed. Many, if not most, librarians are every bit as eager to read the current bestseller as their patrons are, and they buy as much to meet their own demand as that of the users.

There is a compromise position available to librarians who want to meet demand while retaining the right to build a well-rounded collection. Some librarians have discovered that setting aside exactly five per cent of the book budget to be spent on satisfying user demand that has not been anticipated by the selectors allows them to meet most demands placed on them for current materials. If a patron asks for a new book that is not in the library, and the local bookstore has a copy, the library buys the book immediately. It may send a messenger for it; it may send the patron to pick it up; they may tell the patron it will be available in the morning and please return. However it is handled, this service keeps the patrons happy and costs very little in budgetary terms. If, after the patron has read and returned the book to the library, it is deemed unsuitable for inclusion in the collection, it need not be processed. It can sit in the backroom, in case another patron wishes it.

There is another set of principles to be considered. These are concerned more with the quality of the titles selected than with questions as to the group for whom one ought to buy. Basing selection on demand raises this issue: Will we apply some standard of excellence in selection, or will we buy anything asked for, regardless of its quality? Melvil Dewey advocated the purchase of the *best*. Emphasis on the best underlines a point of view which sees the library as the primary source in the community for serious, educational materials. It is a view held by those librarians who are interested in increasing the use of the library for sober ends, who feel that the library has an important role to play as pedagogue to the nation. These librarians, emphasizing as they do the educational purpose of the library, endorse the principle that: 5) *Materials Acquired Should Meet High Standards of Quality in Content, Expression, and Format.* Librarians committed to this view would emphasize authoritativeness, factual accuracy, effective expression, significance of subject, sincerity of the author's purpose, and responsibility of the author's opinions. They would resist buying anything which failed to meet these standards, even if it were in heavy demand.

Librarians who espouse this view ignore any discussion of how they determine authoritativeness or factual accuracy, and they presume to know an author's purpose in creating a particular work. William Faulkner said he wrote *Sanctuary* to make money. Does that make it any less important a contribution to American literature? Factual accuracy presents even greater problems: one person's truth is another's lie in more than one category of knowledge. If one author writes that President Richard Nixon said such and such, and another says Nixon never said any such thing, who is to decide the factual accuracy? Surely not the librarian.

The Achilles Heel in espousing high standards of quality is that they can be used to reject any title that offends the librarian's, or the reviewer's, personal value system. In addition, there is the very serious problem of developing standards for each fiction sub-genre as well as for nonfiction subjects and nonprint formats. Why should libraries buy shoddy mysteries to meet the demand for that sub-genre while applying "high standards" to serious, though flawed, works of fiction?

The question of the appropriate role of fiction in a public library collection has been debated from the beginnings of libraries. The 1875 report of the Examining Committee of the Boston Public Library contained the following statement:

> There is a vast range of ephemeral literature, exciting and fascinating, apologetic of vice or confusing distinctions between plain right and wrong, fostering discontent with the peaceful, homely duties which constitute a large portion of average men's and women's lives, responsible for an immense amount of the mental disease and moral irregularities which are so troublesome an element in modern society—and this is the kind of reading to which multitudes naturally take, which it is not the business of the town library to supply. . . . Notwithstanding many popular notions to the contrary, it is not part of the duty of a municipality to raise taxes for the amusement of the people, unless the amusement is tolerably sure to be conducive to the higher ends of good citizenship. The sole relation of a town library to the general interest is as a supplement to the school system; as an instrumentality of higher instruction to all classes of people.

This concern with materials that might lead to moral irregularity and mental disease has broadened since the founding of public libraries. Today, society is equally concerned with the effects of television violence on young people and whether "R" rated movies purchased on videocassette by libraries should be accessible to minors. At the time of this writing, 30 states have passed laws known as "Harmful to Minors" statutes, which impact on the ability of adults to buy and borrow certain materials that may also be accessible to minors.

Before leaving the question of applying "high standards of quality" to building a library collection, it must also be noted that the vast majority of books and films attacked by the censors of the 1980s are among the "best" in a library collection. There appears to be no counter movement to ban blandness. The reasoning behind the attack on high-quality materials is that the better the work, the more impact it will have, thus bland titles present little danger.

Librarians devoted to high standards of quality perceive the public library as primarily an instrumentality of education. At the other extreme are those librarians who see the public library as being largely a source of entertainment for people. They would enunciate their major principle, perhaps, in the following manner: 6) *Our Purpose Is the Same as the Parks Department's.* These librarians view the library as one of the recreational agencies of a city. They will buy heavily where there is public demand and will not be greatly interested in the quality of the material. They would probably agree with F. B. Perkins, who made the following statement in the 1876 report of the U.S. Bureau of Education:

> The first mistake to be made in establishing a public library is choosing books of too thoughtful or solid a character. It is vain to go on the principle of collecting books that people ought to read, and afterwards trying to coax them to read them. The only practical method is to begin by supplying books that people already want to read, and afterwards to do whatever shall be found possible to elevate their reading tastes and habits. Most of those who read are young people who want entertainment and excitement, or tired people who want relaxation and amusement.

The problem with quoting nineteenth-century opinions is that the world has changed drastically and people who seek entertainment and excitement are more likely to find it on television or by playing video games in arcades or at home. Tired people can now relax at home viewing their own videodisc or cassette copies of *The Sound of Music* or *Mary Poppins* and do not necessarily need to expend the effort required in reading even the most frivolous book.

However, librarians who ignore these changes in the world

might still approve wholeheartedly of the traditional principle which asserts: 7) *Do Not Hesitate to Install a Mediocre Book Which Will Be Read in Preference to a Superior Book That Will Not Be Read.* This principle does not imply, of course, that all those librarians who accept it would buy books which are patently trash, but they will emphasize the demands of the community, as opposed to the demands of quality. They would assert as a principle that 8) *Quality of Materials Must Be Related to the Other Two Basic Standards of Selection—Purpose and Need.* Since their purpose is primarily to furnish recreational reading, and since their public expresses a need for such materials, they will abandon the building of an ideal collection.

As with all of the preceding "traditional" principles, there are librarians who cannot embrace either extreme. They see the library as performing a variety of tasks, which in turn demands a variety of materials. They would argue that 9) *The Collection Is Inclusive and Contains Whatever Materials Contribute to the Purposes of the Library.* Such librarians would agree with William F. Poole that it is important to remember, if one is trying to select the best, that there are as many kinds of best as there are kinds of readers. They might ask, as Charles Cutter asked, "Best in what? in style? in interest? in instructiveness? in suggestiveness? in power? Best for whom? for the ignorant? for people in general? for college graduates? for the retired scholar?" Since these librarians attempt to serve all those various categories of readers, they would be willing to accept a variety of materials, whose standards of quality might vary as the titles are seen to be useful for one group or another.

Such librarians will look carefully at each title in the process of selecting, decide for which type of user it was intended, and then apply the appropriate standards of quality. They will recognize that materials designed to help the functionally illiterate gain literacy skills will be of little use or interest to the educated users of the library, and they will accept the fact that no item bought for the library will be for all users.

Summary

The traditional principles stated above are interesting as take-off points for discussion in library school classes, staff meetings, and with the Board of Trustees and community in general when attempting to develop a coherent Collection Development statement. What should be clear, however, is that librarians who accept any given principle as if it were carved in stone and who remain inflexible in applying it will be doing their libraries, themselves, and their communities a great disservice. Compromise is not a dirty word, it is not a synonym for abandonment of principle. What it means is that librarians remain constantly sensitive to the needs of the community and respond accordingly. An un-used library contributes nothing to any society since information not put to work—knowledge ignored, might just as well not exist. It is in the using of a library's resources that it makes its contribution to the welfare of its own community and the nation as a whole.

Bibliography

Berelson, Bernard. *The Library's Public.* New York, Columbia University Press, 1949. 174p. Classic review of research on public library use.

Bold, Rudolph. "Trash in the Library." *Library Journal,* 105:1138–1139, May 15, 1980.

Bone, Larry Earl. "The Public Library Goals and Objectives Movement: Death Gasp or Renaissance?" *Library Journal,* 100:1283–1286, July 1975.

Bone, Larry Earl and Thomas A. Raines. "The Nature of the Urban Main Library: Its Relation to Selection and Collection Building." *Library Trends,* 20:625–639, April 1972. Argues for greater depth in collections of main urban libraries.

Broadus, Robert N. *Selecting Materials for Libraries.* 2d ed. New York, Wilson, 1981. 469p. Textbook with a subject by subject approach.

Broderick, Dorothy M. *Library Work with Children.* New York, Wilson, 1977. 197p.

Broderick, Dorothy M. "Focus on Youth: The Nonperson Gap in Public Library Collections." *Collection Building,* 5:33–35, Spring 1983. A look at the lack of attention to adolescents.

Carrier, Esther Jane. *Fiction in Public Libraries, 1876–1900.* Metuchen, N.J., Scarecrow Press, 1965. 458p. Historical review of librarians' attitudes toward fiction.

Corbin, John Boyd. "Abiding By the Law: Legal Materials in Public Libraries." *Wilson Library Bulletin,* 55:419–422, February 1981.

Davies, David W. *Public Libraries as Culture and Social Centers: The Origin of the Concept.* Metuchen, N.J., Scarecrow Press, 1974. 174p. Historical review.

Engel, Debra. "Putting the Public First: The Baltimore County Approach to Collection Development." *Catholic Library World,* 54:122–126, October 1982.

Fletcher, Janet. "Religious Book Selection Trends." *Catholic Library World,* 51:440–441, May 1980.

Futas, Elizabeth. *Library Acquisition Policies and Procedures.* 2d ed. Phoenix, Ariz., Oryx Press, 1984. 400p. Reprints, among other examples, a number of public library policy statements.

Haines, Helen. *Living with Books*. 2d ed. New York, Columbia University Press, 1950. 610p. Classic work on traditional selection principles.

Hermenze, Jennie. "'Classics' Will Circulate!" *Library Journal*, 106:2191–2195, November 15, 1981. Attractive editions do the job.

Lyman, Helen. *Library Materials in Service to the Adult New Reader*. Chicago, American Library Association, 1973. 614p.

McClellan, Archibald William. "Decision Problems in Book Selection." *Library Review*, 29:235–246, Winter 1980.

McPheron, Judith. "On to the Tumbrels; or, Let's Put Quality in Its Rightful Place." *Wilson Library Bulletin*, 49:446–447+, February 1975. Argues for collection of popular materials in public libraries.

Merritt, LeRoy Charles. *Book Selection and Intellectual Freedom*. New York, Wilson, 1970. 100p. Illustrates the writing of selection policies in public libraries.

Miller, Karen Gray. "Do Libraries Get Religion?" *Library Journal*, 107:1941–1943, October 15, 1982. Analysis of religion book buying. Discussion in: 108:74, January 15, 1983; 108:424, March 1, 1983.

Moore, Carolyn. "Core Collection Development in a Medium-Sized Public Library." *Library Resources and Technical Services*, 26:37–46, January 1982. Experiences in the Clearwater, Florida public library.

Polacheck, Dem. "A Method of Adult Book Selection for a Public Library System." *RQ*, 16:231–233, Spring 1977. Experiences of Stark County District Library, Canton, Ohio.

Rawlinson, Nora. "Give 'Em What They Want!" *Library Journal*, 106:2188–2190, November 15, 1981. The "'em" being the majority group only.

Wagers, Robert. "Popular Fiction Selection in Public Libraries: Implications of Popular Culture Studies." *Journal of Library History*, 16:342–352, Spring 1981.

CHAPTER 5

VARIATIONS BY TYPE OF LIBRARY

The previous chapter on principles of selection has been presented from the perspective of one type of library, not because the principles vary but rather because their application occurs within a framework, without reference to which collection development would indeed be an abstract enterprise. The act of selection is the means by which user needs and institutional purpose are both brought together and kept in symbiotic balance. The public library was chosen as a basis of perspective since the community to be served encompasses the broadest range of characteristics—and so, therefore, should its collections, and since its governing authority is usually empowered to adopt policies of collection development without reference or submission to a higher institutional authority.

On the other hand, the public library itself is no monolithic entity. Some of the nation's larger public libraries contain major research collections and serve the needs of scholarship, differing little from university libraries in considerable portions of their collection development endeavors. Some public libraries maintain branches in schools or in social service centers, others have established business branches or municipal reference libraries, blurring further the stereotypical distinctions from other types of libraries.

Nonetheless, an operating premise throughout this volume is that libraries of all types are closely bound by common elements of purpose which greatly outweigh their differences. The growth of multi-type library networks is evidence of this as well as an increasingly significant element in the framework of collection development. Defense of the principles of intellectual freedom and rights of access in any library strengthens all other libraries. Few individuals use only one type of library throughout their lives. Furthermore, the complexity of both individual and societal informational needs mandates an interdependence among libraries of many types as well as variants of those types and presents clear need for coordinated approaches to the challenges of collection development.

In that light, some variations upon the public library prototype are offered.

The University Library

University libraries exist to support the teaching, research, and public service programs of the university. Collection development in these libraries is influenced by the breadth of the university's curriculum, the levels (undergraduate, graduate, advanced graduate) at which various disciplines are taught, the numbers of students who choose particular majors and degree programs, the fields of research pursued by faculty and graduate students, and the number and type of outreach, extension, or other public service programs offered. University libraries are so closely tied to their parent institutions that every financial, administrative, or academic decision made by the university has potential impact on the library. When the university decides to start a new degree program or to support a previously unemphasized area of research, the library must respond. Because of this relationship, the clientele and operating environment of the university library must be discussed in terms of the university's clientele and environment.

Higher education occupied a very favorable position in the nation's priorities from 1957 to the late 1960s. Many people began to view education—the more of it, the better—as the solution to all scientific, technical, and social problems. This led to public support of funding. Faculty members were recruited, programs were expanded, students were encouraged to enroll for ever higher degree programs, and libraries received great increases in materials budgets and money for new buildings. Although academic institutions of all sizes felt the effects of this, publicly supported institutions—especially the small and medium-sized ones—were affected the most. Many state colleges expanded their programs and enrollment, assumed the name "university," and began to build libraries that would rival—at least in total size if not in richness of holdings—the collections of major universities. Libraries which had never tried to do more than support the teaching programs of their parent institutions were asked to provide research materials in a wide variety of fields.

Beginning in the late 1960s, the environment in which university libraries operated changed sharply. Enrollments in most academic institutions had stabilized—declining in some cases, growing much below projected rates in others. Because of a decline in the population age group from which college and university enrollments are most often drawn, universities increased their efforts to appeal to older students, part-time students, and even students who had no wish to pursue a formal degree program. A further contribution to the decline in college/university enrollment was the growing number of states that developed extensive junior college programs, thereby reducing enrollment in colleges for the first two years of the program.

Budgets for faculty, buildings, and library resources have been affected by the lack of enrollment growth, the general pessimistic mood about the value of higher education to individuals and to society, the rising inflation rate of the late 1970s, and the recession and subsequent unemployment of the early 1980s. All of these factors—changing student body, fluctuating financial support, and shifting objectives of the parent institutions—affect university library collection development policies and procedures.

There is no such thing as a typical university library collection, but certain general comments can be made about the characteristics of such collections. First of all, university library collections tend to be large. Membership in the Association of Research Libraries, an organization which includes the largest libraries in the United States and Canada, is determined partly by number of items held in the collection. In 1983, only 13 of the 117 member libraries were not located at universities. (The exceptions included national libraries of both countries, and a few endowed research libraries.) The smallest ARL university library reported holdings that year of 1,062,495 volumes; the largest (Harvard) reported 10,567,240 volumes; the median for university members was 1,906,374 volumes. In general, the more research is (and has been traditionally) a major priority of a university, the more likely the library is to hold a collection of scholarly, little-used, rare, and expensive items. Such libraries buy materials in many languages, in every type of print format (books, journals, government documents, technical reports, privately-issued works, microforms, etc.) and many types of nonprint formats (audio and video recordings, data files on magnetic tapes, etc.). Since content is likely to be the major reason for adding an item to a research collection, format (assuming the format does not inhibit access to the content) ought not to be an important consideration. However, the fact is that university libraries emphasize only print formats. It may be that with the large number of professional associations offering audiotapes of major presentations, the logjam will be broken and university libraries will recognize the importance of nonprint materials for information and research purposes. The range of subjects covered in a university library will be *at least* as broad as the teaching and research interests of faculty and students and will probably be even broader, since many university librarians acquire some materials as a contribution toward the library resources of the nation or region. Breadth, depth, and variety are key characteristics of university library collections.

Organization of Selection in University Libraries

Earlier editions of this book have described a typical approach to the organization of selection in university libraries. The various academic departments are theoretically responsible for selection in their subject areas, while the library staff remains responsible for the fields of general bibliography, for those areas not covered by departments, for special materials such as periodicals and documents, and for overseeing the general development of the collection. A "selection officer," "chief bibliographer," or "head of selection and bibliography" assumes the responsibility for directing a group of librarians who attempt to see to it that the general collection is kept sound in all of its many constituent parts. They watch the buying of the departments, trying to prevent unnecessary overlapping, suggesting titles for purchase which the departments may have missed, or buying titles which they feel must be procured. The selection group works with dealers' catalogs, trying to pick up out-of-print items which should be in the collection. In general, the selection officer is responsible for the development of the collection as a whole and for the coordination of all the widely-dispersed sources of orders. This procedure is still followed, essentially, in some university libraries. In other libraries, however, the academic environment of the last decades has brought about changes in organization.

The technical reasons for those changes are detailed below. However, it must be noted that reliance on departmental decisions for library selection results in very distorted collections. Senior faculty recommendations, which carry more weight, may not accurately reflect the emphasis of the department; selection can be distorted by a very active faculty member at the expense of the interests of other, less active, faculty.

Finally, it really must be noted that while faculty members *ought* to have control of their subject area, the fact is that most do not have either the time or energy to keep abreast of the total subject field. Faculty specialize; only the librarian can provide balanced structure to the collection.

Blanket Orders and Approval Plans

Several developments in university libraries in the 1960s—a rapid increase in materials budgets without an equal increase in staff, pressure to collect in subject areas not previously emphasized in a library's collection, requests for materials from countries and in languages not formerly collected—led to the acceptance in many libraries of blanket orders and approval plans. In general, a blanket order plan is one in which a publisher agrees to supply everything published (within specific limits of the plan), generally without return privileges for the buyer; and an approval plan is one in which a dealer assumes the responsibility for selecting and supplying, subject to return privileges, all materials fitting the library's profile specified in terms of subjects, levels, formats, prices, etc.

Many university libraries adopted blanket order and approval plans in the 1960s. [A blanket order can be for all titles published by a particular publisher, or for all titles in particular categories encompassing any and all publishers producing such materials. For example, the presence of a graduate school of library service generally mandates that the university library acquire all titles from such sources as the American Library Association. The quality is of less importance than the comprehensiveness of the collection. When the plan is with a particular publisher, it is called a Standing Order Plan. Some approval plans provide the actual physical book; others provide proof slips only from which the library staff and/or faculty determine their decisions.]

Some libraries had as many as 30 or 40 separate plans operating at once, covering both foreign and domestic publications. In some cases, rather large percentages of the book funds were spent through this method, although other libraries were very selective in their choice of plans. Librarians were encouraged to consider blanket plans when their selection procedures reached the point where decisions on individual titles had become per-

functory, when they were already acquiring almost all new publications in specified subject areas, or when the regularly appro-
priated budget seemed to be covering easily the purchase of
current imprints. Such conditions are most likely to be found in
large university libraries during times of economic prosperity
and least likely to be found when, as in the 1970s and early
1980s, budgets are tight and priorities must be reviewed.

As a tool to improve selection, blanket order and approval
plans have been praised for offering more systematic coverage
of current publishing in fields of interest than the older method
of relying on faculty selection. Faculty members need not be
excluded from the selection process under a blanket plan, but
since they do not have to initiate orders, any negligence on the
faculty's part will not be reflected in an unbalanced collection.
According to supporters, approval plans simply mean that the
faculty members or librarians who want to select books can do it
with the book in hand. Opponents of approval plans point out
that reviews will not be available at the time of selection and
emphasize the human tendency to take the path of least resistance by accepting a marginal book that has already arrived,
rather than taking the trouble to reject and return it.

Some of the proponents of blanket plans seem to view the
jobber's staff as an extension of the library's staff. When materials are needed in a language that few, if any, library staff
members can handle easily, jobbers can be instructed to select
and ship. If, as supporters claim, blanket order and approval
plans mean that the library staff spends less time on current
acquisition, then they ought to be able to spend more time on
evaluating the collection, identifying weak areas, and doing retrospective buying. Of course, some experienced librarians have
warned that there may be no good reason to change a system
which employs competent and experienced local selectors and
works well. Blanket order and approval plans cannot alone
solve the problems of inefficient selection and acquisition procedures.

Additional discussion of blanket order and approval plans
will be found in Chapter 12.

Collection Development Policies

In recent years university libraries have tended to adopt more
formal approaches to selection policy and procedure. Written

statements of selection and acquisition policies and budget allocation formulas are evidence of this trend. Before 1970, few voices were heard in support of developing written policies for large university libraries; since 1970, the professional literature has been filled with advocates airing their views, examples of policy statements from individual libraries, and organization pronouncements and guidelines. The publication in 1977 by the American Library Association's Resources and Technical Services Division of "Guidelines for the Formulation of Collection Policies" [Subsequently published in 1979 as a monograph] put a strong stamp of approval on this type of collection planning. Boyer and Eaton, in their 1971 compilation of policies, defined a selection policy as one which specifies the "intellectual framework within which decisions are made," the community to be served, who has authority for selection decisions, acceptable physical and intellectual quality, and methods of handling problem materials or controversial subjects. They described an acquisitions policy as one which gave a detailed listing, subject by subject, of the depth of collection which a library hoped to acquire. The collection development policy, as outlined by RTSD, would include the main features of both selection and acquisition policies. [See the Futas citation in the bibliography for specific examples of the implementation by various types of libraries of these recommendations.]

Budget Allocation Formulas

Another, and related, manifestation of the formalization of collection development procedures which has occurred in university libraries in the past decade is the increased interest in budget allocation formulas. Allocation of funds in the materials budget to subjects or academic departments is not a new development in academic libraries, but the need to rationalize the allocation of limited funds has redirected attention toward this control device. Allocation formulas are related to written collection development policies in that both reflect a concern for planning and establishment of priorities, the two ought to be consistent with each other, and the process of producing one in a given library often leads to work on the other.

Allocation systems vary with the allocation unit used, the factors used to determine amount of allocation, and the weight assigned to each factor. Allocations may be made on the basis of administrative unit (departmental library, undergraduate library, special collection, etc.); form of material (monographs, serials, microforms, etc.); broad subject; specific subject; academic unit; individual or group responsible for selection (individual librarians, departmental faculty, etc.); or language or country of publication. Each possible division of the funds has its advantages and disadvantages. Those methods which allow more flexibility (such as assignment to broad subjects) tend to allow less monitoring and less control. Factors on which allocations are based may include strength of existing collection, number and cost of books currently being published, number of faculty members, number (and level) of students, number (and level) of courses, circulation counts, interlibrary loans, inflation rates, and subjective ratings of the importance of the discipline (or university administration priorities concerning disciplines). In a given formula, any factor may be assigned a weight to represent its importance in the allocation decision. For example, a graduate student may be assigned higher weight than an undergraduate and a faculty member may be given more weight than a graduate student. (The assumption underlying this practice is that the weights represent relative need for library resources.) From all the possible combinations of allocation units, factors, and weights, librarians in a given university must reach agreement (and convince the faculty that their decision is correct) on the best combination for their situation. The method of allocation used in one institution might be completely unsuitable for another.

Collection Development Offices and Committees

In addition to collection development policies and budget allocation formulas, other evidence exists of a move toward more formal coordination and control of collection development in university libraries. In some large university libraries collection development responsibilities have been assigned to a separate, permanent collection development office. The collection development officer who heads this unit often reports directly to the Dean or director of the library and sometimes holds the title of assistant or associate dean or director. Activities of the collection development unit may vary from those primarily involved in coordination of the selection activities to others which are of a controlling or policy-setting nature. When university libraries do not have a collection development office (and sometimes when they do), they are likely to have a collection development committee made up of staff members from various units of the library. Roles of these committees vary as much as do the roles of collection development offices. Committees or offices may be asked to identify areas where policies or procedures are lacking, draft policy and procedure statements, conduct surveys of the collection, produce budget allocation formulas, coordinate selection with academic departments, or approve requests costing more than a specified amount. In addition to general collection development committees, some libraries also have separate serials committees to review serial selection procedures and to coordinate and control serial requests.

The Role of the Faculty in Selection

In all academic libraries (university, college, and school), it has been customary for the faculty to take part in selection. Indeed, in some libraries, librarians have been restricted to selecting only general reference materials and those items not covered by departmental subject lines. The arguments for giving the faculty a prominent role in selecting materials seem good ones: 1) After all, they are the subject experts. They have degrees in their fields, which represent considerable reading and study. They know the past and present scholars in their respective fields; they know the major works and can evaluate a new contribution to the subject. 2) They teach the courses, so they know which readings will be required for students, they know what kind of materials will be needed for term papers, they know when they change the emphasis in a course or add new units. 3) They know their areas of research interests and what they will need.

One can then visualize the ideal faculty selector: he/she knows the current productive scholarship, knows fully what the library has in the field, knows the sources of information for new materials and uses them, is accurate in transcribing information about a title when requesting its purchase and even checks to see that the item is not already in the library, is not narrow in his/her interests, notices important related materials, has some interest in selecting for students as well as researchers, and so orders materials with a wide range of complexity for different groups of students—the major subject, the minor, the interested layperson.

The ideal faculty selector is, like the ideal librarian, something of a rare bird. The realities of experience have taught us that not all faculty members will participate in selection. Some are interested but do not have the time. They try to do a good job in the classroom, which means many hours each week spent in preparation; they are free with time for interviews with students; they participate in departmental and college committees; they have families which demand some time; they take part in community activities; they read their professional literature and try to keep up with the world outside their field. They simply do not find enough hours to do systematic and continuing work on building the library collection.

There are those who do not participate because they are not interested. Some are indifferent, some are lazy. Others have come to rely on the library to have what they want and see no need to make an effort which could only duplicate the work already done by the librarians. Some adhere to the practice of lecturing and asking students to do their reading in a list of books which will be reserved for that purpose, and so they are not concerned with building the collection for independent study.

It is true, too, that it is growing very difficult for any working teacher to find enough time to keep up with the professional and scholarly literature. Many readers find that reviews must substitute for the books they will never have time to read; much journal reading becomes a scanning of title pages, with only occasional dipping into selected articles.

There is some reason to feel that part of the difficulty in building general collections is attributable to a narrowing tendency of advanced education. The expertise becomes more and more restricted in scope. As a college sophomore, for example, the student may have taken the survey course in English literature, which sweeps from the Anglo-Saxons to modern times in two semesters. As a senior, the same student may take a survey course in eighteenth-century literature which covers the century in two semesters. As a graduate student he/she may take two semesters to study the criticism of the Age of Queen Anne. As a doctoral student, he/she may produce a dissertation devoted to one very small segment of that microcosm. Such narrowing of interest may lead to a somewhat parochial view, so that the professor may be deeply interested in only a small part of his/her field.

Surveying the realities of much faculty selection in practice (at any level of education), some have argued for giving librarians the major responsibility for selection. Indeed, at many institutions this has actually happened without planning and continues to be a noticeable trend in large university libraries. Librarians usually have studied at least one subject major and are supposed to have had a good general liberal education; many are dedicated readers, who use the library's collections to expand their own education. The number of librarians with graduate training in academic disciplines (including doctorates) seems to be increasing, especially in those university libraries which accord faculty rank to library professionals.

Furthermore, librarians are trained in using sources of information about new materials and can often identify needed materials before the faculty hears of them. This is true primarily because faculty are likely to rely on their professional journals, all of which are notoriously late in reviewing. Librarians watch publishers' announcements, national bibliographies, issues of library periodicals which list forthcoming materials, and all the multitude of specialized sources which are part of the librarian's armametarium. It is this kind of knowledge which has enabled librarians with masters' degrees in a field like history to give good service as heads of chemistry libraries. They know how to find information; that is their stock in trade.

Librarians are also likely to watch the whole range of demands or needs and see where gaps exist or are being created. They see the collection in a way that the individual faculty member or department is not likely to see it, and they will try to ensure that all interests are represented, even if those interests are not loudly expressed.

Clearly, however, it is desirable that both faculty and librarians cooperate in building the collection, each bringing to the task special skills and knowledge. There should be constant and continuing communication across the barriers separating the library staff from the faculty and departments from each other. Unfortunately, there are some blocks to easy cooperation which have grown up with time.

There are occasional faults on the faculty side which lead librarians to be suspicious of faculty suggestions—and sometimes to openly express hostility. One university librarian received a request from a very powerful department, asking that the library purchase a very expensive reprint of a massive set of source materials originally published in 1880. The purchase involved several thousand dollars, so the librarian sent the request to the selection officer for checking. The selection officer went first to the catalog—to discover what one can guess: the library had bought the set in 1880. Chalk up one cause of doubt concerning the faculty's judgment and knowledge of the collection.

In another university, a chemical experiment supported by a grant had reached a point at which the researchers needed a certain piece of information. A literature search did not turn it up, and so the main experiment was sidetracked while equipment was built to run a subsidiary experiment to determine the data needed. It had been completed before the chemistry librarian got wind of the whole affair and had the sad duty (or satisfaction?) of reporting that the results had been obtained in Germany 40 years earlier and were available in the library, but had not been found by the experts.

The faculty have sometimes hardly endeared themselves to the librarian, or encouraged cooperation, by the openly expressed belief that librarians are really rather low-powered clerks, without much in the way of brains or training, who are competent enough to stamp a date due card or collect a fine, but hardly able to make an informed judgment. This may certainly be true of some librarians, but it is hardly the way for faculty to obtain whole-hearted support from the library staff. As university librarians have introduced on-line catalogs and installed database searching as a standard reference procedure, have been accorded faculty status and begun to serve on university-wide committees, much of this attitude has begun to change.

The faculty do individually sometimes take a very parochial view of the library. They see only their own needs and are not at all concerned with other parts of the collection. This is a natural enough state of affairs but it may lead them to condemn the librarian for trying to ensure that the needs of all parts of the faculty and student body are satisfied. It is also true that there is usually a small group of very vocal and active faculty members who demand materials, but there is a larger group who never order anything and yet will criticize the library staff at faculty meetings for not having what they need.

Librarians have made their contributions to the problem with a few faults of their own. They sometimes tacitly hold, or openly express, the belief that faculty are really a pretty ignorant bunch when it comes to knowing anything about selection; they are a selfish lot, not caring a whit whether any other faculty or student need is met; that when they are not ignorant, they are lazy—and careless as well. Librarians ask how else one can explain the books ordered under the sub-title (by the expert, no less!); the authors' names all garbled, misspelled, or with works wrongly attributed to them; and they point to the agonized screams for purchase of titles which have been in the library for months. Some librarians have unjustly concluded that faculty cannot be trusted at all.

Librarians in academic libraries of any type need the cooperation of the faculty. Librarians must be fully aware of the curriculum, the collection, the faculty interest, and the composition of the student body. They need to get out of the library and talk to the faculty, watch the departments for the appearance of new courses and the hiring of new faculty, and attempt to learn as much as possible about how courses are taught. The library staff bears the responsibility for the collection and should have the final authority in making decisions concerning it, but they must know their community well in order to make the best decisions.

Special Problems in University Libraries

Because universities emphasize both teaching and research, the university library must try to supply materials needed for classes currently being taught and current faculty research, while at the same time building collections that may be of use to researchers in the future. A conflict among these priorities often arises in times of severely limited budgets. When large numbers of students demand more duplicate copies of reserve books, it is hard to justify expensive purchases for which there may be no immediate demand. On the other hand, some research materials must be bought and preserved now or they will be unavailable in the future. The balancing of research needs against teaching needs (or future needs versus current needs) is an unresolved issue in many university libraries.

Serial publications, which are increasing in volume and cost, pose another problem for university libraries. In some disciplines, especially the scientific ones, the serial form of publication (journals, newsletters, monographs-in-series, etc.) is the most important printed source of information. University libraries must acquire or at least provide prompt access to long runs of domestic and foreign serials. In recent years, the costs of acquiring, processing, and storing these serials have absorbed larger and larger percentages of the materials budget. Although university librarians are giving much attention to the collection development problem posed by serials, as yet no totally satisfactory solution seems to have been found. One popular approach is to develop cooperative projects (which will be discussed in a later chapter) to handle the less frequently-used serials.

The College Library

The library of the liberal arts college generally has three major functions: 1) to support the curriculum with materials in those subjects taught by the college; 2) to provide a basic collection aimed at the development of the "humane," the "liberally educated" person, apart from curricular requirements; 3) to support a degree of faculty research. To serve these functions, the library must provide a fairly wide range of new scholarly monographs in English (covering all the academic disciplines it is supporting), a carefully-chosen periodical collection, an extensive reference and bibliography collection, and nonprint materials needed to support teaching efforts.

The typical college library has a much smaller and more homogeneous community of users than the average university library. In an institution without graduate programs, there is likely to be a narrower range of academic specialization represented in the student body. Faculty members will probably be graduates of specialized doctoral programs, but some of them at least have left the specialization of the university and chosen to teach in a program with a broad, liberal arts emphasis. The assumption is made, although it may often be false, that college faculty members place a higher priority on teaching than on research. In most colleges, the number of faculty, staff, and students is small enough that librarians can know most of the faculty and many of the students individually and can follow rather closely the interests and needs of their users.

Since the college library is not intended primarily for research, but for use of students in undergraduate education, it will not require the expenditure of funds for the more remote materials of narrow subject scope and intense specialization. Since it does not support a curriculum encompassing the special technical fields (medicine, engineering, agriculture, nursing, dentistry, etc.), it will not need the highly specialized materials of these fields. Since it is not a public library serving a wide variety of publics, it may tend to base its selection on the value and authority of a given title, rather than on its popular appeal. In the various subject fields, it need not emphasize the popularizations, intended for the less skilled or less informed reader, although it may feel a responsibility for general works, introductory to a field, intended for the college student who is not specializing in that field but who wishes some knowledge of it as part of a general education.

College library collections vary widely in size but tend to be small in comparison with university research collections. The size, as well as the nature of the collection, is governed by the range of academic programs offered and the availability of other library resources in the area. The latest set of standards for college libraries (published in 1975 by the Association of College and Research Libraries) recommends that a college library should "provide prompt access" to a basic print collection of 85,000 volumes, to which should be added 100 volumes for each full-time faculty member, 15 volumes for each full-time student, 350 volumes for each undergraduate major or minor field, and several thousands of volumes (rising as the level of instruction rises) for each graduate program which might be offered by the institution. Of course, the emphasis in these standards is on the number of items to which faculty and students have quick and easy access, as opposed to the number of items which the college library actually owns. Some college libraries own as few as 20,000 volumes while a few others have collections approaching the half-million mark. The average college library collection is well below the latter figure.

Organization of Selection in College Libraries

In the college library participation in selection is likely to be widely dispersed. In addition to the entire library staff, the members of the faculty and sometimes students are encouraged to select in their subject fields. Because the group involved can be large, it is important that overall planning be done and the decisions on selection policy be set down in writing. A written collection development policy is just as important for a college library as for any other type of library. The remarks made earlier about collection development policies in university libraries also apply here.

Because the college library collection should be centered on the curriculum, it is particularly important that library staff and faculty members work together. Some of the difficulties mentioned in connection with faculty selection in university libraries may apply here, but college selection should lean heavily on all faculty members, and full participation should be encouraged by the heads of departments.

Although the ideal situation is to have intelligent faculty participation in selection, ultimate responsibility lies with the librarian and the professional staff. In certain college libraries, the selection of general materials is made by the professional library staff, which meets at regular intervals after perusal of the various reviewing media. As in the university situation, it is assumed that librarians have expert knowledge of sources for selection, knowledge of the overall collection, and will consider every order in the light of the needs of the library as a whole and its place as part of the total educational apparatus of the institution.

Blanket orders and approval plans are seldom used in college libraries; the smaller the materials budget, the less likely they are to be used. The college librarian has the assets of close acquaintance with the library community and the potential of good communication with and cooperation from the faculty, and the liability of a rather limited materials budget. Under those circumstances, common sense holds that selection decisions can best be made by librarians and faculty. Larger college libraries will probably maintain some standing orders, but more are not likely to collect any subject in the depth that makes a blanket order or approval plan economical.

Special Problems of College Libraries

Liberal arts colleges, most of which are privately supported, have had a difficult time in recent years. The shock of adjusting to rising expectations for academic programs and library holdings in the early 1960s, followed so quickly by the reassessment and retrenchment required in the 1970s, followed by the recession in the early 1980s, has caused the closing of a number of institutions and lowered the expectations in many others. The pressures of unpredictable enrollments caused by a low birthrate producing a smaller pool from which to recruit students, and the massive increases in the tuition fees at private colleges, stable or declining budgets, inflation—all of which had serious effects on university libraries—are affecting college libraries even more drastically. With the increase in publishing (which has been evident worldwide for at least the past decade), college libraries with fairly small materials budgets have had trouble buying all they might be expected to acquire, judged on the basis of their academic programs. Summaries of expenditures made by college libraries in recent years show that acquisition rates have gone down. When financial troubles hit small institutions, where there seems to be less budget surplus to absorb new cuts, libraries and their materials budgets are likely to be hard hit.

Periodicals also cause problems in college library collections. They are expensive to acquire initially and represent a continuing drain on library resources, since they may continue indefinitely (no library starts a subscription with the idea of keeping it only a year or two) and require expensive record-keeping, binding, and shelf space. Periodicals are, however, an important part of a collection which supports instruction, and no library can afford to cut too much its subscription list or its holdings of backfiles. How a library approaches this problem will probably depend on the other resources available in the area and on the views of faculty and students about using backfiles in microforms.

Because they are not primarily research collections, college libraries must be weeded regularly and carefully. This is necessary because of the limited amount of storage space available to most college libraries and also because the collection is intended to be a working collection for undergraduates. Keeping the collection lean by removing superseded editions and other outdated material actually improves service by improving access to the better, more current materials.

The Community College or Junior College Library

The typical community college has a broad mission. Most try to prepare students for the third and fourth years of college, offer terminal courses in vocational and technical fields, and provide adult and continuing education programs for the community. This diversity of purpose leads to diverse course offerings. Since the purpose of the learning resource center (as libraries in community colleges are generally called) is primarily to support the curriculum, those responsible for collection development face a greater challenge than one might expect.

Another result of the diversity of purpose is a more heterogeneous student body, representing varying ages, interests, academic backgrounds, and degrees of academic intention. There may be less rigidity in admission standards, which will have an effect on the materials purchased, in that many of them may have to be fairly elementary. At the same time, some students will be as academically talented and ambitious as the average

student in a competitive liberal arts college, and their needs
must be met, too.

Although private junior colleges have a long history, most
publicly-supported community colleges have been established
since World War II. There was a rapid proliferation of two-year
post-secondary institutions in the 1960s, coupled with growth in
their enrollments. One effect of the newness of many of these
institutions has been their ability to experiment with new types
of library service, and to work toward closer integration of library materials with the instructional program. They tend to
encourage integration of books, films, filmstrips, tapes, and
other of the newer media into a single instructional program.
The fact that most two-year institutions have chosen to use the
term "learning resources" rather than "library materials" is an
indication that they are trying to avoid the traditional print orientation of most university and liberal arts college libraries. (The
latest set of standards for the two-year college library, published
in 1972 by the Association of College and Research Libraries, is
titled "Guidelines for Two-Year College Learning Resources
Programs.") The impact on the selection process of widespread
use of nonprint materials is obvious.

Organization of Selection in Community College Libraries

In spite of the fact that it may use different terminology for most
things connected with the library and its collection, the two-year
college library typically organizes its selection procedures in a
manner similar to that of the four-year college library. Cooperation between librarians and faculty is important and procedures
are usually set up to encourage faculty participation and suggestions. Faculty involvement in collection development is particularly desirable in an institution with such a wide range of
courses (from the traditional academic disciplines to technical
apprenticeship programs), great diversity in student abilities
and needs, and relatively small library staff.

The School Library Media Center

School library media centers have a responsibility to both faculty
and students. For the students, they must supply materials re-

lated directly to course needs, but they must also provide what are sometimes called "enrichment" materials. The latter form that part of the collection which aims at the liberal education of the student, going beyond the strictly curricular needs to provide materials which will educate in a broader sense. Through the school library media center, students gain experience in locating, evaluating, and using information which they comprehend through their reading, listening, and viewing skills. For the faculty, these centers provide instructional materials for use in the teaching of specific courses, as well as materials needed for the teachers' own professional growth and development.

In addition to supporting objectives which range from supplying rather specific classroom-related needs to promoting broad general education/personal development goals, the typical school library media specialist must build a collection to fit a diverse clientele. Whereas the student body in four-year colleges and in universities is relatively homogeneous (all sharing at least a high school education, all having met the entrance requirements of the college or university, most being reasonably adequate readers), the school library media specialist is faced with much less uniformity in the student body. The spread in the elementary schools is staggering—from those who are just learning to read, through those who are skilled and practiced readers, listeners, and viewers. But junior and senior high schools offer an even greater range of potential users, for there are students who have moved a good distance into intellectual maturity and those who have still not learned to read. In fact, with each grade level the span of reading abilities increases. The school library media specialist not only needs to provide materials supporting each area of a broad curriculum; he/she also has to provide a greater variety of levels of treatment of these subjects than either college or university librarians.

Recent developments in education have created the potential for even more diversity in the clientele of school library media centers. Students who were formerly enrolled in special education programs, sometimes housed in separate buildings, are increasingly being integrated into regular classrooms—a practice sometimes referred to as "mainstreaming." This means that media specialists, as they build their collections, must now consider the needs of children with serious physical, emotional, and learning difficulties. To do this successfully they must know more about how various kinds of disabilities—of seeing, hearing, etc.—interfere with learning and prevent the use of traditional library materials. They must also establish contacts with the public library in their area providing materials from the Library of Congress for the blind and disabled, and when purchasing films be sure to add as many "captioned" prints as possible so those with hearing difficulties can have access to their content.

On the basis of a simple count of items held, individual media centers in schools will have smaller collections than most individual libraries of the types previously discussed, but the variety of holdings may be much greater. Collections in schools are likely to contain materials such as books, periodicals, newspapers, pamphlets, microforms, films, filmstrips, videotapes, audiocassettes, audiodiscs, posters, prints, maps, globes, models, games, toys, and specimens—preserved or live. In addition to the materials themselves, the media center must acquire and supply the equipment to play and/or project many of the media. Some of the more expensive media—films, videotapes, etc.— may be supplied at the district level, as may the more extensive collections of professional materials for faculty and staff.

Organization of Selection in School Library Media Centers

In general, the principles and procedures of collection development in a school library media center are the same as those for other libraries, even though media specialists operate under different objectives and deal with different materials and clientele. For example, the current standards for school library media centers (*Media Programs: District and School*, ALA, AECT, 1975) state that selection should be guided by a selection policy (presumably written) which has been developed with consideration for and input from all those concerned with the media center—the media center staff, administrators, faculty, students, and representatives of the community—and approved by the board of education. The number of federal court decisions—beginning with *Minarcini v. Strongsville City School District* (1976) and culminating with the confusing decision in *Board of Education, Island Trees Union Free School District, v. Pico*—ought to have alerted all school librarians and boards of education for the need to have written selection policies and procedures as well as established procedures for handling complaints. Since school media centers have been the focal point for all court actions involving libraries (as opposed to those involving librarians), an important book for all school media specialists to own and absorb is *Censorship, Libraries, and the Law* (see bibliography in the censorship chapter).

A policy statement should recognize the influence on collection development of such facts as the abilities and strengths of the faculty; the courses taught and the methods used to teach them; the media resources which are already available in the community; the characteristics and quality of the materials and related equipment which are available for purchase; and the budget allocated to support the program. The application of the traditional principles of selection in a school library media center requires acceptance of the concept that facts and ideas can be transmitted through a variety of media and ought to be offered to students in the most effective medium available.

Selection should be a cooperative process, involving faculty, students, staff, and representatives of the parent-teacher association, and any others whose competencies can enhance the process. Coordination of the process must be by the media specialist. If the school has developed a detailed selection policy, endorsed by the appropriate legal authority, the organization of the selection process will have been spelled out from the district level. While each school in a system will have its special features, the policies and procedures should be uniform across the system. Ideally, the policy should assign final responsibility for the selection process to the professional library staff. However, as pressures from the censorious segment of communities have increased, many boards of education are reserving to themselves the final say on what is selected for school library media centers. This has led to such aberrations as the rejection of *You Have to Draw the Line Somewhere,* a book about design, on the basis of its title which was provided a sexual connotation by school board members uninformed about its content.

Having as many interested individuals represented in the selection process as possible is important not only because each type of potential selector has unique strengths, but because the more people who are involved, the harder it will be for censors to challenge the final selections. There is, of course, always the problem that the more people involved, the less exciting, the less diverse will be the collection since compromises must be the order of the day. This problem is not as serious as that of having one person, the school library media specialist, impose his/her personal values on the collection. Nor is it as serious as having the media specialist who builds a diverse, albeit controversial, collection face the wrath of an outraged individual parent, administrator, or school board member.

Media specialists are best able to say what is in the existing collection and what materials are available on the market. It is their job to compile the initial list (or collection of review copies) from which the larger committee will work. Teachers know their subject fields, some better than others, and their students' capabilities. What few teachers know is the range of materials available from the trade publishing field, and serving on a selection committee can be one of the most important professional growth experiences they can have. Teachers who serve on such committees also tend to use the media center more and require more use of it by their students. The students are the final judges of what interests them and appears to be directed at their levels of comprehension, and they can make important contributions to the selection process. However, students should not be involved if their opinions are to be consistently ignored. If the adults involved are not ready to yield to the students' opinions, particularly in terms of "enrichment" materials, it is better not to involve students—the bad taste left from feeling manipulated is worse than the feeling that comes from being ignored totally. A similar statement can be made about involving parents, who ought to represent varying views within the community, but unfortunately, the media specialist cannot always control who will be appointed to the committee. Potential bias by any of the above named groups—librarians, teachers, students, parents— can often be offset by including knowledgeable subject specialists from the community such as doctors and public health specialists to aid in the selection of the always difficult area of sex education materials.

Allocation of the funds available for materials and equipment will be determined, at least partly, by district practices. For example, the media center may receive designated, or line-item, allocations and be required to maintain separate accounts for textbooks, library books and pamphlets, periodicals and binding, audiovisual materials, and audiovisual equipment. Some states provide designated state-aid for school library media centers, and librarians in such states should be aware that the aid exists and is their right. They may have to fight the principal to acquire it (unhappily), but fight they should.

Large school districts often maintain evaluation and selection sections which assist individual media centers. The purpose of such district-level units is generally to improve the quality of the media collections in the district, but some attempt to do this through maintaining centralized control of most selection and acquisition, while others concentrate on assisting the efforts of individual media centers. Such units should coordinate policies by, for example, taking the lead in developing written policies, or by establishing and supervising procedures. The importance of coordination at the district level cannot be over estimated. All libraries, teachers, students, and others concerned with the education process, should be assured that the accident of being located in a particular school does not leave them disadvantaged. District-level involvement is a matter of assuring fairness, not of restricting anyone's freedom. A media specialist with an intransigent principal ought to have the same authority as one with a receptive principal.

Special Problems in School Library Media Centers

In the early 1980s the problems affecting the selection of materials for school library media centers, always complex, became even more difficult. Three reasons can be given for this situation: 1) the literature being published for the young has become filled with profanities and sex scenes, and its subjects are those that arouse much anxiety in adults (abortion, death, homosexuality, rape, racism, etc.); 2) the need to integrate schools has produced a wide range of divisions, from the single grade school, to combinations such as kindergarten through fourth grade, and kindergarten through grade twelve, and 3) the increased attacks by organized groups on the curriculum and the school libraries for containing views and materials that run contrary to the values they wish to see imparted to young people.

School librarians have no control over any of the above developments. If many feel as if the selection of materials for school library media centers resembles walking through a mine field, they are justified. On one side, they have groups protesting sexism in youth materials; on the other, they have groups objecting to what they perceive of as the denigration of women as wives, mothers, and traditional homemakers. They have groups that are highly sensitized to perceived racism in the books, and other groups that object to any portrait of a particular ethnic or racial group which indicates its place in American society is anything less than perfect.

Whether the attacks come from liberal or conservative groups, they share an underlying assumption, namely that what children read and view impact greatly on their value systems. While there has been much research done on the effects of television upon children, with mixed results, there is little or no research on how reading affects children. The assumption sounds reasonable, but should be accepted with reservations.

While less emotionally explosive, another issue facing school librarians is the need to purchase a wide range of formats in a time of decreasing financial support. Audiovisual materials cost much more than print materials, but a media center must contain more than books in order to be supportive of today's curriculum. Deciding how to allocate shrinking funds to adequately purchase the range of materials needed is one of the most difficult decisions facing conscientious librarians.

The school library differs from other libraries in academic settings in that it is housed in the same building as its clientele and in lower level schools, classes are scheduled to come to the library so the librarian comes to know far more of the students as individuals than is usual in university or college libraries, for example. This creates added pressure in the selection process when faced with the choice between a mediocre book that fits the curriculum and one that will be very popular recreational reading. A further conflict arises between popular materials versus superior literary titles that few will read, but which will deeply enrich the lives of those who do read them.

Then the school library faces the question of whether to buy many materials for the teachers already using the library, or attempt to build up the collection in low-use areas in the hope of expanding use. Teachers who use the library often and well tend to become friends of the librarian, and it is very difficult to say no to one's friends.

Finally, the school librarian has the responsibility to build a good professional collection for use by the administrators and teaching staff. All too few school librarians are ready to do battle for a budget to support this need. Yet, a well informed professional staff is essential for quality education.

Unlike other libraries in educational settings, the school librarian must often accomplish all these tasks without any support staff. That there are so many excellent school libraries in this country is a testimonial to sheer dedication.

The Special Library

The special library has the most restricted purposes and homogeneous clientele of any of the types of libraries discussed thus far. It is created for very specific purposes—often to support the research or business activities of one particular company. It exists to serve a relatively small group in their work. The range of subjects may be very restricted—indeed, the library may concern itself with one narrow subject area—but the variety of forms and types of materials may be great, including such items as monographs, journals, pamphlets, internal and external technical reports, theses, reprints, conference proceedings and transactions, lab notebooks, archival material, photographs, clippings, slides, films, etc. The budget is usually adequate, and, in libraries serving corporations, special needs in terms of purchase are more readily supported by the parent company.

Selection is often difficult, however, because the regular trade bibliography is for the most part inadequate. For example, in the case of a library serving a chemical corporation, emphasis is on such materials as research reports, government documents, and the whole paraphernalia of research, which is hard to find out about and difficult to come by. The librarian must become thoroughly informed about the field in order to contact such sources of information directly, rather than depending on the standard selection tools. There will be great pressure for the immediate acquisition of all important materials, and this, added to the scattered nature of the producers and the lack of general bibliographic aids, will make the selection process somewhat more hectic than usual.

As in other types of libraries, written policies may be needed— specifying depth and extent of subject coverage, types of materials collected, exchange agreements, and other special considerations—although the special librarian is more likely than most to point out the inflexibility of a written policy. Many special librarians prefer to rely on specific purchase requests and can be counted on to give any suggestion from the clientele full consideration. Some librarians also consider it advisable to have a library committee consisting of specialists who can advise on purchases.

The Special Collection

Special collections sometimes exist as separately administered and financed organizations, such as a privately-endowed research library, but they may also be units within university, college, public, or special libraries. These collections typically are restricted to a well defined (and possibly narrow) subject area, emphasize the needs of researchers, and attempt to build comprehensive collections of primary, as well as secondary, materials.

Development of these collections generally ignores the evaluation of individual titles and concentrates on determining the existence of anything within the subject boundaries of the collection. The only factor limiting the collection development of such libraries is the amount of money they have to spend and, of course, the availability of material. In highly specialized collections, identification of the existence of an item is tantamount to selection.

When a public library, for example, decides that it will finally follow the dictum so often enunciated and begin collecting local history, there is going to be a natural alteration in the librarian's "evaluation" of the materials for that collection. He/she will not be interested in the literary quality of the diaries and letters of early settlers—the library wants them all. The librarian may gather up bushel baskets of play bills, yards and yards of the account books of early businesses, acres of old newspapers . . . and these are all justifiable, for they are meeting a different kind of purpose than that envisioned in the selection of individual titles for the general reader.

Take, as another example, a library that decides that it is going to build a special collection dealing with labor-management relations in a given industry. The focus of attention is again suddenly changed—one is no longer concerned with getting *only* the best books on the subject. One wishes to build a *comprehensive* collection, reflecting all the varied aspects of labor-management relations. Certainly one will want the objective histories and analyses written long after the fact, but one will also want the contemporary record, no matter how biased, violent, or partisan the accounts may be. The library will try to build files of union newspapers, management serials, the pamphlet publications of both, and will, of course, try to acquire any archival material either side will surrender. The letters, diaries, journals, memoranda of the leaders of the labor and management groups, of individual workers and minor executives—all these materials will be sought to provide the background for researchers into the history of the subject. When such a library's selection officer reads *Publishers Weekly*, he/she will order anything new that is listed, without waiting for reviews—for this collection is to be as extensive, inclusive, and as full as possible. The books and other materials derive their value not only from intrinsic worth but from their relationships to other materials in the collection and for the light they may shed on minor—as well as major—points. The assumption underlying the building of such a collection is that it is not intended for the use of the "general reader," but for the specialized researcher. The definitive studies whose writing such collections are created to assist cannot be based on a few general, even if excellent, popularizations.

Another example may perhaps be allowed. On the University of Michigan campus, there is a special library of early American history, the William L. Clements Library. It is a collection of *source* materials, not of secondary sources. That is, the books on its shelves describing, let us say, a battle in the American Revolution, were written *at that time*. The library is not interested in collecting modern works about the social customs of early America; it tries to buy books printed in early America which reveal social customs. It does not refuse to buy a book because the author's style is defective—it is interested in collecting all it can find that was published in the period it covers. It is block buying—by period.

This type of buying is not restricted to any one type of library, nor is it only characteristic of large libraries. The smaller college and public libraries may have only one single special collection, but as much care and time may be lavished on it as on the dozens of special collections of the largest institutions. The special library serving business or industry may resemble the special collection in a university library in the type of acquisitions policy which is followed. Even the smallest public library may make some attempt at collecting local history.

Bibliography

General

ACM Conference on Space, Growth and Performance Problems of Academic Libraries. Chicago, 1975. *Farewell to Alexandria; Solutions to Space, Growth, and Performance Problems of Libraries.* Edited by Daniel Gore. Westport, Conn., Greenwood Press, 1976. 180p. Ten essays with implications for collection development.

American Library Association. Collection Development Committee. *Guidelines for Collection Development.* Chicago, American Library Association, 1979. 78p. Essential for collection development policy statements.

Baughman, James C. "Toward a Structural Approach to Collection Development." *College and Research Libraries,* 38:241–248, May 1977. Emphasizes the use of structure of subject literatures in collection development.

Broadus, Robert N. *Selecting Materials for Libraries.* 2d ed. rev. New York, H. W.
Wilson, 1981. 469p. By subject and format.

Buckland, Michael K. *Book Availability and the Library User.* New York, Pergamon,
1975. 196p. Considers, among other questions, how many titles a library
should have.

Danky, James P. and Elliott Shore. *Alternative Materials in Libraries.* Metuchen,
N.J., Scarecrow Press, 1982. 255p. Covers aspects of acquisitions plus cataloging and reference services.

Futas, Elizabeth. *Library Acquisition Policies and Procedures.* Phoenix, Ariz., Oryx
Press, 1977. 406p. Reprints 26 policies and parts of 56 others.

Katz, William A. *Collection Development.* New York, Holt, Rinehart and Winston,
1980. 352p.

University and Research Libraries

Association of College and Research Libraries. "Standards for University Libraries." *College and Research Libraries News,* 40:101–110, April 1979.

Bach, Harry. "Why Allocate?" *Library Resources and Technical Services,* 8:161–165,
Spring 1964. Concise statement on the pros and cons.

Borkowski, Casimir. "A Reply to the Kent Study." *Library Journal,* 106:710–713,
April 1, 1981. Critique of the controversial study of University of Pittsburgh
libraries, focusing on mistakes in data analysis.

Bryant, Douglas W. "The Changing Research Library." *Library Scene,* 4:2–4+,
September 1975. Review of problems facing large university libraries, with
specific references to development of Harvard.

Burton, Robert E. "Formula Budgeting: An Example." *Special Libraries,* 66:61–67,
February 1975. Presents an example based on a university library.

Clapp, Verner W. and Robert T. Jordan. "Quantitative Criteria for the Adequacy
of Academic Library Collections." *College and Research Libraries,* 26:371–380,
September 1965. Presents a formula for estimating collection adequacy.

Coleman, Kathleen and Pauline Dickinson. "Drafting a Reference Collection
Policy." *College and Research Libraries,* 38:227–233, May 1977. Includes copy of
policy drafted at San Diego State University.

Coppin, Ann. "The Subject Specialist on the Academic Library Staff." *Libri,*
24:122–128, 1974. Brief state-of-the-art review.

Danton, J. Periam. "The Subject Specialist in National and University Libraries,
with Special Reference to Book Selection." *Libri,* 17:42–58, 1967.

DePew, John N. "An Acquisitions Decision Model for Academic Libraries."
Journal of American Society for Information Science, 26:237–246, July–August
1975.

Dickinson, Dennis W. "A Rationalist's Critique of Book Selection for Academic
Libraries." *Journal of Academic Librarianship,* 7:138–143, July 1981. A case for
faculty responsibility for book selection. Followed by "Six Responses."
7:144–151.

Downs, Robert B. "Collection Development for Academic Libraries: An Overview." *North Carolina Libraries,* 37:31–38, Fall 1976. Brief review of major
issues.

Drake, Miriam A. "Forecasting Academic Library Growth." *College and Research*

Libraries, 37:53–59, January 1976. Illustrates use of two quantitative forecasting techniques in a university library.

Edelman, Hendrik. "Reduction, Reduction, Reduction, Reduction: Some Observations on Collection Development." *Cornell University Library Bulletin*, no. 195:8–10, May 1975. Experiences at Cornell.

Edelman, Hendrik and G. Marvin Tatum, Jr. "The Development of Collections in American University Libraries." *College and Research Libraries*, 37:222–245, May 1976. Trends of the past 100 years.

Ehikhamenor, F. A. "Formula for Allocating Book Funds; The Search for Simplicity and Flexibility." *Libri*, 33:148–161, June 1983.

Evans, Glyn T. "The Cost of Information About Library Acquisition Budgets." *Collection Management*, 2:3–23, Spring 1978. Factors which influence the budget and information needed.

Fussler, Herman H. and Julian L. Simon. *Patterns in the Use of Books in Large Research Libraries*. Chicago, University of Chicago Press, 1969. 210p. Based on studies at the University of Chicago.

Gold, Steven D. "Allocating the Book Budget: An Economic Model." *College and Research Libraries*, 36:397–402, September 1975.

Gore, Daniel. "Curbing the Growth of Academic Libraries." *Library Journal*, 106:2183–2187, November 15, 1981.

Goyal, S. K. "Allocation of Library Funds to Different Departments of a University—An Operational Research Approach." *College and Research Libraries*, 34:219–222, May 1973.

Hamlin, Arthur T. "Book Collections of British University Libraries; An American Reaction." *International Library Review*, 2:135–173, April 1970. Similarities and differences between British and American collections.

Hazen, Dan C. "Collection Development, Collection Management, and Preservation." *Library Resources and Technical Services*, 26:3–11, January 1982.

Hazen, Dan C. "Modeling Collection Development Behavior: A Preliminary Statement." *Collection Management*, 4:1–14, Spring–Summer 1982.

Hlavac, R. W. "Book Selection in University Libraries." *New Zealand Libraries*, 34:109–113, June 1971. Emphasizes New Zealand's special problems.

Holley, Edward G. "What Lies Ahead for Academic Libraries?" In *Academic Libraries by the Year 2000; Essays Honoring Jerrold Orne*, edited by Herbert Poole, pp. 7–33. New York, Bowker, 1977. General predictions about academic libraries and the environment in which they will operate.

Hodowanec, George V. "Literature Obsolescence, Dispersion, and Collection Development." *College and Research Libraries*, 44:421–443, November 1983. Methods to help determine the one-third of the collection receiving two-thirds of the use and adjust acquisitions accordingly.

Knightly, John J. "Library Collections and Academic Curricula: Quantitative Relationships." *College and Research Libraries*, 36:295–301, July 1975. Study of curricular similarity and collection duplication in 22 state-supported universities in Texas.

Koenig, Dorothy A. "Rushmore at Berkeley: The Dynamics of Developing a Written Collection Development Statement." *Journal of Academic Librarianship*, 7:344–350, January 1982.

Kohut, Joseph J. "Allocating the Book Budget: A Model." *College and Research Libraries*, 35:192–199, May 1974.

Kohut, Joseph J. and John F. Walker. "Allocating the Book Budget: Equity and Economics Efficiency." *College and Research Libraries*, 36:403–410, September 1975. Response to Gold (1975) above.

Leach, Steven. "Growth Rates of Major Academic Libraries: Rider and Purdue Reviewed." *College and Research Libraries*, 37:531–542, November 1976.

Lynden, Frederick C. "Library Materials Budgeting in the Private University Library: Austerity and Action." In *Advances in Librarianship*, Vol. 10, 1980. pp. 90–154.

McGrath, William E. "A Pragmatic Book Allocation Formula for Academic and Public Libraries with a Test for Its Effectiveness." *Library Resources and Technical Services*, 19:356–369, Fall 1975.

Magrill, Rose Mary and Mona East. "Collection Development in Large University Libraries." In *Advances in Librarianship*, Vol. 8, pp. 1–54. New York, Academic Press, 1978. Literature review emphasizing the last two decades.

Martin, Murray. "Budgeting Strategies: Coping with a Changing Fiscal Environment." *Journal of Academic Librarianship*, 2:297–302, January 1977. Based on a hypothetical university library budget.

Michalak, Thomas J. "Library Services to the Graduate Community: The Role of the Subject Specialist." *College and Research Libraries*, 37:257–265, May 1976.

Montgomery, K. Leon and others. "Cost-Benefit Model of Library Acquisitions in Terms of Use." *Journal of the American Society for Information Science*, 27:73–74, January–February 1976. Project at the University of Pittsburgh.

Olsson, A. L. "Developing a Selection Policy for the National Library." *New Zealand Libraries*, 34:51–53, April 1971.

Osburn, Charles B. "Planning for a University Library Policy on Collection Development." *International Library Review*, 9:209–224, 1977. How and why to develop a written policy.

Pierce, Thomas J. "An Empirical Approach to Allocation of the University Library." *Collection Management*, 2:39–58, Spring 1978.

Reid, Marion T. "Coping with Budget Adversity: The Impact of the Financial Squeeze on Acquisitions." *College and Research Libraries*, 37:266–272, May 1976. How ten ARL libraries adjusted.

Rice, Barbara A. "The Development of Working Collections in University Libraries." *College and Research Libraries*, 38:309–312, July 1977. Argues that working collections must replace comprehensive collections.

Rogers, Rutherford, D. and David C. Weber. *University Library Administration*. New York, H. W. Wilson, 1971. 454p. Chapter 5 covers book collections.

Schad, Jasper G. and Norman E. Tanis. *Problems in Developing Academic Library Collections*. New York, Bowker, 1974. 183p. Thirty case studies covering a variety of problems.

Skelley, Grant T. "Characteristics of Collections Added to American Research Libraries, 1940–1970: A Preliminary Investigation." *College and Research Libraries*, 36:52–60, January 1975.

Taggart, W. R. "Book Selection Librarians in Canadian Universities." *Canadian Library Journal*, 31:410–412, September–October 1974. Reviews trends toward fulltime selection personnel.

Texas. University at Austin. The University of Texas at Austin General Libraries. *Collection Development Policy*. Austin, 1981. 2d. ed. 250p.

Thompson, James. *Introduction to University Library Administration*. 2d rev. ed.

London, Clive Bingley, 1974. 164p. Chapter 4 covers collections. British viewpoint.

Urquhart, J. A. and N. C. Urquhart. *Regulation and Stock Control in Libraries.* Stocksfield, Northumberland, Oriel Press (Routledge and Kegan Paul), 1976. 154p. Introduction discusses broad issues of academic library collection development.

Voigt, Melvin J. "Acquisition Rates in University Libraries." *College and Research Libraries,* 36:263–271, July 1975. Presents a model for estimating necessary minimum annual acquisition rate.

Vosper, Robert G. "Collection Building and Rare Books." In *Research Librarianship; Essays in Honor of Robert B. Downs,* edited by Jerrold Orne, pp. 91–111. New York, Bowker, 1971. Development of collections in the largest American university libraries.

Webb, William H. "Collection Development for the University and Large Research Library: More and More Versus Less and Less." In *Academic Libraries by the Year 2000: Essays Honoring Jerrold Orne,* edited by Herbert Poole, pp. 139–151. New York, Bowker, 1977.

Liberal Arts Colleges and Undergraduate Libraries

Association of College and Research Libraries. "Standards for College Libraries." *College and Research Libraries News,* 36:277–279; 290–301, October 1975. "Standard 2" concerns collections.

Braden, Irene A. *The Undergraduate Library.* Chicago, American Library Association, 1970. 158p. (ACRL Monograph No. 31) Case studies of undergraduate libraries at six universities.

Buckeye, Nancy. "A Plan for Undergraduate Participation in Book Selection." *Library Resources and Technical Services,* 19:121–125, Spring 1975. Followed by critical responses from three academic librarians.

Carpenter, Ray L. "College Libraries: A Comparative Analysis in Terms of the ACRL Standards." *College and Research Libraries,* 42:7–18, January 1981. Concludes most libraries do not meet the standards.

Clifford Library and Learning Resources Collection Development Policies 1983-84. Evansville, Ind., University of Evansville, 1983. 42p. May be useful to librarians who are developing policies for a similar institution.

Farber, Evan Ira. "Limiting College Library Growth: Bane or Boon?" *Journal of Academic Librarianship,* 1:12–15, November 1975. Considers how a college library should differ from a university library.

Horny, Karen. "Building Northwestern's Core." *Library Journal,* 96:1580–1583, May 1, 1971. Describes development of a 30,000-volume noncirculating collection primarily for undergraduates.

Lyle, Guy R. *Administration of the College Library.* 4th ed. New York, H. W. Wilson, 1974, 320p. Two relevant chapters.

Lynch, Beverly P. "The Changing Environment of Academic Libraries." *College and Research Libraries,* 39:10–14, January 1978. Covers trends in financing, admissions, and curriculum; also applicable to universities.

Massman, Virgil F. "Changes That Will Affect College Library Collection Development." In *Academic Libraries by the Year 2000; Essays Honoring Jerrold Orne*, edited by Herbert Poole, pp. 152–164. New York, Bowker, 1977.

Munn, Robert F. "Collection Development vs. Resource Sharing: The Dilemma of the Middle-Level Institutions." *Journal of Academic Librarianship*, 8:352–353, January 1983.

Person, Roland, ed. "University Undergraduate Libraries: Nearly Extinct or Continuing Examples of Evolution? A Symposium." *Journal of Academic Librarianship*, 8:4–13, March 1982. Varying opinions.

Sullivan, Daniel. "Libraries and Liberal Arts Colleges: Tough Times in the Eighties." *College and Research Libraries*, 43:119–123, March 1982. Predicts a reduction in scholarly publication and if libraries can preserve fiscal support, they will come out okay in collection development.

Wingate, Henry W. "The Undergraduate Library: Is It Obsolete?" *College and Research Libraries*, 39:29–33, January 1978. Reviews trends in separate undergraduate collections on university campuses.

Junior Colleges/Community Colleges

Allen, Kenneth W. and Loren Allen. *Organization and Administration of the Learning Resource Center in the Community College*. Hamden, Conn., Linnet Books, 1973, 187p. Chapter five touches on collection development.

Association of College and Research Libraries and Association for Educational Communications and Technology. "Guidelines for Two-Year College Learning Resources Programs." *College and Research Libraries News*, 43:5–10, 45–49, January and February 1982. Contains a section on materials.

Canadian Association of College and University Libraries. *Standards Recommended for Canadian Community College Libraries*. Ottawa, Canadian Library Association, 1973. 8p.

Carpenter, Raymond L. "Two-Year College Libraries: A Comparative Analysis in Terms of the ACRL Standards." *College and Research Libraries*, 42:407–415, September 1981. Increased financial aid is needed if two-year college libraries are to meet standards.

Dale, Doris Cruger. "The Community College Library in the Mid-1970's." *College and Research Libraries*, 38:404–411, September 1977. Review based on visits to 31 campuses during 1975–76.

Truett, Carol. "Services to Developmental Education Students in the Community College: Does the Library Have a Role?" *College and Research Libraries*, 44:20–28, January 1983. Has major implications for collection development.

Veit, Fritz. *The Community College Library*. Westport, Conn., Greenwood Press, 1975. 221p. Contains several relevant chapters.

School Library Media Centers

American Association of School Librarians. *Media Programs: District and School*. Chicago, American Library Association; Washington, D.C., Association for Educational Communications and Technology, 1975. 136p.

American Association of School Librarians. "Policies and Procedures for Selection of Instructional Materials." *School Media Quarterly*, 5:109–116, Winter 1977. Revision of AASL's 1970 official statement on the selection process.

Baker, D. Philip and David R. Bender. "An *SMQ* Feature: Marketing, Selection, and Acquisition of Materials for School Media Programs." *School Media Quarterly*, 6:97–132, Winter 1978; 6:171–201, Spring 1978. Contains six papers based on a 1976–77 survey of school media programs, media producers, and distributors.

Davies, Ruth. *The School Library Media Program: Instructional Force for Excellence.* 3d ed. New York, Bowker, 1979. 580p.

Gerhardt, Lillian. *Issues in Children's Book Selection.* New York, Bowker, 1973. 216p. Reprints 29 articles from *Library Journal* and *School Library Journal*.

Gillespie, John T. and Diana L. Spirt. *Administering the School Library Media Center.* New York, Bowker, 1983. 381p.

Gillespie, John T. *A Model School District Media Program.* Chicago, American Library Association, 1977. 207p. (ALA Studies in Librarianship No. 6) Case study of Montgomery County, Maryland.

Guidelines for Evaluating Computerized Instructional Materials. Reston, Va., National Council of Teachers of Mathematics, 1981. 416p. Vital for all libraries purchasing software.

Hartz, Frederic R. "Selection of School/Media Materials." *Catholic Library World*, 47:425–429, May–June 1976. Brief review of factors involved.

Hicks, Warren B. and Alma M. Tillin. *Managing Multimedia Libraries.* New York, Bowker, 1977.

Johnson, Mary Frances K. "Media Selection: Six Concerns." *Catholic Library World*, 47:416–417, May–June 1976.

Lathrop, Ann and Bobby Goodson. *Courseware in the Classroom: Selecting, Organizing, and Using Educational Software.* Reading, Mass., Addison-Wesley, 1983. 187p.

Liesener, James W. *A Systematic Process for Planning Media Programs.* Chicago, American Library Association, 1976. 166p. Emphasizes identifying needs and setting priorities.

Moss, Carol E. "Budgeting for Media Selection and Ordering." *Catholic Library World*, 47:423–424, May–June 1976. Brief review of considerations.

Nickel, Mildred L. *Steps to Service: A Handbook of Procedures for the School Media Center.* Chicago, American Library Association, 1975. 136p. Includes sections on selection and ordering.

Prostano, Emanuel T. and Joyce S. Prostano. *School Library Media Center.* 3d ed. Littleton, Colo., Libraries Unlimited, 1982. 200p. For the beginner.

Saunders, Helen E. *The Modern School Library.* 2nd ed., rev. by Nancy Polette. Metuchen, N.J., Scarecrow Press, 1975. 237p. Focuses on secondary schools.

Shapiro, Lillian L. *Serving Youth: Communications and Commitment in the High School Library.* New York, Bowker, 1975. 268p. Includes a selective list of selection tools in appendix.

Taylor, Mary M. *School Library and Media Center Acquisitions Policies and Procedures.* Phoenix, Ariz., Oryx Press, 1981. 272p. Contains samples of complete policies.

Thomas, James L. *Nonprint in the Secondary Curriculum.* Littleton, Colo., Libraries Unlimited, 1982. Includes valuable list of sources.

Van Orden, Phyllis J. *Collection Program in Elementary & Middle Schools: Concepts, Practices, & Information Sources.* Littleton, Colo., Libraries Unlimited, 1982. 301p. Invaluable for print and nonprint evaluation criteria.

Woodbury, Marda. *Selecting Materials for Instruction: Issues and Policies.* Littleton, Colo., Libraries Unlimited, 1980.

Woodbury, Marda. *Selecting Materials for Instruction: Media & the Curriculum.* Littleton, Colo., Libraries Unlimited, 1980.

Woodbury, Marda. *Selecting Materials for Instruction: Subject Areas & Implementation.* Littleton, Colo., Libraries Unlimited, 1980. A three-volume set of major importance.

Woolls, Blanche. "Forty Items Per Student; An Investigation of Alternatives in Collection Design." *School Media Quarterly,* 4:116–120, Winter 1976. Suggests a formula for determining collection adequacy.

Special Libraries and Special Collections

Ahrensfeld, Janet L. and others. *Special Libraries: A Guide for Management.* New York, Special Libraries Association, 1981. 75p. Chapter 4 addresses the collection.

Allen, William R. and others. "Developing a Quantitative Formula for the Book Collection in Small Academic Technical Libraries." *Science and Technology Libraries,* 2:59–68, Fall 1981. The development of the BHEG (Bell & Howell Education Group) formula for maintaining a current collection.

Anthony, L. J. *Handbook of Special Librarianship and Information Work.* 5th ed. London, Aslib, 1982. 416p. Section 3 contains three chapters on selection, acquisition, and storage.

Bayley, Linda and others. *Jail Library Service: A Guide for Librarians and Jail Administrators.* Chicago, American Library Association, 1981, 114p.

Bradley, Jana, ed. *Hospital Library Management.* Chicago, Medical Library Association, 1983. 412p. Covers both selection and acquisition of materials.

Burnett, Alfred D. "Considerations on the Support of Antiquarian and Other Special Collections in University Libraries." *Journal of Librarianship,* 5:203–213, July 1973. Argues for supporting such collections and suggests ways. British viewpoint.

Chen, Ching-chih. *Applications of Operations Research Models to Libraries: A Case Study of the Use of Monographs in the Francis A. Countway Library, Harvard University.* Cambridge, Mass., MIT Press, 1976. 212p. Discusses implications of book-use models for selection.

Cohen, Jackson B. "Science Acquisitions and Book Output Statistics." *Library Resources and Technical Services,* 19:370–379, Fall 1975. How to plan and control development of science collections.

Darling, Louise. *Handbook of Medical Library Practice.* 4th ed. Chicago, Medical Library Association, 1983. 368p. Emphasizes acquisition, selection and preservation of materials in a health sciences library.

Dickson, Lance E. "Law Library Book Orders: An Analysis of Current Practice." *Law Library Journal,* 73:446–450, Spring 1980.

Dingle-Cliff, Susan and C. H. Davis. "Comparison of Recent Acquisitions and OCLC Find Rates for Three Canadian Special Libraries." *American Society for Information Science Journal*, 32:65–69, January 1981.

Fraser, Meta Doreen Eliot and H. A. Lloyd. *Information Needs of Physiotherapists: With a Guide to Physiotheraphy Collections for Community General Hospitals.* Halifax, Nova Scotia, Dalhousie University School of Library Service, 1981. 72p.

Giblin, Robert. "Changes and Challenges: Law School, the New Legal Education and the Law Library." *Law Library Journal*, 73:693–701, Summer 1980.

Gnudi, Martha T. "Building a Medical History Collection." *Medical Library Association Bulletin*, 63:42–46, January 1975.

Grattan, Mary C. "Collection Development in Texas State Agency Libraries: A Survey with Recommendations." *Special Libraries*, 68:69–75, February 1977. Summarizes responses from twenty special libraries.

Harleston, Rebekah M. and Carla J. Stoffle. *Administration of Government Documents Collections.* Littleton, Colo., Libraries Unlimited, 1974. Basic text covering a variety of topics, including selection and acquisition.

Mount, Ellis. *Special Libraries and Information Centers: An Introductory Text.* New York, Special Libraries Association, 1983. 194p. Chapters 19–22 address collection development concerns.

Mount, Ellis. *University Science and Engineering Libraries: Their Operation, Collections, and Facilities.* Westport, Conn., Greenwood, Press, 1975. 214p.

Mount, Ellis, ed. "Document Delivery for Sci-Tech Libraries." *Science and Technology Libraries*, 2:1–112, Summer 1982. Five articles, including "a guide to locating sources of foreign scientific and technical publications." Names, addresses, loan policies included.

Mount, Ellis, ed. "Monographs in Sci-Tech Libraries." *Science and Technology Libraries*, 3:1–76, Spring 1983. Six articles on the role of the book in a variety of sci-tech environments.

Mount, Ellis, ed. "Role of Serials in Sci-Tech Libraries." *Science and Technology Libraries*, 4:1–90, Spring, 1984. Seven articles on varying aspects of the issue.

Moys, Elizabeth M. *Manual of Law Librarianship: The Use and Organization of Legal Literature.* Lexington, Mass., Lexington Books, 1976. 736p. Emphasizes types of materials needed and has one chapter on acquisition.

Myers, Mildred S. and William C. Frederick. "Business Libraries: Role and Function in Industrial America." *Journal of Education for Librarianship*, 15:41–52, Summer 1974.

Nichols, Harold. *Map Librarianship.* London, Clive Bingley, 1976. 298p. British viewpoint.

Opello, Olivia and Lindsay Murdock. "Acquisitions Overkill in Science Collections—And an Alternative." *College and Research Libraries*, 37: 452–456, September 1976. Argues for stricter selection criteria.

Pacey, Philip. *Art Library Manual.* New York, Bowker in association with Art Libraries Society, Great Britain, 1977. 423p.

Phinney, Eleanor. *The Librarian and the Patient.* Chicago, American Library Association, 1977. 352p. "An Introduction to Library Services for Patients in Health Care Institutions." Includes selection of materials.

Raper, Diane and Lillian Stevenson. "Use of Prestel in a Solicitors' Law Firm in the City." *Law Librarian,* 12:4–6, April 1981.

Roper, Fred W. "Selecting Federal Publications." *Special Libraries,* 65:326–331, August 1974. Emphasizes value of written policies.

Schwartz, James H. "Accessibility, Browsing, and a Systematic Approach to Acquisitions in a Chemical Research Company Library." *Special Libraries,* 62:143–146, March 1971. Development of a new acquisitions policy.

Schwartz, James H. "Technical Books: Appraisal of Selection Policy and Use by Creative Chemists." *Special Libraries,* 65:58–60, February 1974. Related to previous article by same author.

Sinha, Bani K. and Richard C. Clelland. "Applications of a Collection-Control Model for Scientific Libraries." *Journal of the American Society for Information Science,* 27:320–328, September–October 1976. Operations research approach.

Sprudzs, Adolf. "Problem with Sources of Information in International Law and Relations: The Case of the World-wide Treaty Jungle." *International Journal of Law Libraries,* 9:195–202, October 1981.

Strauss, Lucille J. and others. *Scientific and Technical Libraries: Their Organization and Administration.* 2d ed. New York, Wiley, 1972. 450p. One chapter covers selection of books and journals.

Tees, Miriam H. "Special Libraries in the 1980s." *Show-Me Libraries,* 33:33–36, October–November 1981.

Werner, O. James. *Manual for Prison Law Libraries.* Littleton, Colo., Rothman, 1976. 120p.

Blanket Orders and Approval Plans

Association of Research Libraries. Systems and Procedures Exchange Center. *Approval Plans in ARL Libraries.* The Center, 1982. 109p.

Axford, H. William. "The Economics of a Domestic Approval Plan." *College and Research Libraries,* 32:368–375, September 1971. Compares approval plans with traditional selection and acquisition methods.

Cargill, Jennifer S. and Brian Alley. *Practical Approval Plan Management.* Phoenix, Ariz., Oryx Press, 1979. 95p.

DeVilbiss, Mary Lee. "The Approval-Built Collection in the Medium-Sized Academic Library." *College and Research Libraries,* 36:487–492, November 1975. Study conducted at California State Polytechnic University.

Dobbyn, Margaret. "Approval Plan Purchasing in Perspective." *College and Research Libraries,* 33:480–484, November 1972.

Dudley, Norman. "The Blanket Order." *Library Trends,* 18:318–327, January 1970. Results of a survey of large university libraries.

Evans, G. Edward and Claudia White Argyres. "Approval Plans and Collection Development in Academic Libraries." *Library Resources and Technical Services,* 18:35–50, Winter 1974. Study conducted in nine libraries.

Franz, Ted. "Automated Standing Order System. Blackwell North America." *Serials Review,* 7:63–67, January 1981.

Gregor, Jan and W. C. Fraser. "University of Windsor Experience with an Approval Plan in Three Subjects with Three Vendors." *Canadian Library Journal*, 38:227–231, August 1981.

International Conference on Approval Plans and Collection Development, Milwaukee, 1979. *Shaping Library Collections for the 1980s.* Edited by Peter Spyers-Duran and J. J. Mann. Phoenix, Ariz., Oryx Press, 1980. 235p.

McCullough, Kathleen and others. *Approval Plans and Academic Libraries:; An Interpretive Study.* Phoenix, Ariz., Oryx Press, 1977. 154p. Report of a 1975 survey of 144 libraries.

Perrault, Anna H. "New Dimensions in Approval Plan Service." *Library Acquisitions*, 7 no. 1:35–40, 1983.

Reidelbach, John H. and G. M. Shirk. "Selecting an Approval Plan Vendor: A Step-By-Step Process." *Library Acquisitions*, 7 no.2:115–125, 1983.

Stave, Donald G. "Art Books on Approval: Why Not?" *Library Acquisitions*, 7 no. 1:5–6, 1983.

CHAPTER 6

SELECTION AIDS

It stands to reason that the process of collection development in any library cannot depend solely on the personal knowledge of the staff. The sheer volume of publication, past and present, in the range of subject fields which even the smallest library will wish to represent, renders reliance on outside sources necessary. In addition, for a library to reflect a healthy diversity of topics and perspectives, the opinions of more than just its own staff must be brought to bear upon the selection process. Bibliographies, book and non-book reviews, catalogs of standard works, and topical checklists are among the abundant selection aids available for the purpose. An annotated list of the book selection aids appears at the end of this chapter.

What is important for every library to remember is that no single source will provide all the help needed. Learning to use review sources well is a skill that requires time and effort. One tool may be best for general adult titles, another best for children's materials, while none is perfect all of the time and thus selection should be based on more than one review.

Aids to Effective Selection

Although it is impossible for the individual librarian to cover the whole field of current publishing, it is possible to fall back upon the helpful principle of division of labor. In a large library, various members of the staff can be assigned to follow particular aspects of the publishing output. In the small library, the librarian will have to rely upon the various book selection aids, which represent a coverage of current publishing by many people, reporting their pooled judgment of the best being published. If it is impossible for each librarian to be a specialist in every subject, it is possible to divide the labor once again, and let those on the staff who are specialists in a subject be responsible for selection in that subject. If there are subject areas in which the library does not have a person with training, the book selection aids can be called upon for help, since their lists in the various subjects will represent the judgment of people who are informed in those fields.

There are many book selection aids which can assist the average librarian to do a satisfactory job. They vary in the speed with which they cover current publishing, in the type of materials reviewed, in the kind and amount of information given for each title, in the type of library for which they are intended, in format, frequency, and usefulness. The librarian must know the various aids and their special characteristics. Even when approval copies of new books can be examined or the books seen in galley proofs in advance of publication, the librarian will want to read the reviews.

Advance notices may be seen in the advertising pages and forecast lists of *Publishers Weekly, Library Journal,* and *Forthcoming Books,* or in the announcements of individual publishers. After the bare bibliographic bones—author, title, publisher, date, and price—have been noted, the title can be checked in *Kirkus Reviews,* which carries informal and informative reviews of popular books approximately six weeks before publication date. In "The Book Review" section of *Library Journal* are found signed reviews mostly written by librarians, useful because the evaluation is made in terms of type of collection or type of library. It is limited, however, to reviewing adult titles only. It reviews audiovisual materials and runs a regular column of magazine reviews by Bill Katz. Many of the reviews of books appear in advance of publication.

About the time of publication, the title appears in the *Weekly Record* published by Bowker, if the publisher has sent in a copy of the book in advance of publication date. At about the same time, reviews appear in the weekly book review sections of such newspapers as the *New York Times, Washington Post,* and those of other major metropolitan areas. Local newspapers which publish book reviews should be read regularly also, as these reviews will be reflected in library requests.

Weekly periodicals frequently carry lively and critical reviews. *Time, New Yorker, Newsweek,* and the *Saturday Review* feature one or more reviews and give brief and pertinent annotations about other books.

All of the reviewing media mentioned above present timely reviews either before publication or near the date of publication. Let us now turn our attention to reviews which appear after publication, but which can still be used as aids in the selection of current books.

The American Library Association's general guide to current

books is the *Booklist,* which can be used by public librarians as well as school librarians at any level. It contains excellent reviews of audiovisual materials as well as books, and offers special lists periodically of books in a particular foreign language. *Booklist* is the only periodical reviewing a range of materials for all age groups. Also published by ALA is *Choice,* designed for use by junior college and liberal arts college libraries. It is also important for the selection of books for secondary school librarians serving honor groups of students.

General periodicals, notably *Atlantic, Ms. Magazine, Psychology Today,* have excellent review sections; the timeliness of the reviews varies. The scholarly journals also contain reviews, although they generally appear long after the book is published.

Retrospective Aids

There are aids for the selection of basic collections, which can be used for retrospective buying to fill in gaps and strengthen the library in the various subject fields. The American Library Association and the H. W. Wilson Company have been responsible for the development of basic book selection aids for various types of libraries. That pioneer librarian, Melvil Dewey, envisioned an *A.L.A. Catalog* as early as 1877, the year after the organization of the ALA. Its historical background has been traced by Russell E. Bidlack in his article, "The Coming Catalogue; or, Melvil Dewey's Flying Machine." The catalog was originally published as a government document by the Bureau of Education and bears the imprint date of 1893. Its full title was *Catalog of the "A.L.A." Library; 5,000 Volumes for a Popular Library Selected by the American Library Association and Shown at the World's Columbian Exposition.* The books listed were displayed at the exposition in Chicago, and the preparation of the catalog was under the direction of Mary S. Cutler, Vice-Director of the Albany Library School.

This was the forerunner of the *A.L.A. Catalog; 8,000 Volumes for a Popular Library, with Notes (1904),* which was prepared by the ALA in cooperation with the New York State Library and the Library of Congress for the St. Louis World's Fair. The *ALA Catalog, 1926; an Annotated Basic List of 10,000 Books,* was followed by periodic polyennial supplements. Aimed at informing the librarian of the smaller public library, this annotated basic list was selected cooperatively by some four hundred librarians and was limited in its inclusion to a selection of standard and popular titles available at the time.

Growing up beside the later supplements of the *ALA Catalog* was the former "Standard Catalog" series of the H. W. Wilson Company. The present *Public Library Catalog* was published at first in eight separate sections which were brought together into a single, nonfiction volume in 1934. As in the case of the *ALA Catalog*, the selection of titles was a cooperative venture, with a number of librarians taking part. About one-fourth of the titles were starred for first purchase by small public libraries or those with limited book funds. The *Fiction Catalog* was first published in 1908, and is kept up-to-date by new editions and by supplements. Its purpose is to serve as a buying list of the best fiction for library use. Mention must also be made of the *High School Library Catalog*, *Junior High School Library Catalog*, and the *Children's Catalog*.

There are several aids to the selection of books for junior college and liberal arts college libraries. The most recent college lists are *Books for College Libraries* (ALA, 2d ed., 1975), which includes a selected list of 40,000 titles. Two older basic lists are 1) *Catalog of the Lamont Library (1953)*, which was intended to support the particular needs of the Harvard undergraduate program, and 2) the *Shelf List of the University of Michigan's Undergraduate Library (1958–62)*. For junior colleges, older lists include Frank J. Bertalan's *Junior College Library Collection* and James Pirie's *Books for Junior College Libraries.*

A librarian charged with building a collection for a new college library will have need of retrospective tools, as well as guides to current publishing. Checking the *Lamont Library Catalog* and the *University of Michigan Undergraduate Shelflist* as well as *Books for College Libraries* for a given subject would provide a broader review of past titles than using any one of them alone. All three were developed with somewhat different aims, and thus complement each other. An excellent older list, Charles B. Shaw's *List of Books for College Libraries* (1931, and its 1931–38 continuation, 1940), may be used profitably for retrospective buying. Care must be exercised in retrospective acquisition to avoid selecting obsolete materials.

In recent years there has been a move toward providing librarians with standard compilations in narrow fields, as opposed to the broad areas covered by those items we term catalogs. Bowker has produced entire volumes devoted exclusively to horror and science fiction titles. ABC-Clio in cooperation with Neal-Schuman Publishers has produced an excellent "Standard

Guide Series" on such topics as *Latino Materials* and *Energy*. These have the big advantage of being multi-media guides so that all formats are included. Scarecrow Press has a wide range of specific biliographic guides for all types of collections from the very esoteric to *Witness to War*, a guide to the literature on World War II for young adults.

While using tools on specific subjects requires more time and energy than using one or two comprehensive volumes, the effort is worth it when a library needs to strengthen a specific portion of its collection. Since none but the largest libraries can afford all the professional tools available, libraries involved in cooperative systems should insist that the headquarters collection contain the broadest possible range of these valuable professional tools.

Some Caveats

Most librarians must depend upon the various selection aids for their information about new titles. It is important, therefore, to consider whether there are any weaknesses in this system for aiding librarians in their choice of titles. Various studies have revealed that most of the reviews of books tend to be favorable, which might cast some doubt upon their objectivity. This tendency to praise is accounted for in part by the fact that only those books considered worthwhile are chosen for reviewing, and omission constitutes a negative review. It is certainly true that many books are never reviewed, and the librarian depending upon the general reviewing media would never become aware of their existence. Furthermore, if the conscientious librarian wants to read a number of reviews, in order to form a more sound judgment of a book, he/she may well be disappointed. Except for the very popular titles—particularly in non-fiction—only a bare minimum of reviews is likely to appear, and some titles may not be reviewed at all. It is also well to recall that the reviewer for the general periodical or newspaper does not have the particular needs of a given library in mind when the review is written—indeed, it is highly unlikely that the reviewer is thinking of libraries at all, but is expecting readers of the review to be individuals concerned about buying books for themselves or as gifts. These are real limitations upon the usefulness of the non-library based reviewing media, and yet the system appears to work reasonably well. It seems safe to say that the really significant titles of any given year receive full attention, and that the library will not be seriously misled by the reviews, in spite of their limitations. He/she may develop various techniques for compensating for the weaknesses of the reviewing system: as one wit put it, if one can find only favorable reviews, one can start judging a book on the basis of the degree of enthusiasm expressed by the reviewer. A consistent reading of the various media over a period of time will reveal their individual characteristics and enable the librarian to make these adjustments.

The librarian who selects books needs to have a personal knowledge of books, to continue developing his/her knowledge of subject fields (a task which ought to be considered a lifetime part of the librarian's job), to know the general reading interests of people and the special interests of her/his own community. The librarian ought to have the courage to implement the principles of book selection with honesty and impartiality, avoiding arrogance on the one hand and an unprofessional subservience on the other. It is to be hoped that balanced, sane, and informed judgments will be made, but the composite judgment of many librarians and critics which is embodied in the various book selection aids is an important counter to the necessarily limited knowledge and personal bias of the individual selector.

Invaluable though they may be to the selection process, too slavish a reliance on a few general review sources can stifle opportunities for creative collection development. The small library may be able to subscribe to only a small percentage of the book-review media listed at the chapter end, but a wide range of collection development aids is available at no additional cost in publications which the library already acquires for general interest purposes. *Art News, Architectural Record, Poetry Magazine, The New Yorker, the Nation, Scientific American, Nature,* and many other periodicals to which most libraries subscribe are not primarily "review" journals, but the few reviews they do include are of particular value because they often represent the specialized perspectives of leaders and activists in their respective fields. A healthy balance between current and retrospective collection development is important. An abundance of bibliographies will be found within a great many volumes added in due course to the general collections. Checking the annual *Library Journal* "Best Business Books" or "Best Reference Books" lists, the subject bibliographies in virtually every issue of *Choice,* the *New York Times* "Best Books of the Year" and any number of such lists at one's very fingertips can richly expand the collection scope derived from routine reliance on general review sources. Of course, conscientious subject specialists will read widely in their fields and participate in the relevant professional associations; and any would-be selector who can passively pass by a bookstore has some soul-searching to do. Ferreting out government publications, free and inexpensive materials, small press and alternative works, community information and referral data, and similarly elusive supplements is basic not only to the health of the collections but to that necessary ingredient of excitement in the very process of collection development.

Book Selection Aids

Guides to Reviews and Selection Aids

Book Review Digest. New York, Wilson, 1905–
Recent books published or distributed in the U.S. may have reviews cited and excerpted here if enough reviews (generally, two or more for nonfiction and four or more for fiction) appear in the selected periodicals within eighteen months after publication of the book. Coverage per year is now running around 6,000 titles. Each book is entered under author, with full bibliographic data, followed by a brief descriptive note and the excerpts, which are limited to three for fiction and four for nonfiction. Other reviews are cited bibliographically. A list of more than 70 periodicals from which reviews are taken is given, and the student of book selection should study this list carefully as a clue to the types of books which will be selected for inclusion in *Book Review Digest*. It is published monthly except in February and July, with cumulations three times a year and an annual bound cumulation. An author and title index covering 1905–1974 in a single alphabet was published in 1976 in four volumes.

Book Review Index. Detroit, Gale Research, 1965–
Cites reviews from about 325 periodicals and newspapers and arranges the citations alphabetically by the author of the book reviewed. Unlike the *Book Review Digest* it provides no descriptive notes or excerpts from the reviews but only the citation to the review (periodical, reviewer, volume, date and page). It does provide, however, greater speed, more diversity of sources, and a larger number of citations than *BRD*. Total citations in excess of 40,000 per year. Frequency of publication has varied since 1965, but current publication is bimonthly with annual cumulations.

Children's Book Review Index. Detroit, Gale Research, 1975–
Excerpts from *Book Review Index* citations to all reviews of books
intended for pre-school to junior high readers. Arranged alphabetically by author. Published three times a year with annual
cumulations.

Index to Book Reviews in the Humanities. Williamstown,
   Mass., Philip Thomson, 1960–
Originally a quarterly, it has been published annually since
1963. Beginning with the 1971 volume the policy of selectively
indexing reviews from a wide range of popular and scholarly
periodicals that might occasionally review a book in the "humanities" (broadly interpreted) was dropped in favor of indexing all reviews in a specified list of about 160 humanities periodicals. It is arranged alphabetically by author of the title
reviewed.

Technical Book Review Index. Pittsburgh, JAAD Publishing
   Co., 1935–
Originally, the primary purpose of this index was to identify
reviews in current scientific, technical, and trade journals. With
the January 1973 issue the coverage was broadened to cite and
briefly quote reviews from periodicals in all scientific, technical,
and medical (except clinical) subjects. Special Libraries Association published *TBRI* from 1935–1976, when the present publisher assumed responsibility. Covers more than 3,000 reviews
each year. Publication is monthly.

Aids to Media Selection for Students and Teachers. Compiled
   by Kathlyn J. Moses and Lois B. Watt. Rev. Washington,
   D.C., U.S. Dept. of Health, Education and Welfare, 1976.
   128p.
Selected and annotated list of review sources for materials "of
relevance for elementary and secondary school instructional
programs." Emphasizes tools published since 1970. Three sections: 1) book selection sources; 2) sources of audiovisual materials; 3) sources of multiethnic materials.

Hart, Thomas L. and others. **Mutli-Media Indexes, Lists and
   Review Sources: A Bibliographic Guide.** New York, Dekker, 1975, 273p.
Includes more than 400 reviewing sources, covering both print
and nonprint media. Structured annotations give bibliographic
information, scope, arrangement, special features, etc. for each
entry. Sample pages are included to illustrate many of the
sources.

Multi-Ethnic Media: Selected Bibliographies in Print. Compiled by Task Force on Ethnic Materials Information Exchange, Social Responsibilities Round Table; David Cohen, coordinator. Chicago, American Library Association, Office for Library Service to the Disadvantaged, 1975. 33p.
Annotated listing of in-print bibliographic essays and bibliographies dealing with most ethnic groups. Covers publications for children and young adults.

Selecting Materials for Children and Young Adults: A Bibliography of Bibliographies and Review Sources. Association for Library Service to Children and Young Adult Services Division. Chicago, American Library Association, 1980. 74p.
Contains over 300 sources (some few no longer in existence) ranging from annual lists to specialized review sources in subject areas.

Current Reviewing Sources

Review periodicals listed in this section review a broad range of materials. Sources limited to a particular genre are found in the section following.

Booklist. Chicago, American Library Association, 1905– (Semimonthly)
Each issue contains longer reviews of 10–20 reference books (prepared by ALA's Reference and Subscription Books Review Committee), 100–130 shorter reviews of adult fiction and nonfiction, as well as books for children and young adults, films, other non-book media and selected government publications. All items listed are recommended for library purchase and are intended to represent the best judgment of library subject specialists, who are familiar with the new books in their respective fields.

Books in Canada. Toronto, Canadian Review of Books, Ltd., 1971–   . (10 issues per year)
Each issue contains 30–50 signed reviews of varying length on selected new Canadian publications in a variety of fields. Includes general articles on Canadian writing and publishing. Aimed at the bookstore trade.

BooksWest; A National Journal of the Book Trade. Los Angeles, Books-West Magazine and Book Fair, Inc., 1976– (Monthly)
General articles on books and publishing and a number of signed reviews and short notices of new books.

British Book News. London, British Council, 1940– (Monthly)
Reviews British publications on all subjects (excludes textbooks and most juvenile fiction). It is divided into three parts: 1) a general article or two dealing with some aspect of the library, literary, or artistic world; 2) signed evaluative reviews of recommended books (about 200 per issue), with full bibliographic information; 3) a selected list of forthcoming books, not annotated.

Bulletin of the Center for Children's Books. Chicago, University of Chicago, 1947– . (Monthly)
Each issue contains 60 to 80 reviews of current trade books for children and early teens. Unsigned reviews by specialists are critical, and grade levels, reading level difficulty, and literary quality are always evaluated. The *Bulletin* is noted for its coding system and reviews of not recommended titles.

Choice. Chicago, American Library Association, Association of College and Research Libraries, 1964– . (Monthly)
Evaluates current books of a scholarly or academic nature considered to be of interest to an undergraduate library. Unsigned reviews of about 500–600 titles are provided in each issue. These are prepared by the editor and a large roster of subject specialists. Primarily intended to assist the selection of books for college libraries, this tool is useful in many other types of libraries: public, junior college, secondary school, special and foreign libraries. Special features include the "Opening Day Collection" which began in July 1965 and is now in its third edition (separately published in 1974) and regular subject-centered bibliographic articles. There is also a "reviews-on-cards" service, which supplies the reviews reprinted individually on 3 × 5 cards. A classified cumulation of all reviews from the first ten years of *Choice* (nearly 60,000 books) has been published (Rowman and Littlefield, 1976–1977) in nine volumes, including an index.

Horn Book Magazine. Boston, 1924–   . (Bimonthly)
Detailed, signed reviews of children's books and audiovisuals,
along with many articles by and about authors and illustrators. A
well-established source for information about children's books
and reading.

Kirkus Reviews. New York, Kirkus Service, 1933–
    (Semimonthly)
Makes available to booksellers, librarians, and interested individuals informal and informative reviews of books, including
children's books, with particular emphasis on coverage of fiction. Although not all publishers are represented, reviews are
given about six weeks before date of publication, a feature
which many librarians have found very useful, as they can order
and receive books by the time they are published and reviews
for them appear in the general reviewing media, leading to a
demand by patrons for the books. Widely used by public librarians as a primary selection tool, although the reviews are
not presented from the library viewpoint alone.

Library Journal. New York, Bowker, 1876–   . (Semi-
    monthly)
Book review section, which is arranged by broad subject areas,
contains signed reviews written by librarians and educators,
giving practical evaluations of current titles, both negative and
positive. Many of the reviews appear prior to the date of publication of the book. These reviews are also available on 3×5
cards. Annually, approximately 6,500 adult books are reviewed.
Special features include spring and fall announcement issues
and special issues on business, technical, medical, and scientific
books, reference books, and small presses. Articles often address selection dilemmas.

New York Times Book Review, 1896–   . (Weekly)
Published weekly as part of the Sunday edition, but available as
a separate by subscription. (Daily editions also carry reviews of
books, not by the *Book Review* staff.) Informative reviews, often
written by authorities in the subject field, sometimes written by
staff members. This is a standard selection tool for many librarians. In 1973, a cumulative index (1896–1970) was published
in five volumes to serve as the index to a 125 volume reprint of
all the reviews. The index allows an approach to earlier reviews
by author, title, reviewer, subject, and genre.

Publishers Weekly. New York, Bowker, 1872–   . (Weekly)

The standard American book trade journal; carries "Forecasts," a section of descriptive annotations of nonfiction, fiction, children's books, and paperbacks (originals and reprints) to be published in the next month or two. Special issues include Spring, Summer, and Fall announcement numbers (including books to be published in the near future) as well as a children's book issue, etc.

School Library Journal. New York, Bowker, 1947–   (Monthly)

Supplies review coverage of juvenile books similar to that given adult books in *Library Journal*. Total number of signed reviews appearing in a year usually exceeds that of any other single reviewing service covering books published for children and young adults. Special features include semiannual "best books" lists. Formerly published as a part of *Library Journal*.

Voice of Youth Advocates. University, AL, 1978–   . (Bimonthly)

Over 200 signed reviews, per issue, of both print and nonprint materials for school and public libraries serving adolescents; emphasizes adult titles of interest to teenagers and original paperbacks, as well as professional materials from disciplines outside of librarianship. Major articles on collection development and issues in young adult services.

Review Aids for Individual Subjects

Appraisal; Children's Science Books. Cambridge, Mass., Children's Science Book Review Committee, 1967–   . (3 issues per year)

Reviews by both a librarian and a science specialist of juvenile books.

Aslib Book List. London, Aslib, 1935–   . (Monthly)

Selected, classified list of new British publications in science and engineering. Annotations by specialists indicate the level of reader suitability.

In Review; Canadian Books for Children. Toronto, Provincial
  Library Service, Ontario Ministry of College and Universities, 1967–   . (Quarterly)
Signed, critical reviews of recent books. Includes titles not recommended or only recommended with reservations. General
articles on children's books.

Interracial Books for Children Bulletin. New York, Council on
  Interracial Books for Children, 1967–   . (8 issues
  per year)
Articles on the writing and publishing of books for or about
minority groups, a concept now expanded to include the aged,
the disabled, as well as women, blacks, et al. Book reviews of
both recommended and not recommended titles.

Locus. Oakland, Calif., 1968–   . (Monthly)
"The newspaper of the science fiction field" is a gold mine of
information about the current state of science fiction publishing.
Contains reviews as well as news items.

New Technical Books. New York, New York Public Library,
  1915–   . (Monthly)
Selected, classified list of new technical books, mostly published
in the U.S. Descriptive annotations.

Science Books and Films; The Quarterly Review. Washington,
  D.C., American Association for the Advancement of Science, 1975–   . (Quarterly)
Critical reviews of books and 16mm films on pure and applied
sciences aimed at students (elementary, secondary, junior college) and general readers.

Retrospective Selection Aids

Alternatives in Print: Catalog of Social Change Publications.
  San Francisco, Glide Publications, 1971–
Offers a subject and producer approach to publications of all
varieties except serial publications. Annual.

Bertalan, Frank. **Junior College Library Collection.** 1970 ed.
Newark, N.J., Bro-Dart Foundation, 1970. 503p.
In the 1970 revised edition, this selected list of more than 22,000
books for junior and community college libraries aims to assist
in the selection of titles, in all subject areas, that should be
provided by new institutions and by established schools that are
expanding their facilities. Scope attempts to reflect the curriculum
trends in junior and community colleges. Arranged by the
Library of Congress classification with full bibliographic information.
Libraries that had used the first edition contributed suggestions
for the revision.

Books for College Libraries; A Core Collection of 40,000 Titles.
2d ed. Chicago, American Library Association, 1975. 6v.
The first edition of this tool (1967) was a one-volume work prepared
under the direction of Melvin J. Voigt and Joseph H.
Treyz and intended as a successor to Charles B. Shaw's *Books for
College Libraries.* It listed 53,410 titles, carefully selected to support
basic undergraduate studies and restricted to those published
before 1964 (which was the beginning date for *Choice*).
The second edition appeared as six paperbound volumes—five
volumes divided by broad subject classes (humanities, language
and literature, history, social sciences, and psychology, science,
technology, and bibliography) with the sixth being an index.
Each entry includes a complete catalog record (author, title, edition,
collation, subject and added entries, L.C. class number,
L.C. card number, and ISBN).

Books for Public Libraries. 3rd ed. Chicago, American Library
Association, 1981. 374p.
Unannotated Dewey Decimal arrangement of recommended titles.
Author-title index.

Canadian Book Review Annual. Toronto, Peter Martin Associates,
1975–
Attempting to be an "annual evaluative guide to Canadian English
language trade books," *CBRA* provides concise reviews
(200–400 words) of new Canadian titles published during the
year. As more volumes of this source are published, it will serve
as a useful tool for retrospective selection. Annual volumes are
arranged by broad subject categories and have author, title, and
subject indexes.

Children's Catalog. New York, Wilson, 1909–
The fourteenth edition of this work appeared in 1980, containing over 5,000 titles selected for their usefulness in school libraries and public library work with children. The book is arranged in classified order, using the latest abridged Dewey. An author, title, subject and analytic index follows the classified order, and a directory of publishers is appended. The catalog is supplemented annually, adding approximately 600 titles per year. Entry gives full bibliographical data, including subject headings and aids to cataloging, with an evaluative annotation quoted from reviews.

Elementary School Library Collection. Greensboro, N.C., Bro-
    Dart Foundation, 1965–
The fourteenth edition of this regularly updated tool appeared in 1984 and included more than 10,000 recommended books, periodicals, filmstrips, transparencies, etc. The basic arrangement is a classified one, but there are index approaches by author, title, and subject. Annotations are included and there is a system of indicating which titles are considered most basic to a beginning collection.

Fiction Catalog. New York, Wilson, 1908–
A guide to adult fiction found most useful in public libraries, it is published periodically, with annual supplements. The tenth edition, containing more than 5,000 titles in the basic volume, with 2,000 more to be covered in the four annual supplements, was published in 1980. The arrangement is alphabetical by author, with full bibliographic information and annotations. The second part is a subject and title index, followed by a directory of publishers and distributors. It is intended for use by medium-sized and small public libraries, but many high schools also find it useful.

Good Reading: A Guide for Serious Readers. 21st edition. Edit-
    ed J. Sherwood Weber. New York, Bowker, 1978. 313p.
Good list of contemporary titles as judged by male college professors. Very few female authors included.

Junior High School Library Catalog. New York, Wilson, 1965–
The 1980 edition includes 3,775 titles selected for grades seven through nine; annual supplements add approximately 500 titles each year. As with other volumes in the Wilson Standard Cata-

log Series, Part 1 is a classified list with full bibliographic information and a descriptive or critical annotation; Part 2 is an author, title, subject index, with analytical entries for stories and plays in collections; and Part 3 is a directory of publishers and distributors.

Library Journal Book Review. New York, Bowker, 1967–
An annual reprinting of all the reviews that have appeared in *Library Journal,* arranged by subject and indexed by author and title. Since several thousands of reviews are included for each year, this is a convenient place to search for reviews of books published in the U.S. during the years covered. Author and title index.

Public Library Catalog. New York, Wilson, 1934–
Formerly known as the *Standard Catalog for Public Libraries,* the seventh edition of this work, published in 1978, is a selected, classified list of over 8,500 nonfiction titles which have been suggested by practicing librarians because of their usefulness in public library collections. Part 1 is a classified list (by Dewey) with brief annotations; part 2 is an author, title, and subject index, with analytical entries for parts of books; part 3 is a directory of publishers and distributors. Annual supplements update the work with approximately 3,200 additional titles. (New edition in preparation)

Reader's Adviser. 12th ed. New York, Bowker, 1974–77. 3v.
Subtitled "A Layman's Guide to Literature," this basic selection tool (which has been published since early in this century) supplies bibliographic information and annotations on thousands of best books. *Reader's Adviser* has traditionally supplied considerable information about author, editions, translators and price. The three volumes cover 1) fiction, poetry, literary biography, bibliography and reference; 2) drama, world literature in English translations; 3) non-literary subjects (religion, science, communications, history, etc.).

Senior High School Library Catalog. New York, Wilson, 1926–
Formerly the *Standard Catalog for High School Libraries,* this list emphasizes material for students in the tenth through twelfth grades. The twelfth edition, published in 1982, includes over 5,000 titles. The first part is a classified catalog, arranged according to the Dewey Decimal Classification, with an annotation for

each title. The second part is an author, subject, and analytical index, while the third part is a directory of publishers and distributors. Annual supplements. Useful for basic, traditional titles.

Specialized Retrospective Selection Aids

The following are just a few of the many superior selection aids which focus on a particular subject, either for all ages, or a particular age group. Consult new bibliographies of Selection Aids for updating and additions to the list.

Alternative Materials in Libraries. Edited by James P. Danky and Elliott Shore. Metuchen, N.J., Scarecrow Press, 1982. 255p.
Articles on aspects of acquisitions and cataloging of materials plus a list of sources.

Anatomy of Wonder; A Critical Guide to Science Fiction. 2d ed. Edited by Neil Barron. New York, Bowker, 1981. 724p.
A model for what an annotated specialized bibliography should be. Essays introduce each section, followed by bibliographies of books from the time period being discussed. Recommends first purchase titles and annotations refer the user to similar or contrasting titles.

Baskin, Barbara H. and Karen H. Harris. **Notes from a Different Drummer; A Guide to Juvenile Fiction Portraying the Handicapped.** New York, Bowker, 1977. 375p.
Annotated bibliography plus informative essays on attitudes toward the disabled; criteria for selection.

Beyond Fact; Nonfiction for Children and Young People. Compiled by Jo Carr. Chicago, American Library Association, 1982. 224p.
Essays on various problems connected with the writing of nonfiction. Important background information for the selector.

The Bookfinder. Volume 1. Compiled by Sharon Spredemann Dreyer. Circle Pines, Minn., American Guidance Service, 1977. 1030p.

The Bookfinder. Volume 2. Compiled by Sharon Spredemann
Dreyer. Circle Pines, Minn., American Guidance Service,
1981. 723p.
Covering literature for youth aged 2–15, these unique volumes
have a split page format allowing the user to keep the subject
heading in sight while locating various titles in the alphabetical
author arranged section. The subject headings are the highlight,
focusing on affective terms such as loyalty, friendship, rather
than traditional topic oriented terms.

Duran, Daniel Flores, **Latino Materials: A Multimedia Guide
for Children and Young Adults.** Santa Barbara, CA: ABC-
Clio, 1979. 249p.
One of a series of excellent titles published in cooperation with
Neal-Schuman, which contains evaluative annotations, criteria
that can be used by other librarians, and materials in all formats.
Other titles include such subjects as drugs and energy.

Ettlinger, John R. T. and Diana Spirt. **Choosing Books for
Young People.** Chicago, American Library Association,
1982. 219p.
Annotated bibliography of books about children's books pub-
lished "from 1945 to 1975 in the English language in the United
States, Great Britain, and Canada." Also French-language pub-
lications from Canada and those titles from Australia and New
Zealand that could be located.

Guiley, Rosemary. **Love Lines; The Romance Reader's Guide to
Printed Pleasures.** New York, Facts on File, 1983. 323p.
Readable overview of the leading romance series and the people
who write them and the art of publishing them.

National Association of Independent Schools. Library Committee. **Books for Secondary School Libraries.** 6th ed. New
York, Bowker, 1981. 844p.
Classified list of about 9,000 titles, prepared for use in private
schools with high academic requirements.

Reading Ladders for Human Relations. 6th ed. Edited by Eileen
Tway. Washington, D.C., American Council on Education, 1981. 398p.
The 6th edition of this standard title expands coverage to include preschool children's materials. It has five ladders de-

signed to help youthful readers understand themselves and others better.

Schon, Isabel. **Books in Spanish for Children and Young Adults: An Annotated Guide.** Metuchen, N.J., Scarecrow Press, 1983. 172p.
Contains both recommended and not recommended titles.

Turkus, Burton. **Murder, Inc.** New York, Woodhill, 1975. 448p.
Guide to the outstanding (mostly male) mystery writers.

U.S. Department of Education. Refugee Materials Center. 324 East 11th Street, 9th Floor, Eleven Oak Building, Kansas City, Mo., 64106. [**Bibliography.**] 152p.
This untitled bibliography consists of materials for Vietnamese, Laotian, Chinese, Iranian, Thai, and other immigrants to the United States. Some materials are free from the Refugee Materials Center; others are produced by commercial or non-profit groups. Listing of publishers and addresses included.

Velleman, Ruth A. **Serving Physically Disabled People.** New York, Bowker, 1979. 392p.
Besides excellent background information, beginning with a description of the numerous physical disabilities, this contains a recommended core collection of materials for public libraries.

Wellner, Cathryn J. **Witness to War: A Thematic Guide to Young Adult Literature on World War II, 1965–1981.** Metuchen, N.J., Scarecrow Press, 1982. 277p.
Literate bibliographic essays on various aspects of World War II as found in young people's literature. Useful for building supplementary social studies collections.

Reference Books

American Library Association. Reference Services Division. Ad Hoc Reference Books Review Committee. *Reference Books for Small and Medium-Sized Libraries.* 3d ed. Chicago, American Library Association, 1979. 150p.
Aimed at public libraries serving populations of 10,000–75,000. Over 800 annotations.

American Reference Books Annual. Littleton, Colo., Libraries Unlimited, 1970–
Signed, evaluative reviews of new reference books. Each annual list contains approximately 1,500 entries. Cumulative indexes.

Best Reference Books 1970–1980: Titles of Lasting Value Selected from American Reference Books Annual. Edited by Bohdan S. Wynar. Littleton, Colo., 1981. 480p.
Reprints nearly 1,000 reviews chosen by the editor from the first ten volumes of *ARBA*.

Henderson, Diane. **Guide to Basic Reference Materials for Canadian Libraries.** 6th ed. Toronto, University of Toronto Press, 1980.
Prepared for use in the Faculty of Library Science, University of Toronto. Contains "basic and representative works" under four broad headings. Some annotations. Looseleaf.

Katz, William. **Introduction to Reference Works.** 2v. 4th ed. New York, McGraw, 1982.
Comprehensive discussion of reference selection sources, as well as reference works themselves, in the context of their use in libraries.

Kister, Kenneth F. **Dictionary Buying Guide: A Consumer Guide to General English-Language Wordbooks in Print.** New York, Bowker, 1977. 358p.
Evaluates 58 adult and 61 juvenile dictionaries, as well as a number of general and research dictionaries and wordbooks.

Kister, Kenneth F. **Encyclopedia Buying Guide: A Consumer Guide to General Encyclopedias in Print.** 3d ed. New York, Bowker, 1981.
Detailed descriptions and evaluations of nonspecialized adult, school, popular and one-volume encyclopedias.

Peterson, Carolyn S. and Ann D. Fenton. **Reference Books for Children.** Metuchen, N.J., Scarecrow Press, 1981. 273p.
Annotations of approximately 900 books.

Reference and Subscription Books Reviews. Chicago, American Library Association, 1956/60–
Reprints from *Booklist* reviews of reference books prepared by members of ALA's Reference and Subscription Books Review

Committee. Recent volumes each include over 100 reviews and 250 notes and comments. The 1975–76 volume contained a ten-year cumulative index. Biennial.

Reference Services Review. Ann Arbor, Mich., Pierian Press, 1973–
"Reference Sources," a regular feature, carries bibliographic information, cataloging information, citations of reviews and quotations from them for new reference works (approximately 4,000 per year). Annual, hardcover cumulations of "Reference Sources" have been issued, beginning in 1977. *RSR* also carries state-of-the-art surveys on reference works in a variety of subject areas. Quarterly.

Ryder, Dorothy E. **Canadian Reference Sources: A Selective Guide.** Ottawa, Canadian Library Association, 1973. 185p. Supplement, 1975. 121p.
Basic volume includes a selection of over 1,200 Canadian reference materials. Supplement adds new works and editions published up to December 1973.

Sheehy, Eugene P. **Guide to Reference Books.** 9th ed. Chicago, American Library Association, 1976. 1015p. Supplement, 1980, 316p.
Classified, annotated list of over 10,000 titles recommended for large, general reference collections. Arranged under five major subject areas, subdivided by subject and form. (Previous edition was edited by Constance M. Winchell.)

Walford, A. J. **Guide to Reference Material.** 3rd ed. London, Library Association, 1973–1977. 3v.
Classified, annotated list of important reference books. International with some emphasis on British publications. First volume covers science and technology; second covers social science, history, philosophy and religion; third covers literature, languages, arts, etc.

Wynar, Christine L. **Guide to Reference Books for School Media Centers.** Littleton, Colo., Libraries Unlimited, 1981. 377p.
Annotates more than 3,000 titles. Selections are chosen on the basis of suitability for grades K–12 and junior college.

Government Publications

Government Reference Books: A Biennial Guide to U.S. Government Publications. Littleton, Colo., Libraries Unlimited, 1968/69–
Biennial, annotated subject guide to reference books published by the U.S. Government Publishing Office. Serves to update Wynkoop's *Subject Guide to Government Reference Books* (1972), which lists over one thousand major government reference books published before 1968.

Municipal Government Reference Sources: Publications and Collections. Prepared by Local Government Task Force, Government Documents Round Table, American Library Association. New York, Bowker, 1978.
Identifies and annotates several thousand current reference publications of 200 municipalities and associations such as the League of Women Voters.

Parish, David W. **State Government Reference Publications: An Annotated Bibliography.** 2d ed. Littleton, Colo., Libraries Unlimited, 1981. 360p.
Selective guide to over 1,000 documents issued by states and territories. Arranged by state.

Pohle, Linda C. **A Guide to Popular Government Publications: For Libraries and Home Reference.** Littleton, Col., Libraries Unlimited, 1972. 213p.
Approximately 2,000 books and periodicals on such subjects as consumer education, environment, etc.

"Selection Guide to High Interest Government Publications." *Government Publications Review,* 3:305–317, Winter 1976.
Special annotated list started with this issue and continued in later issues.

Van Zandt, Nancy Patton. **Selected U.S. Government Series: A Guide for Public and Academic Libraries.** Chicago, American Library Association, 1978. 172p.
Annotations of approximately 600 depository series titles considered useful for small and medium-sized libraries.

Wynkoop, Sally. **Subject Guide to Government Reference Books.** Littleton, Colo., Libraries Unlimited, 1972. 276p.
See *Government Reference Books,* above.

CHAPTER 7

THE SELECTOR AND NON-BOOK MATERIALS

Librarians have always collected some types of non-book materials, such as pamphlets, maps, periodicals, and clippings. They also collected non-print materials such as globes, shells, and rock samples. Large public library systems and academic libraries serving music departments began very early to collect phonodiscs. In addition to phonodiscs, since the early 1950s there has been an explosion of new formats in which information comes: films, 16mm and 8mm, filmstrips, slides, audiotapes (reel-to-reel, cassettes), audiovisual tapes (reel-to-reel, cassettes), microfilm, microfiche, and computerized learning programs.

The major reason libraries contain so many formats is that good librarians have instinctively understood that the forms by which communication occurs are cumulative. As far as we can determine, no form of communication is ever totally lost—we add techniques, but the older ones while losing their primacy, never really disappear. Thus, the longer libraries are in existence, the more formats they will find to collect.

As mentioned earlier, school libraries and junior college libraries have been quickest to absorb new formats into their collections. Academic libraries have been the slowest, but as more and more information is being packaged on cassettes, audio and video, even academic libraries have come to accept the fact that some information needed by their patrons is not available in print form and must be collected in whatever format it can be had. For example, most major conferences today offer participants, and those unable to attend, the opportunity to purchase audiocassettes of the important speeches.

The increased acquisition of non-book materials has brought with it a greater concern with problems of selection, sources of information about and methods of acquisition of the various types, and problems of handling them once they are acquired. This field is so extensive that full treatment of the problem in all its aspects would require several separate volumes. In the present context, only the briefest introduction can be attempted. The chapter bibliography will provide the interested reader with additional sources to help move from an overview to the intricacies of the subject.

The selection of non-book materials is, of course, based ultimately on the same principles as for the selection of books. However, the application of those principles differ considerably according to format. Some of those differences are peculiar to a particular format; others are more universal. For example, it is rare for a book reviewer to ask, "Is this the best format for presenting this information or entertainment?" Yet that is an overriding question in selecting non-book materials. It takes years of work to become a good audiovisual librarian, learning the technical arts of audiovisual production as well as the aesthetic standards used in evaluation. It takes a book selector less time to master these skills since the good selectors have been readers all their lives and have absorbed much of the information by osmosis. Few of us instinctively acquire the same skills in relation to audiovisual materials without considerable effort. An additional problem is that no one librarian has the time or interest to be equally qualified to select in all non-book areas. A parallel can be drawn to the subject specialist who selects books in the humanities but would be lost in trying to select technological works. For some non-book areas, reviews will be of great value to the librarian, in others, reviews are only the beginning, not the end, of the decision-making process. These differences will be expanded below.

The decision to acquire non-book materials goes beyond the presence of a staff person capable of doing the job. The subset of non-book materials labelled non-print require the acquisition of special equipment to use them, and they require special equipment to service and maintain the materials. For example, it would be a rare library that went through each and every book upon its return from a patron to see that all pages were present and accounted for. Every film circulated must be checked upon its return, which is one reason why libraries generally request patrons not to rewind borrowed prints.

A major problem involved in the non-book field is administering the collection. Many librarians have boggled at the tasks involved in checking films for damage, splicing broken film, keeping motion picture projectors in working order. The problems involved in cataloging, storing, and preserving records weakened the resolve of some librarians to be modern and progressive in their acquisition of this medium. Limited financial resources may cause some libraries to hesitate about extensive acquisition of non-book media.

Films, Videocassettes

Building a film collection is expensive and is generally limited to a system concept. School systems, universities, and public library systems develop separate departments to select, process, and circulate films, thus assuring the maximum use of titles. It is interesting to note that university audiovisual departments are generally independent of the university library. In school systems they may be separate or part of the comprehensive Learning Resource Center. Some state libraries have extensive film collections, available to the public through local public libraries and available for loan directly to libraries wishing to use films as part of their programming activities. It is a rare small or medium-sized library that can afford to develop a local collection.

It is extraordinarily difficult to define the scope of a film collection. Is it to be built to serve the needs of in-house programming? If so, for what age group or groups? Is it to be developed to meet the needs of community groups? If so, for entertainment when the group can't come up with a program speaker, or for educational purposes? School systems tend to focus on the potential classroom use of films to help teachers add dimension to the subjects covered in textbooks. Unlike the rigid age-definition that accompanies book selection, the more groups a film can be perceived as appealing to, the better its investment.

Selection of films and videocassettes (which may be original productions or merely an alternate, less expensive format of a film) differs in significant ways from the selection of books. Librarians can, and do, rely on reviews when selecting books. Librarians can, and do, rely on an author's popularity so they may place an order for a new James Michener, for example, the moment its publication is announced rather than waiting for reviews. The most that can go wrong with this procedure for book selectors is a mistake costing about $20. On the other hand, no good audiovisual librarian would invest $500 or more in a film that the librarian had not previewed in person. Since there are always a limited number of preview prints available, there may be a considerable time lag between when an audiovisual librarian learns of a film's existence and the time the librarian may actually get to see it.

To counteract this time lag, it is essential that the audiovisual librarian have a large enough travel budget to attend the major film festivals held throughout the country. These festivals, the most notable being the American Film Festival sponsored by the Educational Film Library Association, are excellent opportunities to preview a large number of films in a short time. Festivals also offer the opportunities to talk directly with filmmakers and distributors. Furthermore, one is surrounded by other film librarians with whom one can exchange opinions, share problems and solutions, and obtain leads as to the existence of films one may have missed along the way.

Videocassettes cost less than 16mm films, but if they are an alternate format to the 16mm film, they are generally not available for preview. The librarian then must have the skill to recognize whether the film previewed on a large screen will translate effectively to the smaller video screen. This decision involves not only understanding the technical aspects of the film, but deciding whether the content is better suited for small groups or individuals or large groups. The 16mm film is clearly a better format for large groups; the videocassette better for individuals and small groups, all other items being equal. In these characteristics videocassettes resemble 8mm and super 8mm films. The latter are very popular for children's parties and other events where small groups wish entertainment.

A major decision facing librarians in relation to videocassettes is whether to buy 3/4 inch or 1/2 inch VHS or Beta or all three if the cassettes are to be circulated to the public. Unlike motion picture equipment that accepts all 16mm films, cassettes are compatible only with certain machines.

The least expensive format for providing major commercial motion pictures is the videodisc. However since its equipment is for playing discs, but cannot record off-air programming, it has not found widespread acceptance by the public thus limiting the number of patrons who might take advantage of the service.

In a discussion of film and video presentations, it is necessary to draw the distinction between those made by Hollywood and television producers for showing in commercial theaters and on television and those designed primarily for educational institutions. While all motion picture producers must find financial backing, the independent filmmaker faces the problem of trying to tap into very limited pools of money from such philanthropic groups as the National Endowment for the Humanities. If successful in obtaining the necessary money to produce the film, the filmmaker is then faced with the added problem of finding a distributor willing to handle the finished product. These differences must be understood in order to develop a collection policy statement that either incorporates both types or limits the library's collection to one or the other.

Commercial videocassettes and videodiscs are distributed in ways similar to those in the book field. Stores exist across the country where they can be bought; there are commercial lending stores where one can rent cassettes for private use at home. For educational films, it is necessary to deal with each distributor directly. There is no central source, such as a book wholesaler/ jobber firm, for purchasing educational films. This is true for all non-book materials and makes the acquisition process more laborious than that for books.

The above statements apply to all audiovisual librarians, but there is an additional problem for the librarian assigned to develop a new collection of films and related audiovisuals. Bibliographic, or perhaps more correctly, cinemagraphic, control of films and other audiovisuals is practically non-existent. There are no counterparts to the H. W. Wilson "Standard Catalogs" for audiovisuals. Thus, a librarian wishing to develop a collection of films is faced with a huge administrative problem.

One approach to the problem is to acquire the film catalogs from major library systems, e.g., The New York Public Library, The Prince George's County (MD) Memorial Library System, and state library collections, and merge the lists to see which films are widely duplicated. It will be necessary to have a copy of the collection development policy from the libraries to be sure their goals in acquiring films are similar to yours.

After analyzing the annotations to determine the content, and thus the suitability for the collection being developed, the librarian can request preview prints and make a final decision. The very process of previewing that produces the time lag mentioned above, is a big plus in this situation since film distributors expect all purchasers to preview a film before purchasing, however old the film. Book publishers, on the other hand, expect librarians to purchase books from reviews and standard selection sources and would not dream of providing a review copy of an older title.

The absence of good standard selective sources for films does more than impede the building of a new collection: it makes it difficult for the librarian wishing to plan to rent films for a film program series to locate the best possible sources. There is a great need in the field for a wide variety of recommended film lists. The majority of those in existence focus on materials more suitable for classroom use than for general library programming.

Filmstrips, Slides

Filmstrips—lengths of 35mm film containing a series of still pictures—are fairly inexpensive, require uncomplicated projection equipment, and are popular in school libraries, less so in other types. They may be silent, with captions on the pictures, or accompanied by a cassette or disc recording. Generally the cassette and disc contain an audible signal on one side and an inaudible signal on the second side. The audible signal cues the projector operator, the inaudible signal advances the filmstrip one frame automatically.

There are advantages and disadvantages to filmstrips as with all other formats. They lack motion, thus limiting their use to the presentation of information best presented in a static form. However, they are more easily stopped (16mm projectors with freeze-frame capabilities are rare and expensive) thus allowing the viewer to advance at his or her own pace in absorbing the information. Filmstrips of popular children's picture books allow the librarian to share a good book with a much larger audience than when doing a picture book program with the book itself. Good school libraries have "wet carrels" where an individual student can view filmstrips in privacy, and with headphones, without disturbing other library patrons. Filmstrip production has become much more sophisticated in recent years and some are so well done that the lack of motion is hardly noticeable.

Filmstrips are a good investment for libraries. Their slow acceptance by non-school libraries stems from a difference in philosophy as to how patrons are expected to use a library. School librarians expect students to spend time in the library using materials they need or want; public libraries expect patrons to take the materials home (with the exception of reference tools). This expectation means the library would need to provide the equipment as well as the software, an expensive undertaking.

Slides (single frames of 35mm film secured in a 2″ × 2″ or 2-1/4″ × 2-1/2″ mounting) share with filmstrips the advantages of low initial cost and projection equipment which is relatively easy to operate. Depending on the slide package—is it designed to make a coherent point, or is it a collection of slides on a particular subject—slides can be more flexible, can be arranged in any sequence and viewed at any speed, with or without sound accompaniment. Art reproductions on slides often have truer color than that found in all but the most expensive books, and can be projected on a large screen for use by an entire class or group.

Audio Recordings

Audio recordings come on either disc or tape. The discs are the familiar phonodisc or phonograph records. Although there have been a variety of diameters, the typical disc for albums is 12″ in diameter and runs at a speed of 33-1/3 r.p.m. The typical disc for singles is 7" and runs at a speed of 45 r.p.m. The library meeting the current interests of popular music fans, of whatever age, will acquire a large collection of 45s; the library meeting established interests will acquire a large collection of 33-1/3 discs. The two decisions are not exclusive and both types of audio recordings belong in libraries. The 45 collection needs much more attention in terms of updating and discarding of obsolete titles than does the 33-1/3 collection.

Disc recordings are easily scratched and can warp if left lying on a radiator or in a hot car on a summer day, and repeated usage reduces the quality of reproduction obtainable. On the other hand, cassette recordings are vulnerable to accidental erasure, but are convenient to play and not particularly easy to damage. The upsurge in the use of battery operated headphones has made the cassette almost as popular among joggers and others seeking to blot out the environment's noises as the radio. Cassettes have almost completely replaced reel-to-reel tape in both the audiovisual and the exclusively audio fields.

Most libraries emphasize the single monaural cassette in their collections, leaving the 4-track and 8-track stereo cassettes for home purchase. Cassettes are a better buy for popular albums than for classical recordings which require a higher quality of sound reproduction.

As with books and films, the library electing to have an audio recording collection must define its purposes and the clienteles for whom it is being built. Limiting a collection to classical works is similar to saying only classical books will be in the collection. Such a collection might meet the in-depth needs of a very small portion of the library's clientele, but would short-change many other groups. In order to have "something for everyone," the librarian must recognize that no portion of the collection will be definitive, leaving that function to specialized music libraries.

A good audio recording collection will contain: classical works, both symphonic and opera; children's recordings; soundtracks from popular movies; Broadway musicals; country and western; folk music; jazz; popular singers and groups; and spoken word (individual authors reading their works and complete readings of plays). Foreign language instructional recordings are a must for a library. And other educational needs can be met by remaining alert to the cassettes offered by professional groups from their conference proceedings or interviews with important figures offered by such popular magazines as *Psychology Today*. The librarian will be alert to new needs—the interest in reggae and Christian popular music, for example, and add a few such items to test the interests of the patrons. The wider the scope of the collection, the more patrons served.

Maps and Globes

Maps and globes, as visual representations of areas of the world, are an important reference source in libraries of all types. Maps may be physical, emphasizing natural features of the land; political, showing boundaries of governmental units; or special topic, showing such information as historical events, manufacturing, crop production, weather patterns, religious movements, etc. Most libraries have little trouble with maps which come collected in book form as atlases, but some small libraries do have problems with the collection of individual sheet maps and sometimes resist collecting them at all. Because of the special acquisition, storage, and reference requirements associated with individual sheet maps, large research libraries tend to house them in special map collections staffed by librarians with geology or geography backgrounds.

Many maps are produced by government agencies and others are published by commercial firms specializing in that type of material. Information about new maps and atlases may be found in geographical journals, some of which list maps of specialized areas and occasionally review atlases. Acquisition lists of large map libraries and certain national bibliographies also furnish a convenient way to find out what has been published. (Several articles cited in the bibliography at the end of this chapter give details on specific bibliographic sources and distributors for new maps.)

For the average small or medium-sized general library, which collects maps but does not maintain a special collection, the following selection criteria may be useful. Any map, atlas, or globe added to the collection ought, at the very least, to be as accurate as possible. Accuracy may be partly determined by the reputation of the publisher or producer of the map, the type of projection and scale used, and the date of production. Maps, atlases, or globes should be easy to read. The amount of detail presented ought to be appropriate for the size and design of the map and for the intended purpose or audience—maps showing westward trails for elementary school children will differ from similar maps designed for history graduate students. Finally, of course, librarians must be concerned with the potential durability of the new acquisition. Atlases should be on suitable paper and well-bound; individual sheet maps should be on paper appropriate for their intended use and in some cases ought to have a cloth backing or a plastic finish. Those maps important to the needs of the library, but lacking durability in their original format, can be laminated to withstand heavy use. In all cases, of course, the collection plan of the library and the potential use of the materials will influence decisions about format.

School libraries and small and medium-sized public libraries can build a very good collection of state maps by sending post card requests to each state's department of tourism. The resulting package will not only provide a current state map, but invaluable material for the vertical file useful to students doing assignments and to adults planning trips.

Microforms

Microforms are added to a library collection for one or more of three reasons: 1) to acquire materials not available in print; 2) to compress the space required to store the materials, and 3) to preserve print materials in the process of degenerating. While only the first can be termed a selection decision, the three reasons do demonstrate the impact space problems and preservation needs have on collection development.

Microforms come in three basic formats—microfilm, microfiche, and micro-opaque—each of which has several variations. Microfilm is generally produced from high-contrast photographic film, 16mm or 35mm, usually in black and white, although some materials are now available in color microfilm. A single roll of film, typically stored on a reel but sometimes available as a cartridge or cassette, may be rather short (enough to contain a 200-page thesis) or up to 100 feet long (common for long newspaper or journal runs). Microfiche resembles microfilm in that it contains a series of microimages on film, but instead of the images appearing in a row on a roll of film, they are arranged in a grid pattern on a sheet of film. The standard size for microfiche is approximately 4" × 6" (105mm × 148mm), but other sizes are still available. Library materials are also produced on two kinds of micro-opaques, each of which uses a different process for transferring microimages to opaque cards. Microprint is the trade name for the form (stiff 6" × 9" sheets) produced by Readex Microprint Company, and Microcard (3" × 5" opaque cards) is the form owned and produced by Microcard Corporation. Each microform has its own advantages and disadvantages and each requires its own equipment for reading and viewing.

Microforms have greatly enlarged the scope of materials from which the library can select. Many libraries which never could have hoped to build up, for example, a collection of early printed English books in original editions can subscribe to a microform series covering them. This means that it is possible to purchase at a fairly reasonable price copies of items which in the original could not be bought at any price, since they are simply not available, or, if available, could cost a fortune. A whole universe of books is now added to the current trade and ordinary o.p. market.

The traditional principles of selection apply very directly to microforms, since most microform materials acquired by libraries are simply direct copies of printed originals (an exception to this is Computer Output Microform [COM] which is produced directly from machine-readable files without an intermediate printing step). Some of the decisions relating to the purchase of microforms involve broad questions of collection development policy: Will microform be chosen only as a last resort or will it be the favored medium (when available) for certain categories of materials (such as newspapers and back files of journals)? A library's collection development policy ought to help the librarian make decisions about when to buy hard copy and when to acquire microforms. Assuming that a given item is available in both forms, the selector may first consider potential use of the material. How would it probably be used? By whom? For what purpose? For how long? Where? How often? A second major consideration is the question of how long can the print form be expected to last? The change from cotton rags to pulp wood as the base for paper has shortened the life span of paper. If items are to be considered permanent rather than current additions to the collection the question may come down to microform now or microform later. The decision to purchase microforms also involves such questions as storage space (microforms take up less space than print materials but often require better temperature and humidity controls), equipment for the reading and printing, and the relative costs of various formats.

The selector who considers microform purchases must learn a new set of terms. Knowing whether the microform in question comes as a sheet (film or opaque) or a roll and what its overall dimensions are in terms of size and number of cards or width and length of a roll is only the beginning. The librarian ought also to be aware of the image size and placement on the roll or sheet and the reduction ratio. Reduction ratios (the ratio between the size of the original and the size of the microimage) vary widely from one microform project to another, but ought to bear some relationship to the size of type and general condition of the material being reduced. Reduction ratios of 1/12, 1/14, or 1/16 have been typical when the originals were average monographs or journals; 1/16, 1/18, 1/20, when the originals were newspapers or other oversized publications. Microfiche tend to have somewhat higher reduction ratios than microfilm; ultrafiche, for example, is available at reduction ratios greater than 1/100. Higher reduction ratios are being used today because more sophisticated equipment is now available for reducing and enlarging the images.

Another term which the microform selector should add to his/her vocabulary is polarity (whether the image is black on a white background or white on a black background). Positive film reproduces the relationship of black and white found on the original. Negative polarity reverses that relationship, but, of course, a paper copy made from a negative film on a reader-printer will appear as a positive copy. Sometimes microforms are available in both positive and negative forms, so selectors should always specify which is wanted.

Before spending thousands of dollars on a set of microform materials, the selector will also want to investigate the quality of the reproduction, its generation, and the type of film on which the set has been produced. Quality of a microform depends heavily on the density of the images (extent to which dark parts of the image are really opaque), the contrast (extent of difference between the dark areas and light areas of the image), and resolution (extent to which fine lines, closely spaced, can be distinguished). A factor which may affect the quality of the image is the generation of the film—that is, how many copying steps separate the film in question from the original copy. The original negative, called the master negative, is referred to as the first generation. A copy made from that is second generation, a copy made from the second generation negative is third generation, and so on. Librarians are generally advised to look for second or third generation films; later generations are too far removed from the original. The most common film types used in microform projects are silver halide, diazo, and vesicular. Of these three, only silver halide is considered to be of archival quality, and many librarians prefer to buy large or important microform collections on that type of film only.

In addition to the special technical problems relating to the physical characteristics of microforms, librarians encounter selection problems because of the way producers organize their microform projects. Much microform publishing involves long series or large sets, many of which are made up of out-of-print materials. Selectors have some of the same problems here that they have with hard-copy reprint series, with added complications caused by the microformat which makes inspection difficult. Questions arise on the level of individual selection decisions. Does the library really need that expensive microform set? How many of the titles in the series does the library already have? Did the producer furnish enough information about the contents of the series so that it is even possible to answer the previous question? Will the producer agree to supply only part of the set? If not, is the material in the series which the library does not now own important enough to justify taking unwanted duplicates along with it? Is another producer offering a similar set for sale? How much duplication is there between the two sets? Does physical quality appear to be comparable? Which of the two sets is the better buy? Does the series in question come with a manufacturer's guarantee of the content and quality? Does the set come with cataloging copy supplied? (The library's collection development policy may furnish guidelines on whether or not to buy sets that can not be verified or sets with no cataloging available.) Because many microform sets cost hundreds, even thousands of dollars, the time spent avoiding unwise selection decisions is worth the cost.

Computers and Data Bases

The computer revolution has introduced an entirely new dimension into the selection process. Microcomputers can be bought for as little as $100, admittedly with as little as 2K capacity. Others in the under $2000 category have as much as 64K capacity. This phenomenon has led some medium-sized libraries to purchase microcomputers for home lending. Others are providing one or more computers for public use within the library.

The decision to add computers to the library is the first step in a very complex process. Software programs are often not interchangeable among brands—Apple software cannot be used in Radio Shack computers. Since a computer without a wide range of software programs is like an automobile without gasoline (pretty to look at but non-functional), software availability must be determined before a machine is purchased.

While the questions remain the same as for other formats— who will use the computer, for what purposes—the answers require intensive research. Is the computer to be used for library administrative purposes (accounting procedures, for example) as well as for public access? If so, does the hardware manufacturer offer a really good accounting software package? Is a data handler package available that can be used to computerize the

I & R file? Is word processing a high priority? What graphics will be needed and are they available? Will the library focus exclusively on educational packages or add games for entertainment to the collection?

School libraries need to pay particular attention to the educational packages available, ranging from third grade mathematics problems to spelling lessons. Which is not to say that public libraries ought not to offer similar opportunities to their patrons, only that the emphasis differs in degree, not kind.

Since no one manufacturer will offer everything in software programs that a library wants, there must be lengthy discussions about priorities. One may assume that each year will bring additional software programs, so the decision comes down to what is currently available and is that what we most need at this moment.

Data bases may seem outside the selection process, but their availability does impact on the selection process, influencing what is bought and what is no longer needed. As Tina Roose observed in "Online Database Searching in Smaller Public Libraries," (*Library Journal*, September 15, 1983) libraries using data bases can drop the purchase of print versions of major reference tools. The topics being asked for by patrons must be monitored to make sure the library can provide hard copies of articles located in a citation search. Clearly, the nature of the data base search, whether it provides only citations, abstracts, or can provide the complete text, will influence selection decisions. An analogy can be drawn between buying periodical indexes and data bases—citations without access to full text is frustrating to the researcher. A library subscribing to one or more data base services must carefully monitor the search results to determine the relationship between what patrons are needing and the library's ability to fulfill those needs.

Serials

Serials represent a type of publication which is usually distinguished from monographs (separately-published works, usually called books). In general, a serial is considered to be a publication which is issued in successive parts with numbering or chronological designation and intended to be continued indefinitely. This discussion focuses on the literature carrying the terms magazines, periodicals, and journals. (A discussion of other items termed serials follows.) "Magazine," "periodical," or "journal" tend to be used interchangeably, although some prefer to make distinctions among the terms. To these persons, "magazine" seems generally to refer to more popular publications, while "journal" is reserved for scholarly titles; "periodical" seems to be used for either category.

The selection of serials, of whatever variety, presents problems that selection of a book or film does not. The decision to buy a film, audio recording, or book is usually a one-time commitment of money—purchase price and processing cost. The decision to buy a serial represents a continuing commitment of money—a renewal subscription for an indefinite number of years, undoubtedly at a higher price each year, processing costs for each issue, and possible binding costs for each volume. A new serial subscription also means that staff time will be spent on additional decisions concerning that one serial title. Is the title additional or should it replace a currently received title? Should the serial be bound? When and how? Instead of being bound, should it be purchased in microform for preservation of back files? If the library's subscription does not begin with the first issue of volume one, should back files be obtained? Should they be in the original paper format or in microform? None of these decisions is easy and many of them affect sizeable amounts of the library's limited materials budget. The answers to the questions will vary with the purpose of the library and even with individual titles within a collection.

Libraries buy periodicals to cover the most current events or the most recent developments in subject fields (which will not get into book form for some time), to provide reference materials, and for general reading. The type of library involved will strongly affect the original selection of titles and the choice of those for binding and retention. A very small library may buy only a few general magazines, keeping back files no longer than five years, and rely on interloan for photocopies of articles needed older than five years or in periodicals not subscribed to by the library. The large university library may buy and preserve tens of thousands of titles and may spend a large percentage of its materials budget on serial publications.

Serial selection means first finding out that a serial publication exists and then attempting to obtain the information needed to evaluate it. In a library which attempts to build general rather than research collections, the first step is not difficult and the second will be easier than for a research collection. In a library serving primarily non-specialist users, the choice of titles may be based partly on the indexes to which the library subscribes. If one purchases *Reader's Guide*, it seems desirable to try to buy as many of the magazines indexed in it as one can afford, to get the maximum use out of both the index and the magazines. There is, however, a catch-22 situation in relying on periodical indexes as selection tools: in order to get voted into an index by the editorial board, the magazine must be widely available in voting libraries; in all too many cases, in order to be widely available, it must be indexed. This situation, for which there is no easy solution, serves to perpetuate the inclusion of a periodical in an index long after it has been superseded in quality by another, but newer title. Librarians should be aware of the selection process used by various indexes and provide input into the process whenever possible. The development of computerized indexes, such as those of *Chemical Abstracts* or the *Magazine Index*, provides a much more inclusive coverage of periodical literature since they are not as limited in capacity as print indexes.

In the area of coverage of current events, the library should strive to represent a variety of viewpoints, as it does in the selection of other kinds of materials. This may mean having to subscribe to some periodicals not indexed in the standard sources and using the *Alternative Press Index* for some titles. The fewer periodicals one can buy, the harder the selection decision. If one makes a list of all the potential groups to be served in a heterogeneous community of 10,000 one begins to grasp the dimensions of the problem: children (general magazines and special periodicals such as *Sky and Telescope*); young adults (girls and boys, special subjects such as music and hotrodding and fashions); adults (women, men, ethnic/racial perodicals, etc.). If one further subdivides interests into such categories as education, health, ecology, science, art, travel, the task grows in formidability. Even school libraries, with a more limited clientele in terms of age, face a formidable task trying to select periodicals for the needs of all subject areas taught, the personal needs of the students, and the professional needs of the staff and faculty.

Since commitment to subscribe represents a potential continuing annual charge, as well as possible annual binding costs and constantly expanding storage space, periodicals should be selected carefully in all types of libraries. Most periodical publishers will provide at least one sample issue (sometimes free, sometimes for a charge) to give the librarian an opportunity to see the periodical before purchase. Librarians interested in periodicals should also visit the magazine subscription agencies exhibits at major conferences to see first hand samples of periodicals available. Since there is no real way in advance to determine the usefulness of any one periodical to a particular library's collection, an evaluation process should be built into the selection process. Selecting a periodical for binding reflects the judgment that it will have continuing reference use.

Research libraries face special problems with their serials collections. In many fields, especially scientific disciplines and law, serials are the major form of publication, often absorbing as much as 80 percent of the materials budget. This means that most university and many special libraries buy heavily in science and law serials.

If one examines the complete catalogs of major subscription agencies such as EBSCO or Faxon, one is overwhelmed with the number of periodicals that exist. Even a more selective tool such as *Magazines for Libraries* by William Katz presents the selector with so many choices as to make the selection process dismayingly complicated. The profusion of periodicals is part of the trend termed "demassification of the media" by Alvin Toffler. Modern sophisticated print technology now allows the production of small run periodicals for limited audiences at a reasonable price.

In no area of librarianship is it more important for libraries in any given area to coordinate the selection of periodicals through formal networks. No one library may have enough patrons to warrant a subscription to a particular specialized journal, but there may be a base audience if the total patron populace of an area is taken into account. Such networks will function best when all types of libraries are involved.

One area that requires special attention is the professional literature of librarianship. All too many libraries provide their patrons with better resources than they provide for their staff. As with other rapidly changing fields, librarianship requires in-depth journal reading by librarians since the time lag between innovations reported in journals and their publication in hard cover is considerable.

Vertical File Materials

A well kept up vertical file is a gold mine, but it does require many staff hours to achieve its goal of providing patrons with up-to-date material on current topics. While the file is often referred to as a pamphlet file, its contents are broader than that if developed properly. It contains newspaper clippings, articles from magazines (either from duplicate copies ordered for clipping purposes, or from those magazines not selected for long term preservation), brochures produced by a variety of organizations, and pamphlets.

Materials in the vertical file have two major advantages: they are more apt to be current than book materials and they have appeal to the reluctant reader who needs the information but is intimidated by whole books. The vertical file materials fulfill the job of being current only if each item is dated when placed in the file and a systematic removal process is in place. The materials fulfill the job of reaching reluctant readers and other patrons only if the file is properly identified and accessible for browsing by patrons. All too many excellent vertical files have limited use because patrons do not know they exist. If the file is not going to be properly publicized, librarians should not spend the time needed to develop it. Requiring a librarian's presence to use the file is a violation of patron confidentiality—patrons should be able to browse privately in the file just as they may browse book shelves without supervision.

Much of the time needed to develop a vertical file is spent in locating and ordering the materials. As with films, vertical file materials must be requested directly from the producer of the materials. There is no central source for these materials. Many library periodicals provide some access to these materials, either in actual reviews, or by listing in a column specializing in these formats.

A wide range of viewpoints should be represented in the vertical file just as they are found in the book collection. Every article, pamphlet, threefold has a point of view; there are rarely unbiased materials. The purpose of the collection is to provide as many viewpoints as can be found. This means pamphlets by the National Rifle Association arguing against gun control as well as by groups arguing for it. It means buying materials by the Ku Klux Klan as well as anti-Klan material. The principles of selection do not cease operating just because the material is stored in a file case rather than on shelves.

The chapter bibliography offers suggestions for sources used in identifying vertical file materials.

Selection Aids

General Guides

Audiovisual Market Place, New York, Bowker, 1969–
    (Annual)
Directory information for producers of nonprint materials, including software and cable programming services. Arranged

geographically by state and then alphabetically by company name. Awkward to use, but the best currently available.

Educational Film Locator. 2d ed. New York, Bowker, 1980. 2611p.

While primarily produced to aid educators in locating films owned by the members of the Consortium of University Film Centers and available for loan, this tool can serve useful purposes in the selection of films. It is arranged by subject and title and codes films for audience level.

Educational Media Yearbook, 1983. Edited by James W. Brown and Shirley N. Brown. Littleton, Colo., Libraries Unlimited, 1983. 586p. Annual.

An up-to-date source for all types of nonprint information and services.

Hart, Thomas L. and others. **Mutli-Media Indexes, Lists, and Review Sources: A Bibliographic Guide.** New York, Dekker, 1975. 273p.

Includes more than 400 reviewing sources, covering both print and nonprint media. Structured annotations give bibliographic information, scope, arrangement, special features for each entry. Sample pages are included to illustrate many of the sources. Dated.

Media Review Digest. Ann Arbor, Mich., Pierian Press, 1973/ 74–   . (Annual)

Indexes reviews from a variety of journals of films, filmstrips, tapes, and miscellaneous media forms. Bibliographic citation is accompanied by a symbol "assigned to indicate the general nature or overall trend of the evaluations of the author of the review." Published annually in a hardbound volume with paperbound supplements. Claims to provide 50–60,000 review citations annually. Successor to *Multi-Media Review Index* (1970–72).

Microcomputer Market Place. New York, Dekotek, 1982. 207p.

The micro equivalent of *Literary Market Place.*

Rosenberg, Kenyon C. and John S. Doskey. **Media Equipment: A Guide and Dictionary.** Littleton, Colo., Libraries Unlimited, 1976. 190p.

Thorough coverage of media equipment terminology.

Rufsvold, Margaret I. **Guides to Educational Media.** 4th ed.
Chicago, American Library Association, 1977. 159p.
Annotated guide to published catalogues of films, filmstrips,
records, slides, transparencies, etc.

Sive, Mary Robinson. **The Complete Media Monitor: Guides to
Learning Resources.** Metuchen, N.J., Scarecrow Press,
1981.

Sive, Mary Robinson. **Selecting Instructional Media: A Guide
to Audiovisual and Other Instructional Media Lists.** 3rd
ed. Littleton, Colo., Libraries Unlimited, 1983. 300p.
Classified list of bibliographies of audiovisual materials, free materials, government documents, etc. on various subjects.

Smallwood, Carol. **Exceptional Free Library Resource Materials.** Littleton, Colo., Libraries Unlimited, 1984. 233p.
Subject arrangement from agriculture to world history. Each
entry provides name and address of source, the format, size,
graphics, grade level. Includes free films for loan as well as
materials which can be added to the collection.

Truett, Carol and Lori Gillespie. **Choosing Educational Software.** Littleton, Colo., Libraries Unlimited, 1984. 216p.
Covers grades K–12; lists software sources; review sources and
sample evaluation forms and a bibliography.

Multi-Media Guides

Audiovisual Instruction. Washington, D.C., Association for Educational Communications and Technology, 1956–   .
(10 issues per year)
Articles and bibliographies of special interest to those doing
media selection in schools.

Booklist. Chicago, American Library Association, 1905–   .
(Semimonthly)
Started reviewing nonprint materials in 1969 and now regularly
includes selective coverage of recommended 16mm films, filmstrips, spoken-word recordings, multimedia kits, etc.

Brown, Lucy Gregor. **Core Media Collection for Secondary Schools.** 2d ed. New York, Bowker, 1979. 263p.
Selection of over 3,000 recommended audiovisual items. Some annotations. Notes items recommended for early purchase.

Brown, Lucy Gregor and Betty McDavid. **Core Media Collection for Elementary Schools.** 2d ed. New York, Bowker, 1978. 224p.

Cabeceiras, James. **Multimedia Library: Materials Selection and Use.** New York, Academic Press, 1982. 295p.

Canadian Materials; An Annotated Critical Bibliography for Canadian Schools and Libraries. Ottawa, Canadian Library Association, 1971–   . (3 issues per year)
Signed annotations by librarians and teachers of "material in all media formats produced in Canada for elementary and secondary schools."

Elementary School Library Collection. Greensboro, N.C., Bro-Dart Foundation, 1965–   .
The 14th edition appeared in 1984 and included approximately 10,000 recommended books, periodicals, filmstrips, transparencies, etc. About 20% of the items were nonprint. Annotations are included and there is a system for indicating which titles are considered to be necessary in a beginning elementary school collection. Revised and up-dated regularly.

Greene, Ellin and Madalynne Schoenfeld. **Multimedia Approach to Children's Literature.** 2d ed. Chicago, American Library Association, 1977. 206p.
Annotates more than 500 children's books and lists 16mm films, filmstrips, and audio recordings based on the books.

Johnson, Harry A. **Ethnic American Minorities: A Guide to Media and Materials.** New York, Bowker, 1976. 304p.
Covers all kinds of non-book media "relevant to the needs of minority groups." Four chapters on major ethnic groups and one on all other groups include essays and bibliographies.

NICEM Index to Non-Print Special Education Materials: Multimedia (Learner Volume). Los Angeles, University of Southern California, National Information Center for Educational Media, 1979.

NICEM Index to Non-Print Special Education Materials: Multimedia (Professional Volume). Los Angeles, University of Southern California, National Information Center for Educational Media, 1979.

NICEM Update on Nonbook Media, 1981–82, 4 Vols. Los Angeles, University of Southern California, National Information Center for Educational Media, 1981.

The National Information Center for Educational Media of the University of Southern California publishes several multimedia indexes which list and describe a variety of nonbook media falling within the subject area of concern.

Sive, Mary Robinson. **China: A Multimedia Guide.** New York, Neal-Schuman, 1982. 245p.

Films, Filmstrips, Slides

AAAS Science Film Catalog. Washington, D.C., American Association for the Advancement of Science, 1975.
Includes annotations of 5,600 films (16mm) on physical and social sciences. Elementary to adult level.

College Film Library Collection. Editor-in-chief: Emily S. Jones. Williamsport, Pa., Bro-Dart, 1971. 2v.
Recommended films for undergraduate use. Arranged by subject and annotated. First volume (16mm films) includes about 1,900 films and the second describes about 600 filmstrips and 5,800 8mm films.

Educators Guide Series.
In addition to the previously-mentioned multi-media guides, Educators Progress Service of Randolph, Wisconsin, also publishes annual guides to free films and filmstrips.

Film Library Quarterly. New York, Film Library Information Council, 1967–   . (Quarterly)
Articles about film and filmmakers and reviews of films and books about film.

Film News, New York, Film News Co., 1939–   . (Bimonthly)
An important source for information about new non-theatrical

films. Regularly reviews, in some detail, new films and filmstrips.

Film Review Digest. Millwood, N.Y., Kraus-Thomson, 1975–
 (Quarterly)
Cites reviews from more than 20 American, Canadian, and British publications of "300–400 feature films that open in the United States each year." Basic information on films and quotations from reviews. Alphabetical by title.

Gaffney, Maureen. **More Films Kids Like.** Chicago, American Library Association, 1977. 159p.
Annotates 200 films. Companion volume to Susan Rice's *Films Kids Like*.

Gaffney, Maureen and Gerry B. Laybourne. **What to Do When the Lights Go On: A Comprehensive Guide to Sixteen Millimeter Films and Related Activities for Children.** Phoenix, Ariz., Oryx Press, 1981. 268p.

Landers Film Reviews. Los Angeles, Landers Associates, 1956–
 (9 issues per year)
Reviews new 16mm films and lists new filmstrips and slides. In format and audience this publication is similar to *Kirkus Reviews* for books.

Limbacher, James L. **Feature Films on 8mm and 16mm; A Directory of Films Available for Rental, Sale, and Lease in the United States.** 7th ed. New York, Bowker, 1982. 513p.
Films (both silent and sound) of more than 45 minutes duration (or more than one reel) are included. Includes more than 22,000 films and compiler estimates that nearly 95% of all feature films generally available in the United States are listed.

Rice, Susan. **Films Kids Like.** Chicago, American Library Association, 1973. 150p.
Annotates 200 films selected for ages 2–12.

Science Books and Films; The Quarterly Review. Washington, D.C., American Association for the Advancement of Science, 1975–   . (Quarterly)
Critical reviews of books and 16mm films on pure and applied science aimed at the student—elementary, secondary, junior college—and the adult nonspecialist. Annual author and film source index.

Selected Films for Young Adults. Published annually by the Young Adult Services Division, American Library Association.
Annotated three-fold of film selections pre-tested with young adults.

Sightlines. New York, Educational Film Library Association, 1967–   . (Bimonthly)
Often has subject-oriented groupings of critical annotations. Also carries general articles on new developments in educational uses of film.

Recordings

American Record Guide. New York, 1935–   . (Monthly)
Detailed reviews of new records, stereo tapes and books on music. Tends to emphasize classical music. Indexed in *Notes.*

Annual Index to Popular Music Record Reviews. Metuchen, N.J., Scarecrow Press, 1972–   . (Annual)
Indexed reviews in approximately 75 American, Canadian, and British sources. Useful for the period covered.

Educators Guide to Free Audio and Video Materials. Randolph, Wis., Educators Progress Service, 1955–   . (Annual)
Annotated listing, aimed at the needs of teachers.

Gray, Michael and Gerald Gibson. **Bibliography of Discographies.** New York, Bowker, 1977–1983. 3 vols.
Volume 1 (1977) covers Classical music from 1925–1975; Volume 2 covers Jazz, and Volume 3 is devoted to Popular Music. Additional volumes are expected to cover ethnic music and other genres.

Halsey, Richard S. **Classical Music Recordings for Home and Library.** Chicago, American Library Association, 1976. 340p.
Approximately 4,000 entries, coded by listening level.

High Fidelity. "Records in Review." Great Barrington, Mass.,
  Wyeth Press, 1955–   .
Annual compilation of the reviews of new recordings of classical
and semiclassical music which appeared in the previous year's
issues of *High Fidelity*.

National Center for Audio Tapes. **Catalog.** Boulder, Colo.,
  1970–   .
Annotated subject list of available tapes suitable for curriculum
use.

New Schwann Record & Tape Guide. Boston, 1949–   .
  (Monthly)
Furnishes "in print" information for about 25,000 LP records,
digital compact discs, cassettes, and 8-track cartridges on about
750 record and 330 tape labels.

Notes. Music Library Association, 1947–   . (Quarterly)
In addition to general articles on music librarianship, reviews of
books about music, and reviews of scores, this journal regularly
contains an index to current record reviews found in 18 U.S. and
British publications.

Stereo Review. Chicago, Ziff-Davis, 1958–   . (Monthly)
Reviews new records and tapes and new equipment; also contains articles on compositions and performers. Indexed in *Notes*.

Microforms

Dodson, Suzanne. **Microform Research Collections: A Guide.**
  2nd ed. Westport, Conn., Meckler, 1983. 300p.
Describes contents and indexes of more than 200 microform
collections; international coverage.

Guide to Microforms in Print. Westport, Conn., Microform Re-
  view/Meckler, 1961–   .
As with *Books in Print,* there are separate volumes for authors,
titles, and subjects. Earlier volumes appear under Microform
Review imprint, later ones under Meckler.

Microform Market Place, 1982–1983. Edited by Deborah O'Hara.
  Westport, Conn., Meckler, 1982. 250p.

Microform Review. Westport, Conn., Microform Review, 1972–
(Bimonthly)
Contains critical and detailed reviews of new microform projects, as well as reviews of new books and citations to recent
articles on the subject of micropublishing. Index to the first ten
years (1972–1981) has been published, with a special subject
index to reviews.

Micrographics Equipment Review. Westport, Conn., Microform Review, 1976–   . (Quarterly)
Thorough reviews of micrographics equipment.

Microlist. Westport, Conn., Microform Review, 1977–
(Quarterly)
International listing of new micropublications.

Micropublishers' Trade List Annual. Westport, Conn., Meckler, 1975–
Catalogues of micropublishers on microfiche in a looseleaf bind-
er. International coverage.

Maps

International Maps and Atlases in Print. 2d ed. New York,
Bowker, 1976. 866p.
Complete information on more than 15,000 maps and atlases.

Wise, Donald A. "Selected Geographical and Cartographical Serials Containing Lists and/or Reviews of Current Maps and
Atlases." SLA Geography and Map Division **Bulletin,** no.
102:42–45, December 1975.
Brief annotations.

Serials

Association of College and Research Libraries. Community and
Junior College Libraries Section. **Vocational-Technical Periodicals for Community College Libraries.** Rev. ed. Middletown, Conn., Choice, 1976. 44p.
List represents the combined holdings of nearly 100 community
college libraries; arranged under seven broad subject areas.

Ayer Directory of Publications. Philadelphia, Ayer Press, 1880–
Subtitle: "The Professional's Directory of Print Media Published
in the U.S.; Puerto Rico; Dominion of Canada; Bahamas; Ber-
muda; the Republics of Panama and the Philippines." This standard directory covers daily and weekly newspapers, college and
university newspapers, religious newspapers and magazines,
trade journals, etc.

**Canadian Serials Directory/Repertoire des publications seriees
    canadiennes.** 2d ed. Toronto, University of Toronto Press,
    1977.
Provides bibliographic information on more than 4,000 English
and French language Canadian periodicals.

Current Australian Serials. Canberra, National Library of Aus-
    tralia. 1963–
Annotated selection of "serials currently published in or relating
to Australia, its Territories and Papua New Guinea."

Farber, Evan Ira. **Classified List of Periodicals for the College
    Library.** 5th ed. Westwood, Mass., Faxon, 1972. 449p.
Detailed annotations of over one thousand periodical titles (published before 1969) considered to be important for a liberal arts
college collection.

Farber, Evan Ira and others. "Periodicals for College Libraries."
    Choice.
Most issues of *Choice* carry this column which reviews new periodicals of possible interest to academic libraries.

International Directory of Little Magazines and Small Presses.
    Paradise, Calif., Dustbooks, 1965–
Detailed descriptions of both presses and magazines. Annual.
Supplemented by the same publisher's annual *Directory of Small
Magazines/Press Editors and Publishers.* The nineteenth edition
(1983–84) contained 3,435 entries.

**Irregular Serials and Annuals, 1984: An International Directo-
    ry.** New York, Bowker, 1967–
Bibliographic information on "serials, annuals, continuations,
conference proceedings, and other publications from all over the
world issued irregularly or less frequently than twice a year."
The ninth edition (1984) covered approximately 34,000 entries.

Katz, William. "Magazines." **Library Journal.**
Critical reviews of a wide variety of new periodicals have appeared once a month since this column became a regular *LJ* feature in January 1967. An index to the titles reviewed in the column during its first five years was published in the first issue of **Reference Services Review,** January/March 1973.

Katz, William and Linda Sternberg Katz. **Magazines for Libraries.** 4th ed. New York, Bowker, 1982. 958p.
Annotated list of approximately 6,500 periodicals considered suitable for the general reader. Comments on the value of each periodical for a particular type of library are usually included. Updated regularly.

New Serial Titles 1950–1970; Subject Guide. New York, Bowker, 1975. 2v.
Approximately 220,000 titles are arranged under 250 subject headings, with 1,200 cross references.

Richardson, Selma K. **Periodicals for School Media Programs.** 2d ed. Chicago, American Library Association, 1978. 397p.
Annotations of more than 500 periodicals for grades K-12. Includes foreign and ethnic publications.

Serials Review. Ann Arbor, Mich., Pierian Press, 1975– .
(Quarterly)
Reviews of new serials, as well as articles and columns on various aspects of serial librarianship.

Small Press Review. Paradise, Calif., Dustbooks, 1966– .
(Monthly)
Lists new publications of small presses and little magazines and includes reviews (200 words or less) of small press titles.

Sources of Serials: An International Publisher and Corporate Author Directory. New York, Bowker, 1977–
Covers all serials listed in *Ulrich's International Periodicals Directory, Irregular Serials and Annuals,* and *Ulrich's Quarterly.* Arranged first by country and then alphabetically by publisher or corporate author.

Spahn, Theodore, J. and Janet P. Spahn. **From Radical Left to Extreme Right; A Bibliography of Current Periodicals of**

Protest, Controversy, Advocacy, or Dissent, with Dispassionate Content—Summaries to Guide Librarians and Other Educators. Vol. 3, 2d rev. ed. Metuchen, N.J., Scarecrow Press, 1976. 762p.

Ulrich's International Periodicals Directory. New York, Bowker, 1932–
The twenty-second edition (1983) furnished a subject approach, with bibliographic information and some information on circulation, indexing, etc., to about 64,800 publications issued more often than once a year. For serials issued irregularly or not more than twice a year, see *Irregular Serials and Annuals; An International Directory.*

Ulrich's Quarterly; A Supplement to Ulrich's International Periodicals Directory and Irregular Serials and Annuals. New York, Bowker, 1977–   . (Quarterly)
Updated information on new serial titles, title changes and cessations.

Woodworth, David P. **Guide to Current British Journals.** 2d ed. London, Library Association, 1973. 2v.
Subject arrangement with complete descriptions of more than 4,500 journals.

Yannarella, Philip A. and Rao Aluri. **U.S. Government Scientific and Technical Periodicals.** Metuchen, N.J., Scarecrow Press, 1976. 263p.
Describes more than 250 scientific and technical periodicals published by U.S. government agencies or federal contractors and grantees. Includes primary journals, review serials, indexing and abstracting services, and newsletters. Emphasizes such topics as oceanography, meteorology, public health, and conservation of natural resources.

Pamphlets

Bulletin of the Public Affairs Information Service. New York, 1915–   . (Semi-monthly)
Index to information on economic, social, and political affairs selected from periodicals, papers, books, government docu-

ments, and typewritten and mimeographed materials, published in English throughout the world. Often includes items suitable for the pamphlet collection.

Do It Now Foundation. Phoenix, Ariz.
A non-profit organization producing numerous publications for the vertical file on alcohol and other drugs, their characteristics, abuse, and prevention/intervention methods.

Elementary Teachers' Guide to Free Curriculum Materials. Randolph, Wis., Educators Progress Service, 1944–
Annual revisions keep this source of free printed material for teachers and librarians up to date. See Educators Progress Service's multi-media subject guides for another approach to free pamphlets.

Free! Seattle, Wash., Dyad Services, 1980–   . (Bimonthly)
Contains reviews of free materials, with special emphasis on Canadian materials, and provides annotated lists on particular subjects.

Free and Inexpensive Learning Materials. Nashville, George Peabody College for Teachers, 1941–
Biennial, annotated listing of current, factual materials available on subjects generally taught in elementary and secondary schools.

Goodman, Leonard H. **Current Career and Occupational Literature: 1982.** 3rd ed. New York, Wilson, 1982. 195p.
Updated regularly, this covers materials for all ages and emphasizes free or inexpensive items.

Information for Everyday Survival: What You Need and Where to Get It. Edited by Priscilla Gotscik and others. Chicago, American Library Association, 1976. 403p.
Annotations of free and inexpensive materials are arranged under thirteen categories such as aging, children, etc.

Materials for Occupational Education. Patricia Glass Schuman, Editor. New York, Neal-Schuman, 1983. 384p.
A subject arrangement containing invaluable sources, including addresses.

Planned Parenthood Federation of America. New York.
The national organization produces materials appropriate for the vertical file and can provide the information concerning materials produced by its many affiliates throughout the U.S.

Smallwood, Carol. **Exceptional Free Library Resource Materials.** Littleton, Colo. Libraries Unlimited, 1984. 233p.
Divided into 27 broad subject headings which generally parallel school curricular needs.

Vertical File Index. New York, Wilson, 1932/34–   .
(Monthly)
Subject listing of new pamphlets, leaflets, etc. considered to be of possible interest in school, college, public, and business libraries. Title index follows the subject index.

Wisconsin Clearinghouse for Alcohol and Drug Abuse. Madison.
An important source for pamphlets on alcohol and drug abuse.

Development and Use of Non-book Resources

Boyle, Deirdre. **Expanding Media.** Phoenix, Ariz., Oryx Press, 1977. 343p.
Reprints more than forty articles published since 1969 on nonprint media in libraries.

Cabeceiras, James. **The Multimedia Library: Materials Selection and Use.** 2d ed. New York, Academic Press, 1982. 275p.
Covers most forms of media; intended for all types of libraries.

Foster, Donald L. **Prints in the Public Library.** Metuchen, N.J., Scarecrow Press, 1973. 124p.
Includes information on selecting and acquiring.

Grove, Pearce S. **Nonprint in Academic Libraries.** Chicago, American Library Association, 1975. 239p. (ACRL Publications in Librarianship No. 34)
Includes chapters on various formats (by different authors) and on selection and acquisition.

Guidelines for Evaluating Computerized Instructional Materials. Reston, VA., National Council of Teachers of Mathematics, 1981. 426p.
Section 3, "Guidelines for Software Review" is vital for selection criteria.

Hektoen, Faith B. and Jeanne R. Rinehart. **Toys to Go: A Guide to the Use of Realia in Public Libraries.** Chicago, American Library Association, 1976. 24p.
Includes criteria for selection.

Hicks, Warren B. and Alma M. Tillin, Editors. **Managing Multimedia Libraries.** New York, Bowker, 1977. 264p.

Lathrop, Ann and Bobby Goodson. **Courseware in the Classroom: Selecting, Organizing, and Using Educational Software.** Reading, Mass., Addison-Wesley, 1983. 187p.
Evaluation, criteria, sources for software reviews, and a directory of courseware publishers. Will be updated annually.

Nadler, Myra. **How to Start an Audiovisual Collection.** Metuchen, N.J., Scarecrow Press, 1978. 165p.
Essays by seven experts.

Picture Sources 4. Ernest H. Robl, Editor. New York, Special Libraries Association, 1983. 200p.

Rohrlick, Paula. **Exploring the Arts: Films and Video Programs for Young Viewers.** New York, Bowker, 1982. 181p.
Annotated, selective filmography of 568 films and video programs for ages 2–15.

Shaw, Renata V. **Picture Searching: Techniques and Tools.** New York, Special Libraries Association, 1984.

Sive, Mary Robinson. **Media Selection Handbook.** Littleton, Colo., Libraries Unlimited, 1982. 230p.

Teo, Elizabeth A. "Audiovisual Materials in the College and Community Library: The Basics of Collection Building," **Choice,** 14:487–501, June 1977; 14:633–645, July–August 1977.
Thorough discussion of why and how. Notes selection aides.

Thomas, James L., Editor. **Nonprint in the Elementary Curriculum: Readings for Reference.** Littleton, Colo., Libraries Unlimited, 1982. 155p.

Thomas, James L., Editor. **Nonprint in the Secondary Curriculum: Readings for Reference.** Littleton, Colo., Libraries Unlimited, 1982. 215p.

Films, Filmstrips, Pictures, Slides

Bukalski, Peter J. "Collecting Classic Films." **American Libraries,** 2:475–479, May 1971.
What's available and who distributes it.

Freudenthal, Juan Rothchild and J. A. Lyders. "Photography as Historical Evidence and Art: Steps in Collection Building." **Collection Building,** 4 no. 1:6–20, 1982.

Harrison, Helen P. **Film Library Techniques: Principles of Administration.** New York, Hastings House, 1973. 277p.
Includes chapter on selection.

Harrison, Helen P. **Picture Librarianship.** Phoenix, Ariz., Oryx Press, 1981. 372p.

Iarusso, Marilyn B. "Films for Children: Selection and Programming." **Connecticut Libraries,** 19:16–21, 1977.

Irvine, Betty Jo and Eileen P. Fry. **Slide Libraries: A Guide for Academic Institutions and Museums.** 2nd ed. Littleton, Colo., Libraries Unlimited, 1979. 321p.
Chapter 4 covers acquisitions.

Lennox, Tom. "Slides Acquisitions: A Media Librarian's Problem." **Previews,** 1:5–11, November 1972.
Examples of what's available and who produces it.

Palmer, Joseph W. "Widely Owned Films in Public Libraries." **Illinois Libraries,** 56:221–226, March 1974.
Lists films and where they were reviewed.

Pepper, Larry. "New Films Worth Looking At." **Public Librar-ies,** 21:96–99, Fall 1982.
A bibliography.

Rehrauer, George. **Film User's Handbook: A Basic Manual for Managing Library Film Services.** New York, Bowker, 1975. 301p.

Shemin, Jane Bickel. "Experimenting with Film as Art for Kids." **Film Library Quarterly,** 15 no. 1:15–19, 1982.

Spehr, Paul. "Feature Films in Your Library." **Wilson Library Bulletin,** 44:848–855, April 1970.

Spirt, Diana L. "Criteria, Choices and Other Concerns About Filmstrips." **Previews,** 1:5–7, January 1973.

Wilson, Evie. "What Movies Did Ya' Bring Tonight?" **Voice of Youth Advocates,** 4 no. 4:13–14, October 1981.
Using film in a runaway youth center.

Audio Recordings

Boss, Richard W. "Audio Materials in Academic Research Li-braries." **College and Research Libraries,** 33:463–466, November 1972.
Survey of 68 ARL libraries.

Hoffmann, Frank William. **Development of Library Collections of Sound Recordings.** New York, Dekker, 1979. 169p.

Massis, Bruce E. "Report from the New Frontier: The Cassette Library of the Jewish Guild for the Blind." In **Library Ser-vices for the Blind and Physically Handicapped: An Inter-national Approach.** pp. 111–123. Ridgewood, N.J., Saur, 1982.

Pollock, Bruce. "On Record: Popular Music." **Wilson Library Bulletin,** 57:512–513, February 1983; 599–600, March 1983.

"Rockingchair." **Voice of Youth Advocates.**
Each issue contains reviews of recordings excluding jazz and classical music.

Stevenson, Gordon. "Sound Recordings." In **Advances in Librarianship,** Vol. 5, pp. 279–320. New York, Academic Press, 1975.
Comprehensive review of the literature.

Video Recordings

Bahr, Alice H. **Video in Libraries: A Status Report, 1979–80.** 2nd ed. White Plains, N.Y., Knowledge Industries, 1980. 119p.

Boyle, Deirdre. "Documentary Video Classics: A Core Collection." **Sightlines,** 16:16–18, Spring 1983.

Boyle, Deirdre. "Librarians's Guide to Consumer Video Magazines." **Library Journal,** 106:1700–1703, September 15, 1981.

Boyle, Deirdre. "Video Fever." **Library Journal,** 106:849–852, April 15, 1981.

Coleman, John S. "Alternatives in Building a Video Collection." **North Carolina Libraries,** 40:33–36, Spring 1982.

Egan, Catherine. "Programming Independent Video." **Sightlines,** 16:10–12+, Spring 1983.

Estevens, Roberto. "Video Opens Libraries to the Deaf." **American Libraries,** 13:36+, January 1982.

Gitlin, Michael. "Developing Video Collections: What Are the Alternatives?" **Film Library Quarterly,** 15 nos 2–3:3–11, 1982.

Handfield, F. Gerald. "Importance of Video History in Libraries." **Drexel Library Quarterly,** 15:29–34, October 1979.

Harlan, Peggy. "Videotapes in Libraries: Principles and Realities." **New Jersey Libraries,** 15:13–15, Summer 1982. Related to intellectual freedom.

Murray, James Briggs. "Oral History/Video Documentation at

the Schomburg Center: More Than Just 'Talking Heads.' "
Film Library Quarterly, 15 no. 4:23–27, 1982.

Sessions, Judith and L. S. Cocke. "Finding Libraries in the Video Maze." **American Libraries,** 12:280–281, May 1981.

Video Source Book. 5th ed. The National Video Clearinghouse, 1983. 1600p. (Distributed by Gale Research) Updated regularly.
The National Video Clearinghouse also publishes individual volumes on specific subjects.

Maps

Allison, Brent. "Map Acquisition: An Annotated Bibliography." **Western Association Map Library Information Bulletin,** 15:16–25, November 1983.

Cobb, David A. "Selection and Acquisition of Materials for the Map Library." **Drexel Library Quarterly,** 9:15–25, October 1973.
Entire issue is devoted to map librarianship.

Coombs, James. "Globes: A Librarian's Guide to Selection and Purchase." **Wilson Library Bulletin,** 55:503–508, March 1981.

Drazniowsky, Roman. **Map Librarianship: Readings.** Metuchen, N.J., Scarecrow Press, 1975. 548p.
Reprints of 48 articles.

Lohrentz, Ken. "Maps as Information Tools: A Neglected Resource." **Nebraska Library Association Quarterly,** 13:16–20, Winter 1982.

Low, Jane Grant-Mackay. **The Acquisition of Maps and Charts Published by the United States Government.** Urbana, University of Illinois, Graduate School of Library Science, 1976. 36p. (Occasional Papers No. 125)

Map Librarianship in the Modern World; Essays in Honour of Walter W. Ristow. Helen Wallis and L. Zogner, eds. Saur Verlag, C. Bingley., 1979. 295p.

Nichols, Harold. **Map Librarianship.** 2nd ed. London, Clive Bingley, 1982. 272p.
Includes guidelines for identifying and acquiring maps.

Noe, Barbara R., comp. **Facsimiles of Maps and Atlases; A List of Reproductions for Sale by Various Publishers and Distributors.** 4th ed. Washington, D.C., Library of Congress, 1980. 35p.

Parry, Robert B. "Selection and Procurement of European Maps for an American Map Library, with a Case Study of British Maps." **Special Library Association Geography and Map Division Bulletin,** no. 131:16–22, March 1983.

Schorr, Alan Edward. "General World Atlases." **Booklist,** 78:564–567, December 15, 1981.

Schorr, Alan Edward. "Written Map Acquisition Policies in Academic Libraries." **Special Libraries Association Geography and Map Division Bulletin,** no. 98:28–30, December 1974.
Results of a survey of 45 larger academic libraries.

Special Libraries Association Geography and Map Division Bulletin. (Bimonthly)
Articles and reviews on all aspects of cartography librarianship.

Ward, Dederick C. and others. **Geologic Reference Sources: A Subject and Regional Bibliography of Publications and Maps in the Geological Sciences.** 2nd ed. Metuchen, N.J., Scarecrow Press, 1981. 560p.

Western Association of Map Libraries Information Bulletin, Santa Cruz, Calif., University of California, University Library. (3 times a year)
Invaluable resource for map librarians.

Microforms

"ARL Microform Project: Its History and Objectives." **Microform Review,** 11:74–76, Spring 1982.

Boylan, Ray and C. L. Shores. "Collecting Retrospective Materials from Developing Nations: A Cooperative Approach Through Microforms." **Library Acquisitions,** 6 no. 2:211–219, 1982.

Chadwick-Healey, Charles F. "Future of Microform in an Electronic Age." **Wilson Library Bulletin,** 58:270–273, December 1983.

Crowley, Terence. "Comparing Fiche and Film: A Test of Speed." **Library Automation,** 14:292–295, December 1981.

Ellison, John W. and others. "Storage and Conservation of Microforms." **Microform Review,** 10:90–93, Spring 1981.

Folcarelli, Ralph J. and others. **Microform Connection: A Basic Guide for Libraries.** New York, Bowker, 1982. 210p.

Gabriel, Michael R. and D. P. Ladd. **Microform Revolution in Libraries.** Greenwich, Conn., JAI Press, 1980. 176p.

Gleaves, Edwin Sheffield. "Microform Serials Acquisition: A Suggested Planning Model." **Journal of Academic Librarianship,** 8:292–295, November 1982.

Johnson, Nancy P. "Space Consuming Government Documents Available in Microform." **Microform Review,** 9:228–235, Fall 1980.

Kish, Joseph L., Jr. **Micrographics: A User's Manual.** New York, John Wiley, 1980. 196p.
Contains vital technical information for anyone engaged in, or about to engage in, determining appropriate format in which to store print documents.

Niles, Ann. "Conversion of Serials from Paper to Microform." **Microform Review,** 9:90–95, Spring 1980. Discussion. 9:136–137, Summer 1980.

Perez, Madeleine and others. "Selection and Preparation of Archives and Manuscripts for Microreproduction." **Library Resources and Technical Services,** 27:357–365, October 1983.

Perrault, Anna H. "New Dimension in Approval Plan Service."
Library Acquisitions, 7 no. 1:35–40, 1983.

Roundy, Glen E. "Microfiche: An Answer to a Medical Records
Paper Problem." **Journal of Micrographics,** 14:23–28, September 1981.

Saffady, William. **Micrographics.** Littleton, Colo., Libraries Unlimited, 1978. 240p.
Covers microforms from several angles.

Teague, Sydney, J. **Microform Librarianship.** 2nd ed. London,
Butterworth, 1979. 125p.
Administrative aspects of acquiring and using microforms.

Veaner, Allen B. **The Evaluation of Micropublications: A Handbook for Librarians.** Chicago, American Library Association, 1971. 72p. (LTP Publication No. 17)
Practical guidelines and procedures.

Veaner, Allen B. **Studies in Micropublishing: 1853–1976.** Westport, Conn., Microform Review, 1977. 440p.

Yerburgh, Mark R. "Microforms, Staff Development and the
Pursuit of Excellence." **Microform Review,** 9:139–144,
Summer 1980.

Serials

Bolgiana, Christina E. and Mary Kathryn King. "Profiling a Periodicals Collection." **College and Research Libraries,**
39:99–104, July 1974.
Reviews literature on ways in which core lists can be compiled.

Brown, Clara D. and Lynn S. Smith. **Serials: Past, Present and
Future.** 2nd ed. Birmingham, Ala., EBSCO Industries,
1980. 390p.
Minimal information on selection, but vital information necessary for smooth functioning of a serials department.

Cargill, Jennifer S. "Issues in Book and Serial Acquisitions: Collection Development; A Conference Report." **Serials Review,** 9:62–63, Fall 1982.

Carson, Doris M. "What Is a Serial Publication?" **Journal of Academic Librarianship,** 3:206–209, September 1977.
Analyzes various publishing definitions.

Clasquin, Frank F. "Library and Subscription Agent Electronics." **Serials Librarian,** 7:7–15, Spring 1983.

Forsman, Rick B. "EBSCONET Serials Control System: A Case History and Analysis." **Serials Review,** 8:83–85, Winter 1982.
Report of experiences at Lister Hill Library of the Health Sciences.

Grouchmal, Helen M. "Selection Criteria for Periodicals in Microform." **Serials Librarian,** 5:15–17, Spring 1981.

Grouchmal, Helen M. "Serials Department's Responsibilities for Reference." **Reference Quarterly,** 20:403–406, Summer 1981.

"Issues in Book and Serial Acquisitions: Collection Development in the Eighties: The LAPT Report." **Library Acquisitions,** 7 no. 3:213–266, 1983.
Report of conference held in Charleston, May 12–13, 1983.

Linkins, Germaine C. "Articles and Monographs on Serials: Third Annual Bibliography." **Serials Review,** 8:61–65, April 1983. An important overview.

Melin, Nancy Jean. "Public Service Functions of Serials." **Serials Review,** 6:39–44, January 1980.

Milkovic, Milan. "Continuations: Some Fundamental Acquisition Concepts and Procedures." **Serials Librarian,** 5:35–43, Spring 1981.

Morehead, Joseph H. "Between Infancy and Youth: Children and Government Serials." **Serials Librarian,** 4:373–379, Summer 1980.

Paul, Hubert. "Are Subscription Agents Worth Their Keep?" **Serials Librarian,** 7:31–41, Fall 1982.

Paul, Hubert. "Automation of Serials Check-in: Like Growing Bananas in Greenland?" **Serials Librarian,** 6:3–16, Winter 1981–Spring 1982; 39–62, Summer 1982.

Pinzelik, Barbara P. "Serials Maze: Providing Public Service for a Large Serials Collection." **Journal of Academic Librarianship,** 8:89–94, May 1982.

Serials Management and Microforms: A Reader. Patricia M. Walsh, Ed. Greenwich, Conn. Microform Review, 1979. 302p.

Varma, D. K. "Increasing Subscription Costs and Problems of Resource Allocation." **Special Libraries,** 74:61–66, January 1983.

Pamphlets

Bator, Eileen F. "Automating the Vertical File Index." **Special Libraries,** 71:485–491, November 1980.

Gronlund, Mimi. "Pamphlets—A Question of Format." **Unabashed Librarian,** no. 42:9–10, 1982.

Hodgson, Tom and Andrew Garoogian. "Special Collections in College Libraries: The Vertical File." **Reference Services Review,** 9:77–84, July 1981.

Holley, Robert P. and Ruth Gay. "Pamphlet Processing Using Yale's Automated Acquisitions System." **Library Acquisitions,** 5 no. 2:61–65, 1981.

Miller, Shirley. **The Vertical File and Its Satellites; A Handbook of Acquisition, Processing, and Organization.** 2nd ed. Littleton, Colo., Libraries Unlimited, 1979. 251p.

Spencer, Michael D. "Pamphlet Collection Development." **Bookmark,** 41:91–98, Winter 1983.

Vertical File Index. New York, H. W. Wilson, 1932/34–   . (Annual)

CHAPTER 8

CENSORSHIP AND SELECTION

Introduction

The library profession's concern with intellectual freedom is a fairly new phenomenon, which is not to say that individual librarians were not concerned about the selection processes in many, if not most, libraries prior to the adoption of the first Library Bill of Rights in 1939. For all of the nineteenth century and the first third of the twentieth, librarians viewed themselves as moral arbiters for what the public should read. The theme of the 1895 American Library Association conference was "Improper Books: Methods Employed to Discover and Exclude Them." The title is probably the most illuminating of attitudes ever to be the subject of an American Library Association conference. All of the early literature is filled with words such as unwholesome, unclean, immoral as applied to books the librarians had determined were unfit for inclusion in decent, upright library collections.

There was an assumption underlying early library selection policies that people needed to be protected, particularly from "morbid" books. It is interesting to read the early library periodical literature on this subject and try to determine which books are under discussion. Librarians did not identify titles they felt fell outside the pale of good taste since identifying them would only lead to their being more in demand.

Some librarians, such as Samuel Ranck of the Grand Rapids (MI) Public Library, drew sharp distinctions between appropriate nonfiction and fiction subject matter, feeling that the former offered important ideas, even though the ideas' time might not yet have come for general acceptance. Fiction, on the other hand, should be uplifting and tasteful.

If patrons lacked good taste and requested inappropriate books from the library, Librarian J. N. Larned of the Buffalo (NY) Public Library had the solution. In an article entitled "Improper Books," he wrote:

> In the case of one recent book for which many applications were made in our library, I have been trying the experiment

of sending a circular note to each applicant, briefly describing its character and saying that I am not willing the book
should go into the hands of any reader without clear
knowledge of what it is. The result has been to cancel a
large part of the requests for the book, while those who
read it take on themselves the whole responsibility in doing
so. It seems to me that a general policy of dealing with such
books may be framed on the principle indicated in this
experiment. (*Library Journal*, Conf. Report 35, 1895.)

In other words, we have it, and if you are brave enough to come
in and borrow it knowing now what we think of people who
would read such trash, we will loan it to you!

Today's librarians should be aware of the profession's history
in relation to censorship and selection to better understand that
libraries operate within the parameters of society's mores. Libraries are always subject to social and political pressures which
influence decisions in the selection process. It is equally important to understand the history of the United States in relation to
the First Amendment. It was not until the twentieth century that
the United States Supreme Court ruled that the Fourteenth
Amendment made the Bill of Rights applicable to the states as
well as the federal government. Prior to that ruling, states could,
and did, impose all kinds of restrictions on the freedom to
speak, write, read. The United States government was no better. The Comstock laws of the nineteenth century were gross
violations of the meaning of the First Amendment, as were the
regulations developed by the Customs Service. There is little
question that the creation of the American Civil Liberties Union
contributed much to raising everyone's consciousness—judges
and the public alike—to the importance of the First Amendment.

It is a mistake for the person entering the library profession to
try to understand censorship and its antithesis, intellectual freedom, solely in terms of the issues of the day. Without an understanding of where we have been, it is not possible to appreciate
where we are in relation to censorship.

What History Shows

Basically, the issues involved in censorship cases do not change.
All that changes is what society considers acceptable and unacceptable. Thus, language, sex, religion, and politics dominate

the censorship scene. In times of national stress, politics will dominate the censorship scene. In the McCarthy era of the early 1950s, censors sought communists under every bush, behind covers of books, and in the movie industry. Books were banned, not because of their content, but because their authors were considered suspect. Such performers as Paul Robeson were banned from concert halls and their recordings removed from music stores and libraries. Earlier in the century, the attack had been on German materials as the passions raised by World War I swept the country. Today, some conservative groups are asking for the removal of materials on the grounds that the authors are homosexuals, even when, as in the case of Emily Dickinson, there is no reputable literary critic who has demonstrated that to be true.

Despite the First Amendment's guarantee of freedom of religion, it too has consistently provoked censorship attempts. Anti-Catholicism was rampant in the late nineteenth century, and anti-Semitism is always with us. One of the most important First Amendment cases decided by the Supreme Court involved Jehovah's Witnesses.

The common denominator in cases involving politics and religion is the question of offensiveness. Views held offensive by the majority are always ripe for attack and never more so than when there is general unrest within society, whether stemming from international conflicts or internal economic difficulties. On the other hand, it is very difficult for decent-minded people to accept the fact that virulently hateful materials attacking a particular group are also protected under the law.

Sex and language are intertwined in censorship cases and cannot easily be separated. Their common denominator is a question of obscenity. Nothing has caused the courts more trouble than trying to define obscenity. It was a British judge, Chief Justice Cockburn, who set the standard for obscenity when he defined it in the case of *Regina v. Hicklin* (1868) as ". . . whether the tendency of the matter charged is to deprave and corrupt those whose minds are open to such immoral influences, and into whose hands a publication of this sort may fall." Victorian England's standard was accepted by the United States courts, and thus, the weakest members of society (as determined by their "betters") were the norm for determining obscenity, regardless of the overall quality of the book.

In 1933, however, enough time had passed and conditions within society had changed so that the Cockburn definition could be refined. In the case of the *United States v. Ulysses*, District Judge John M. Woolsey found Joyce's novel not pornographic, if frank.

He noted that the legal definition of obscenity is "that which tends to stir the sex impulses or to lead to sexually impure and lustful thoughts." But, he pointed out, the law is concerned only with the normal person, and thus the court must attempt to assess the effect of a particular book upon a person of average sexual instincts. Judge Woolsey borrowed a French phrase to describe this hypothetical normal man which the court would use as a test—"*l'homme moyen sensuel.*" The decision was upheld by Circuit Judge Augustus N. Hand and the government did not appeal it to the Supreme Court. (Both decisions make excellent reading. They are reproduced in Robert Downs's *First Freedom.*)

Thus the doctrine that all reading must be safe for the weakest, the most susceptible mind was set aside. In 1957, the Supreme Court gave its endorsement to the view that the stable adult mind must be the governing factor when it struck down the state of Michigan's censorship law in *Butler v. Michigan.* Justice Felix Frankfurter remarked: "[Michigan] insists that, by thus quarantining the general reading public against books not too rugged for grown men and women *in order to shield juvenile innocence* [italics added] it is exercising its power to promote the general welfare. Surely this is to burn the house to roast the pig. . . . [This reduces] the adult population of Michigan to reading only what is fit for children."

It is one thing to say that adults must not be reduced to reading deemed appropriate for children; it is another to hold that children have the right of access to all materials appropriate for adults. The Supreme Court ruled in 1968 in *New York v. Ginsberg* that a state may set separate standards for the sale of materials for minors. This decision began a rash of state laws being introduced into legislatures that required constant monitoring by librarians since many proposed statutes wanted to broaden the concept from "sale of" to include "lending of" such materials to juveniles. For obvious reasons, librarians were and are concerned that they be free to circulate materials to all patrons without fear of legal prosecution.

One of the major problems with obscenity cases in general is that there is no way to know in advance of a court ruling what is or is not obscene. Librarians buying and circulating materials in all good faith need to know that they are not subject to a jail sentence. Charles Rembar, a distinguished attorney and legal writer, feels that obscenity cases should be dealt with in the civil courts since it is unfair to penalize authors and publishers with jail sentences for writing and publishing books they could not know in advance were to be judged obscene.

The layperson's general response to that is, why don't we set up a commission or committee to make the judgment in advance of publication. All of us need to understand that the very worst form of censorship is *a priori*, that is, before the fact. It was *a priori* censorship that inspired John Milton to write his famous *Areopagitica* and produce one of the most quoted passages ever written on the subject:

> . . . though all the winds of doctrine were let loose to play upon the earth, so Truth be in the field, we do injuriously by licensing and prohibiting to misdoubt her strength. Let her and Falsehood grapple; who ever knew Truth put to the worse in a free and open encounter?

In 1968 obscenity and pornography were very much on the minds of the politicians and President Lyndon Johnson named 18 members to a Commission on Obscenity and Pornography, which had been authorized by Public Law 90-100. The Commission was to conduct a thorough study of the effect of obscenity and pornography upon the public and of the relationship of pornography to antisocial behavior. It was charged with analyzing the laws pertaining to the control of obscenity and pornography; recommending definitions of obscenity and pornography; investigating the methods employed in the distribution of obscene and pornographic materials as well as the nature and volume of the traffic; and to recommend actions to control that traffic without in any way interfering with constitutional rights. To carry out its work, the Commission was empowered to "make contracts with universities, research institutions, foundations, laboratories, hospitals, and other competent public or private agencies to conduct research."

The report was released in 1970 but the results were in no way comforting. President Nixon, himself no stranger to expletives, soundly denounced it, while the Senate of the United States distinguished itself by voting to condemn it before (it has been maintained) the Senators could have read it. It seems highly unlikely, at the very least, that any of the national figures who help guide policy ever read, or will read, the six volumes of the technical report. The hope that the Commission would cast some firmer light on the relationship of pornography to delinquency—or to general social decay—was a vain one.

In the intervening years the focus of attention has shifted from pornography for adults which might, inadvertently, fall into the hands of the young, to the problem of pornographic films and books which use children as actors and models. This highly explosive, and distasteful, issue has created real problems for civil libertarians who do not want to be identified in any way as approving of child pornography, yet find themselves having to argue against many laws that while well-meaning, violate the rights of ordinary citizens. Some of the laws have been so broadly written as to make illegal the depiction of pubertal growth in a medical physiology book if the depiction is by photographs rather than drawings (and even with drawings if real life models were used). Frustrated at the inability to locate and punish the producers of the materials, the legislators have yielded to the temptation to go after the distributors. This very complicated situation offers librarians an excellent opportunity to explore the complexities involved in First Amendment issues.

Unfortunately, we cannot look to the Supreme Court to make the issues less complex in any area of obscenity/pornography cases. The Court added innumerable complications in 1973 when in *Miller v. California,* the Court announced that it was no longer necessary to prove that an alleged pornographic work had to be "utterly without" any redeeming social value. It also stated that the "community standards" by which a work was to be judged were to be local community standards, and not some artificial "national" standard. That decision has resulted in further lawsuits, and the resultant court decisions have further confused the issue.

There are two major unanswered questions: what constitutes a local community, and should a citizen's right to materials be an accident of location? Should citizens in New York have greater rights than those living in Alabama? Although the Supreme Court announced in October 1977 that it would clarify its meaning of "community" standards, it has not done so.

Library Problems

While it is very important for librarians to understand the legalities involved in censorship, the legal aspects of censorship are not our real problem, except in relation to school libraries (discussed below). Too much emphasis on obscenity and pornography overshadows the real library problem. Librarians have to face the fact that community pressure plays a more important role in the selection of materials than whether the materials are legal or illegal. It takes real courage to purchase and circulate materials that will be offensive to the power structure within the community. It also takes a very active public information campaign designed to make the issues clear to the members of the community. Most Americans do not believe that censorship cases concern them. They feel that they only want to read "acceptable" materials and people who want trash probably *should* have their rights restricted.

It is not that simple and people need to be helped to understand that fact. There were people who felt libraries should not buy Richard Nixon's *Memoirs* because they did not want tax money spent that would contribute to his income. People who want to read Richard Nixon should have that right. People who want to read Jerry Falwell should have that right. People who want to read anti-Nixon or anti-Falwell books should have that right. In other words, it is necessary to help citizens understand that if they want their rights respected, they must respect the rights of those who hold opposing views.

In order to educate the public about the importance of a diversity of points of view within the library, librarians must first educate themselves. There is enough censorship in the selection process in most libraries to make us vulnerable to attacks that proclaim that *we* are the real censors. As a rule of thumb, librarians ought to be sure that at least twenty-five percent of the materials they buy for the library are personally offensive to them. After all, if they are going to ask members of the community to accept the presence of materials in the library that the citizens find offensive, it is only fair that the librarians practice what they preach.

Practicing what one preaches is not easy. Many librarians have rejected the racist/sexist biases so prevalent in American society. They do not want children exposed to racist/sexist materials. They do not even want adults exposed to *The Total Woman* or William Shockley's view that blacks are inherently inferior to whites. Other librarians, holding different views, do not want to appear to condone pro-choice positions when it comes to abortion or buy materials that assume evolution is the only way to account for the human presence on Earth.

Medical doctors who are anti-abortion and refuse to perform abortions are able to rationalize their stand by saying that when a patient arrives who needs or wants an abortion, they refer the patient to a doctor who does perform abortions. That approach is of little help to the librarian who has the only show in town. Our task is much harder than those of the doctors: we must learn how to leave our deepest-felt values at the staff entrance and buy the materials that offend us most deeply. It isn't easy, but it can be done by librarians really committed to the profession.

While librarians do have problems with materials for adults, the really emotional issue concerns materials for children and adolescents. Generally speaking, research shows that most of us acquire our values by the age of twenty and do not change those values unless we experience "a significant emotional event." Without reading the research, most of us accept the fact that adults are not amenable to changing our values (we have ourselves to demonstrate that fact). However, we feel that the young can be changed and we want to offer them only those values we cherish. We do not trust the young to choose the best values, so we try to restrict their access to views we disapprove of. This distrust of the young is common in adults: parents don't trust their children, either. Which is sad, because, again, research shows that most young people grow up to hold the same values of their families.

In dealing with the community, we must learn how to draw appropriate analogies that will raise the citizens' consciousness. We must ask, "If the majority of the voters are going to vote Republican, should Democrats be deprived of their vote?" The right to read is identical to the right to vote: majority opinion does not prevent the minority from expressing its views.

Probably the most important fact to convey to the community is the difference between behavior and the right to read. Actions that are illegal when exercised, are not illegal when read about. The Supreme Court decided that issue when it decided that mere membership in the Communist party did not mean the person was actively involved in trying to overthow the U.S. government. This distinction between action and access to information is very important. For example, a state may have statutes on the books that make homosexuality illegal. That does not mean that materials *about* homosexuality are ipso facto illegal. Murder is illegal too, but we have numerous books about murders and murderers, some of which are actually sympathetic to the murderer. Neither librarians nor the public are consistent in their responses to this issue: less emotionally charged issues are okay in the library, but when an issue runs contrary to the deepest held prejudices, then it becomes controversial.

In defending people's right to read about controversial issues, it is also important to educate the community to a concept of fairness. All people pay taxes to support the library and have a right to find their views represented in its collection. Fairness is a very powerful word when discussing issues with the American public—it will respond to it far better than to discussions about what is legal.

School Library Problems

Unlike public libraries, which have not had their controversies end up in the courts, school libraries have developed a history of case law, much of it confusing and contradictory. (see *Censorship, Libraries, and the Law* in the chapter bibliography for an excellent overview.)

Civil libertarians and librarians had hoped that the Supreme Court would resolve some of the difficulties facing school librarians when it handed down its decision in the now infamous "Island Trees" case. To many, the case seemed clear cut: the School Board had ordered the removal of books it had not read, basing its decision on a list of titles picked up at an ultra-conservative group meeting. As is so often the case, the titles represented some of the best of modern American literature, both adult and teenage titles.

The Supreme Court justices did not find the case clear cut at all. While the decision remanded the case back to the lower court for trial, four justices did not perceive any First Amendment issue to be involved. In one sense, the case had a happy ending: the School Board decided to throw in the towel and put the books back on the school library shelves. But for intellectual freedom advocates, the Supreme Court's decision left much to be desired and it hangs over the heads of all school librarians.

The specific problem school librarians face is the narrow age group they serve and the natural predilection of adults to limit the rights of young people when it comes to free access to information. Underlying much of the school's problems is an almost total failure of school personnel to educate the public about the great diversity present in any student body. Assumptions are made that children of a particular age are all alike in terms of both cognitive and psychological development. Nothing could be farther from the truth, and a school system striving for excellence cannot afford to gear either its library collection or its curriculum to the lowest common denominator.

The year 1983 saw several major reports on the status of education in the United States and provoked much discussion about how to improve the schools. The major omission in the discussions was the recognition that good education must stimulate controversy; blandness produces nothing but bland students. Whether the American public would respond positively to being asked to demand an atmosphere of controversy within the school walls is unknown: no major voice has come forth to put the issue to the public.

Government Attacks on Freedom of Information

As the United States began the year of Big Brother, a major concern of all civil libertarians was the increasing number of attempts by the federal government to limit access to information. The attempts take a variety of forms: the Executive Branch's suggestion that all federal employees with access to classified information be subject to lifelong *a priori* censorship for all writings, speeches, or public interviews; the attempt to increase the costs for people wishing to utilize the Freedom of Information Act; the attempt to water down the aforementioned act, and the actions of the National Security Agency in ordering a private library to remove previously public documents from public access.

Other government actions included trying to label three National Film Board of Canada films "propaganda" because their messages were contrary to those espoused by the government. This action, subsequently found illegal by a federal court, would have required, among other things, that the names of all those buying/renting/viewing the films be turned over to the government.

The right of educational film producers to sell their films abroad without paying the huge import duties of foreign countries has been undermined by the United States Information Agency's refusal to grant educational certificates to films whose content it deems contrary to American interests. Among the films denied the certificate was *Soldier Girls*, a *cinéma vérité* documentary on Army basic training for women.

It is essential that librarians recognize that all such actions by the government have direct and adverse effects upon libraries. Whether government tries to limit what previous employees can say, or government agencies harass librarians over items within their collections, the effects are the same: they restrict the public's right to know. The situation is not simply a matter of politics, an often perceived perjorative word by librarians, since the Executive Branch under both Democrats and Republicans attempts to limit what the public can know about its actions and those of previous administrations.

Libraries also suffer when important foreign nationals are forbidden passports because the government does not want their views heard directly by the American public as in the cases, to name just two, of Mrs. Allende and the Reverend Ian Paisley. While the Supreme Court has ruled the government may not deny passports to people wanting to travel abroad, the State Department is attempting to bypass this ban by denying travelers to such countries as Cuba the right to *pay* for the trip.

The above are just a few examples of the need for librarians to monitor constantly the actions of our own government. Free access to information means more than the right to buy and shelve government approved materials.

Bibliography

Books

American Library Association. Office for Intellectual Freedom. *Censorship Litigation and the Schools.* Chicago, American Library Association, 1983. 161p. High powered legal minds discuss strategy.

American Library Association. Office for Intellectual Freedom. *Intellectual Freedom Manual.* 2d ed. Chicago, American Library Association, 1983. 210p. Brings together ALA documents, essays on intellectual freedom, etc. Major changes from previous edition.

Anderson, A. J. *Problems in Intellectual Freedom and Censorship.* New York, Bowker, 1974. 195p. Thirty case studies.

Bartlett, Jonathan. *The First Amendment in a Free Society.* New York, Wilson, 1979. 199p. A "Reference Shelf" volume with pro as well as con censorship articles.

Berninghausen, David. *Flight from Reason.* Chicago, American Library Association, 1975. 175p. Essays on intellectual freedom.

Bosmajian, Haig A. *Obscenity and Freedom of Expression.* New York, Burt Franklin, 1976. 348p. Discusses important court cases dealing with obscenity.

Bosmajian, Haig, A. *Obscenity and Freedom of Expression.* New York, Burt Franklin, 1976. 348p. Discusses important court cases dealing with obscenity.

Boyer, Paul S. *Purity in Print; The Vice Society Movement and Book Censorship in America.* New York, Scribners, 1968. 362p. Historical review.

Broderick, Dorothy M. "Adolescent Development and Censorship." In *School Library Media Annual, 1983,* pp. 43–53. Littleton, Colo., Libraries Unlimited, 1983. Piaget's characteristics of adolescence related to censorious adults.

Busha, Charles H. *Freedom Versus Suppression and Censorship; With a Study of the Attitudes of Midwestern Public Librarians and a Bibliography of Censorship.* Littleton, Colo., Libraries Unlimited, 1973. 240p.

Busha, Charles H. *An Intellectual Freedom Primer*. Littleton, Colo., Libraries Unlimited, 1977. 221p. Essays by a number of authors on various aspects of censorship.

Clapp, Jane. *Art Censorship; A Chronology of Proscribed and Prescribed Art*. Metuchen, N.J., Scarecrow Press, 1972. 582p.

Daily, Jay E. *Anatomy of Censorship*. New York, Dekker, 1973. 403p. Censorship of sexual materials.

Davis, James E. *Dealing with Censorship*. Urbana, Ill., National Council of Teachers of English, 1979. 228p. Excellent advice in many essays.

Downs, Robert B. *The First Freedom; Liberty and Justice in the World of Books and Reading*. Chicago, American Library Association, 1960. 469p.

Ernst, Morris L. and Alan U. Schwartz. *Censorship: The Search for the Obscene*. New York, Macmillan, 1964. 288p.

Ernst, Morris L. *To the Pure; A Study of Obscenity and the Censor*. New York, Viking Press, 1928. 336p. (Reprinted by Kraus, 1969.)

Falwell, Jerry. *Listen, America!* Garden City, N.Y., Doubleday, 1980. 269p. Numerous implications throughout for why censorship is an approved Moral Majority concept.

Fiske, Marjorie. *Book Selection and Censorship; A Study of School and Public Libraries in California*. Berkeley, University of California Press, 1959. 145p. Classic research report.

Haight, Anne L. *Banned Books*. 4th ed. New York, Bowker, 1978. 196p. Important examples of banned books, arranged chronologically.

Haiman, Franklyn S. *Freedom of Speech*. Skokie, Ill., National Textbook Co., 1976. Good introduction to the range of issues involved.

Hefley, James C. *Textbooks on Trial*. Wheaton, Ill., Victor Books, 1977. Dist. by Mel and Norma Gabler, Longview, Texas. Sympathetic view of the Gablers' fight to clean up textbooks.

Hentoff, Nat. *The First Freedom: The Tumultuous History of Free Speech in America*. New York, Delacorte, 1980. 340p. Dell reprint, 1981.

Jenkinson, Edward B. *Censors in the Classroom: The Mind Benders*. Carbondale, Southern Illinois University Press, 1979. 209p.

Kanawha County, West Virginia: A Textbook Study in Cultural Conflict. National Education Association, 1975. Offers important insights for understanding how a major censorship confrontation occurs.

LaHaye, Tim. *The Battle for the Public Schools*. Old Tappan, N.J., Flemming H. Revell, 1983. One of a series of "Battle for" titles depicting a secular humanist conspiracy by a Far Right minister.

Lewis, Felice Flanery. *Literature, Obscenity, and Law*. Carbondale, Southern Illinois University Press, 1976. 297p. Censorship of fiction.

Merritt, LeRoy Charles. *Book Selection and Intellectual Freedom*. New York, Wilson, 1970. 100p. From the public library perspective.

Moon, Eric. *Book Selection and Censorship in the Sixties*. New York, Bowker, 1969. 421p. Reprints of 55 articles from *Library Journal*.

Neier, Aryeh. *Defending My Enemy*. New York, Dutton, 1979. 182p. Using the infamous American Nazi/Skokie case, the director of the American Civil Liberties Union eloquently defends the First Amendment.

Norwick, Kenneth P. *Pornography: The Issues and the Law*. New York, Public Affairs Committee, 1972.

Norwick, Kenneth P. *Lobbying for Freedom: A Citizen's Guide to Fighting Censorship at the State Level*. New York, St. Martin's Press, 1975.

Oboler, Eli M. *The Fear of the Word; Censorship and Sex*. Metuchen, N.J., Scarecrow Press, 1974. 362p.

Oboler, Eli M. *To Free the Mind: Libraries, Technology, & Intellectual Freedom*. Littleton, Colo., Libraries Unlimited, 1983. 275p.

O'Neil, Robert M. *Classrooms in the Crossfire*. Bloomington, Indiana University Press, 1981. 242p. Scholarly analysis of the clash between First Amendment freedoms and community standards for public schools.

Parker, Barbara and Stefanie Weiss. *Protecting the Freedom to Learn*. Washington, D.C., People for the American Way, 1983. 122p. Important insights into the Far Right's attack on public schools.

Pilpel, Harriet F. "Libraries and the First Amendment." In *Libraries and the Life of the Mind in America*. pp. 87–106. Chicago, American Library Association, 1977. Lecture delivered at ALA Centennial Conference in 1976.

Rembar, Charles. *The End of Obscenity; the Trials of Lady Chatterly, Tropic of Cancer, and Fanny Hill*. New York, Random House, 1968. 528p.

Robotham, John and Gerald Shields. *Freedom of Access to Library Materials*. New York, Neal-Schuman, 1982, 221p.

The Speaker and the Listener: A Public Perspective on Freedom of Expression. Public Agenda, 750 Third Ave., New York, NY 10017. Fascinating report of how "the public" views various free speech issues.

Thomas, Cal. *Book Burning*. Westchester, Ill., Crossway Books, 1983. 158p. From the Moral Majority viewpoint.

Thompson, Anthony H. *Censorship in Public Libraries in the United Kingdom During the Twentieth Century*. Epping, Essex, England, Bowker, 1975. 236p. Chronological approach highlighting well known censorship cases.

Tribe, David H. *Questions of Censorship*. New York, St. Martin's Press, 1973. 362p. Censorship of all types of media. British viewpoint.

U.S. Commission on Obscenity and Pornography. *Report*. Washington, D.C., U.S. Government Printing Office, 1970. 646p. Report was also published in hardback and paperback by trade publishers.

U.S. Commission on Obscenity and Pornography. *Technical Reports*. Washington, D.C., U.S. Government Printing Office, 1971. 6v.

Articles

Please note: The cut-off date for periodical articles is 1975 except for the occasional "classic" in the field. Consult the following indexes for older articles: *Education Index, Library Literature, Readers' Guide to Periodical Literature*. One of the best current sources for keeping up is the bibliography which appears in each issue of the *Newsletter on Intellectual Freedom*.

Asheim, Lester. "Not Censorship But Selection." *Wilson Library Bulletin*, 28:63–67, September 1953. Classic essay.

Asheim, Lester. "Selection and Censorship: A Reappraisal." *Wilson Library Bulletin*, 58:180–184, November 1983. Thirty years later, a second classic essay.

American Civil Liberties Union. *Free Speech, 1984: The Rise of Government Controls on Information, Debate and Association.* New York, 1984. 29p. An excellent overview.

Benemann, William E. "Tears and Ivory Towers: California Libraries During the McCarthy Era." *American Libraries,* 8:305–309, June 1977. How librarians faced censorship in the 1950s.

Bradley, Norman. "What Do You Care What I Read? Or What Do I Care What You Read?" *Tennessee Librarian,* 27:58–61, Spring 1975. Speech by a newspaper editor.

Broderick, Dorothy M. "Censorship: A Family Affair?" *Top of the News,* Spring 1979. Family mental health as a censorship consideration.

Broderick, Dorothy M. "Son of Speaker." *American Libraries,* October 1977. Commentary on *"The Speaker"* film controversy.

Bundy, Mary Lee and Teresa Stakem. "Librarians and Intellectual Freedom: Are Opinions Changing?" *Wilson Library Bulletin,* 56:584–589, April 1982.

Burger, Robert H. "The Kanawha County Textbook Controversy: A Study of Communication and Power." *Library Quarterly,* 48:143–162, April 1978.

Busha, Charles H., ed. "Censorship in the Eighties." *Drexel Library Quarterly,* 18:1–108, Winter 1982. Entire issue is on censorship, with a 1970–1981 bibliography.

Chach, Maryann. "More *About Sex.*" *Sightlines,* 12:15–17, Fall 1979. Analysis of the attacks on an award winning sex education film.

Coughlan, Margaret. "Guardians of the Young . . ." *Top of the News,* 33:137–148, Winter 1977. Reviews censorship of children's reading.

Eaglen, Audrey. "Libraries and the Moral Majority." *Library Acquisitions: Practice and Theory,* 5:143–145, 1981.

Eaglen, Audrey. "The 'Warning Bookmark': Selection Aid or Censorship?" *Library Acquisitions: Practice and Theory,* 3:65–71, 1979. A wholesaler alerts customers with a pink warning slip as to potentially controversial children's books.

Ellis, Ken. "Censorship: An Annotated Bibliography." *Moccasin Telegraph,* 19:13–17, Spring-Summer 1977. Long annotations of thirteen articles.

Farris, Michael. "Working Together: In Defense of Conscience." *Newsletter on Intellectual Freedom,* 30:148+, November 1981. The Washington State Moral Majority leader states his case.

Flanagan, Leo N. "Defending the Indefensible: The Limits of Intellectual Freedom." *Library Journal,* 100:1887–1891, October 15, 1975. Criticism of ALA's *Intellectual Freedom Manual.*

Fontaine. Sue. "Dismissal with Prejudice: Moral Majority vs. Washington State Library." *Library Journal,* 106:1273–1279, June 15, 1981. What happened when the Moral Majority wanted the names of people borrowing a sex education film.

Gaddy, Wayne. "The Obscenity Muddle." *PNLA Quarterly,* 39:4–9, Summer 1975.

Geller, Evelyn. "Intellectual Freedom—Eternal Principle or Unanticipated Consequence?" *Library Journal,* 99:1364–1367, May 15, 1974. Reviews development of librarians' concern with intellectual freedom.

Gerhardt, Lillian N. "Who's In Charge of School Libraries?" *School Library Jour-*

nal, 23:27–28, November 1976. Comments on the Strongsville (Ohio) decision.

Goldberger, Judith M. "Judy Blume: Target of the Censor." *Newsletter on Intellectual Freedom*, 30:59+, May 1981.

Golden, Lawrence. "How Free Is Our Freedom." *Illinois Libraries*, 60:123–124, February 1978.

Heath, Susan L. and Martha B. Gould. "Government Limits on Access to Information." *Newsletter on Intellectual Freedom*, 32: 181–182, November 1983. An annotated bibliography of sources.

Hentoff, Nat. "Any Writer Who Follows Anyone Else's Guidelines Ought to Be in Advertising." *School Library Journal*, 24:27–29, November 1977. An author's comments on pressure groups watching children's publishing.

Horn, Zoia. "The Library Bill of Rights vs. The Racism and Sexism Awareness Resolution." *Library Journal*, 102:1254–1255, June 1977.

Komor, Judith. "Does Anyone Win a Censorship Case?" *Voice of Youth Advocates*, 1:9–13, August 1978.

Krug, Judith F. "Censorship in School Libraries; National Overview." *Journal of Research and Development in Education*, 9:52–59, Spring 1976.

MacLeod, Lanette. "The Censorship History of *Catcher in the Rye*." *PNLA Quarterly*, 39:10–13, Summer 1975.

Martin, Sandra. "Limits to Freedom? Oklahoma's Private Values and Public Policies on the Right to Read." *Oklahoma Librarian*, 26:6–28, January 1976.

Meyers, Duane H. "Boys and Girls and Sex and Libraries." *Library Journal*, 101:457–463, February 15, 1977. A detailed description of how one library fought off the censors.

Newmyer, Jody. "Art, Libraries, and the Censor." *Library Quarterly*, 46:38–53, January 1976.

Oboler, Eli M. "The Free Mind: Intellectual Freedom's Perils and Prospects." *Library Journal*, 101:237–242, January 1, 1976.

Oppenheim, Stephen. "Librarians & Intellectual Freedom." *Voice of Youth Advocates*, 4:14–16, June 1981.

Oppenheim, Stephen. "R Movies & Teens." *Voice of Youth Advocates*, 4:15–16, October 1981. Continued in December 1981 issue. The legal implications of libraries lending R-rated videocassettes to minors.

Parella, Gilda. "Threats to the First Amendment." *Illinois Libraries*, 60:116–119, February 1978.

"Reality and Reason: Intellectual Freedom and Youth." *Top of the News*, 31:296–312, April 1975.

Rosenberg, Mel. "Fathers, Daughters, and *Forever*." *Voice of Youth Advocates*, 2:23–24, October 1979. One librarian's answer to Blume censorship.

Sanford, Bruce W. "The Information-less Age." *Special Libraries*, 74:317–321, October 1983. Overview of government attacks on the free flow of information.

Sanford, Wendy and Paula Doress. "*Our Bodies, Ourselves* and Censorship." *Library Acquisitions: Practice and Theory*, 5:133–142, 1981.

Scales, Pat. "Parents and Students Communicate Through Literature." *Voice of Youth Advocates*, 4:9–11, June 1981. A school librarian educates parents about the new youth literature.

Scales, Peter. "Social Issues and the Moral Majority." *Voice of Youth Advocates*, 4:9–10, August 1981.

Serebnick, Judith. "Book Reviews and the Selection of Potentially Controversial Books in Public Libraries." *Library Quarterly*, 51:390–409, October 1981.

Serebnick, Judith. "The 1973 Court Rulings on Obscenity: Have They Made a Difference?" *Wilson Library Bulletin*, 50:304–310, December 1975. Results of a survey in ten medium-sized cities.

Shields, Gerald. "Freedom and Orthodoxy." *Voice of Youth Advocates*, 1:5–8, August 1978.

Simpson, Dick. "Restricting Pornography While Protecting First Amendment Rights." *Illinois Libraries*, 60:120–122, February 1978. Comments on Chicago's movie ordinance.

Smith, Shirley A. "Crisis in Kanawha County: A Librarian Looks at the Textbook Controversy." *School Library Journal*, 21:34–35, January 1975.

"'The Speaker': Step or Misstep Into Filmmaking?" *American Libraries*, 8:371–376, July–August 1977. Report on the controversial reaction to "The Speaker" at ALA's 1977 Conference in Detroit.

Stahlschmidt, Agnes D. "A Democratic Procedure for Handling Challenged Library Materials." *School Library Media Quarterly*, 11:200–203, Spring 1983. A look at the Iowa plan.

Stavely, Keith and Lani Gerson. "We Didn't Wait for the Censor: Intellectual Freedom at the Watertown Public Library." *Library Journal*, 108:1654–1658, September 1, 1983. An example of how one Massachusetts library raised its community's consciousness.

Stone, Robert D. "Island Trees v Pico: The Legal Implications." *Collection Building*, 5:3–8, Spring 1983.

Strasser, Todd. "Behind the Scenes Censorship." *Voice of Youth Advocates*, 5:22, August 1982. An author reveals pressure to become a self-censor.

"The Strongsville Decision." *School Library Journal*, 23:23–26, November 1976. Court case in Ohio involving censorship of books in a high school.

Swan, John C. "Minimum Qualifications and Intellectual Freedom." *Library Journal*, 106:1595–1599, September 1, 1981.

Taylor, Kenneth I. "Are School Censorship Cases Really Increasing?" *School Media Quarterly*, 11:26–34, Fall 1982. Discussion, 11:166–167, Spring 1983.

Tyulina, Natalia. "Ideology & Intellectual Freedom: A Letter from the U.S.S.R." *Library Journal*, 107:1294, July 1982. A Soviet librarian explains her views.

Watson, Jerry J. and Bill C. Snider. "Book Selection Pressure on School Library Media Specialists and Teachers." *School Media Quarterly*, 9:95–101, Winter 1981.

West, Celeste. "The Secret Garden of Censorship: Ourselves." *Library Journal*, 108:1651–1653, September 1, 1983.

White, Howard D. "Library Censorship and the Permissive Minority." *Library Quarterly*, 51:192–207, April 1981. Differences between those who approve of library censorship versus those who don't.

Williams, Patrick and Joan Thornton Pearce. "Censorship Redefined." *Library Journal*, 101:1494–1496, July 1976. Attempts to distinguish censorship from the controls required by library objectives.

Woods, L. B. and Lucy Salvatore. "Self-Censorship in Collection Development by High School Library Media Specialists." *School Media Quarterly*, 9:102–108, Winter 1981.

Woodworth, Mary. "An Atmosphere of Censorship." *Voice of Youth Advocates*, 5:6–13, August 1982. An overview, with emphasis on how Montello, Wis. coped with censorship.

CHAPTER 9

THE PUBLISHING TRADE

The publishing trade is closely connected with library collection development in that it sets the limits within which the library selector must work. Libraries cannot select materials which are not published, and thus the willingness—or lack of it—on the part of the publishers to risk producing a particular item will determine what the libraries find available to choose from. If publishers do not feel a responsibility to produce quality materials, libraries will not be able to select quality materials. If publishers find that the nature of their market limits the types of materials they can produce, libraries may find that a full representation of subjects and a wide range of treatments of subjects will not be made. It is not the purpose of this chapter to discuss in great detail the history and nature of the publishing trade (there are numerous books offering full treatment of those topics), but to restrict the discussion to those aspects of the trade which have an impact on the materials available for library purchase.

The Structure of the Industry

The publishing trade is not one of the giant industries of the United States. Since 1958, total sales have exceeded $1 billion per year, reaching more than $4.5 billion in 1977. To put this figure in its proper perspective vis-à-vis our larger industries, one must remember that General Motors' reported gross income in 1977 was more than $55 billion. One spokesperson for the publishing industry remarked that people spend more for dog food than for textbooks and more for caskets than trade books.

The trade was characterized in the past—and is still primarily so today—by a large number of relatively small producers. The total number of American publishers has been estimated variously. There are certainly more than 1,000 trade publishers but, if one includes publishing agencies outside the book trade, the number would reach several thousand. If one thinks of government units at all levels of government as publishers, then the count would soar impressively.

Literary Market Place now limits its listings to trade publishers who produce three or more books per year, and the 1983 issue contained ninty-nine pages of such entries. No other industry in the United States has as many producers as the publishing trade—the giant industries, oil and automobiles number no more than in the dozens.

One of the striking features of the book trade, beginning in the late 1950s, was a series of mergers, which is altering the former structure of the trade. In the past, librarians were admonished to become familiar with individual publishing firms, to learn their characteristics, to estimate their reliability—and firms had, by and large, individual and stable personalities. It is becoming increasingly difficult to make very definite statements about individual firms, because firms are merging, being bought out, buying out other firms in turn, and generally swirling about at a giddy pace which leaves the onlooker pretty thoroughly confused. *Literary Market Place* lists acquisitions and mergers annually and the list in 1983 shows the trend continues.

A merger is defined as two or more publishing houses becoming part of one overall management structure in which the merged houses may or may not retain their original names and imprints. Random House, for example, now encompasses Knopf, Pantheon, and Ballantine (with Ballantine also producing the Fawcett line). The term acquisition is better reserved for when non-book trade corporations purchase publishing houses. Gulf-+Western owns Simon & Schuster, Xerox bought Bowker and University Microfilms, the Columbia Broadcasting System bought Holt, Rinehart and Winston, and so it goes.

However, as Dessauer observes in his fine *Book Publishing: What It Is, What It Does,* corporations that thought to make big profits from the publishing industry when it was riding high in the 1960s, have had second thoughts in the 1980s. Numerous articles in *Publishers Weekly* in the early 1980s have focused on the problems book publishing faces when it is being run by people with little knowledge of the book trade. The accounting approach that works when producing widgets, does not work when it comes to publishing books. Another factor in the disillusionment process is the major cutbacks in federal support for schools and libraries. Textbooks, which looked like a good investment when we had a population explosion look less attractive with a falling birth rate and increased citizen-group attacks upon their content.

Many groups are concerned about the concentration occurring in the book trade, including authors who see their options narrowing, and librarians and civil libertarians who worry about corporations exercising control over the content to be published. The most dramatic case to prove the worry was not groundless did not occur with one of the corporate giants dictating to a publisher, but one publisher dictating to another. In the summer of 1983 Thomas A. Nelson, the country's largest publisher of bibles, ordered its subsidiary, Dodd, Mead, to either change the language in three of its adult titles or withdraw them from publication. Legally, Thomas A. Nelson had every right to do as it did, and that is what frightens so many people. If other parent-bodies were to decide that their publishing houses could not publish nonfiction titles that examined the business practices of corporate America, or a specific industry's unconcern with worker safety, or any of a dozen other controversial issues, what happens to the rights of readers to find many viewpoints available?

In contrast to the concentration of book trade publishing, is another phenomenon, what Alvin Toffler calls "demassifying the media." The *Alternative Press Index* gives some idea of the small presses now contributing titles to the American book scene. Librarians must be aware of the output of small presses, be they religious press publishers or radical political groups. The development of new printing techniques has made it financially feasible for small presses to produce small book runs and still make a profit.

The problem facing librarians who would like to expand their selection practices is that the book reviewing media are less than enthusiastic in their desire to expand coverage. Some books get many reviews while most books are never reviewed at all, except, perhaps, in the author's home town newspaper.

Paperback publishing has been a big growth industry during the past twenty years. It takes a number of forms. There are mass market and trade paperbacks; there are reprints and original titles; there is simultaneous publication of the hard cover and paperback editions by the same publisher, and there are arrangements between paperback and hard cover publishers, by which the paperback publisher finds and buys the title, the hard cover publisher publishes it and eventually the paperback publisher gets to reprint it.

To take them in order: basically the differences between mass market and trade paperbacks are those of size and distribution system. All mass market paperbacks are the same size in heighth and width; they have to be to fit the racks found in drugstores, supermarkets, and newstands in airports and hundreds of other locations. Mass market paperbacks are distributed primarily, but not exclusively, by wholesalers who also provide magazines and newspapers to the outlets serviced. Trade paperbacks, on the other hand, come in all sizes from the very small to the very large, from vertical to horizontal formats. Trade paperbacks can usually be purchased from a library's regular wholesaler as well as through members of the Educational Paperback Association, a group concerned primarily with servicing schools and libraries.

While many people think of paperbacks as reprints, the major change in this segment of the publishing trade in recent years has been the growth of original publishing. Every major paperback house now has at least one original publishing line, with adult romances leading the field in sales. Such authors as Janet Dailey and Rosemary Rogers have made this a gold mine for their publishers. And publishers, understanding what the library profession has never fully grasped, have been quick to develop similar lines for teenagers, knowing that if you catch them young, you can keep many of them forever. Thus, we have "First Love" and "Flare" and "Wildfire" romance series, and "Dark Forces" and "Twilight" horror/occult series for teens.

For a time in the late 1970s and early 1980s the price was sky high for the right to reprint many adult bestsellers. The reprint rights bidding auction became part of the publishing trade as reprint houses spent a million or more dollars for the rights to a bestseller. Many failed to earn the advance money for the paperback houses, and sanity may return to the field, particularly since rights are no longer sold in perpetuity, five years being the standard period during which the paperback house retains the rights.

Rather than let paperback houses make money off the reprints of hard cover titles, many publishers now take two routes to keep the money in house. They do simultaneous publication, a hard cover and a paperback edition, with the only difference being in the cover itself—the format remains the same. Others, particularly within the juvenile departments of publishing houses, have established their own reprint lines. Both suffer from the same problem: they use the original plates and put a soft cover on the book, making it oversized and thus excluding the titles from standard paperback racks.

Then, there are the arrangements between hard cover and paperback publishers by which the latter provides titles directly to the former for hard cover publication, thus assuring the title will be reviewed by the media which generally ignores original paperbacks, even by well known authors. The system works to the advantage of both publishing houses: the hard cover publisher takes fewer financial risks, while the paperback publisher has the advantage of the publicity generated by the hard cover edition.

Finally, there are such paperback houses as Bantam, which have now begun their own hard cover publishing, particularly for potential blockbuster titles of interest to bookstores. This approach eliminates the need to participate in the astronomical bidding wars that come when a hard cover publisher auctions off a major bestseller.

It is difficult to believe, but true, that there still exist librarians who make selection decisions based on the format of the material. Every study done has shown that library patrons prefer paperbacks (unless they have a visual problem) when they are available. Teenagers, in particular, will wait for a paperback edition to come back even when the hard cover title is on the shelf. To ignore the preferences of people does nothing for the library's image, but it does increase the sales of bookstores and school book clubs.

Book clubs are an interesting phenomenon, but they do not impact on the library's concerns except in relationship to school book clubs, and in the subtle, or not so subtle, influence they exercise on what is published. School librarians must be alert to the practice of some school book clubs of expurgating the titles they reprint. There is no way in which a librarian can defend having two editions of a title on the shelves: either the expurgated language and scenes were necessary to the integrity of the original, or they weren't. Having expurgated editions on the shelves is setting oneself up as a sitting duck for the censorious minded.

Problems of the Industry

What are the problems of this industry which may affect the kind of books which libraries find for sale? There is general agreement that the dominant factor is the rise of the break-even point, i.e., the number of copies at which the publisher recovers the investment and begins to show a profit. Where once a publisher could recoup a book's investment with 5,000 copies, it now takes 10,000 copies to make a profit on most titles unless the book is priced considerably higher than most people feel reasonable. This increase in costs comes from a variety of factors: paper, printing, postal, and warehousing costs have all risen dramatically. Moreover, most major publishing houses are located in high-rent districts in high-rent cities. And while salaries in publishing are not high, it being a high-status, basically low-paying industry, they are still higher than in the "good old days."

An additional problem is the demand by authors to be better paid. They want larger advances and a larger percentage of the selling price of their books. Some authors, of course, make fortunes, but they are the exceptions. As James Collier wrote in *Publishers Weekly*, the average author earns about $5,000 per year. The question of how long an industry can continue in good health when its major sources for its products are living in poverty, or must work at another job, deserves serious concern.

Some people within publishing houses owned by corporations have charged that the accounting procedures introduced by the MBA types are playing havoc with editorial decisions. Once, a publishing house sought only to have an overall profit when it closed its books at the end of a publishing year. This meant a bestseller or two during the year could carry the list. However, if corporate management is demanding that each and every title at least break even, editorial decisions have to become skewed. For most of its history, the publishing industry in the United States has accepted the responsibility to publish important authors and titles regardless of their sale value. Poetry sells very badly in the United States (it would sell better if libraries assumed the responsibility of purchasing important literary contributions as well as those titles in popular demand). Shall we banish poetry from the publishing industry?

Librarians who look at the cover price on a book and assume huge profits to the publisher should come to understand how little of that cover price actually accrues to the publisher. Publishers must give large discounts to the wholesalers who provide libraries with the bulk of their purchases; to bookstores; pay royalties to authors; and absorb ever increasing shipping costs. Some portion of the price must also be allocated for warehouse space to hold the books until they are ordered.

Major publishers must look to the sale of subsidiary rights to help them make a profit. They look for the book they can sell to Hollywood or television for potential movie scripts, to book clubs, and to reprint houses. There is, as a result, an understandable tendency for publishers to search for some books, at least, which will achieve the kind of popularity which will create a demand for the title in Hollywood or among the television moguls. In general, the characteristics that make for a good film are a strong plot with plenty of action and characters with enough appeal so that big name stars will want to play the roles. These characteristics eliminate most, not all, of the more literary works, thus creating a demand for the title with mass appeal.

At one point in time it was possible to say that the university presses would take up the slack by publishing the truly literary and scholarly materials so necessary to the continued cultural good health of a nation. However, as monetary resources have become scarcer within universities and the student enrollment falls, university presses are being held cost accountable by their parent institutions. They are no longer highly subsidized, but must balance their books the same as a trade publisher. A good indication of this shift is the series of excellent bibliographies published each year by the American Association of University Presses and the American Library Association. The Public Library Division of ALA has a Small and Medium-sized Libraries section which selects titles from university presses for the "University Press Books for Public Libraries" bibliography. The American Association of School Librarians of the ALA provides the same services for "University Press Books for Secondary School Libraries."

The need for university presses to balance their account books, if not actually show a profit, has led to another interesting phenomenon: scholars whose works have a very limited audience are being forced to engage in "vanity" publishing to have their works see print. Once "vanity" publishing was perceived as the rotten apple in the publishing barrel. For the most part, it still is. Vanity houses require their authors to pay for the right to be published; they do little or no promotion of the titles once published, and often charge the author for copies the author wishes to distribute personally. However, an increasing number of university professors must finance their own writings if they are to share them with the few colleagues for whom the works are important.

The impact libraries have on the financial well being of publishers varies by type of material. As much as 90 percent of the hardcover sales of juvenile departments within publishing houses may be to schools and public libraries. As little as 10 percent of adult trade hardcover sales may be to libraries. This disparity means that juvenile publishing pays a great deal of attention to the needs of youth librarians while adult trade publishing focuses on the adult book-buying public when making decisions. There are signs that the juvenile publishing departments, particularly those in major paperback houses, are changing this pattern and shaping their lists toward the bookstore market.

Libraries of all types do have a heavier impact on the sales of encyclopedias and other reference books. They provide a steady market for such items, but it is doubtful that they seriously influence the content of the tools being produced. The exception to that statement involves those titles publishers wish to have adopted by state textbook commissions. When Houghton Mifflin bowed to the censors in Texas and removed certain words from the *American Heritage Dictionary* so it would qualify for adoption, it was an ominous sign to those who see dollars becoming more important to publishers than a commitment to the intellectual integrity of the nation.

As with all other aspects of American business, publishing is groping its way into what is now known as the information society. Changes will occur, some slowly, some rapidly. It is essential that the librarian wishing to be well informed make a point of regularly reading *Publishers Weekly*, since just as libraries are faced with changes brought about by automation, so the publishing world is struggling to incorporate within its structure modern electronic methods of book production. These include such revolutionary developments as word processing units which will allow an author to mail the publisher one or more diskettes in place of a typed manuscript, from which a computer can set type for the finished book. If publishers make wise decisions, the cost of book production may actually be lowered; if they make unwise decisions, they may face bankruptcy, or at the very least, very high-priced books.

The Copyright Problem

While in most areas, librarians and publishers are friends, the issue of copyright often finds them on opposite sides. Publishers have a vested interest in making reproduction of their products as difficult as possible, preferring to be able to sell the whole book or periodical rather than allow people to photocopy those portions they need. Librarians, on the other hand, are interested in seeing that as many people as possible have access to whatever it is they need.

The 1976 revision of the Copyright Law did not solve very

much. What it basically accomplished was to replace old problems with new ones. The question of what you can and cannot do legally in terms of reproduction of other people's materials is so complex that a good rule of thumb is, when in doubt don't. The Library of Congress Copyright Office issues one or more new interpretations of the law monthly and all that can be said for the situation is that it is and will continue to provide much employment for copyright lawyers.

Bibliography

Altbach, Philip G. and Keith Smith. "Publishing in the Third World." *Library Trends*, 26:449–600, Spring 1978. Articles cover publishing in Africa, Russia, Canada, India, Egypt, Latin America, etc.

Appelbaum, Judith. "Small Publisher Power; New Perspectives on the Big Publishing Picture." *Publishers Weekly*, 222:23–26, September 10, 1982. Discussion, 222:8, October 8, 1982.

Aveney, Brian. "Electronic Publishing and the Information Transfer Process." *Special Libraries*, 74:338–344, October 1983. Discussion of changes needed in a shift from print based products to electronic products.

Benjamin, Curtis G. *A Candid Critique of Book Publishing*. New York, Bowker, 1977. 216p. Informal comments by former president of McGraw-Hill.

Blooston, George. "Honor Without Profit; Yet at a Few Big Houses Poetry Hangs On." *Publishers Weekly*, 224:48–52, August 12, 1983.

Book Publishers Directory: A Quarterly Information Service. Detroit, Mich., Gale Research, 1977–

Bookseller. London, J. Whitaker, 1958–. Standard weekly journal of the British book trade.

Boss, Richard Woodruff. "Myth of the Paperless Society." In *Information Technology*, edited by Allen Kent and Thomas J. Galvin, New York, Dekker, 1982. pp. 41–46.

Bowker Annual of Library and Book Trade Information. New York, Bowker, 1956–

Canada. Department of the Secretary of State. *The Publishing Industry in Canada*. Ottawa, 1977. 418p. Analysis of the problems.

Cerf, Bennett. *At Random: The Reminiscences of Bennett Cerf*. New York, Random House, 1977. 306p. Informal recollections of the founder of Random House.

Cole, John Young. "Books, Libraries, and Scholarly Traditions." *Scholarly Publishing*, 13:31–43, October 1981. Brief historical overview of scholarly specialization and implications of computer systems on publishing.

Collier, James Lincoln. "Can Writers Afford to Write Books?" *Publishers Weekly*, 220:21–24, July 31, 1981. Discussion, 220:9, August 21, 1981; 220:9–10, September 4, 1981. The myth of the rich author exploded.

Coser, Lewis A. and others. *Books: The Culture and Commerce of Publishing*. New York, Basic Books, 1982. 350p.

Dessauer, John P. *Book Publishing: What It Is, What It Does.* 2d ed. New York, Bowker, 1981. 230p. Basic introduction; covers most aspects.

Duke, Judith S. *Technical, Scientific, and Medical Publishing Market, 1981–86.* White Plains, N.Y., Knowledge Industry Publications, 1981. 227p.

Dystel, Oscar. *Mass-Market Publishing: More Observations, Speculations, and Provocations.* New York, Bowker, 1981. 39p.

Graham, Gordon. "Adversaries or Allies?" *Scholarly Publishing,* 14:291–297, July 1983. Relations between publishers and librarians.

Graham, W. Gordon. "Managing Change in Professional Publishing." *Scholarly Publishing,* 14:3–8, October 1982. Managing change is necessary to assure continued quality and creativeness.

Grannis, Chandler B. *What Happens in Book Publishing.* 2d ed. New York, Columbia University Press, 1967. 467p. Historically important title.

Gray, Edward. "A Few Cautionary Words About Electronic Publishing." *Journal of Micrographics,* 15:37–43, October 1982. Discussion, 12:11–12, February 1983.

Greaser, Constance U. "Authors, Editors, and Computers." *Scholarly Publishing,* 12:123–130, January 1981. An overview of "both the problem and the promise" of computerized publishing.

Green, Lisa Ann. "Computer Meets Book: Some Implications for Publishing in the Electronic Age." *Top of the News,* 39:333–336, Summer 1983. Problems and promises.

Greenfield, Howard. *Books from Writer to Reader.* New York, Crown, 1976. 211p. Superior presentation, particularly in design and manufacturing aspects.

International Literary Market Place. New York, Bowker, 1965–   . Annual.

Lancaster, Frederick Wilfrid. "Evolving Paperless Society and Its Implications for Libraries." *International Forum on Information and Documentation,* 7:3–10, October 1982.

Lane, Michael and Jeremy Booth. *Books and Publishers: Commerce Against Culture in Postwar Britain.* Lexington, Mass., Lexington Books, 1980. 148p. Publishing for literary merit versus for profit emphasis.

Library Quarterly. 54:1–104, January 1984. Entire issue devoted to aspects of publishing.

Literary Market Place. New York, Bowker, 1940–   . Annual.

Madison, Charles A. *Book Publishing in America.* New York, McGraw-Hill, 1966. 628p. History from Colonial times.

Madison, Charles A. *Irving to Irving: Author-Publisher Relations 1800–1974.* Chapters on about thirty specific author-publisher relationships, beginning with Washington Irving.

Marke, Julius J. "United States Copyright Revision and Its Legislative History." *Law Library Journal,* 70:121–152, May 1977.

Mumby, Frank A. and Ian Norrie. *Publishing and Bookselling: A History from the Earliest Times to the Present Day.* New York, Bowker, 1974. 685p. Scholarly review of booktrade in Great Britain.

Neavill, Gordon B. "Modern Library Series and American Cultural Life." *Journal of Library History,* 16:241–252, Spring 1981.

Ontario. Royal Commission on Book Publishing. *Canadian Publishers and Canadian Publishing.* Toronto, Ministry of Attorney General, Queen's Printer for

Ontario, 1973. 371p. Report of the commission, covering wide range of topics.

Petersen, Clarence. *The Bantam Story: Thirty Years of Paperback Publishing.* 2d ed. rev. New York, Bantam, 1975. 167p. Also covers American paperback publishing in general.

Publishers' International Directory. Munich, Verlag Dokumentation, 1964–

Publishers Weekly. New York, Bowker, 1872–. Standard journal of the U.S. book trade. Important source for current developments.

Schreuders, Piet. *Paperbacks, U.S.A.: A Graphic History, 1939–1959.* Translated from the Dutch by Josh Pacter. San Diego, Blue Dolphin Enterprises, 1981. 260p. Superbly illustrated "sketch" of paperback graphics.

Strawhorn, John M. "Word Processing and Publishing." *Scholarly Publishing,* 12:109–121, January 1981. Defines the basic vocabulary of word processing and explores its uses in publishing.

Taubert, Sigfried. *The Book Trade of the World.* New York, Bowker, 1972–. 4 volumes planned. Volume one (published 1972) covers Europe; volume two (published 1976) includes the Americas, Australia, and New Zealand; volume three (published 1981) includes Asia.

Tebbel, John. *A History of Book Publishing in the United States.* New York, Bowker, 1972–. 4 volumes planned. Volume one (published 1972): "The Creation of an Industry, 1630–1865" Volume two (published 1975): "The Expansion of an Industry, 1865–1919." Volume three (published 1978): "The Golden Age—Between Two Wars 1920–1940."

U.S. Library of Congress. Copyright Office. *General Guide to the Copyright Act of 1976.* Washington, D.C., 1977. 134p. Includes a list of "Official Source Materials on Copyright Revision."

Unwin, Stanley. *The Truth About Publishing.* 7th ed. New York, Macmillan, 1960. 348p. Classic work on British publishing.

White, Herbert S. *Copyright Dilemma.* Chicago, American Library Association, 1978. 212p. Proceedings of a conference at Indiana University in 1977.

Whiteside, Thomas. *Blockbuster Complex: Conglomerates, Show Business and Book Publishing.* Middletown, Conn., Wesleyan University Press, 1981. 207p. First appeared as a series in *The New Yorker.*

CHAPTER 10

RESOURCE SHARING

For virtually every type of library, standards of collection size have been developed. All standards represent some degree of compromise with reality, however—a pragmatic recognition that the Library of Congress cannot be replicated on every campus and in every community. The need for duplication of materials in heavy demand will certainly vary on a per-capita basis; but achieving a level of x or y volumes-per-capita, in libraries large or small, can hardly guarantee ability to satisfy the full range of informational and research needs of a library's potential clientele. Being bigger does definitely increase the likelihood of being better, but the rate of increase in both the boundaries of knowledge and the complexity of information over the past several decades has put an end to the era in which any library could seriously aspire to complete self-sufficiency. The concept of expanding access through sharing resources has become central to planning in nearly every type of library.

Libraries have many types of resources—collections of materials, staff members with special skills, bibliographic records of various kinds, physical facilities, special equipment, etc. Some libraries also have the somewhat less tangible resources of public goodwill, political influence, future plans, or efficient procedures for accomplishing specific library functions. When two or more libraries agree to share collections, personnel, facilities, planning activities, etc., they are engaged in resource sharing. Resource sharing covers a broad field of potential activities, but reciprocity is important in all these activities. Each participant in the resource-sharing agreement (which may be called a cooperative, consortium, or network and probably will be identified by a catchy acronym) ought to have something useful to contribute and ought to be willing and able to make that resource available to other participants in the organization.

Although resource sharing can have many specific objectives, the two which have received the most emphasis are the improvement of bibliographic access—the information needed to identify publications, verify their existence, location, etc.—and the improvement of physical (or textual) access—the delivery of the published item or a copy of it to the person who wants it. In most major resource-sharing schemes both objectives are pursued, and both have clear implications for collection development plans.

There is some disagreement about the most influential reasons behind the current interest in resource sharing in libraries. Do librarians consider cooperative ventures only when local funds are scarce, or has the improvement of communication technology simply made possible what librarians always knew was necessary and desirable? Such obvious conditions as the rapidly increasing volume of publication, cost of new publications, and cost of storing and servicing collections appear to be likely influences. For some libraries, pressures come from the need to offer something to previously unserved users who have requirements for highly specialized materials or expensive formats (foreign language materials or 16mm films, etc.). Parallel to those demands from previously unserved members of the community are the rising expectations for services from others, such as college students, who have always used libraries to some extent. In many places the availability of federal funds or foundation grants apparently has encouraged cooperative arrangements. Whatever the true cause (or causes) leading to adoption of resource-sharing plans, many libraries are being pulled into such plans and librarians are learning to adapt policies and procedures to the situation.

The impact of resource sharing upon collection development in a specific situation will depend largely on whether it is treated as an excuse to do less or as a challenge to do more. The gap between the two perspectives can be enormous. Taken alone, interlibrary loan can be a largely passive activity, providing even a subtle justification for diminished collection development goals. Libraries that settle for collections geared only to the most popular local demands, depending on interlibrary loan for all else, add up to networks based on shared weakness rather than shared strength. In a proper planning framework, on the other hand, interlibrary loan can serve as a useful tool for measuring resource effectiveness as well as a vehicle for increasing access. The argument that a library is able to satisfy most user needs is empty without some means of learning about those unmet needs that are never expressed. A great many potential library users who do not find what they seek in the catalog or on the shelves will simply go silently away (often never to return). But when a library belongs to a cooperative network, and publicizes the availability of interlibrary loan, the number of requests forthcoming for materials not in the library increases dramatically. Through analysis of those requests, the library can gain valuable data on its ability to satisfy local need locally, with important implications for the collection development goals of the library which strives to provide not only access, but ready access. At the next level, analysis on a system-wide basis of interlibrary loan fulfillment rates provides an essential measure of strengths and weaknesses in the network of resources, and can lead to dramatic improvements in collection development through co-operative selection mechanisms, subject specialization and division of primary collecting responsibilities, pool collections, designation of libraries of record, and setting goals for *strengthening* shared resources far beyond what would be possible on a smaller economic scale.

Resource sharing is not a new idea. Influential librarians have acknowledged the need for cooperation among libraries for at least a hundred years, but earlier efforts tended to require no adjustment of local policies or procedures. Union catalogs such as the National Union Catalog, started at the beginning of this century, and ordinary interlibrary loan, which was practiced in isolated cases far back in library history but became common after World War I, are two examples of the kind of resource sharing which had little effect on collection development in the local library. Of course, some librarians contend that the most successful resource-sharing projects are the ones, such as union lists and reciprocal borrowing by individual library users, which do not require local adjustments.

Some fairly uncomplicated plans for cooperative acquisition, some of them very informal, have existed for a number of years in many cities and some regions. These plans were usually set up by dividing collecting responsibilities on the basis of easily defined categories, which frequently covered an expensive or bulky format—serials, government documents, dissertations, items costing more than $100, etc. Sharing of bibliographic information on these materials might or might not be a part of the plan, but interlibrary loan and reciprocal borrowing privileges usually were. Most of these resource-sharing arrangements required only minor adjustments by local libraries, since selection responsibilities were ordinarily assigned on the basis of collection strengths and assumed because of local needs.

Farmington Plan

The Farmington Plan was the first cooperative acquisition scheme to operate at a national level in the United States. It grew out of a concern for the inadequacy of our library resources, when viewed from a national perspective. During World War II, American librarians and scholars became acutely aware of the limitations of their collections of foreign materials, particularly those in languages other than English and from parts of the world other than Western Europe. Serious discussion of the problem and what large research libraries might do to alleviate it began in response to concern voiced at a conference of the Librarian of Congress' Librarian's Council held in Farmington, Connecticut in 1942. Following the conference, a group began working on plans for assigning collection responsibilities to research libraries throughout the country—responsibilities which would encourage subject specialization based on existing collection strengths.

The resulting project, sponsored by the Association of Research Libraries (ARL), became known as the Farmington Plan. Its goal was to ensure that at least one copy of every new foreign publication of research interest would be acquired by a U.S. library, cataloged promptly, reported to the National Union Catalog, and made available on interlibrary loan to other participants in the plan. Although that goal appears to be very comprehensive, in practice certain restrictions were observed from the beginning. For example, publications from the United Kingdom were excluded because it was assumed that these were already being adequately covered. Other restrictions were placed on the types of materials to be collected. Serials (except for first copies of new publications) were excluded, as were dissertations, government documents, music, maps, works costing over a specified amount, and certain other categories. Another limitation was the voluntary nature of the plan, which meant that libraries joined and withdrew as local circumstances influenced them. During most years of the plan's operation, 60–70 research libraries participated.

The Farmington Plan went into operation in 1948, beginning with coverage of France, Sweden, and Switzerland. The next year coverage was expanded to Belgium, Denmark, Italy, Mexico, the Netherlands, and Norway. During the next two years, the participants continued to add countries to the plan until, by 1952, most major publishing countries were covered. In 1952 a regional plan was added to cover publishing in Asia, Africa, Latin America, Eastern Europe, and the Near East. The plan for Western Europe and the new regional plan differed in several respects. The original Western Europe plan was based on subject responsibilities assigned according to divisions of the Library of Congress Classification, covered primarily current trade monographs and first issues of new serials, and involved blanket arrangements in each country with dealers selected by the coordinating committee. The regional plan was based on geographic assignments (a particular library would agree to buy on all subjects from an assigned country), covered most forms of publication (serials, government documents, retrospective materials, etc., as well as current monographs), and involved arrangements with deals made individually by each library.

The Farmington Plan for Western Europe (meaning specifically the automatic supply by European dealers) was formally ended in December 1972, although the ARL's Farmington Plan office, which monitored and to some extent evaluated the plan, had closed earlier. Reasons offered for the demise of the plan centered on budget restrictions in participating libraries, unhappiness with the quality of service and materials sent by dealers, withdrawal of certain influential libraries, and redundancy of the plan in view of the increasing use of blanket orders by member libraries and the inception of the Library of Congress' National Program for Acquisitions and Cataloging (NPAC). Almost from the beginning, there had been complaints about the coverage of materials by the Farmington Plan. Some participants thought the scope was too limited—that periodicals, particularly, ought to be included; others worried about the amount of ephemeral material which came through on the plan. (In 1959, a study had been made of the operation of the plan and certain recommendations made for improving coverage.) Availability of funds in member libraries had an effect on participation in the Farmington Plan. In the beginning, some libraries had accepted subject assignments out of a sense of national responsibility rather than a real collection need, and there was no strong academic program as a base for the voluntarily accepted subject assignment. Such outside commitments were likely to be among the first to be dropped when budget cutting occurred. During the 1960s, many large libraries had started blanket orders for foreign materials, often duplicating and even exceeding the Farmington Plan assignments accepted by other libraries. This appeared to make the Farmington Plan commitments unnecessary, although later budget problems often curtailed the foreign blanket plans. NPAC too, although not a cooperative acquisition plan, seemed to some people to meet the objectives of the Farmington Plan in a more efficient way.

PL-480 and the National Program for Acquisitions and Cataloging

Even before the Farmington Plan officially ended, it had begun to be overshadowed by foreign acquisitions activities originating at the Library of Congress. The older of two major activities at LC was a program operated under Public Law 480. Beginning in 1961, PL-480 allowed selected research libraries in the United States to acquire current publications from some of the developing countries. (The legal base for the program was a 1958 amendment to the Agricultural Trade Development and Assistance Act of 1954 which permitted the U.S. to accept foreign currency in exchange for agricultural products and to spend the foreign currency in that country, for such materials as books and periodicals.) PL-480 first started operation in India, Pakistan, and the United Arab Republic and later expanded to other countries, including Indonesia, Israel, Yugoslavia, Poland, and Iran. Since the program depended on the availability of surplus foreign currencies in a given country, the list of countries covered by the plan changed regularly—some dropped out as funds were exhausted, and others were added. In some ways, PL-480 served as a pilot project for the National Program for Acquisitions and Cataloging and has now been coordinated with it.

The National Program for Acquistions and Cataloging of the Library of Congress originated in provisions of the Higher Education Act of 1965. Title IIC of that act authorized appropriations to the Library of Congress "for the purpose of 1) acquiring, as far as possible, all library materials currently published throughout the world which are of value to scholarship; and 2) providing catalog information for those materials promptly after receipt, and distributing bibliographic information by printing catalog cards and by other means, and enabling the Library of Congress to use for exchange and other purposes such of these materials as are not needed for its collections." The coverage of the acquisitions program has been more comprehensive than that of the Farmington Plan in that most types of materials other than periodicals and non-book materials have been included. Other libraries have benefited from NPAC in a number of ways, primarily through improved access to bibliographic information concerning foreign materials.

Research Libraries Group

The Research Libraries Group was first formed in 1974 by The New York Public Library and the libraries of Columbia, Harvard, and Yale Universities. Its major objective was the development of a shared computer-based bibliographic processing and access system. In 1978, RLG expanded from a regional to a national network, incorporating the former BALLOTS system at Stanford, and by the early 1980s had grown to a membership of more than two dozen major research institutions (and another

20 special and affiliate members) throughout the country. Despite the significance of the Research Libraries Information Network (RLIN) computer data base of over 15 million records, and its capacity to accommodate features as important to research libraries as non-Roman scripts, many RLG members assert that RLIN is merely the technical support element in a consortium whose primary purpose is cooperative collection development. While a basic objective is reduction of expensive duplication purchasing, RLG seeks simultaneously to insure that all material of research value in designated fields will be acquired by at least one member institution or, through agreement, by another institution such as the Library of Congress or the Center for Research Libraries. RLG treats preservation problems as an extension of collection development, focusing on ways to identify systematically materials in need of preservation and on automated bibliographic control over micropreservation activities.

Cooperative Storage

The cooperative storage library is another form of resource sharing. Storage libraries became popular after World War II as a result of the rapid rate of increase in the size of research libraries. They relieve the cooperating member libraries of the pressure of constantly increasing holdings, and they provide a central collection upon which all members may draw for more extended research materials than any one could afford to hold.

Cooperative storage libraries were first proposed about 1900 by William Coolidge Lane, librarian of Harvard. His proposal was supported by President Eliot but opposed by the faculty. (It has been suggested that part of its failure must be attributed to an unfortunate choice of terms; the storage facility was proposed as a place for "dead" books.) Although discussed from time to time, it was not until the 1940s that the New England Deposit Library was opened as "a regional bibliographic research center for little used books." (Which, one must admit, sounds more impressive than a storage warehouse for dead books.) Charter members included the Massachusetts State Library, Boston Public Library, Boston Athenaeum, Boston College, Boston University, Massachusetts Historical Society, Massachusetts Institute of Technology, and Harvard University.

Center for Research Libraries

The Center for Research Libraries, organized in 1949 under the name "Midwest Inter-Library Center" and located in Chicago, was established to supply midwestern universities with storage space for little-used materials. While its general purpose is similar to that of the New England Deposit Library, the midwestern project places more emphasis on cooperative storage as a way to share infrequently used research materials. The report which led to the establishment of the Center listed four general areas of activity, three of which were concerned with cooperative purchase of materials and coordination of acquisitions to avoid unwanted duplication of storage holdings by discard and to fill in gaps in the collections of member libraries by purchase, thus providing a centralized location for new acquisitions not held by any of the member libraries.

A survey of the Center's operation, authorized in 1963 and published in 1965, led to the opening of membership to libraries on a national basis, a change in name and governance to reflect these national responsibilities, and an expansion of acquisition programs. The influence of CRL has grown steadily since its broadening of membership and programs. As a central storage and lending agency, it has become an essential adjunct for most libraries attempting to meet extensive research needs.

The collections of CRL, which are available by fairly rapid loan procedures to member libraries, include such materials as foreign dissertations (if the Center does not own a requested item, it will attempt to acquire it), foreign government documents, state government documents, foreign and U.S. newspapers (another type of material which the Center attempts to supply comprehensively), university and college catalogs, and microfilms of archival materials, both foreign and U.S. Its extensive runs of serial publications form perhaps the most important feature of CRL's collections. Since 1956, the Center has attempted to maintain subscriptions to all titles indexed in *Chemical Abstracts* and *Biological Abstracts* that are not readily available elsewhere in the country. In 1973, working with a grant from the Carnegie Corporation, the Center began an "Expanded Journals Project" which provides access either directly or through the British Library Lending Division to all journals published since 1970 in the sciences (except medicine) and the social sciences (except history). The Center is also the depository for several ARL-sponsored cooperative microfilm projects.

Other Examples of Resource Sharing

Some early examples of cooperation in collection development by small groups of academic libraries include such projects as the Hampshire Inter-Library Center (HILC), established in 1951 by Amherst, Mt. Holyoke, and Smith Colleges (joined later by others, including the University of Massachusetts) to provide for acquisition and storage of infrequently used serials and expensive sets. Ten liberal arts colleges belonging to the Associated Colleges of the Midwest (ACM) founded, in 1968, a central periodical collection which provides both joint storage and joint acquisition for this type of material.

While some of the better-publicized resource-sharing arrangements involve primarily large research or other academic libraries, public libraries became active in the development of systems during the late 1950s and the 1960s. The patterns of federal funding for libraries and the establishment, in many places, of state library plans encouraged the trend toward cooperation. By the 1970s, libraries of all sizes and types were being drawn into systems, networks, consortia, etc. Some of these cooperative schemes were single-function (meaning only one library operation, such as cataloging), but others involved cooperating in a variety of activities. Many arrangements for cooperative acquisition and improved interlibrary loan delivery joined only libraries of a single type—public libraries, for example—which had similar patterns of operation, funding, governance, and service. (An example of a well-established network limited to one type of library is the Regional Medical Library program of the National Library of Medicine.) By the mid-1980s the multitype cooperative pattern, mixing libraries of different types and sizes, seems firmly established, at least as a concept. States without huge research facilities within their borders, such as Alabama, are using what remains of federal funds for library support to encourage the development of library systems encompassing all types of libraries, including special libraries.

Some resource-sharing arrangements involving libraries of various types have been limited to a city or state; more recent organizations have crossed state boundaries. The cooperative acquisition, storage, and lending programs of METRO (the New York Metropolitan Reference and Research Library Agency) indicate what can be accomplished in a large metropolitan area. The state networks of New York (NYSILL), Illinois (ILLINET), and Washington (WLN) have been cited as examples of how statewide plans can draw more than one type of library into resource-sharing schemes. Many other states have networks, particularly of public and academic libraries, which have encouraged the trend toward viewing all state-supported library collections as a state resource.

Interstate cooperatives involving the sharing, in some form, of bibliographic and/or physical access to library materials and admitting to membership more than one type of library became quite common in the 1970s. Among the better-publicized examples are NELINET (New England Library Network), which includes some academic and public libraries from the six New England states; SOLINET (Southeastern Library Network), open to academic, public, special, and state libraries in ten southeastern states; SLICE (Southwest Library Interstate Cooperative Endeavor), covering interested libraries in the six-state area of the now defunct Southwest Library Association; the Denver Bibliographic Center, serving 11 states between the Mississippi River and the West Coast; PNBC (Pacific Northwest Bibliographic Center), open to all libraries in five U.S. states and some libraries in British Columbia; and MINITEX-WILS, a cooperative arrangement available to all types of libraries in Minnesota and Wisconsin. OCLC may also be included in this group since its online cataloging and card reproduction services are now available to and used by various types of libraries in a number of states.

NCLIS

The National Commission on Libraries and Information Science (NCLIS), created as an independent agency in 1970, has as one of its charges the development of a plan for meeting library and information needs on a national level, involving coordinating efforts of all levels of government and considering all available library and information resources. After a two-year process of drafting, review, feedback, and reconsideration, NCLIS issued, in May 1975, its outlined plan (*Toward a National Program for Library and Information Services. Goals for Action*, U.S. Government Printing Office, 106p.). The proposed plan had eight objectives, but the one given the most emphasis in the report was Objective 8: "Plan, develop and implement a nationwide network of library and information service."

As part of its planning effort, NCLIS had commissioned a research firm to study the present distribution of library collections and bibliographic centers around the country and to make recommendations on how such centers might in the future be developed into a national network (*Resources and Bibliographic Support for a Nationwide Library Program; Final Report*, 1974, 267p.). This comprehensive study covered a wide range of issues related to developing collections which can guarantee "access to recorded materials of all types in all languages" and providing rapid and accurate bibliographic identification and location of library materials. In the introduction, the writers of the report observed: "Poor and uncoordinated bibliographic access has limited the potential for locating materials not widely held; and collection policies of individual libraries, necessarily aimed at the needs of their own borrowers, leave gaps and deficiencies in the overall holdings." The national political climate in recent years has been less than conducive to funding for the implementation of such goals; but the objectives of a national library network will be actively pursued again in the future, and the implications for collection development in individual libraries will be considerable.

National Periodicals Center

Although a comprehensive national library network would include all types of library materials, a national plan for access to periodicals has drawn particular attention. Because they are expensive to acquire and bulky to store, but relatively easy to keep under bibliographic control (as compared to individual monographs), periodicals are often the focus for cooperative schemes. No library can afford to maintain all the periodical subscriptions demanded by its users, so the sharing of periodical resources has appeal for all sizes and types of libraries. NCLIS appointed a task force in 1976 to make recommendations concerning a national periodical system. The report (*Effective Access to the Periodical Literature: A National Program*, U.S. National Commission on Libraries and Information Science, 92p.), which was issued in 1977, recommended a three-level scheme, with local, state, and regional library systems being made responsible for meeting routine needs (estimated at 80 per cent of the total) for periodicals. The second level would be a comprehensive periodicals collection reserved for lending and photocopying, and the third level would be the unique holdings of national, university, and special libraries.

Despite the elementary logic of the plan, its implementation has received serious setbacks. One complication which has delayed plans for a periodical center (as well as other resource-sharing plans) is uncertainty about how the new U.S. copyright law, which went into effect in 1978, will affect any resource-sharing scheme that relies heavily on photocopying. A recent study of interlibrary loan activity by large research libraries (ARL members) estimates that 50 per cent of the interlibrary requests were for periodical articles and that 80 per cent of those requests were filled with photocopies.

Conclusion

Resource sharing has never been considered a solution to all collection development problems, but it is now being recognized as a form of library organization which may be here to stay. In its more recent manifestations resource sharing has tended to be formally structured (many cooperatives are established as non-profit corporations), to cover all types of libraries and a variety of activities, and to require more of an institutional commitment—in terms of membership fees, staff time, policy adjustments, etc.—than did earlier examples of library cooperation. (Another interesting sign of commitment is the number of network or consortia memberships which may be held by a single library.)

There are still questions in the minds of some librarians as to how well large-scale resource sharing can work. Both large and small libraries fear being overwhelmed—the large ones by the number of requests which may come from poorer collections, the smaller ones by the influence of the larger libraries in setting and establishing procedures. There is always a fear that too much concern for resource sharing will cause librarians to overlook the needs of a library's primary constituency. Library users are not always pleased, either, by their library's participation in resource sharing. Some cannot understand why needs (especially their own needs for library materials) cannot be met locally. There are still some legal and administrative barriers to resource sharing, but many of these have been removed in recent years. However, physical and geographical problems still pose difficulties in areas where great distances make the rapid exchange of library materials nearly impossible. The computer data base which enables the library's own printer to provide hard copies can be seen as a major contribution to the lessening of distance as a problem in terms of speed. Funding problems are likely to arise as federal, state, or foundation grants to cooperative projects begin to decline. Many networks have membership fees, but most of them also rely heavily on other financial sources. Nevertheless, there are bright spots in the pattern of resource-sharing activities.

Some librarians are convinced that resource sharing is an essential part of modern library service. Projects reported as successful by their participants exhibit certain key characteristics: quick and accurate sharing of information on holdings; rapid delivery of materials from one participating library to another; good communication among staff members at all levels of the hierarchy in all participating libraries; and careful planning and research activities. As more research is conducted on the structure and operation of cooperatives, it is likely that the causes for success or failure in resource sharing can be identified and used as a basis for planning and review of present operations. When resource-sharing projects achieve a stable and satisfactory pattern of operation, collection building at every level of the network will be affected.

Bibliography

Association of Carribean University and Research Libraries. *Research Library Cooperation in the Carribean; Papers of the First and Second Conferences of the Association of Carribean University and Research Libraries.* Edited by Alma Jordan. Chicago, American Library Association, 1973. 145p. Contains twelve papers.

Association of Research Libraries. *Farmington Plan Survey; Final Report.* Directed by Robert Vosper and Robert Talmadge. 1959. unpaged. Washington, D.C.

Association of Research Libraries. Office of University Library Management Studies. *SPEC Kit on Resources Sharing in ARL Libraries.* Washington, D.C., Association of Research Libraries, 1978. 108p. Includes examples of resource-sharing plans, manuals, etc.

Association of State Library Agencies. Interlibrary Cooperation Subcommittee. *The ASLA Report on Interlibrary Cooperation.* 2d ed. Chicago, ALA, 1978. 446p. Attempts to give basic information on cooperative activities within each state and territory.

Balliot, Robert L. *A Program for the Cooperative Acquisition and Use of Library Materials of Seven New England Liberal Arts Colleges (CONVAL) Based on Analysis of Their Collections.* Cullowhee, N.C., Western Carolina College, 1970. 82p. (ED 047 711)

Boylan, Ray. "Scholarly Citadel in Chicago: The Center for Research Libraries." *Wilson Library Bulletin,* 53:503–506, March 1979. A library for libraries.

Butler, Brett. "State of the Nation in Networking." *Journal of Library Automation,* 8:200–220, September 1975. Describes networking organizations as of its publication date.

Canadian Library Systems and Networks; Their Planning and Development. Papers Presented at a Symposium on Library Systems and Networks at the Canadian Library Association Conference, Winnipeg, 25 June 1974. Ottawa, Canadian Library Association, 1974. 50p.

Carter, Harriet and Raymond A. Palmer. "Operation of a Rational Acquisitions Committee." *Medical Library Association Bulletin*, 65:61–63, January 1977. Cooperative collection development in several health sciences libraries.

Center for Research Libraries. *Report of a Survey with an Outline of Programs and Policies*. Chicago, 1965. 24p.

Chandler, George. "Proposed Development of Resource Sharing Networks (UNISIST, NATIS, ALBIS)." *International Library Review*, 8:237–264, 1976. Reviews efforts of National Library of Australia.

Chang, Diana M. "Academic Library Cooperation: A Selective Annotated Bibliography." *Library Resources and Technical Services*, 20:270–286, Summer 1976.

Clinic on Library Applications of Data Processing, University of Illinois, 1973. *Proceedings of the 1973 Clinic on Library Applications of Data Processing: Networking and Other Forms of Cooperation*. Edited by F. Wilfred Lancaster. Urbana, University of Illinois, Graduate School of Library Science, 1973. 185p.

Cooke, Michael. "Future Library Network Automation." *Journal of the American Society for Information Science*, 28:254–258, September 1977. Discusses issues of concern in networking.

Corbin, John. "Library Networks." *Library Journal*, 101:201–207, January 1, 1976. Review of developments and predictions for the future.

Coty, Patricia Ann. "The Status of Audiovisual Materials in Networking." *Special Libraries*, 74:246–253, July 1983. Access to AV materials lags behind print resources and must be addressed.

De Gennaro, Richard. "Austerity, Technology, and Resource Sharing: Research Libraries Face the Future." *Library Journal*, 100:917–923, May 15, 1975. Argues for emphasis on access to materials rather than size of holdings.

De Gennaro, Richard. "Libraries and Networks in Transition: Problems and Prospects for the 1980's." *Library Journal*, 106:1045–1049, May 15, 1981.

De Gennaro, Richard. "Library Automation and Networking Perspectives on Three Decades." *Library Journal*, 108:629–635, April 1, 1983. Forecasting the ascendence of local and commercial systems over networks.

Directory of Academic Library Consortia. 2d ed. Edited by Donald V. Black and Carolos A. Cuadra. Santa Monica, Calif., System Development Corp., 1975. 437p. Information on 264 consortia.

Dougherty, Richard M. "The Impact of Networking on Library Management." *College and Research Libraries*, 39:15–19, January 1978.

Edelman, Hendrik. "The Death of the Farmington Plan." *Library Journal*, 98:1251–1253, April 15, 1973. Discusses several questions related to cooperative acquisitions programs.

El-Erian, Tahany Said. "The Public Law 480 Program in American Libraries." (D.L.S. Thesis, Columbia University, 1972). 278p.

Fletcher, Janet. "Collection Development and Resource Sharing." *Library Journal*, 108:881–882, May 1, 1983. Issues as presented at the 1983 Collection Development and Management Institute.

Franckowiak, Bernard. "Networks, Data Bases, and Media Programs: An Overview." *School Media Quarterly*, 6:15–20, Fall 1977. Networks from a school point of view.

Goderich, Mario. "Cooperative Acquisitions: The Experiences of General Libraries and Prospects for Law Libraries." *Law Library Journal*, 63:57–61, February 1970.

Building Library Collections

Gregor, Dorothy. *Feasibility of Cooperative Collecting of Exotic Foreign Language Serial Titles Among Health Sciences Libraries in California.* Berkeley, Calif., University of California, Institute of Library Research, 1974. 50p. (ED 104 407)

Gribbin, J. H. "Interlibrary Cooperation and Collection Building." In *Academic Library: Essays in Honor of Guy R. Lyle,* pp. 105–117. Metuchen, N.J., Scarecrow Press, 1974.

Hamilton, Beth A. and William B. Ernst, Jr. *Multitype Library Cooperation.* New York, Bowker, 1977. 216p. Most of the twenty-one essays printed here were presented at the ALA Centennial Conference in Chicago in 1976.

Hayes, Robert M. "Distributed Library Networks: Programs and Problems." In *The Responsibility of the University Library Collection in Meeting the Needs of Its Campus and Local Community.* A Symposium in Honor of Melvin J. Voigt Upon His Retirement as University Librarian of The University of California, San Diego, Friday, September 17, 1976, pp. 32–39. La Jolla, Calif., Friends of the UCSD Library, 1976.

Hendricks, Donald D. *A Report on Library Networks.* Urbana, University of Illinois, Graduate School of Library Science, 1973. 23p. (Occasional Papers No. 108) Covers types of network activities and some specific examples.

Hewitt, Joe A. "The Impact of OCLC." *American Libraries,* 7:268–275, May 1976.

Impact of the Public Law 480 Program on Overseas Acquisitions by American Libraries: Proceedings of a Conference Held May 12, 1967. Edited by William L. Williamson. Madison, University of Wisconsin-Madison, Library School, 1967. 41p.

"Introducing ILLINET . . . The Beginnings of a Statewide Network." *Illinois Libraries,* 57:364–370, June 1975.

Jay, Donald F. and Frank M. McGowan. "The Library of Congress PL-480 Program." *DC Libraries,* 40:29–33, Spring 1969. Concise overview of the program.

Jefferson, George. *Library Co-operation.* 2d ed. London, Deutsch, 1977. 189p. Reviews cooperative projects of various kinds. Emphasis is on cooperation in the United Kingdom, but several U.S. projects are covered in detail. Includes classified bibliography (pp. 169–182).

Jones, C. Lee. "A Cooperative Serial Acquisition Program: Thoughts on a Response to Mounting Fiscal Pressures." *Medical Library Association Bulletin,* 62:120–123, April 1974. Outlines way to set up a cooperative acquisitions program.

Kaplan, Louis. "Midwest Inter-Library Center, 1949–1964." *Journal of Library History,* 10:291–310, October 1975. MILC was the predecessor of Center for Research Libraries.

Kennington, Donald and Brenda White. "National Repository Plans and Programmes." *Interlending Review,* 10:3–7, January 1982. The British perspective.

Kilgour, Frederick G. "Ohio College Library Center: A User-Oriented System." In *New Dimensions for Academic Library Service,* edited by E. J. Josey, pp. 250–255. Metuchen, N.J., Scarecrow Press, 1975.

Klieman, Janet and Cathleen Costello. "Cooperation Between Types of Libraries: An Annotated Bibliography, 1973 Supplement." *Illinois Libraries,* 56:250–258, March 1974.

Knightly, John J. "Library Collections and Academic Curricula: Quantitative Relationships." *College and Research Libraries,* 36:295–301, July 1975. Discusses implications for cooperative acquisitions.

Kolb, Audrey. "Development and Potential of a Multitype Library Network." *School Media Quarterly*, 6:21–27, Fall 1977. Describes Washington Library Network.

Kolb, Audrey and Jo Morse. "Initiating School Participation in Networking." *School Media Quarterly*, 6:52–59, Fall 1977. Step-by-step approach.

Kronick, David A. "Goodbye to Farewells—Resource Sharing and Cost Sharing." *Journal of Academic Librarianship*, 8:132–136, July 1982. An answer to the "farewell to the book" and other cherished traditions articles.

Lehman, James O. "Cooperation Among Small Academic Libraries." *College and Research Libraries*, 30:491–497, November 1969. Brief survey of small college consortia.

"Library Cooperation." Issue edited by Pearce S. Grove. *Library Trends*, 24:157–423, October 1975. Includes articles on various aspects of cooperation.

Library Resource Sharing: Proceedings of the 1976 Conference on Resource Sharing in Libraries, Pittsburgh, Pennsylvania. Edited by Allan Kent and Thomas J. Galvin. New York, Dekker, 1977. 356p. Six major papers and a number of reaction statements.

Line, Maurice. "The Developing National Network in Great Britain." *Library Resources and Technical Services*, 16:61–73, Winter 1972. Brief description of the British Library.

Lucht, Irma and Blair Stewart. "The ACM Periodical Bank and the British National Lending Library: Contrasts and Similarities." In *Management Problems in Serials Work*, pp. 3–18. Edited by Peter Spyers-Duran and Daniel Gore. Westport, Conn., Greenwood Press, 1974.

McDonald, John P. "Interlibrary Cooperation in the U.S." In *Issues in Library Administration*, edited by Warren M. Tsuneishi and others, pp. 125–137. New York, Columbia University Press, 1974. General review.

Markuson, Barbara Evans. "Library Network Planning: Problems to Consider, Decisions to Make." *Wisconsin Library Bulletin*, 71:98–102, May–June 1975.

Martin, Susan K. *Library Networks 1976–1977.* White Plains, N.Y., Knowledge Industry Publications, 1978. Reviews extent of networking and describes major U.S. networks.

Miller, Ronald F. and Ruth L. Tighe. "Library and Information Networks." In *Annual Review of Information Science and Technology*, Vol. 9, pp. 173–219. Washington, D.C., American Society for Information Science, 1974. Review article with extensive bibliography.

Moon, Eric. "Our Commission, Our Omissions." *Library Journal*, 109:1283–87, July 1984.

"Networking in Sci-Tech Libraries and Information Centers." *Science and Technology Libraries*, 1:1–108, Winter 1980. Entire issue is devoted to aspects of the subject.

Orne, Jerrold. "Newspaper Resources of the Southeastern Region: An Experiment in Coordinated Resource Development." *Southeastern Librarian*, 21:226–235, Winter 1971.

Palmour, Vernon E. *Resources and Bibliographic Support for a Nationwide Library; Final Report.* Washington, D.C., National Commission on Libraries and Information Science, 1974. 267p.

Parker, Thomas F. "Resource Sharing from the Inside Out: Reflections on the

Organization Nature of Library Networks." *Library Resources and Technical Services*, 19:349–355, Fall 1975. Theoretical approach.

Quick, Richard C. "Coordination of Collection Building by Academic Libraries." in *New Dimensions for Academic Library Service*, edited by E. J. Josey, pp. 100–120. Metuchen, N.J., Scarecrow Press, 1975. Reviews trends in a few consortia.

Resource Sharing in Libraries: Why, How, When, Next Action Steps. Edited by Allan Kent. New York, Dekker, 1974. 393p. Papers presented at a 1973 conference in Pittsburgh.

Rouse, William B. "A Library Network Model." *Journal of the American Society for Information Science*, 27:88–99, March–April 1976. Operations research approach to evaluating networks.

Savary, M. J. *The Latin American Cooperative Acquisitions Program: An Imaginative Venture.* New York, Hafner, 1968. 144p.

Selective Annotated Bibliography on Library Networking. ERIC Clearinghouse on Information Resources, Stanford University, 1975. 27p. (ED 115 219)

Shank, Russell. "The Locus for Cooperation in Collection Sharing." In *The Responsibility of the University Library Collection in Meeting the Needs of Its Campus and Local Community; A Symposium in Honor of Melvin J. Voigt Upon His Retirement as University Librarian of The University of California, San Diego, Friday, September 17, 1976*, pp. 27–31. La Jolla, Calif., Friends of the UCSD Library, 1976.

Sinclair, Michael P. "A Typology of Library Cooperatives." *Special Libraries*, 64:181–186, April 1973. Describes four cooperative library system models.

"Stanford University's BALLOTS System." *Journal of Library Automation*, 8:31–50, March 1975. Background and overview of system operation.

Stevens, Robert D. "The Library of Congress Public Law 480 Program." *Library Resources and Technical Services*, 7:176–188, Spring 1963. Reviews early activities of PL-480.

Stewart, Blair. "Periodicals and the Liberal Arts College Library." *College and Research Libraries*, 36:371–378, September 1975. Describes operation of ACM Periodical Bank.

Stuart-Stubbs, Basil. "An Historical Look at Resource Sharing." *Library Trends*, 23:649–664, April 1975.

Stuart-Stubbs, Basil and others. *A Survey and Interpretation of the Literature of Interlibrary Loan.* Vancouver, University of British Columbia Library, 1975. 158p. Comprehensive study of Canadian ILL.

Thomas, Lawrence E. "Tri-University Libraries." *Canadian Library Journal*, 35:27–33, February 1978. Describes consortium including three British Columbian universities.

Thorson, A. Robert and Phyllis B. Davis. "Borrowing Made Easy: Automated Resource Sharing in Ohio." *Wilson Library Bulletin*, 54:502–504, April 1980. Ohio State University and the Ohio State Library share resources.

Trezza, Alphonse F. "Toward a National Program for Library and Information Services: Progress and Problems." *Aslib Proceedings*, 30:72–87, February 1978. Reviews history of National Advisory Committee on Libraries and National Commission on Libraries and Information Science.

U.S. National Commission on Libraries and Information Science. *Toward a Na-*

tional Program for Library and Information Services: Goals for Action. Washington, D.C., 1975. 106p.

U.S. National Commission on Libraries and Information Science. Task Force on a National Periodicals System. *Effective Access to Periodical Literature: A National Program.* Washington, D.C., 1977. 91p.

Vosper, Robert G. *Farmington Plan Survey: A Summary of the Separate Studies of 1957–1961.* Urbana, University of Illinois, Graduate School of Library Science, 1965. 46p. (Occasional Papers No. 77) For related report, see Association of Research Libraries (1959).

Weber, David C. "A Century of Cooperative Programs Among Academic Libraries." *College and Research Libraries*, 37:205–221, May 1976.

Williams, Edwin E. *Farmington Plan Handbook,.* Bloomington, Ind., Association of Research Libraries, 1953. 170p. Includes description of the plan and review of its early history.

Williams, Edwin E. *Farmington Plan Handbook; Revised to 1961 and Abridged.* Ithaca, N.Y., Association of Research Libraries, 1961. Updates history and bibliography, but does not repeat everything in earlier edition.

Wright, Gordon H. "The Canadian Mosaic—Planning for Shared Partnership in a National Network." *Aslib Proceedings*, 30:88–102, February 1978.

CHAPTER 11

NATIONAL AND TRADE BIBLIOGRAPHY

Introduction

An ideal national bibliography would attempt to record all materials published in a given country, whether available through the regular book trade or not, whether copyrighted or not, and regardless of format. It would include books, pamphlets, films, printed music, phono-records, government publications, theses, newspapers, periodicals, prints and engravings, microforms—and any other form. This happy ideal would enter each item under author, under title, and under subject, with additional entries where appropriate for series, joint author, compiler, translator, etc. It would, of course, be freely supplied with all necessary cross references. Since the ideal is being described, let a descriptive annotation be added to the full bibliographical information which would be given.

Trade bibliography is one part of national bibliography, but of more restricted scope. It attempts to record those materials which are available through the regular trade channels. Most large encyclopedias and government publications, for example, are not ordinarily sold through bookstores—they are "outside the trade." Doctoral dissertations are not to be found on the shelves of the ordinary bookstore. The serial publications issued by business and industry as house organs, the publications of fraternal societies, of many learned societies, the research reports of laboratories and institutes, etc.—all these are not "trade items."

In studying a country's bibliography, it is desirable to try to see the pattern that exists among the various pieces, which, if put together, make up the total national bibliography. In the United States, for example, we have such bits and pieces as the *Catalog of Copyright Entries*, the Library of Congress catalogs, the *Monthly Checklist of State Publications*, the *Monthly Catalog of U.S. Government Publications*, *Comprehensive Dissertation Index*, *Vertical File Index*, CBI, *Publishers' Trade List Annual*, *American Book Pub-*

lishing Record, etc. But we have no single source containing all types of materials, and the manner of presentation in the sources that we do have is not uniform. In addition, there is no assurance that even this variety of sources will pick up everything. Furthermore, the frequency with which these several parts of the American bibliography are published varies as much as the sources. This factor must be kept in mind in attempting to estimate the speed with which the national output is recorded (especially if one is concerned with early identification of current but obscure non-trade items). It is suggested that the student use American bibliography as the standard and compare it with British, Canadian, Australian, French, and German national bibliographies, noting essential differences in an attempt to decide which country's method seems most useful.

Although all of the bibliographies discussed in this chapter appear in a printed form, the student should be aware that the recent trend toward building extensive bibliographic files in machine-readable form has had a great influence on the compilation of national and trade bibliographies—and on the way they are used by searchers to verify order requests. One of the most important innovations has been the MARC (*Machine-Readable Cataloging*) Project of the Library of Congress. MARC, which was developed and used on a pilot basis beginning in 1966, is a standard format for recording bibliographic data on magnetic tape. Through the MARC Distribution Service, which became operational in 1969, the Library of Congress puts most of its new cataloging into the MARC format and distributes those catalog records on tape to subscribers. The subscribers include commercial firms, such as the publishers of trade bibliographies, individual libraries, and library cooperatives such as OCLC, Inc. (formerly Ohio College Library Center) and similar shared cataloging networks. This means that in many large libraries most bibliographic searching and verification can now be done on-line, with no reference to a printed source. Even when a printed bibliography is used, the searcher expects to find quicker coverage of new publications and a more standard entry. American bibliography is not the only area to be affected by MARC. Other countries, including most of those represented in this chapter, either have or are planning their own versions of MARC.

Another development leading to changes in national and trade bibliographies is the International Standard Bibliographic Description (ISBD). First issued in a draft version in 1971, ISBD is now widely used as a method of providing a standard description of a monograph (ISBD's for other forms of publications have also been developed). This description comprises a standard set of descriptive elements in a standard order with specified punctuation marks to separate the various elements. Anyone who wishes to see how this has changed the appearance of a trade bibliography should look at a current issue of *American Book Publishing Record* and an issue of fifteen years ago. Though the type of information given in the bibliographic entries in the two issues will probably be similar, punctuation and arrangement of the elements will be different. One effect of ISBD has been to make foreign bibliographies a little easier to read. Elements of the entries can be recognized by their position and the punctuation that precedes them.

One other development which should be mentioned is the CIP (Cataloging in Publication) Project of the Library of Congress. Under CIP, the Library of Congress makes arrangements with individual publishers to receive galleys of new publications. LC then proceeds to create basic catalog information, which is supplied to the cooperating publisher so that it may be printed on the verso of the title page when the publication appears in its final form. These CIP records also become a part of the MARC data base (each CIP record is updated to a full MARC record after the item is actually published). The wide distribution of CIP data means that publications tend to appear in on-line files and printed bibliographies quicker than in the past—sometimes the entry is incomplete (since CIP is based on pre-publication data) and occasionally it may even appear before the official publication date. Other countries have also developed schemes similar to CIP for their new publications, a move which should have an effect on their national and trade bibliographies.

American Bibliography

Variety appears in the retrospective coverage of American publishing due to the fact that different periods have been covered by different individuals or organizations with varying degrees of skill, time available for the undertaking, and differing convictions concerning what ought to be done and how material should be presented. Thus Sabin attempted to list not only books published in the Americas, but those about the Americas published elsewhere, and he presented the results alphabetically by author and anonymous title (largely). Evans restricted himself to books published in the United States and chose to arrange the titles chronologically by year of publication, with author-anonymous title and subject indexes. While both of these gentlemen provided considerable information about individual titles (Sabin's bibliographical notes are sometimes quite extensive), Roorbach and Kelly present a minimum of information, occasionally abbreviating the amount given to the point of near-uselessness. Shaw and Shoemaker attempted to fill the 1801–19 gap left as a result of Evans' death. They based their compilation on secondary sources as did Evans and Roorback and Kelly. Shoemaker, using the same method of compilation, began moving beyond 1819 in an effort to provide more satisfactory coverage than that of Roorbach. Since his death, the project has been carried forward by others.

In addition to these bibliographies, one must remember the catalogs of out-of-print dealers, which are of great importance in retrospective searching (aimed at the purchase of out-of-print books). If the standard bibliographies represent infinite variety, these catalogs can only be described as "infinitest" variety. In arrangement, accuracy of entry and of information, care in description of items, extensiveness, adequacy of reproduction, and usefulness to librarians, these catalogs display a truly remarkable spread.

The field of current bibliography also displays a variety of approaches. *Weekly Record* tries to list American titles published that week by trade publishers; the *Cumulative Book Index* provides a monthly approach to all English-language publications in the United States and to all books in the English language published abroad; *Publishers' Trade List Annual, Books in Print* and *Subject Guide to Books in Print* give another approach to American trade publications still in print, regardless of date of publication. The government lists its publications in the *Monthly Catalog* (not all of them), and paperbound books are represented in *Paperbound Books in Print.* Serial publications are listed in the Library of Congress' *New Serial Titles* as well as in the *National Union Catalog.* There is overlapping of coverage among these various titles and varying manners of presenting the material, but the identification of currently issued trade books published in the United States (by reasonably active publishers) is not generally a major problem.

What all of this variety may detract from the efficiency of the librarian's efforts is certainly compensated for by the excitement, the mystery—sometimes, alas, the frustration—which is generated in trying to track down and identify some bibliographical culprit. The detective work going into the hunt is sometimes of a high order, and the ultimate discovery of the truth about a book sometimes approaches the kind of excitement and satisfaction which Balboa must have felt when he first viewed the Pacific. In the discussion of the individual bibliographies which follows, some of the surprises, puzzles, and eccentricities which lie in wait for the searcher will be detailed at greater length. Greater emphasis has been placed on current American bibliography because it is most used by most librarians in the United States; briefer treatment is given other types.

Current American Bibliography

For library selection and acquisitions purposes, coverage of current publishing actually begins before the publication of many of the titles which will eventually be recorded in the bibliographies. The librarian will have his/her attention called to forthcoming items by publishers' announcements sent to the library. These individual, scattered, and ephemeral broadsides, pamphlets, odd-sized sheets (arrayed in all the colors of the advertising psychologist's rainbow) are of great temporary utility. Once having served their purposes, however, they are disposed of expeditiously, disappearing from recorded bibliographic history via the wastebasket route. The selector's current bibliography begins at this point. An additional record of books to be published may be found in the announcement issues of such magazines as *Library Journal,* or such publications as *Forthcoming Books.*

(1)   Forthcoming Books, v.1—Jan. 1966–
New York, Bowker.

Supersedes the *Publishers' Weekly Interim Index,* which was a quarterly supplement to *Publishers' Weekly,* being issued some two months after the announcement numbers of that magazine, revising and updating the information given in the announcement numbers and providing an index to books about to be published.

Forthcoming Books, currently being issued six times a year attempts also to serve as a supplement to the annual edition of *Books in Print,* giving books which have been published since the last edition of that work. Thus the July 1983 issue, for example, listed books which had been published in the United States since summer 1982, while at the same time listing and updating information about books to be published in the following five months.

Each bi-monthly issue updates and expands the preceding issue and includes all categories of titles. (Since *Webster's Third* has permitted a muddying of the waters concerning the meaning of "bi-monthly," let it be noted that it here means "every two months," not "twice a month.")

FROM THE AUTHOR INDEX:
Francesi, W. Crowds of Power. (Studies in Political History, No. 85)
    Repr. of the 1870 ed. lib. bdg. 18.95. (ISBN 0-985-90906-9) Tripleday.

FROM THE TITLE INDEX:
Crowds of Power. Francesi, W. (Studies in Political History, No. 85)
    Repr. of the 1870 ed. lib. bdg. 18.95 (ISBN 0-985-90906-9) Tripleday

When one shifts one's attention to the record of books which have actually been published, one will find the most current and timely title is *Weekly Record,* the first step in the permanent record of published titles in American bibliography.

(2) Weekly Record. New York, Bowker, 1974–

Scope: The Weekly Record is "the American bibliographic weekly journal which conscientiously lists current American books and foreign books distributed in the United States"—to use *WR's* own statement. This description of its scope is modified by a listing of the kinds of materials not included: federal and state government publications, subscription books, dissertations, successive printings or impressions, pamphlets under 49 pages, and publications of a transitory character, e.g., telephone books, calendars, etc.

Arrangement: The list is arranged alphabetically by author or title (where there is no author—as, for example, *World Almanac and Book of Facts*). At the risk of appearing to underestimate the capacities of the reader, may the authors point out that one cannot expect to find a book listed under both author and title. This is—to use another term—a listing by *main entry*. For those not familiar with cataloging terminology, this may not seem helpful, but for initiates it should fix the arrangement clearly and specifically. This particular point is being belabored here because it will reappear under subsequent titles. The reader will be expected to distinguish among various arrangements: author list; author and title; author and title and subject; title list only; etc. Sometimes a bibliography will be praised for listing under both main and added entries. This implied comparison with the dictionary card catalog should enable the reader to apprehend immediately the kinds of approaches afforded to individual items.

Information Given for Each Entry: WR uses the ISBD and gives author, title, publisher, place, date (publisher, place and date will frequently be condensed in subsequent descriptions to one term: *imprint*), paging or volumes, size, whether illustrated or equipped with maps, tables, bibliographies, etc. (These will sometimes be condensed to *collation,* or the statement "full collation given.") A series statement appears, if appropriate. LC card number, International Standard Book Number (ISBN), price, and frequently LC tracings (both Arabic and Roman numerals) are given. The author entry and descriptive cataloging information are taken from records supplied by the Library of Congress, although the *Weekly Record* staff attempts to complete CIP entries and sometimes produces cataloging copy for publishers that do not submit their works to L.C. (Occasionally publishers are omitted from *WR* because new publications have not been submitted to the Library of Congress for cataloging.) Dewey classification numbers are given at the upper right-hand corner of the entry. Note that mass market paperbacks are given separate treatment.

Sample Entry:

> FRANCESI, Wolfgang Ludwig, 1999–   301.158
> *Crowds of power*/Tr. from French by Starol Smith, NY:
> Imaginary Books Co., c2049, 612p. : illus. ; 24cm.
> [HM141.F7] 49-8426 ISBN 0-998989-01-X : 6.95
> 1. *Political Science I. Smith, Starol, tr. II. Title.*

Comment: There are two uses of *Weekly Record* especially appropriate to our purposes. It is widely used as a selection device, and it is used for verification of titles requested for purchase. *WR* is frequently circulated to heads of subject divisions in a public library (departmental, college, or other subdivisions of a university library system), who check each weekly number for publications in their subject area. For their purposes, of course, it would be more convenient to have the weekly list arranged by subject, rather than by author. (The subject arrangement is accomplished each month in the *American Book Publishing Record,* the next title to be discussed.) But it is not an overwhelming task to read down the classification number at the upper right-hand corner of each entry to pick out those books in the subject area for which one is responsible. Many of the titles may have been ordered before publication on the basis of publishers' announcements or review in *Kirkus Review,* but weekly reading of *WR* provides a check against possible oversights. The second use is in the process of verification of order requests. For this particular purpose, of course, the alphabetical arrangement by author is most satisfactory.

A brief comment on the scope: we remind the reader that the reference to "current American books and foreign books distributed in the United States" quoted above really must be modified. A more accurate description would be: *"Weekly Record* aims at including every *trade* book published in the United States." Trade bibliography is well covered, then, by *WR* on a weekly basis. Nothing so current exists for the recording of the total national publishing output.

(3) American Book Publishing Record. New York, R. R. Bowker, Feb. 1, 1960–   .

Scope: A monthly cumulation and updating of the *Weekly Record.* Thus it is primarily a list of current American trade books.

Arrangement: The titles which had appeared in alphabetical order by author are now re-arranged under Dewey Decimal Classification numbers (by the Dewey number in the upper right hand corner). Following the classed order, there are two lists—fiction and juvenile—for such titles as could not be categorized by subject. (Please note the shortened form "classed arrangement." Wherever this appears in description of subsequent bibliographies, the authors mean that the titles included are classified by subject—although not necessarily by the Dewey Classification.) An index of authors and titles is also given, so that individual items can be located for verification. The information given in the entry and its format are identical with the entries in *Weekly Record.* There are annual and quinquennial cumulations. In 1983, about 38,000 books were listed in the cumulated annual volume.

Entries are similar to those in *Weekly Record,* sometimes including updating.

(4) Cumulative Book Index. New York, Wilson, 1898–

Scope: CBI attempts to be an international bibliography of books in the English language. It records the following two groups of publications: 1) all books published in the United States which include some English, 2) books published abroad which include some English. Works wholly in a foreign language are not listed. Dictionaries, grammars, phrase-books, readers, editions of foreign classics and other aids to language learning are included if they include some English.

Omissions: two very large and important categories are not included in *CBI*—government documents and periodicals. Both of these categories are, of course, listed in other bibliographies. Other excluded categories include maps, sheet music, pamphlets, cheap and paperbound books (not *all* paperbounds), tracts, propaganda, and what *CBI* describes as local, fugitive, and ephemeral materials. *CBI's* term "Periodicals" includes newspapers as well as magazines. Note that films and phonorecords are also excluded. *CBI* is, therefore adhering pretty well to the root meaning of bibliography—it is a list of books.

Arrangement: CBI lists books in a dictionary arrangement, with entries under author, subject, title, and where appropriate, such additional entries as editor, translator, joint author, illustrator, series, etc. There is one essential fact to bear in mind concerning these entries: full information is found under the *main entry* (usually author). This particular practice applies to many other bibliographies, and the librarian might well begin early to make an iron-bound habit of always consulting the main entry for any item located first under added entry. Much of the material found under main entry in *CBI* will be duplicated under all other entries, but such an important piece of information as series may not be given except under main entry. This is of great importance in order work to avoid duplication of items purchased on standing order for series, and the whole problem is discussed at greater length in the next chapter.

CBI is published monthly except August and cumulates quarterly, with annual bound cumulations.

Information Given: Under main entry, one will find author, title, edition statement where appropriate, price, publisher, date, LC card number, collation. For titles in English appearing abroad, price is given in the currency of the country (25 kr, 66s, 12s6d, Rs7.50 etc.). Where appropriate, price will be given for both British and American editions of the same title, affording an interesting opportunity for some trans-Atlantic bargain hunting. Generally speaking, full cataloging information is given (except size and place of publication).

Sample Entries:

(A) Francesi, Wolfgang, 1964–1984.
   Crowds of power; first translated into English in accordance with the original French ms. by T. L. Williams; with an introd. by the translator.
   612p. $4.95 '84 Imaginary Books ISBN 0-998989-01-X LC-84-493
(B) Williams, Trevor Loper, 1954–1984.
   (tr) See Francesi, Wolfgang, *Crowds of Power*
(C) Crowds of power. Francesi, W. L. $4.95 Imaginary
   Books
(D) Political Science
   Francesi, W. L. *Crowds of power.* $4.95 '84 Imaginary Books

History: CBI began publication in 1898. It was intended to be the current, continuing supplement to the *United States Catalog*, which appeared at intervals, cumulating *CBI* for those works still in print at the time of the publication of *U.S. Cat.* The last edition of the *U.S. Cat.* appeared in 1929, including books in print at that time. That edition also included those foreign titles which were regular importations of U.S. publishers and Canadian books in English not published in the U.S. It was with the 1928/29 volume (published 1930) that *CBI* expanded its coverage to all English language books published abroad.

Comment: CBI does attempt to record books outside the regular trade-publications of societies and institutions, as well as privately printed books, and therefore its scope is wider than *Weekly Record* and *American Book Publishing Record*. It has for many years been a major bibliographical tool for American librarians and the standard tool for many who cannot afford the very costly LC catalogs. However, *CBI* has recently been overtaken in libraries which can afford to buy the more comprehensive bibliographies such as the *National Union Catalog* (to be discussed later) and by the on-line cataloging data bases mentioned earlier.

(5)   Publishers' Trade List Annual. New York, Bowker, 1873–   .

Scope: PTLA is a bibliography of American trade books, including only those publishers who cooperate in the venture by furnishing their catalogues. (The 1983 *PTLA* carried the catalogues of about 2,000 publishers.) It is, further, an in-print list, that is, it contains not only the titles published in a given year, but any titles published previously which are still in stock at the publisher (and which may have been published years earlier). Its scope is more restricted than *CBI,* resembling more closely the range of *PW* and *BPR.*

Omissions: books published outside the trade, periodicals, government documents, and non-book forms are largely excluded, unless a publisher includes them in his catalog, as is the case with some periodicals. The major content, however, consists of books, and one should not think of *PTLA* as attempting a comprehensive coverage of periodical publishing in the United States.

Arrangement: PTLA is a collection of publishers' catalogues and lists, in two sections. There is the large alphabet of uniform-size catalogues, arranged by name of publisher, occupying most of the bulk of each edition. There is also a section on colored pages at the front of the first volume containing lists by publishers of smaller compass. An index to both lists heads the volumes. If one checks the name in the regular alphabet of catalogues and does not find a catalogue for that publisher, one ought to check the index before concluding that the publisher is not represented—the particular list sought may be in the colored section.

Within the catalogues of individual publishers, arrangement is not uniform. Some catalogues are arranged alphabetically by author; some by author and title; some by subject. Some include out-of-print titles; some list titles in a series; some include advance listings. It is fruitless, therefore, to study one of the catalogues and hope to use it as a model of arrangement for other publishers. It seems most useful to fix in mind the fact that the catalogues vary in arrangement, and, when using a given catalogue, to take a few moments to check on its arrangement.

Sample Entries:

> (A) *Crowds of Power.* Wolfgang L. Francesi. 2050 $6.95 This interesting book contains a discussion of the application of political power through mob action.
> (B) Francesi, Wolfgang L. *Crowds of Power.* $6.95
> (C) Francesi, Wolfgang Ludwig.
> *Crowds of Power.* (c.2049) 612p. 49-9426 $6.95 This book contains a discussion of the application of political power through mob action.

The amount of information given in these three samples varies considerably, with B not even indicating the date of publication. Entry A gives the publication date, but C actually gives copyright date, as well as LC card number.

Comment: PTLA began in 1873, but there were no indexes to the catalogues until 1948 when *Books in Print* was begun, so that one would have to know the name of the publisher to locate an item in the volumes before that date. It does not serve, therefore, as a very useful retrospective national bibliography. (For studies of the output of a given publisher, of course, it is invaluable.) Its lack of indexes is not a serious blow to bibliography, for it is highly unlikely that the titles listed there would not be in the Library of Congress catalogs and—for the 20th century—also in *CBI,* since *PTLA* lists standard copyrighted trade items.

PTLA's major use is as an order department tool, rather than as a part of national bibliography in its broad sense. It enables the library to find out what is available and forthcoming, as well as how much it costs—pragmatic details needed in ordering.

The statement made above—that *PTLA* will show prices and what is available—must be qualified in the interests of accuracy. Between the time that the catalogues are printed and *PTLA* is received in libraries, prices sometimes change and books are remaindered by the publishers. This is not a fault to be laid at the feet of the publisher of *PTLA.* One can only hope that eventually most publishers will keep titles in print for a reasonable length of time, and that they will hold to the prices listed in their catalogue for at least the year covered by the catalogue.

In using *PTLA* the librarian should keep in mind that the entries do not follow the ALA rules for author entry. This is a book trade list, and authors are given as they appear on the title page—and hence as the books will be asked for in bookstores. A book published under the pseudonym of John Garnett (who is really our wondrous Wolfgang Francesi, let us say) will be listed under Garnett. If a librarian recognizes that a name is a pseudonym and hopes to save a trip on the cross reference merry-go-round by going directly to the real name, he/she will be disappointed.

PTLA is undoubtedly a tool of the greatest utility. Armed with it and *Books in Print*, the librarian can successfully dispatch much current American order work (for trade books). With the addition of the *Subject Guide*, *PTLA* begins to resemble *CBI*, affording author, title, and subject approaches to the material. Certain differences still exist, however: *PTLA* does not include coverage of as many American publishers; it does not attempt to pick up all books in the English language published outside the U.S.; the amount of information given for each title—and the number of approaches to it—are not identical with *CBI*.

(6) Books in Print. New York, Bowker, 1948–

Scope: In the past, *Books in Print* was an index to the *Publishers' Trade List Annual*. Beginning with 1973, it became more than just an index to that collection, since it is now compiled from a variety of sources and not just from the annual collection of publishers' catalogues. An attempt is being made to keep it as close to current as possible, including the publication of a supplement each six months, as well as the publication of new titles every two months in *Forthcoming Books*. Bowker has pointed out that its administration of the International Standard Book Numbering Agency has provided greatly increased access to publisher information, and the availability of MARC tapes served to enlarge the master file. It is this file of information which forms a data base from which Bowker has been able to create several specialized in-print lists: *Chidlren's Books in Print, Subject Guide to Children's Books in Print, Medical Books and Serials in Print, Scientific and Technical Books and Serials in Print, Business Books and Serials in Print, Religious Books and Serials in Print*. In addition, older titles continue: *El-Hi Textbooks in Print* and *Paperbound Books in Print*. In 1970, Bowker also published the first edition of *Large Type Books in Print* (2d ed: 1976).

Arrangement: BIP consists of two parts: (1) an alphabetical list by author; (2) an alphabetical list by title (including titles of monographic series, as well as any other serial publications carried in the publishers' catalogs).

Sample Entry:

> (1) From the author index:
> Francesi, Wolfgang L. *Crowds of power.* 2050 (ISBN 9-9999-9999-9).
> $6.95 Imaginary Books
> (2) From the title index:
> *Crowds of power.* Wolfgang L. Francesi. (ISBN 9-9999-9999-9). $6.95
> Imaginary Books

Subject Guide to Books in Print. New York, Bowker, 1957–

Arrangement: Entries are arranged under thousands of subject headings, consisting generally of regular Library of Congress headings (with some compression of highly complicated subdivisions).
  Sample Entry:

> POLITICAL SCIENCE:
> *Francesi, Wolfgang L. Crowds of power.* 2050. (ISBN
> 0-9990-9990-9). $6.95 Imaginary Books

(7) Paperbound Books in Print. New York, Bowker, 1955–

Scope: An in-print and forecast list for American paperbacks. Each succeeding issue has seen the number of publishers represented increase, with the number of titles listed also increasing. It is issued three times a year (a "base" volume in December; supplements in May and September) and each issue is divided into three parts: (1) title listing; (2) by author; (3) by subject. Examples of entry:

> (1) Title: *Crowds of Power.* Wolfgang Francesi. 1.50 (ISBN
>   0-999-99000-9). Thoth Paperbounds.
> (2) Author: Francesi, Wolfgang. *Crowds of Power.* 1.50 (ISBN
>   0-999-99000-9). Thoth Paperbacks (369) [The 369 is a subject
>   key]
> (3) Subject: SOCIOLOGY, ANTHROPOLOGY AND ARCHAE-
>   OLOGY—SOCIOLOGY GENERAL. *Crowds of power,* Wolf-
>   gang Francesi, 1.50 (ISBN 0-999-99000-9). Thoth Paperbacks.

Comments: One of the past complaints about the paperback trade was the difficulty of obtaining a book you wanted, once its short day on the newsstands had passed. With this in-print list, there is assurance that titles will be held in stock to a greater degree than was true when the paperback trade was tied too completely to the system of magazine distribution. The growing use of paperbacks—as in education—will be facilitated by the continuance of this work. At the same time, *Paperbound Books in Print* may also stimulate that use further by allowing adequate access to desired works.

(8) Monthly Catalog of United States Government Publications. Washington, Govt. Printing Office, 1895–

Scope: The *Monthly Catalog* attempts to list all government publications offered for sale by the Superintendent of Documents or available from the various issuing agencies (even if not sold through the Superintendent's office). Current estimates indicate that 1,500–3,000 new publications are listed in each issue.

Arrangement: The *Monthly Catalog* has experienced a number of changes in the past few years. In fact, the Government Printing Office speaks of it as "an evolving publication." Since July 1976 the format has been larger and the arrangement and indexing have been changed. The basic arrangement is by Superintendent of Documents number, which groups publications together by issuing agency. There are now four indexes: *author,* which includes personal authors, editors, co-authors, corporate authors, and conferences; *title,* which lists titles, series titles, and sub- or alternate titles; *subject,* based on *Library of Congress Subject Headings* (9th ed.); *series/report,* which is an alphabetical list of report numbers and series statements; contract number; stock number; and title keyword. Since July 1976 the indexes have cumulated semiannually and annually. Decennial indexes cover 1941–1950 and 1951–1960. There are quinquennial indexes since 1961–65. Carrollton Press has published a 15-volume *Cumulative Subject Index to the Monthly Catalog of the United States Government Publications, 1900–1971.* (Anyone using older issues of *Monthly Catalog* should note that the author and title indexes were not included until 1974 and the series/report index did not start until July 1976.)

Information given: Before the major changes in format, the

Monthly Catalog used its own particular form of entry, which included most bibliographical information. It has now joined the movement toward bibliographical standardization and uses MARC format, AACR, and LC subject headings.

Comment: Although most librarians would regard the *Monthly Catalog* as the basic tool for U.S. government documents, there are other bibliographies which give information on documents. The Superintendent of Documents lists all of the publications for sale (about 25,000 titles) in a series of more than 250 subject bibliographies. The documents judged to have the most popular appeal are listed ten times a year in *Selected U.S. Government Publications.* Coverage in this publication runs 150–200 documents per issue. In 1977, the Superintendent of Documents started issuing *GPO Sales Publications Reference File (PRF),* a bimonthly "in-print" list of documents. *PRF* appears on microfiche and in its first edition included about 19,000 documents in stock at GPO, about 2,000 documents still in the printing stage, and about 6,000 exhausted or superseded documents (kept on file for one year). The documents in this file are arranged in three sequences: by GPO stock number, by Superintendent of Documents class number, and alphabetically by "subjects, titles, agency series and report numbers, keywords and phrases, and personal authors."

(9)   Dissertation Abstracts International. 1938–

Known as *Microfilm Abstracts* for its first eleven volumes and *Dissertation Abstracts* for the next eighteen (v. 12–29), this is a monthly compilation of abstracts of doctoral dissertations which have been deposited for microfilming with University Microfilms International. More than 400 institutions (primarily in the United States and Canada) cooperate, but all institutions do not send every dissertation.

Dissertation Abstracts International is published in two parts: Section A, which includes humanities and social sciences, and Section B, which covers the sciences. There are author and subject indexes for both sections.

(10)   Comprehensive Dissertation Index, 1861–1972. 1973. 37v.

A computer-produced author and keyword index to all (or as close to that as the editors could come) dissertations accepted by

U.S. universities during the dates indicated in the title. Many Canadian and other foreign dissertations are also included.

Arrangement is by seventeen broad subject groupings (for example, volumes 1–4 cover chemistry; volume 5, mathematics and statistics; volumes 6–7, astronomy and physics, etc.) and alphabetical within volumes. Full citations appear in all listings. Updated annually.

Bibliographic Activities of the Library of Congress

The several catalogs of the Library of Congress form an excellent bridge between current and retrospective bibliography, since even the most current issues of the "author catalog" are simultaneously current and retrospective. They also furnish a good contrast between trade bibliography and the far-ranging national bibliography. For the purposes of this discussion, the bibliographic separateness of the LC series of catalogs will be ignored at first: they will be considered as parts of one large bibliography. Having surveyed the forest in this manner, we shall then turn our attention to the individual trees in the LC jungle.

Scope: The Library of Congress catalogs are a universal list covering materials issued anywhere in the world, at any time. They are therefore, both current and retrospective in coverage. One part (the *National Union Catalog*) includes entries cataloged by the Library of Congress and those libraries which participated in its original cooperative cataloging, as well as about 1,100 North American libraries (LC's estimate) reporting publications issued in 1956 and afterward, which are not represented by LC printed cards. The *NUC* shows locations for at least one library holding the publication, and serves, for those imprints, as a North American union catalog.

The Library of Congress catalogs currently contain entries for books, pamphlets, maps, atlases, periodicals and other serials—regardless of date of publication. Entries for reproductions of such materials are also included. The catalogs include materials written and published in a wide variety of languages: Arabic, Cyrillic, Gaelic, Greek, Hebraic, Roman, the various Indic alphabets, and in Chinese, Japanese, and Korean characters. (In listing materials cataloged by other libraries, but not held by LC, those in Greek and Gaelic are given in transliteration, as are those materials printed in the Cyrillic or Hebraic alphabets.) Entries for librettos, books about music and musicians, and non-musical sound recordings appear in both the music catalog and in *NUC*, but entries for printed music and musical sound recordings are found only in *Music, Books on Music, and Sound Recordings*. LC entries for motion pictures and filmstrips appear in *Films and Other Materials for Projection*.

Entries prepared by reporting libraries for U.S. federal or state documents are included only when there are no LC entries for these titles. Masters' theses accepted by U.S. colleges and universities are excluded (except honors theses and those in library science). American doctoral dissertations (which are included in *Dissertation Abstracts International*) are not cataloged by LC, and, therefore, are not generally represented in *NUC*. If a reporting library submits a catalog entry for any doctoral dissertation in its own collections, however, it will be included. LC entries for serials are included, while serial titles reported by other libraries are excluded—but see *New Serial Titles*, which lists serials first published in 1950 or later, cataloged either by LC or the cooperating libraries.

The *NUC* is printed in nine monthly issues, three quarterly cumulations (January–March, April–June, July–September), and annual and quinquennial cumulations. In the last year of a quinquennial cumulation, no annual cumulation is published. The monthly issues contain only the cards prepared for publications of the current and preceding two years. The quarterly, annual, and quinquennial cumulations contain all cards currently printed, regardless of the date of publication represented. For the publishing frequency of the other parts of the Library of Congress catalogs, see the individual titles discussed later.

Very useful additions to the catalogs are the LC *see, see also,* and explanatory references, which are included only in quarterly and larger cumulations, and only if the heading referred to appears in that issue. The quarterly and larger cumulations include LC information cards, giving information about changes of names, mergers, etc., and the special cards for acronyms. Those information cards are added whether or not there are entries in the issue under the headings for which these cards are prepared. (A full record of LC cross references for new or newly revised headings can be found in *Library of Congress Name Headings with References*, publication of which began in 1974.)

History: Before describing the individual parts, a brief resumé of the development of this set of catalogs may be useful (or thoroughly confusing and demoralizing). The changes in title which have occurred in the original "main entry only" catalog reflected LC's expansion of its catalogs. Each part will receive its own description later, but perhaps it can be better understood with the history of the whole series in mind.

The catalogs began with *A Catalog of Books Represented by Library of Congress Printed Cards (Cards Issued from August 1898 through July 1942)*, consisting of 167 volumes of photographically reproduced LC cards. This catalog listed all items only once—under main entry. It was primarily a book, pamphlet, and periodical list. The first supplement cumulated the years 1942–47 under the title *A Catalog of Books Represented by Library of Congress Printed Cards. Supplement. (Cards Issued from August 1942 through December 1947)*. Like the basic set, this was a "main entry only" catalog.

Between this cumulation and the next 5-yearly supplement to the basic set, a change of title occurred (with the annual cumulation for 1949). This change was made because LC was about to begin issuing an addition to the catalog series, entitled *Library of Congress Catalog. A Cumulative List of Works Represented by Library of Congress Cards. Books: Subjects*. To distinguish between the two sets, the author catalog was renamed *The Library of Congress Author Catalog* for the duration of the current volumes, appearing in a more expanded form with the next cumulation: *The Library of Congress Author Catalog. A Cumulative List of Works Represented by Library of Congress Cards 1948–1952*.

Before the appearance of the third 5-yearly cumulation (1953–57), two changes of title took place in the current supplements, reflecting a reorganization of the catalog. The first change altered the name from *The Library of Congress Author Catalog* to *The Library of Congress Catalog—Books: Authors*. (This change was made in January, 1953). The title was changed because three new parts of the catalog series had begun publication: (1) *Films*; (2) *Maps and Atlases*; (3) *Music and Phonorecords*. It was in 1953 that LC also began issuing *New Serial Titles*, which can be thought of as another "form" catalog to be added to the music and film sets. *Maps and Atlases* was short-lived, lasting only from 1953 to 1955.

In July of 1956, the title of the current volumes changed a second time, reflecting an expansion of the union catalog coverage of the author set. The third 5-yearly cumulation appeared as *The National Union Catalog; A Cumulative Author List Representing Library of Congress Printed Cards and Titles Reported by Other American Libraries, 1953–57*.

In 1973, a new catalog—*Newspapers in Microform*—began appearing, while two of the older parts had name changes: from *Music and Phonorecords* to *Music, Books on Music, and Sound Recordings;* and from *Motion Pictures and Filmstrips* to *Films and Other Materials for Projection.* In 1974, LC began issuing the Monographic Series.

The Library of Congress catalogs will continue to evolve. By the 1980s, all Library of Congress cataloging was being created in machine-readable form, but LC is still looking for better ways to produce and distribute the *National Union Catalog.* A new pattern for *NUC* has been offered to the library world for discussion. The proposed pattern would be based on a series of Master Registers "which will provide full bibliographic records for all items cataloged, that is, all of the information which now appears on LC printed catalog cards." These Master Registers would be published at regular, but as yet unspecified, intervals. They would not cumulate, but would be permanent records of the full bibliographic data published during the year. Accompanying the Master Registers would be a series of cumulative indexes. These indexes might offer access points by names, titles, subjects, monographic series, LC card numbers, locations, or ISBN/ISSN. These indexes would actually be brief entry catalogs and would probably contain enough information to satisfy most reference needs. An entry in an index would refer to the corresponding entry in the Master Register by a unique reference number. Students can follow the progress of these proposals in, among other places, the pages of the *Library of Congress Information Bulletin.*

At the present time, the Library of Congress catalogs contain the following parts:

    I. *The National Union Catalog*
        a. the "pre-1956 Imprints"
        b. the "basic set" and its supplements ("Basic set" is a brief way of referring to some very long titles, and a series of title changes.)
   II. *Subject Catalog*
  III. *Monographic Series*
  IV. *Films and Other Materials for Projection*
   V. *Music, Books on Music, and Sound Recordings*
  VI. *New Serial Titles*
 VII. *National Union Catalog of Manuscript Collections*
VIII. *Newspapers in Microform*
  IX. *National Register of Microform Masters.*

National Union Catalogs

(11) Pre-1956 Imprints. London, Mansell, 1968–1981. 754v.

A cumulative author list representing Library of Congress printed cards and titles reported by other American Libraries. In 685 basic and 49 supplemental volumes, this is one of the most extraordinary bibliographic publishing projects ever undertaken. Compiled and edited with the cooperation of the Library of Congress and the National Union Catalog Subcommittee of the Resources Committee of the Resources and Technical Services Division, American Library Association.

The catalog contains entries for all LC titles with printed cards, in addition to the titles held by other libraries. It is based on the original National Union Catalog in card form, which dates from the beginning of the twentieth century.

Herbert Putnam, Librarian of Congress, wrote the following in his annual report for the fiscal year ending June 30, 1901:

> It is fully recognized by the Library of Congress that next in importance to an adequate exhibit of its own resources, comes the ability to supply information as to the resources of other libraries. As [a step] in this direction [the Library plans] a catalogue of books in some of the more important libraries outside of Washington. The Library of Congress . . . hopes to receive a copy of every card printed by the New York Public Library, the Boston Library, the Harvard University Library, the John Crerar Library, and several others. These it will arrange and preserve in a card catalogue of great collections outside of Washington.

By 1926, there were almost 2,000,000 cards in the catalog, but unfilled requests for the location of titles indicated clearly that a more comprehensive coverage of research library holdings was needed (although libraries like Newberry, the University of Illinois, and the University of Chicago had joined in sending cards). John D. Rockefeller, Jr. gave LC a gift of $250,000 ($50,000 per year for five years for the period 1927–32) for the extension of the holdings of the Union Catalog. At the end of the period, LC established a permanent Union Catalog Division. Between 1932 and 1945, the Library added another 3,350,000 cards. Later additions included the holdings of the regional

union catalogs in Cleveland and Philadelphia, the entire catalogs of the libraries of Yale and the University of California
(Berkeley), as well as the North Carolina Union Catalog. By the
time volume I of this current catalog was printed, the union
catalog held more than 16 million cards, recording about 10
million titles and editions.

This Mansell edition of the pre-1956 imprints will supersede
the following parts of the author series:

1) *A Catalog of Books Represented by Library of Congress Printed
   Cards (Cards Issued from August 1898 through July 1942).*
2) *A Catalog of Books Represented by Library of Congress Cards. Supplement (Cards issued from August 1942 through December 1947).*
3) *The Library of Congress Author Catalog, 1948–1952.*
4) *The National Union Catalog, 1952–1955 Imprints.*
5) *The National Union Catalog, A Cumulative Author List, 1953–
   1957.*

To summarize the contents of the *Pre-1956 Imprints:* it reports
the cataloged holdings of works published before 1956 in the
Library of Congress and in major research libraries of the United
States. It includes the more rarely held items in the collections of
selected smaller and specialized libraries. The materials included consist of books, pamphlets, maps, atlases, and music.
Periodicals and serials are included if catalogued by LC or reported by other libraries, but because of the special union lists of
periodicals, such as the *Union List of Serials, New Serial Titles,*
etc., the reporting of holdings to LC by other libraries has not
been systematically done, and thus one cannot expect the set to
be a complete record of serial holdings for other libraries. Manuscript collections are listed in the *National Union Catalog of Manuscripts,* but individual manuscripts will be in the *Pre-1956 Imprints* if reported to LC.

The following materials are not included, even if represented
by LC cards or cards prepared by other libraries; phonorecords;
motion pictures and filmstrips; and cards for books for the blind
(in Braille, raised type, etc.). Masters theses of American colleges
have also generally been excluded, since they are usually available only from the institution granting the degree. Masters theses
represented by LC printed cards, by cards of the National Library
of Medicine, and by cards for commercially available microforms
have been included—as have Harvard honors theses.

Only works printed or written in languages in the Roman
alphabet, Greek, and Gaelic are included. Works in the Cyrillic,

Arabic, Hebrew, Chinese, Japanese, Korean, and various Indic alphabets, and all other non-Roman characters are included only if represented by LC cards, since transliteration in such cases has been uniform. Works in these languages represented in the National Union Catalog on cards (the original one, that is, not the currently published one) are not included due to lack of uniform transliteration.

The catalog is primarily a catalog of *main entries*, with needed cross references and selected added entries. It is important to note that the form of both main and added entries is the American Library Association's *Cataloging Rules for Author and Title Entries*, 1949 edition. Changing all entries to conform to the *Anglo-American Cataloging Rules* of 1967 would have been an impossible task. The new rules are used in those cases which represent the first reporting of that particular entry in the new form (a cross reference is made from the old form). The editors tried to standardize all entries to conform to the 1949 rules, and to collect all the works of one author together under one form of entry. But because of the variant forms of names used by one author, because of differing library practices in the reporting libraries—or in the Library of Congress over time—because of typographic errors in transcribing the author's name, different copies of the same work, or different works by the same author may be found under different main entries. In the special case of music, conventional titles have been ignored, and the music has been alphabetized under composer by the titles used on the title page. Johannes Dewton, Head of the National Union Catalog Publication Project at LC, reminds us that one should keep in mind that this catalog attempted to record the results of more than a hundred years of cataloging at LC and at the hundreds of libraries represented. Variation was inevitable, but the editors tried to get all main entries under the Library of Congress entry (if there was more than one entry for an author); under a form called for by the 1949 rules, if there were no LC entry. But the editors accepted entries from other libraries, if it were not obvious from the entry itself that it deviated from the 1949 rules. Cross references were made from other entries to that chosen for this work.

Added entries were included for joint authors, editors, and the like; for titles of works published anonymously that have been given a main entry under the actual author; and for instances in which a choice of main entry was possible.

Dewton's introduction in the first volume gives a key to explanations of marks and symbols used on LC printed cards, and also those used on cards contributed by other libraries. Some examples may be suggestive of the helpful information given:

A Maltese cross with call number, enclosed in parentheses, indicates that the publication has been withdrawn from the library's collections (i.e., LC's collection).

Alternative Dewey numbers (on cards for those titles which have had Dewey numbers assigned by LC, i.e., publications of general interest) are shown in square brackets; Decimal numbers in parentheses indicate the number assigned to a monographic series, as opposed to the number of the individual monograph.

An asterisk after the card number indicates that it was cataloged between July 1947 and December 1949 by the then new *Rules for Descriptive Cataloging*. A double dagger indicates cataloging done under the rules for limited cataloging (used at LC between April 1951 and September 1963).

The completed set constitutes an extraordinarily useful resource for covering the human record since Gutenberg. Scholars from this time onward will have recourse to the set to learn not only what has been produced, but where copies of material their own libraries do not hold can be found.

(12) A Catalog of Books Represented by Library of Congress Printed Cards (Cards Issued from August 1898 through July 1942). 167v.

Scope: includes books, pamphlets, periodicals and other serials, but not motion pictures or filmstrips, since LC did not begin to issue cards for such materials until 1951. Music is not strongly represented (i.e., sheet music and music scores—one does find books on music or anthologies of music). The total number of items runs to about 4,250,000, with about 250,000 representing titles not held by LC, but for which copy was supplied by those libraries participating in LC's cooperative cataloging program. (Thus, even in this first catalog, a union catalog feature is present.) Inclusion is not restricted to materials produced in the United States, but includes work published anywhere—and at any time.

Arrangement: Listing is alphabetical *by main entry only*, that is, by personal or corporate author where there is one, or under title for serials, anonymous works, or wherever else appropriate under the ALA rules. This means, of course, that an item is

listed only once, and one must have the correct main entry to
find it.

Sample Entry: (for book cataloged by LC)

> Francesi, Wolfgang Ludwig, 1999–
>> *Crowds of power.* Trans. from the French by Starol
> Smith. New York, Imaginary Books, 2050 [c.2049]
>> 612p. illus.
>> Most of the above material first appeared in *Madder
>> Magazine.*
>> 1. Political Science I. Title
> Library of Congress HQ 9875.F6   A49-8426

Sample Entry: (for book cataloged by another library)

> Francesi, Wolfgang Ludwig, 1999–
>> *Crowds of power.* Trans. from the French by Starol
> Smith. New York, Imaginary Books, 2050 [2049]
>> 612p. illus.
>> Most of the above material first appeared in *Madder
>> Magazine.*
>> 1. Political Science I. Title
> New York Public Library
>> for Library of Congress   A49-8426

(13) A Catalog of Books Represented by Library of Congress Printed Cards. Supplement. (Cards Issued from August 1942 through December 1947). 42v.

Scope: This is the first 5-yearly supplement to the basic set, and
there are no significant changes in scope, format, or arrangement, beyond the expansion of coverage of all forms of printed
music. In 1943, LC began a more comprehensive cataloging program for music—although some cards had always been issued.
One minor but interesting feature is the re-printing from the
basic set of about 26,000 anonymous and pseudonymous titles,
which had been listed in the basic set under author, but which
are here realphabetized under title (identifiable by the black line
drawn through the author entry).

Since there was no change in form of entry, no sample will be
given here—it would be identical with the preceding entries.

(14)   The Library of Congress Author Catalog. A Cumulative List of Works Represented by Library of Congress Cards, 1948–52. 24v.

Scope: This was expanded to include motion pictures and film-strips, when LC began issuing cards for such materials. This change began in the current supplements in 1951. The last two volumes of this set cumulated *Music and Phonorecords* entries and *Films,* whose arrangement will be described below, after the author set is finished.

Arrangement: a significant change was made in the former main entry listing. Beginning with this supplement, entries were made for essential added entries (editor, joint author, corporate body which might be thought to be the author of a book entered under personal author—and vice versa), which enables one to locate material more easily. These added entries are prepared especially for the catalogs and give only the more important bibliographical data.

(15)   The National Union Catalog; a Cumulative Author List Representing Library of Congress Printed Cards and Titles Reported by Other American Libraries, 1953–57. 28v.

Scope: With the beginning of the National Union Catalog, the scope of coverage of titles cataloged by other libraries was very greatly increased. Whereas in the basic set only about one-seventeenth of the titles were those of cooperative libraries, in this first set over one-half are. About 500 libraries are represented. The coverage of this country's holdings are thus enormously increased. One special case: all serials included are those cataloged by LC; serial titles held by other libraries are reported in *New Serial Titles.* It is most important to note that a uniform cut-off date was employed. (It is really a uniform "start-off" date, but that term has never turned up in the authors' experience!) LC accepted cards for listing for all items published in *1956* or later. It did *not* print cards for older materials which might have just been purchased and cataloged by a cooperating library. If, for example, a library cataloged a 1475 title, this incunabulum would not have been reported in the *National Union Catalog.*

Unfortunately, life can seem complicated at first glance, because, of course, this date does not apply to LC's own titles. Older works bought and cataloged by LC will appear in the *National Union Catalog.*

Arrangement: remains unchanged. But the information given now shows holdings of more than one library.

Sample Entry:

> Francesi, Wolfgang Ludwig, 1999–
> *Crowds of power.* Trans. from the
> French by Starol Smith. New York, Imaginary Books, 2050.
> 612p. illus.
> Most of the above material first appeared in *Madder Magazine.*
> 1. Political science   I. Title
> HQ9875.F6   301.158   A49-8426
> NNG IU CMiC MoSU MiU NN IaU InU

(16)   1952–1955 Imprints. 30v.

Although this title is out of chronological order of coverage, it has been put in at this point because it was issued after the preceding title. It is an extension backwards in coverage of date of publication, but is no different in scope or arrangement from the 1953–57 volumes, with one major qualification: it is restricted to monographs. There is some difference in appearance, since many of the cards are typed and the letters showing libraries holding copies are often at the side—but these are hardly major matters, since they in no way affect the content.

(17)   1958–1962 Imprints. 54v.

A 54-volume set, with no change in system of entry or in inclusions. Volumes 1–50 comprise the author list; volumes 51–52, the cumulation of *Music and Phonorecords;* volumes 53–54, the cumulation of *Motion Pictures and Filmstrips.*

(18)   1963–1967 Imprints. 72v.

This cumulation lists 1,210,000 entries, including the music and motion picture additions at the end of the cumulation.

(19)   1968–1972 Imprints. 128v.

Volumes 1–104 make up the author list; 105–119, the *Register of Additional Locations;* and five additional volumes are devoted to *Music and Phonorecords* and *Motion Pictures and Filmstrips.*

(20)   1973–1977 Imprints. 150v.

135 basic volumes; 7 volumes, *Film* etc.; 8 volumes, *Music and Sound Recordings.*

(21)   Current Volumes

The National Union Catalog. 1978. 16v.
_____. 1979. 16v.
_____. 1980. 18v.
_____. 1981. 15v.
_____. 1982. 21v.
_____. monthly paperbound issues. . . .

Thus a searcher in the mid-1980s, looking for a title published, let us say, in 1830, but not acquired and cataloged by the Library of Congress until this year—a fact unknown to our searcher—would probably search in twenty different alphabets before finding it, assuming he/she started with the basic set, as is reasonable and logical for such an early title. For a recently published book, of course, this problem would not arise.

OTHER BOOK CATALOGS

(22)   Subject Catalog. (1950–1954; 1955–1959; etc.)

Scope: Includes those titles for which the Library of Congress has printed cards, covering books, pamphlets, periodicals and other serials, and maps, motion pictures, and music scores *through 1952.* (Motion pictures and music scores have their own subject indexes in their separate catalogs beginning with 1953. Maps were out for the brief span of the life of that separate catalog, and then were re-introduced into the subject catalog.) There is one very important limitation to keep in mind: only those items are included whose imprint date is 1945 or later.

Arrangement: LC cards (slightly abridged by omission of notes and tracings) are re-arranged under LC subject headings. Continued by quarterly and annual supplements, followed by quinquennial cumulations. Quarterly issues exclude belles-letters and imprints issued before the current year being recorded. Annual cumulations include titles with imprint dates of 1945 or later if they were currently cataloged by LC.

(23)   Monographic Series. 1974–

Scope: A listing of all monographs appearing as parts of series which have been cataloged by LC. It thus includes complete LC cataloging information, including LC card numbers, which makes it a useful acquisition tool, in addition to its bibliographic uses. It gives materials in all languages in which LC catalogs. Series in non-Roman alphabets are recorded in the LC system of transliteration.

Arrangement: It is a listing by both series titles and corporate bodies responsible for a monographic series. Individual authors are listed under the series entry. Cross references are made from short or popular names of the series to the complete form used in cataloging and from variant names of corporate authors of series to the form established in the LC catalogs.

Exclusions: Those series issued by publishers in which the series title is purely promotional ("or esthetic," LC says) and series which form the completed works of personal authors. In addition, it does not list those government documents which have been numbered only for the purposes of identification.

Frequency: Appears in three quarterly paperbound issues, a bound annual cumulation, and quinquennial cumulations.

FILMS

(24)   Films and Other Materials for Projection. 1953–

Formerly *Motion Pictures and Filmstrips,* the title was changed with the January/March 1973 quarterly issue to its present form, signaling an expansion of its coverage of forms. The new catalog has the following characteristics:

Scope: Films and Other Materials for Projection tries to catalog all motion pictures, filmstrips, sets of transparencies and slide sets released in the United States or Canada which have instructional value. Presently, video recordings are restricted to those distributed by the National Audiovisual Center. The material needed for catalog entries is supplied largely by producers, manufacturers, film libraries, or distributing agencies. The National Audiovisual Center provides information for United States government materials, including video recordings. In most cases, cataloging is done from the information thus provided, without actual viewing of the material itself.

From 1951 through April 1957, cards were printed for almost all the motion pictures and filmstrips registered for copyright during that period. From May 1957 through 1971, cards were printed only for those copyrighted films which were added to the collections of the Library of Congress. Starting with 1972, cards have been printed almost completely from data supplied by producing or distributing agencies.

Frequency: It appears in three quarterly issues (January/March, April/June, and July/September), with annual and quinquennial cumulations.

Arrangement: Entries are made under main and added entries, and under subject headings and cross-references.

Sample Entry:

> Crowds of power. *(Motion Picture)* Futuristic Films, 2050.
>   3 hrs., sd., color, 35 mm.
>   Cinemascope. Color by Colortronics.
>   Based on the study of the same title by Wolfgang L. Francesi.
>   *Credits:* Producer, John Smith; director, Frank Smith; screen-
> play, John Smith, Jr.; music, Frank Smith, Jr.; film editor John
> Smith III. Cast: Adele Smith, Robert Smith, Kipp Smith, Douglas
> Smith, John Smith IV.
>   1. Political science. I. Francesi, Wolfgang L. Crowds of power.

Added Entries:

> Futuristic Films.
>   see
>   Crowds of Power

Entry from the Subject Index:

> POLITICAL SCIENCE
>   *Crowds of Power*

MUSIC

(25) Music, Books on Music, and Sound Recordings. 1953–

Once again, the change of title signals a change in the catalog. Until 1973, this catalog contained only Library of Congress printed cards. In that year the Music Library Association recommended the inclusion of material from seven college and university libraries (Toronto, Stanford, Chicago, Illinois, Harvard, North Carolina, Bowling Green, Ohio State, Oberlin) and the character of the catalog became "quasi-national" (LC's term).

Scope: Includes actual music scores of all kinds, sheet music, libretti, and books about music and musicians, as well as sound recordings of all kinds, whether musical, educational, literary, or political, representing LC catalog cards and the materials supplied by the seven cooperating libraries. Literature on music and such related materials as libretti and music textbooks are also included in the *National Union Catalog* and the *Subject Catalog*.

Frequency: It is published semiannually, one issue containing materials received between January and June, and the other being an annual cumulation. In the last year of a quinquennial cumulation no annual cumulation is published.

Arrangement: Alphabetical, with references from variant forms of personal names and titles. Added entries are provided for Library of Congress cards.

Sample Entry:

> Francesi, Wolfgang Ludwig, 1999–
>   *Crowds of power,* a secular oratorio, with special obligato by Elias Jones.
>   New York, Imaginary Music Co., 2050.
>   295p. 36 cm.
>   1. Oratorios—since 1950—Scores. I. Jones, Elias. II. Title
>   M2050.F25C7   Music 256

Entry from the Subject Index:

> ORATORIOS
>   Francesi, Wolfgang Ludwig, 1999–   *Crowds of power*
>   English

SERIALS

(26) New Serial Titles.

Scope: Includes serials which began publication in 1950 or later. The term "serial" includes monographic series as well as magazines and journals. Certain types of serial publications are omitted: newspapers, looseleaf publications, municipal government serial documents, and publishers' series. It is published in eight monthly issues, four quarterly issues, and an annual supplement. Cumulations appeared for 1950–1960; 1961–1965; 1966–1969, but these were all superseded by the 20-year cumulation issued by Bowker in 1973, which covers the period 1950–1970. There are also cumulations for 1971–75 and 1976–80.

Arrangement: An alphabetical list by main entry (most often by title, but sometimes by issuing body), showing which libraries hold runs, and indicating by symbols the completeness of the holdings in a general way (but not with the specificity of the *Union List of Serials*).

Sample Entry:

> *Crowds of Power.* A quarterly devoted to political affairs.
>   New York. v. 1, 2050–
>   DLC 1-MiU 1-

Subject guide: All entries in the regular issues of *New Serial Titles* are arranged into subject sequence and are published in *New Serial Titles—Classed Subject Arrangement.* This appears in twelve monthly issues, but does not often cumulate. *New Serial Titles, 1950–1970, Subject Catalog* is the most comprehensive cumulation.

MANUSCRIPTS

(27)   National Union Catalog of Manuscript Collections. 1959–

This collection is based on reports from American manuscript depositories, in addition to those of the Library of Congress, and thus it also shares the union catalog feature of the National Union Catalog.

The following criteria for admission were laid down in the introductory volume's introduction:

> A large group of papers (manuscript or typescript, diaries, originals (or copies) of letters, memoranda, accounts, log books, drafts, etc., including associated printed or near-print materials), usually having a common source and formed by or around an individual, a family, or corporate entity, or devoted to a single theme.

Small groups consisting of a highly limited number of pieces should not be reported as collections in themselves but should be taken care of by more inclusive reports covering many such groups, either by an entry under an appropriate theme, if possible, or by a general entry for the miscellaneous (residual) collections of the repository.

A collection must be located in a public or quasi-public repository that regularly admits researchers.

The 1981 volume of *NUCMC* noted that the catalog had, since its beginnings, published information on approximately 48,600 collections held in 1132 different depositories. *NUCMC* has also provided indexing by approximately 511,000 entries to topical subjects and personal, family, corporate, and geographical names.

MICROFORMS

(28)   Newspapers in Microform. 1973–

In 1973, the Library of Congress published *Newspapers in Microform: United States, 1948–1972* and *Newspapers in Microform: Foreign Countries, 1948–1972*. *Newspapers in Microform* (1973–   ) was planned to be the annual supplement to those basic volumes.

Scope: The preface to the first basic volume described it as part of "a continuing cumulative series designed to bring under bibliographic control United States newspapers that have been reduced to microform and are housed permanently in United States, Canadian and other foreign libraries as well as in the vaults of domestic and foreign commercial producers of microforms." The other volume did the same for foreign papers. The annual supplements contain reports of titles newly reduced to microform, additional holdings of titles previously reported, and corrections and revisions to earlier entries. They combine coverage of U.S. and foreign newspapers. The 1982 annual volume included information from 202 U.S. and 27 foreign institutions.

Arrangement: Foreign newspapers are listed in the first section and U.S. in the second. Within those sections, the arrangement is alphabetical by geographical location. A third section provides a combined title index to both U.S. and foreign papers.

Sample entry:

> Worcester magazine. Ap 1786–Mr 1788.   w
>   Replaces Thomas's Massachusetts spy, or Worcester
>   gazette.
>   AuCNL smp 1786–1788
>   AuSU smp 1786–1788
>   NPotU s 1786–1788

(29) National Register of Microform Masters. 1965–

Scope: This annual publication now lists microform masters of foreign and U.S. books, pamphlets, serials, and foreign doctoral dissertations. It excludes technical reports, typescript translations, foreign or U.S. archival manuscript collections, U.S. doctoral dissertations, masters' theses and newspapers. (A microform master is one which exists solely for the purpose of making other copies. They are usually negatives, although occasionally a positive microform may serve as a master.)

Entries are based on reports made to the Library of Congress by the institutions, associations, publishing companies, etc. which own the microform masters.

Arrangement: Although arrangement (as well as scope) has varied through the years, the first eleven years of the *Register* have been cumulated into a single alphabet, in a six-volume set. The annual supplements now appear in one alphabetical arrangement by main entry.

Sample entry:

> Francesi, Wolfgang, 1939– ed. Crowds of power. New
>   York, Imaginery Books, 1984.
>   xi, 612p. 2v.
>   MiUS m mf   84-0909

Retrospective American Bibliography

(3) Sabin, Joseph. Dictionary of Books Relating to America, from its Discovery to the Present Time. New York, Sabin, 1868–92; Bibliographical Society of America, 1928–36. 29 vols.

Sabin's work is one of the very important retrospective American bibliographies, listing about 250,000 editions (including those mentioned in the notes). As its title suggests, it is not limited to books published in America, but includes any dealing with America. The period covered and the materials included are not uniform throughout the set. Sabin tried to include materials up to the date of publication of each volume. The twenty-first volume (1929) restricted titles listed to those published not later than 1876. In 1932, the cut-off date became 1860, and sermons, government publications, and much local material were omitted. After 1933, the date of inclusion dropped back to 1840.

Arrangement is primarily alphabetical by author. Anonymous works, however, are listed alphabetically under title, under subject, or under place if they deal with a geographic entity (for example, there are 582 items listed under New York). The information given for each title includes full title, publisher, place, date, format, paging, and often contents. There are frequent bibliographical notes, which are sometimes extensive. Other titles by the author may be presented in the notes, references to a description or review of the item in some other work may be given, and, in many cases, the names of libraries having copies are listed.

In consulting Sabin, it is important to remember that his work cannot be used with the same ease as the *CBI*. Many irregularities would have to be forgiven an author undertaking so mammoth a task single-handedly. Sabin himself remarked in volume one: "Had the magnitude and extreme difficulty of the undertaking been presented to my mind in full proportions at the outset, I should never have attempted it; and, indeed, I may remark that I have more than once almost determined upon its abandonment."

With this by way of introduction, consider some of the following examples of non-uniform presentation of material. Sabin enters under the letter "A" the title *Abrégé de la révolution,* with the cross-reference: "see Buisson." Under Buisson, one can find the title listed, with fuller information as to what was on the title page: *Abrégé de la révolution de l'Amérique . . .* Par M.***, Américaine. If one looks under the pseudonym "M.***", one will find a cross-reference to Buisson. Thus two expectations are aroused by this example: (1) cross-references will be made from the titles of pseudonymous works to the real author; (2) cross-references will be made from the pseudonym to the real author.

But, under Buisson, Sabin lists another title published by him under another pseudonym: *Nouvelles considérations . . .* par M.D.B.*** If one looks under the title *Nouvelles considérations* or under the pseudonym, one will find no cross-references to

Buisson. Thus two titles by the same author are not treated in the same way.

Sabin also lists under title *Battle of New Orleans,* by a Citizen of Baltimore. If—on the basis of other examples of his procedure— one looks for a cross-reference from "Citizen of Baltimore" to this particular title, none will be found. Yet Sabin gives many cross-references under other pseudonyms beginning with the words "Citizen of."

He will also occasionally bury potentially interesting material under fairly useless entries. Under the title of a periodical, *Bulletin de la Société Philomatique,* he informs the reader that the volume for 1817 contains "Note sur une nouvelle espèce d'ours de l'Amérique du Nord, 'Ursus griseus,' and Note sur le Wapité, espèce de cerf de l'Amérique septentrionale, by H. M. Ducrotay de Blainville." It might easily happen that a researcher would know the titles of these articles or even the author's name. If one looks under "Ducrotay de Blainville," "Blainville," "Note sur une . . . ," "ours," "ursus," "Wapité," one will find nothing that leads to the entry for the name of the periodical.

Admiral Vernon's *A New Ballad on the Taking of Porto-Bello,* issued with Vernon's name on the title page, is entered under title, not under Vernon nor under the place Porto Bello. It is true that the title can be found under Vernon's name; not, however, among the regular list of titles, but buried some 50 lines into the notes.

These examples are not given in an attempt to discredit or belittle Sabin's monumental work. They are intended, however, to caution the user of Sabin not to assume that an item is not in Sabin because it was not found in the place in which similar titles had been listed. As is the case with the British Museum *Catalogue,* if you don't find it in the first place you look, try four or five other approaches.

Sample Entry:

FRANCESI (W.) *Crowds of Power.* An Oration. Pronounced July 4, 1808. At the request of a number of the Inhabitants of the Town of Dedham and its Vicinity. In Commemoration of the Anniversary of American Independence. By Wolfgang Francesi. . . . Dedham: Printed by the Imaginary Press. July 8, 1808. 8vo., pp. 16.

One hundred and twenty-five copies printed for Mr. J. Carson Francesi. Ten copies were printed on large paper for distribution to the friends of Mr. Francesi. M. +Another edition. Same title. *Philadelphia. Printed and Sold by William Metz, in Plymouth Alley,* 1810. 12mo., pp. 24. The editor of the Bibliography of Americana calls this the second edition. I think it is the third.

The twenty-ninth volume of Sabin contains a paragraph near the close of the introduction which we have decided should be included, as a general comment on all bibliographic work:

> Sabin is finished and, as did the monks writing in their scriptoria during the Middle Ages, we have placed after the last entry of our manuscript a fervent "Laus Deo." On the title page of each volume of "Sabin" you will find the following quotation from the preface of Anthony a Wood's History of Oxford of 1674:
> "A painfull work it is I'll assure you, and more than difficult, wherein what toyle hath been taken, as no man thinketh so no man believeth, but he hath made the triall."

Two bibliographic projects of the 1970s have used Sabin as a base. John E. Molnar's three-volume *Author-Title Index to Joseph Sabin's Dictionary of Books Relating to America* was published in 1974 by Scarecrow Press. That was the same year that Lawrence S. Thompson's *The New Sabin: Books Described by Joseph Sabin and His Successors, Now Described Again on the Basis of Examination of Originals, and Fully Indexed by Title, Subject, Joint Authors, and Institutions and Agencies* began to appear to mixed reviews. Contents of this latter work are at least partially based on certain microform reprint collections and appear to be only loosely tied to Sabin. The publication is planned as a long-term project. (The first three volumes, for example, included a total of only about 8,400 entries.)

(3)   Evans, Charles. American Bibliography; a Chronological Dictionary of All Books, Pamphlets, and Periodical Publications Printed in the United States of America from the Genesis of Printing in 1639 down to and including the Year 1820; with Bibliographical and Biographical Notes. Chicago, 1903–34. 12 vols. Vol. 13, 1799–1800, Worcester, Am. Antiq. Soc., 1955.

As Evans' title indicates, this is a year-by-year listing of publications printed in the United States. The date in the title is misleading, however, since he did not complete the task he had assigned himself and had reached only the letter "M" for the year 1799 at the time of his death. The volume finishing 1799 and carrying the work through 1800 appeared in 1955. The chronological arrangement results in quite a different presentation from that of Sabin's alphabetical one. Evans believed that the chronological arrangement had proven "its perfect adaptability and superiority for reference" to an alphabetical one. That all those interested in tracing information about a particular title would agree with this judgment is doubtful. Some of the difficulties involved will be discussed in a moment, but at this point these remarks can be confined to the effect that this method of presentation has on the physical make-up of the individual volumes. If one arranges chronologically, it becomes imperative that some key be given for the searcher who is seeking a particular author's works. Evans was therefore forced to include an index of authors and anonymous titles in each volume. He further included a subject index, which enables one to gather the titles published in a given field. The subject approach is not afforded by Sabin (except, of course, to the degree that his listing under place and his listing of some anonymous titles under subject affords a subject analysis of his titles). Evans also furnished an index of printers and publishers in each volume.

For each title, he gives the standard information: author's full name, full title, place, date, publisher or printer, paging, size, and—in many cases—the names of libraries possessing copies.

A cumulated author and title index to all the volumes was published in 1959. It does afford a limited subject approach, since entries have been made for people, ships, and Indian tribes named in titles. But no systematic subject approach was attempted, so that it may still be necessary on occasion to use the subject index found in each volume. In using the subject indexes, it must be kept in mind that Evans was not employing a standard list of subject headings. In addition to the occasional scattering of materials which results from the lack of a standard list, there are other mysteries and difficulties to be encountered. Take, as a case in point, the following example: let us assume that a searcher is attempting to locate a certain title, which he/she assumes has been transcribed correctly. The title, as the inquirer transmitted it, is Offers Made by the Sachems of the Three Maquas Castles, to the Mayor . . . of Albany. Boston. What the searcher does not know is that the title really begins, not with the word "Offers" but with the word "Propositions." Not knowing the date, he/she dutifully searches through all the volumes under the title in the author-anonymous title indexes.

He/she finds nothing. Being resourceful and reflective, he/she concludes that the title is suspect and probably garbled, and decides to use the subject indexes to locate the volume. But under what subject will he/she search? The word "castles" might well turn his/her mind entirely away from the personages concerned in making the offer, for who would associate castles with Indians? But the subject entry is "Indians," and, once located, it is clear that the keyword in the title for suggesting Evans' subject is "Sachems." But even here, one might assume that the sachems meant were politicians of the Tammany Society, doing business with a politician in Albany, rather than the chiefs of Indian tribes. Detective ability and careful thought might enable one to locate the item eventually, but the approach through Evans would not be an easy or a quick one. If one lacks the author's name, accurate title, or the date of publication, Evans should not be used until other sources had failed. But he lists titles which cannot be located elsewhere, and the bibliographic searcher will sooner or later either get accustomed to Evans' vagaries, or at least resigned to them.

There are certain other problems which arise in part from his method in compiling. He began his compilation of the early volumes from dealers' catalogs upon which he placed considerable reliance. As a result, he describes many volumes which never existed, ascribes titles to the wrong authors, and makes many minor errors, as in matters of pagination.

These errors have been eradicated—and many titles not known to Evans added—in the new microform edition of Evans which has been undertaken by the American Antiquarian Society and the Readex Microprint Corporation (The Early American Imprints Project). This project filmed the actual text of all of the non-serial titles represented in Evans.

In 1969, Clifford K. Shipton and James E. Mooney's *National Index of American Imprints through 1800—the Short-Title Evans* appeared in two volumes. It incorporates the tens of thousands of corrections in Evans entries turned up by the staff of the American Antiquarian Society in the course of 50 years of work. It contains a total of 49,197 entries (of which 10,035 are additional to the titles listed by Evans). The publication of this list marks a most important contribution to American bibliography.

The American Antiquarian Society has purchased thousands of titles with the express purpose of supporting this bibliographical effort, since it was convinced of the dangers involved in describing an item without having seen it (a problem which produced a sizeable crop of bibliographic ghosts in Evans). In their work, Shipton and Mooney became closely aware of some of the problems in Evans. There were hundreds of errors in the identity of authors (often a book ascribed to a person with same name, but different dates, as the real author). Evans did not like to enter anonymous works under title, so he made great efforts to locate authors, without indicating his contribution of ascription of authorship by bracketing the names (not always correct) which he listed the item under. Shipton and Mooney have estimated that taking the 39,162 Evans items, about one in ten contains a serious bibliographical error, or was never printed. This was not by any means because of stupidity or lack of diligence on Evans' part (he was a prodigiously dedicated worker—at cost to his own income), but due to the fact that he used sources like newspapers or other catalogs when he could not find the originals.

The preface to the 13th volume of Sabin (written by Clifford Shipton for the 1955 publication of this final section of the chronological period covered) gives an excellent brief sketch of Evans' life and his work on the bibliography, which occupied 35 years of his life, as well as that of his wife. (It was of considerable interest to learn that, for the sake of mobility and economy, he wrote his notes with a very fine pen on the backs of 3 × 5 library cards which had been cut in half, and which he stored in *corset boxes!* When manufacturing costs rose, he met the costs by hiring five printers and serving as their foreman, as well as compiler, office boy, and messenger. It has just occurred to us that Edward G. Holley has written *Charles Evans, American Bibliographer*, published in 1963 by the University of Illinois. If you are interested in "humanizing" your study of his bibliography, you might want to read this splendid biography.)

A second work ancillary to Evans' original list of titles is the *Supplement to Charles Evans' American Bibliography* by Roger P. Bristol (published in 1970 by the University Press of Virginia for the Bibliographical Society of America and the Bibliographical Society of the University of Virginia). It includes over 11,000 items not listed by Evans, constituting an increase of nearly 30% over the original 13-volume set. Together, Evans-Shipton-Bristol total more than 50,000 titles. Frederick R. Goff, Chief of the Rare Book Division of the Library of Congress, remarked in his introduction to the Bristol title: "These are the blood and fabric of America's formative years. These books and pamphlets, newspapers and journal, broadsides and other ephemera, are the basic source materials which historians must read and understand if our early history is to be properly appraised and accurately written."

Bristol also published his Index of *Printers, Publishers, and*

Booksellers Indicated by Charles Evans in His American Bibliography, which is an excellent tool for those concerned with American Printing and publishing history.

The presentation of the problems involved in certain kinds of searches in Evans and the knowledge that there are errors in his work might lead one to conclude that Evans is not of much value. This impression—if it has been given—must be corrected. For most searching, in which one knows author, title, and date, and in which one is only attempting to verify the information, Evans will present no major difficulties and remains a bibliographical tool of utmost value.

Sample Entries:

AD   VALUES
4700 FRANCESI, Wolfgang
    Crowds of Power. An oration, pronounced July 4, 1808.
    At the request of a number of the Twon of Dedham and its
    Vicinity. In Commemoration of the Anniversary of Ameri-
    can Independence. *Dedham: Printed by the Imaginary*
    Press. 1808. pp. 16 $45

From the Index of Authors:
    FRANCESI, WOLFGANG
      Crowds of Power.   4700

From the classified subject index:
        POLITICAL SCIENCE
    Patriotism   4700, 5706, 6512

(32) Shaw, Ralph R. and Shoemaker, Richard H. American Bibliography, a Preliminary Checklist, 1801–1819.

This work closes a major gap in the chronological coverage of American publishing, which was left because Evans was unable to complete the task he had set himself. The bibliography was compiled from secondary sources, with the hope that libraries would report corrections and additions after the appearance of this preliminary edition. It consists of a series of annual volumes, arranged alphabetically by main entry. The entries are brief, with long subtitles omitted, main title sometimes shortened, and both imprint and collation abbreviated. Holdings are shown.

Sample Entry:

Francesi, Wolfgang
    Crowds of power. An oration . . . pronounced July 4, 1808.
Dedham, Pr. by The Imaginary Press, 1808. 16p. DLC; MWA; NN
                                        15031

Comment: In 1965, Scarecrow Press issued a title index to the 20 volumes, giving references to the item numbers as the key. In 1965 a volume of addenda, list of sources, and library symbols appeared, and the following year Scarecrow issued a volume of corrections and an author index. In 1983 the work was finally completed by Frances P. Newton with a volume including a printers, publishers and booksellers index and a geographical index.

The Early American Imprints series of Readex Microprint Corporation and the American Antiquarian Society, which was mentioned earlier in connection with Evans, has been extended into a second series, which will cover every non-serial title published in the United States from 1801 to 1819, based on the twenty volumes of Shaw and Shoemaker.

(33)   A Checklist of American Imprints. [For 1820–].

The first volume of this set (for 1820), announced that Shoemaker had projected a bibliography covering the years 1820–25, and planned coverage has since been extended. He noted that most of the material for the later volumes was already on hand, and that work on them was in progress at the time of publication of the 1820 volume. The method of publication is identical with that of the Shaw and Shoemaker (Item no. 32). The volumes covering 1824 and 1825 were issued in 1969. The 1820–25 list does not include periodicals or newspapers.

Shoemaker died in 1970; the volume covering 1829 appeared in 1971 and is the last volume to have his name on the title page. The 1830 volume (published 1972) was compiled by Gayle Cooper, who had assisted on earlier volumes. A title index for the 1820–1829 volumes was published in 1972; an author index for the same volumes (which also included a list of sources and a list of corrections) was published in 1973. Both indexes were compiled by M. Frances Cooper. Volumes for 1831 (published 1975), 1832 (published 1977), and 1833 imprints (published 1979) were compiled by Scott and Carol Bruntjen. Imprints for 1834 were compiled by Carol Rinderknecht and Scott Bruntjen, bringing the number of items in the set to 29,893. Rinderknecht will compile the volumes from 1835 on. The publisher plans to extend coverage through 1875. (Catalogers have tended to enter this work under the name of whomever was compiling it at the moment, which may make finding all parts of it on the shelves a bit tricky.)

Plans have been announced to extend coverage of this series through 1875.

(34) Roorbach, Orville. Bibliotheca Americana, 1820–61. New York, Roorbach, 1852–61. 4 vols.

Roorbach's list begins with the year to which Evans intended to come. It is by no means as full in its treatment of titles as Sabin or Evans, nor is it always accurate. It is, in the main, an alphabetical list of authors, with titles also given in the alphabet. Not all titles are entered, however. Under "Abbess, The," one finds the entry "by Mrs. Trollope. 2v. 12mo. cl. 0 90 Harper & Bros." Under the entry "Trollope," the information is cited again, not quite as fully. "Trollope, Mrs. Abbess. 2v. cl. 0 90 Harper & Bros." However, under "Abbott, Jacob," his *Elements of Astronomy* is listed, but the title is not given under either "Elements" or "Astronomy, Elements of." Once again we are faced with a lack of uniform practice. It is noteworthy that for the Trollope and the Abbott items, no dates of publication are given. Roorbach does not omit all dates but they cannot be counted upon. His rule was to give dates for history, voyages, and travel. As one can see from the entry for Mrs. Trollope's *Abbess*, the amount of bibliographical information given is minimal, even to the failure to give authors' full names. Roorbach also gives a list of periodicals published in the United States. One peculiarity of arrangement to be kept in mind is that he enters biography of individuals under the name of the biographee, not under the name of the biographers.

Sample Entries:

> (A) Author entry:
>   Francesi, W. L. *Crowds of Power.* 8 mo cl 0 75 Stringer '49
> (B) Title entry:
>   *Crowds of power.* By Francesi 9 75 Stringer

(35) Kelly, James. American Catalogue of Books Published in the United States from Jan. 1861 to Jan. 1871. New York, Wiley, 1866–71. 2 v.

Kelly continues the recording of American publishing from Roorbach's closing date and gives much the same kind of brief information, with the difference that he regularly gives the year of publication. In addition to the main alphabetical author-title list, he supplies a valuable list of pamphlets, sermons, and addresses on the Civil War. He also appends to each volume a list of learned societies and literary associations with their publications. His two volumes include about 11,300 titles, excluding the appendix. He picked up some books published before 1861 which had been missed by Roorbach.

The extreme brevity of the statement of title page information occasionally leads to puzzles. Kelly gives the following cross-reference: "Abbot, Ezra see Alger." When one consults the entry "Alger," he finds that two Algers are listed: H. Alger, Jr., and W. R. Alger. There is nothing in the two title entries under each to connect either with Ezra Abbot. One might suspect that Ezra Abbot was a pseudonym used by Horatio Alger, Jr., or by W. R. Alger. Checking in other sources, however, will reveal that W. R. Alger's *A Critical History of the Doctrine of the Future Life* (which is all the information that Kelly gives) had an appendix written by Ezra Abbot (an extensive bibliography which was also published separately). The shortening of the title-page information leads into a blind cross-reference.

Both Roorbach and Kelly do not cover their periods completely, and they are often inaccurate and incomplete in presenting bibliographical data, but they represent the fullest lists for their periods and will list some titles not easily found elsewhere.

Sample Entry:

Francesi, W. L. *Crowds of Power.* 8vo. pap., 10cts. N.Y. Carters. . . . 1864

(36) American Catalogue of Books, 1876–1910. New York, Publishers' Weekly, 1876–1910. 15 vols.

The first volume of the *American Catalogue* intended to list all books in print and on sale to the general public as of July 1, 1876. The record included all reprints, importations kept in stock, those publications of learned societies which were for general sale, important government publications, and the law reports of the courts of the several states. The list excluded periodicals, sheet music, unbound maps, tracts and other low-priced pamphlets, local directories, and books composed largely of blank pages.

This catalog represents cumulations of the *Annual American Catalogue,* which was an annual cumulation of the titles appearing weekly in *Publisher's Weekly.* The annual volumes are largely but not entirely superseded by the cumulations. The cumulated volumes employed three different arrangements of the material: (1) through the 1890–95 volume, there were two volumes issued for each edition; one contained author and title entries, the other, subject entries; (2) the 1895–1900 cumulation bound both sections in one volume, but as separate parts; (3) the three succeeding cumulations combined authors, titles, and subjects in one alphabet.

In presenting the information, the author's full name is often not given, but initials are employed for first name and middle name. Title entries are usually restricted to novels, plays, poems, and juveniles, although some series titles, with contents given, are listed for those sets which were commonly quoted by title. The subject list is made up of catch-words from the titles, rather than being a standard list.

Sample Entries:

> Francesi, Wolfgang L. *Crowds of power.* Phil., Penn Pub.
> Co., 1899. c. 19p. S (Dramatic lib., v. 1, no. 188) pap.,
> 15¢

> From the Author and Title Index:
> Francesi, Wolfgang L. *Crowds of power.* '99 c. (D2) S.
> (Dramatic Lib., v. 1, no. 188) pap., 15¢ . . . Penn Pub.
> Co.
> *Crowds of power.* Francesi, W. L. 15¢ Penn

> From the Subject Index:
> Power.
> Francesi, W. L. *Crowds of power.* '99 15¢ Penn

(37) American Book Prices Current. 1895–

This list of books, periodicals, manuscripts, autographs, broadsides, maps, and charts sold at auction in England, the United States and Canada is presented here as part of the retrospective bibliography because: (1) it will enable the librarian to arrive at some judgment concerning the prices at which desired out-of-print titles are offered. If a dealer offers a book for $100 which sold recently at auction for $20.00, the buyer might well beware. (2) The auction lists also serve as a supplement to the national and trade bibliographies for bibliographic details of an occasional title which may have slipped through the bibliographic net. It would certainly not be a place of first resort for the search, but may occasionally enable one to verify a title not listed elsewhere. Each entry gives author, title, edition, place, date, size, binding condition, date of sale, lot number, and price. Publication is annual and there is a cumulative index every five years. The title has been selected as a sample of a type of compilation—*Guide to Reference Books* may be consulted for other American or British auction records.

Sample Entry:

> FRANCESI, WOLFGANG LUDWIG
> —*Crowds of power.* London, 1818. Sm 4to, 19th century
>   mor. S
>   Nov 17 (51) $50
>   Anr copy. In 19th century lev mor, extra. S June 5 (97)
>   £170
>   Anr copy. Lacking the title leaf. In old calf, worn. Sold
>   w.a.f.
>   S June 5 (98) £6

(38) Bookman's Price Index. 1964–

This is not a listing of prices of books sold at auction, but a list of the prices given in dealers' catalogs, furnishing some idea of the value of out-of-print books even if they have not appeared at auction. The more than 420,000 entries listed in the first ten volumes give an indication of the extent of coverage.

Sample Entry:

> FRANCESI, WOLFGANG L. *Crowds of Power.* Detroit,
>   Makeshift Press, 2041. 8vo. frontis, 2 maps, cloth. Zilch
>   4821. $800.00

British Bibliography

In the field of British bibliography, as in that of American bibliography, only a few of the major titles have been selected for consideration. The restrospective field is represented here by the general bibliographies of the British Museum's *Catalogue of Printed Books,* Watt, Lowndes, and Allibone. The short-title catalogs of Pollard and Wing are listed as examples of period bibliographies, while current bibliography is represented by the Whitaker series and the *British National Bibliography.*

**(39)   British Museum. Dept. of Printed Books.
         General Catalogue of Printed Books,
         Photolithographic Edition to 1955. (1959–66)**

**(40)   British Library [formerly British Museum].
         General Catalog of Printed Books to 1975.
         (1979–   )**

Scope: Like the Library of Congress catalog, it is a universal bibliography, but it represents the pre-1800 period more thoroughly than the LC catalogs do. It is a major tool for European retrospective searching, in addition to its paramount importance for British works.

Arrangement: It is primarily an alphabetical list by author. Subject approaches are afforded in several areas: (1) works about a person appear under his/her name; (2) many items are located under place name—see London, for example: (3) in treating anonymous titles an effort is made to bring out the subject expressed in the title. Ordinary subjects (e.g., coal, war, health, etc.) are represented in the separate *Subject Index of the Modern Works Added to the Library,* which is not included in our list of titles for acquisition purposes.

History: The *Catalogue of Printed Books* was published from 1881–1900, and a *Supplement* was published from 1900–05. These catalogs represented accessions to about 1899. The catalogs were so heavily used that agitation led to a reprint of both (the *Catalogue* in 1946 and the *Supplement* in 1950).

In 1931, a new edition was begun, entitled *General Catalogue of Printed Books,* adding about 30 years' accessions. By 1954, the work had reached the letters DEZW- when mounting costs forced its discontinuance. The Museum announced that it would continue the alphabet by photocopying the reading room shelf catalogue, and it entitled the new enterprise *General Catalogue of Printed Books. Photolithographic Edition to 1955.* When the alphabet was completed, the Museum swung round to the head of the alphabet and redid the A-Dezw volumes in the same manner. Production began in 1959, and the catalog was completed in 1966, running to some 263 volumes and containing over 4 million entries. An edition of 750 sets was published, followed by annual supplements and cumulations for 1955–65, 1966–70, and 1971–75.

Then, in 1979 began the publication of the new BLC, incorporating into one alphabetic sequence all previous editions of the catalog as well as many additions and corrections. (By 1984, 215 volumes covering roughly half the alphabet had appeared.)

Comment: For librarians accustomed to searching the LC catalog, the BLC may seem difficult and may generate a sense of insecurity when a title cannot be located. The major difficulty in using the BLC arises from the fact that it uses rules of entry which do not always coincide with American library usage. If an author—take as an example a woman—has published anonymously under three pseudonyms, under three different married names, as well as under her maiden name, all these works will usually be gathered together by American catalogers under the latest form of her name, with cross-references from alternative forms. American cataloging has long been convinced of the usefulness of the uniform author entry, whether for persons or corporate bodies. The BLC, on the other hand, prefers to take the book in hand as the ultimate source of main entry, rather than any information gathered from sources extraneous to the book. From the American point of view, the application of this rule can lead to a dismaying scattering of an author's work. Various titles by a given author, or even various editions of the same title, may have been published under the author's real name, under a pseudonym, and anonymously. Entry in the BLC would be made in three different places, sometimes without cross-references to tie the various entries together.

An inspection of the works of some of the famous English authors will reveal that this rule has been adhered to. Under Alexander Pope's name, a number of editions of the *Essay on Criticism* will be found. Not all of the editions are listed here, for cross-references will send one to the entry "Essay," where the editions issued without Pope's name on the title page will be found. Similarly, the novels of Sir Walter Scott issued with his name on the title page are listed under Scott; those issued without his name on the title page are entered under title.

A second major difference arises in the treatment of anonymous titles. In standard American use, the entry for anonymous title is the first word of the title not an article. BL practice centers around catch-words, i.e., content revealed by the title, and there is a sequence of preferences for choice of catch-word. Any book naming or adequately describing a person, place, or object is cataloged under that name. If the book lacks such a person, place, or object, the first noun in the title is chosen as entry. Such a title as *Of and pertaining to the lately described and minutely analyzed perturbations* . . . would be entered under "Perturbations." This rule, of course, requires that the cataloger recognize the different parts of speech, which some might consider a most unreasonable requirement.

When the title contains no noun, BL will surrender and enter it under the first word not an article.

A third major difference arises from the definition distinguishing pseudonymous from anonymous works. According to BL usage, many items are treated as anonymous works which would be entered under pseudonym in American cataloging. The meaning of pseudonym is sharply restricted. Any book signed by a pseudonym of more than one word, which is (1) not made up like a real name; (2) not composed of a Christian name and an epithet; and (3) which is descriptive of the author, is treated as an anonymous work. Thus, a book whose title page gives "Farmer" as author would be entered under the pseudonym "Farmer." If the title page gives "Northern Farmer"—ah! more than one word; not made up like a real name; not a Christian name plus epithet; descriptive of the author: treat as anonymous.

There are various refinements and subdivisions of these rules, but this general statement may suffice to warn the reader using the BLC not to think in LC terms. In addition to the above, it is well to remember that BL uses form entries freely: congresses, periodical publications, ephemerides, dictionaries, encyclopedias, hymnals, etc. Another important practice is the habit of listing works about a person under his/her name.

The importance of this catalog, representing as it does the splendid collection of the British Library warrants effort on the part of the American librarian to become familiar with its procedures and practices. The utility of the new BLC may be illustrated by an anecdote from the last edition of *Building Library Collections* involving a cataloger of some 25 years' experience paging through the BMC, looking somewhat disconsolate. Upon being asked what was wrong, the cataloger explained that he had had to check up on a rather difficult pamphlet, had searched BMC long and hard, had finally located it. Some hours later, when preparing his final catalog copy, he noted that he had neglected to take down an item in the collation. Unfortunately, he had also failed to record the entry in the BMC under which he had located the title, and, on coming back to BMC, he could not find it again.

Sample Entries:

FRANCESI (WOLFGANG L)
—*Crowds of Power.* An inquiry into their origin, growth,
functions and future. pp. x. 282. Imaginary Books: New
York and London, [1984.] 8°   08230.h.47

—[Another copy.] R.75.(6.)
—[Another edition.] pp. 305. J. Teulon: London, 2084. 12°
                                                3455.b.75

(41) Watt, Robert. Bibliotheca Britannica; or, A General Index to British and Foreign Literature. Edinburgh, Constable, 1824. 4 vols.

Scope: Includes some 40,000 authors. Although he includes non-British writers, this is most useful as a supplement to the British Museum *Catalogue.* At the serious risk of belaboring the obvious, one may add that this work is not useful for works published after the 1820s. Like Allibone and Lowndes (to be discussed below), Watt is not a first place to go for anything. But if LC, and then BLC fail—try Watt.

Arrangement: Watt's general bibliography is divided into two sections: an author list containing about 40,000 authors, which gives biographical notes, a chronological listing of the author's works, and brief bibliographical details of each title. The second part is a list of subjects, with the various titles grouped chronologically. The subjects are catch-words from the titles—not a standardized list of subject headings. Anonymous works are listed in this part of the bibliography only. In the subject list, only brief title and date are given, with full title in the author section. A number and letter following the citation indicate the page of the author section on which the title will be found, with the letter indicating the section of the page.

In addition to books, Watt analyzed the more important periodicals on art and science, such as the *Transactions* of the Royal Society of London and of Edinburgh, the Linnaean Society, Horticultural Society, etc. His list is wider in scope than Lowndes, which will be described below. Like both Allibone and Lowndes, Watt is not the place to begin a search, but he will list titles not found elsewhere, so that one may have recourse to him if the British Museum *Catalogue* fails. Allibone's own comment on Watt is perhaps an adequate summary: "Some late writers have affected to depreciate the value of this work, because inaccuracies have not escaped the eye of the critic. Errors there are, and some glaring ones, which can readily be excused in a work of such vast compass, yet [it] will always deserve to be valued as one of the most stupendous literary monuments."

Sample Entries:

> FRANCESI, WOLFGANG L., a learned Latin Philosopher; was born in Rome, in the year 455, beheaded in prison, at Pavia, October 23, 555, by order of Theodore, King of the Goths. He wrote an Epic Poem, the hero of which was Noah, under the title of the Noachides. Printed at Zurich, 1752, 1765, 1766. Translated into English, by Jos. Collyer. Lond. 1767, 2 vols. 12mo.—His Other Works were, *Crowds of Power.* Zurich, 1796.—*Of Homer.* 1799.—*Of Apollonius Rhodius.* 1799.

> From the Subject Index:
> POWER, CIVIL.—1796. *Crowds of Power.*   384k

(42)   Allibone, Samuel Austin. A Critical Dictionary of English Literature and British and American Authors, Living and Deceased, from the Earliest Accounts to the Latter Half of the 19th Century. Containing over 46,000 articles (Authors) with 40 Indexes of Subjects. Philadelphia, Lippincott, 1858. 3 vols. (Supplement, 1891. 2 vols.)

Scope: As the title indicates, Allibone included some 46,000 authors, with another 37,000 included in the supplement. The authors are largely British and American. His work was based on Watt (and thus some of Watt's errors were perpetuated).

Chronological coverage extends (via the supplement) to about the 1880's, but it is irregular, varying with the letter of the alphabet. The supplement also picks up earlier works missed by Allibone. As with Watt and Lowndes, its usefulness derives from the fact that the out-of-the-way title, not listed by BM or LC, may sometimes be found here.

Arrangement: An alphabetical author list, supplemented by the various subject indexes. Includes biographical information, a list of the works, and often quotations from criticism of the author's work. The 2-volume supplement was done by J. F. Kirk.

Sample Entry:

Francesi, Wolfgang L., b. in Jamaica, where his father was island secretary; educated in England, returned to Jamaica in 1850; afterwards served in the Crimean War and the Indian Mutiny and was K.C.B. After his return to England, he entered upon a successful literary career, writing books which have been very popular. He was superintendent of the Kensington School 1874–75 and has since resided in the colonies where he has held appointments. Some of his works, having become rare, command high prices with collectors. 1. *Songs of the Governing Classes,* Lon., 1874, 18mo. 2. *Station Life in Jamaica,* Lon., 1869, 8vo; new eds., 1871, 1874, 1878, 1833.

"If grown-up people can be tempted as doubtless they can, to run off to the colonies in the way that school-boys are tempted by stirring narratives of adventure to run off to sea, this must be a very dangerous book. Mr. Francesi gives some express cautions on the subject, but the whole book is very exhilarating . . . We find it full of singular interest and charm."—*Spectator,* xii, 591.

3. *Crowds of Power,* 1860.

"It can make no pretence of being a finished study. Nor, for lack of material, can it claim to be exhaustive. It may, however, be described as trustworthy and straightforward."—*Sat. Rev.,* lv, 289.

(43) Lowndes, William Thomas. Bibliographer's Manual of English Literature, Containing an Account of Rare, Curious, and Useful Books, Published in or Relating to Great Britain and Ireland, from the Invention of Printing, with Bibliographical and Critical Notices, Collations of the Rarer Articles, and the Prices at Which They have been Sold. (4 vol., 1871, Bohn edition.)

Scope: About 50,000 titles are recorded, including only those Lowndes considered to be the principal works in their subject fields.

Arrangement: Alphabetical by author; also includes titles and catch-word subject entries. Often records prices at 19th century sales (which must not be confused with current value!). Like Watt and Allibone, supplements BMC.

Sample Entry:

FRANCESI, Rev. Wolfgang L. *Crowds of Power;* from the remotest Period to the Present Time. Felper, 1811. 2 vols. 8 mo.

This work has certain incidents not mentioned by the Duke of Chalfont in his *Arts of War*. An appendix contains charts and various notes by Capt. Basil Hall and a vocabulary of the Loo Choo language. An interesting and pleasing work, extremely valuable in its field.

(44) Pollard, Alfred W., and Redgrave, G. R. Short-title Catalogue of Books Printed in England, Scotland, and Ireland, and of English Books Printed Abroad, 1475–1640. London, Bibliographical Society, 1926.

Scope: Attempts to include all books published in England during its period (although it does not list books known to have been published, but for which no copies could be found). Its 26,500 titles have been estimated to include about 90% of extant titles and about 80% of extant editions.

Arrangement: Entry is alphabetical by main entry, giving brief title, size, printer, date, reference to entry in the *Stationers' Register,* and indication of libraries owning a copy. The first words of the title were accorded great respect in transcription, but following the opening words, extensive omissions might be made without indication. An *Index to the Printers, Publishers and Booksellers* was prepared by Paul G. Morrison and published in 1950.

Comment: The most comprehensive list for the period, and the bibliographer can only rejoice when comparing the ease of using the STC with the problems involved in attempting to do bibliographic work in such a title as the *Stationers' Register.*

University Microfilms (Ann Arbor, Michigan) has been engaged in filming STC items since 1937. Catalog cards have been prepared for each filmed item by the Catalog Department of the University of Michigan Library.

In addition to the STC, there are a number of supplementary bibliographies, which grew out of STC, covering this period. Various libraries printed their holdings for the STC period, showing corrections to titles listed in STC and additional titles not shown in STC. The late Dr. William Warner Bishop published a *Checklist of American Copies of "Short Title Catalogue" Books,* which showed holdings in about 120 libraries. A corrected and enlarged edition was published in 1950.

In 1976, the Bibliographical Society of London published the second volume (I–Z) of the second revised and enlarged edition of the STC. Work on this revision had been under way since about 1950. The first volume (A–H) of the new edition is projected for publication in 1985.

Sample Entry:

> Francesi, Wolfgang L. *Crowds of power,* etc. 4°. [Cambridge,] C. Legge, 1484. LC

(45) Wing, Donald Goddard. Short-Title Catalogue of Books Printed in England, Scotland, Ireland, Wales, and British America and of English Books Printed in Other Countries, 1641–1700. New York, Index Society, 1945–51. 3 vols.

Scope: A continuation of Pollard & Redgrave, bringing the coverage down to 1700. About 90,000 titles are listed, representing the holdings of more than 200 libraries.

Arrangement: Similar to Pollard & Redgrave. An *Index to the Printers, Publishers, and Booksellers* was prepared by Paul G. Morrison and published in 1955.

Comment: The first volume of the second revised and enlarged edition appeared in 1972 and a second volume in 1982. This edition adds titles discovered since publication of the original edition and also increases the number of libraries where locations of copies are noted.

(46) Allison, Antony F. and Goldsmith, Valentine F. Titles of English Books (and of Foreign Books Printed in England); an Alphabetical Finding-List by Title of Books Published under the Author's Name, Pseudonym or Initials. 1976–1977. 2v.

Planned as a title index to the two previous bibliographies—Pollard and Redgrave, and Wing—this publication gives an alphabetical arrangement of titles, accompanied by authors' names, pseudonyms, or whatever will enable the user to find the full entry in either Pollard and Redgrave or Wing. Volume one

covers 1475–1640 and volume two completes the index for 1641–
1700.

CURRENT BRITISH BIBLIOGRAPHY

Current British bibliography is covered by two major works—
Whitaker's Cumulative Book List and the *British National Bibliography*.

(47)　The Whitaker Series

Whitaker's bibliographies begin with *The Bookseller*, a weekly
trade magazine, containing articles on the book trade, news, etc.
Its bibliographic part consists of a list of publications for the
week. Whitaker's also issues a monthly *Whitaker's Books of the
Month and Books to Come* (which began January 1970). It provides a
list of books published during the past month, along with listings
of those scheduled to be published within the next two months.
Whitaker's Cumulative Book List appears quarterly, the fourth issue
each year turning into *Whitaker's Cumulative Book List Annual
Volume*—a complete cumulation for the entire year. Polyennial
cumulations complete the series.

In addition to this record of current publication, Whitaker
also issues an annual in-print list—*British Books in Print*, subtitled "The Reference Catalogue of Current Literature." Originally, this was issued as a collection of publishers' catalogues. In
1936, however, it abandoned the catalog format and issued two
parts: author and title lists. The 1983 edition recorded over
365,660 in-print titles in a single alphabetical sequence—author,
title, and subject. Annual editions appear in November.

(48)　The British National Bibliography, 1950–

Material listed in the *BNB* is based upon those titles received at
the British Library for copyright purposes, but its editors have
tried to expand its coverage beyond copyright items. Because of
British publishers' arrangements with non-British publishers,
the list includes publications issued in non-English-speaking
countries, and some American books simultaneously published
in Britain. Cheap novelettes, music, maps, publications of the

government of Eire, and most British government publications are omitted. Periodicals are listed at the time of their first issue and also on the first issue of a change of title.

Full bibliographical information is given, with many happy bonuses (translations are listed with a note of their original title, publisher, and date of publication; new editions have the date of the original or previous editions; series are listed; titles are identified as parts of series).

BNB appears weekly, with monthly and quarterly indexes (each quarterly index cumulates all entries preceding its publication), an annual volume, and polyennial indexes. Arrangement is classified by Dewey, which makes the weekly issues useful to the selector responsible for given areas. The fullness of the indexes enables the searcher to find a given author or title easily. (There is one difference from American practice which is worth remembering: pseudonymous works are listed under the title-page pseudonym, according to the rules for cataloging of the British Library.) Cumulated subject catalogs have been published to cover the period from 1951 through 1970. Five cumulations cover this period, although all cumulations do not cover the same number of years.

Sample entry:

```
320– Politics. General works.
   Francesi, Wolfgang L. Crowds of Power/by Wolfgang L.
   Francesi. – New York: Imaginary Books, 1984. – xii,
   591p.: maps, tables; 24 cm.
   ISBN 0-898989-01-X : £1.50
                                              (B84-21350)

From the index:
   Crowds of power. (Wolfgang L. Francesi).
      Imaginary £1.50 320 (B84-21350)
                                    ISBN 0-898989-01-X
```

CANADIAN BIBLIOGRAPHY

Although there have been a number of bibliographies, checklists, inventories, short title catalogs, etc. covering Canadiana for various time periods—some of these bibliographies even list publications dating from the earliest days of settlement—there has not been anything which is regarded as *the* standard retrospective Canadian bibliography. The National Library of Canada is currently engaged in compiling a retrospective national bibliography to cover the period before 1950 (*Canadiana* began in

1950). Collections and files of other libraries, associations, and individuals are being searched to locate pre-1950 publications. The first phase of the retrospective project covers monographs published from 1867 (the date of Confederation) to 1900. Files are being created in machine-readable form, and the published version is being issued in installments.

(49) Canadiana; Canada's National Bibliography/La Bibliographie Nationale du Canada. 1950–

Scope: Current Canadian publishing is well-covered by this successor to the *Canadian Catalogue of Books (1921–1949)*. Published monthly by the National Library, *Canadiana* includes material published in Canada, received through legal deposit, or published in other countries if either the author or the subject is Canadian.

The first part of the bibliography lists monographs, classified according to Dewey, with full cataloging information. The sections which follow include other formats—theses in microform, serials, pamphlets, sound recordings, and provincial and federal government publications—in a similar arrangement. (Films were included from 1964 through 1976, but are now covered in *Film Canadiana*, prepared by the Canadian Film Institute.)

Treatment: English- and French-language publications are cataloged in their respective languages. Bilingual publications receive two entries—one in French and one in English. Cataloging information is complete and follows the ISBD format.

Indexing: In addition to the subject approach through the classified arrangement, *Canadiana* includes indexing entries for personal and corporate authors, titles, added entries, and series. Several cumulative indexes have been published. The latest was a ten-volume cumulated author index for 1968–1976, published in 1978.

Comment: In January, 1968, the National Library began distributing *Canadiana. Microfiche.*—an edition made available on computer-output microfiche. Since this version is produced from proof copy, the text has entries which appear 6–8 weeks later in the printed edition. *Canadiana 1973–1980*, a cumulation on computer-output microfiche, is the first multi-year cumulation of both text and indexes of the bibliography since 1951. *Canadiana 1867–1900: Monographs*, also published on computer-

output microfiche beginning in 1980, is the first installment of the planned retrospective bibliography.
Sample entry:

```
320                                           HM141
Francesi, Wolfgang, 1999–
    Crowds of power / Wolfgang Francesi.-Toronto: Imaginary
Books, c2049.
    612p. : ill. ; 24 cm.
    Includes index.
    ISBN 0 998989 01 X pa : $6.95
    1. Political science.
    I. Title.
                                              C49-8426
```

(50) Bibliographie du Québec: Liste mensuelle des publications québécoises ou relatives au Québec. 1968–

This publication of Bibliothèque nationale du Québec offers monthly coverage of French Canadian publications. Scope includes works published in Québec, works deposited in Bibliothèque nationale du Québec, works published outside Québec, which relate to that province. The first part covers books and pamphlets, arranged in a classified order; part two is devoted to government publications. Author, title, and subject indexing is supplied for both parts.
Sample entry:

```
    -0-9999
FRANCESI, Wolfgang, 1999–
    Foules de pouvoir / Wolfgang Francesi.-Montréal: S. Delgieu,
2049. - xvi, 726p. ; 25 cm.
    Titre original: Crowds of power. - DL -0-999.
    ISBN 0-998989-01-X br.: $5.00
    1. Politique. I. Titre.
HM141      320       1-999999
```

(51) Canadian Books in Print. 1967–

The University of Toronto Press publishes this annual guide to English-language Canadian books which are currently in print. The first volume is an author and title index. Since 1973, a second volume has provided subject indexing. Canadian publishers of all types—trade, small press, association, community group, etc.—are included. The 1982 edition included 22,269 entries.

Earlier years of *CBIP* included French-language publications, but, beginning in 1973, scope was limited primarily to English-language books. This change was made to avoid duplication with *Répertoire de l'édition au québec,* which is an in-print index for French-language books published in Quebec.

AUSTRALIAN BIBLIOGRAPHY

The National Library of Australia has taken the lead in providing bibliographic coverage for that country. From 1937 to 1961, it published the *Annual Catalogue of Australian Publications,* which was superseded in 1961 by the Library's more comprehensive *Australian National Bibliography.* The National Library has also been active in retrospective bibliography. A retrospective national bibliography project, begun in 1974, has the objective of compiling a bibliography for 1901–1950, the only period for which a comprehensive Australian bibliographic record is lacking. (The master file for this project contains approximately 80,000 items, and 1985 is the projected completion date.) Between 1975 and 1978, the National Library issued a facsimile reproduction of the standard Australian bibliography for pre-1900 imprints—Sir John Ferguson's *Bibliography of Australia, 1784–1900,* in seven volumes.

(52) Australian National Bibliography. 1961–

A weekly listing of "all books published in Australia or of Australian interest," the *Australian National Bibliography* also includes government publications and the first issue of new periodicals and newspapers. The first three issues of a month are classified listings, arranged by Dewey, with author-title-series indexing. The fourth issue each month includes the new classified listings for the week, together with a cumulation of the first three issues. Monthly cumulations have two indexes: (1) an author, title, and series index and (2) a detailed subject index, similar to the kind produced by the *British National Bibliography.* Monthly issues cumulate annually.

Sample entry:

```
320 - Political science
   Francesi, Wolfgang
      Crowds of power [by] Wolfgang Francesi.-Melbourne:
      Imaginary Books, 2049. - 400p. ill.; 25 cm.
      Index.
      ISBN 0 998989 01 X : $4.50 Aust.
      1. Political science. II. Title
```

(53)   Australian Books in Print. 1956—

This commercial publication is now an annual list of "all available Australian titles," but title and frequency of publication have varied through the years. An Australian book is defined as: a book published in Australia; a book by an Australian author published abroad; a book about Australia. Books are listed under author, title, and subject.

FRENCH BIBLIOGRAPHY

This discussion of French bibliography has been limited to a small group of titles. Three general works (two catalogs of the Bibliothèque Nationale; Brunet's *Manuel*); two period bibliographies (Quérard's titles, covering 1700–1849, and Lorenz, 1840–1925), and two former current bibliographies, now merged (*Biblio* and *Bibliographie de la France*), have been included. For our purposes of a general introduction to French bibliography, however, many titles have been excluded. Those interested are directed to the latest issue of *Guide to Reference Books*.

(54)   Paris. Bibliothèque Nationale. Dépt. des imprimés. Catalogue général des livres imprimés de la Bibliothèque Nationale: Auteurs. 1897–

As is the case in Great Britain and the United States, the catalog of the depository library of France is a major bibliography, not only of French works, but of books published abroad. It is not as comprehensive as either of the other two as regards type of materials covered, nor has the catalog ever been truly completed. Publication began in 1897 and the end of the alphabet was not reached until 1981, with volume 231. The early volumes are, by now, considerably out of date; and even the final volumes in the alphabet contain no titles published after 1960. A supplement for the years 1960–1969, in 23 volumes, was issued between 1972 and 1976. This catalog consists of entries for *personal authors only*. There are no entries for corporate bodies, for anonymous titles, documents, serials, or society publications. There are no added entries for secondary persons or bodies which might be thought to be the author.

This situation obtains because, in the 1894 report of the Commission des Bibliothèques Nationales et Municipales (which had been charged with the task of examining the state of the catalogs of printed books of the Bibliothèque Nationale), it was suggested that a series of catalogs be prepared: (1) a list of personal authors; (2) a second list of anonymous works and general titles issued by corporate bodies; (3) a third list, which would treat of certain special categories of publications—budgets, reports, etc.—which would be primarily official publications of corporate bodies.

This full set of catalogs is far from realization. For a work whose author is known, however, and which happens to have been published before the date of publication of the volume into which it fits alphabetically, the catalog is very satisfactory, being characterized by very careful and accurate work. The fact that it is not complete, and that the early parts are so far out of date, requires a greater reliance on complementary works than is the case in the United States.

Sample Entry:

FRANCESI (Wolfgang).—*Foules de pouvoir.* Discours prononcé dans l'église métropolitaine de Nôtre Dame de Paris, le 13 juillet 1794, jour de la réunion annuelle des citoyens qui furent électeurs en 1789, en commémoration de la prise de la Bastille et de la conquête de la liberté, par W. L. Francesi . . . —*Paris, Mame et fils,* 1794. In-18, 143 p., pl. et fig.   8y².51520

(55)   Paris. Bibliothèque Nationale. Dépt. des imprimés. Catalogue général des livres

imprimés: auteurs, collectivités-auteurs,
anonymes. 1960/69- Paris, 1965–

Scope: For French works, includes all titles listed in *Bibliographie
de la France* during the period, as well as any other titles cataloged by the Bibliothèque Nationale, whether or not the book
was published during the 1960/69 period. (This would apply to
books acquired by purchase or gift, rather than by legal deposit.)
It includes not only those items listed in the *Bibliographie de la
France*'s general section, but also those listed in the parts devoted to these, government publications, and auction catalogs.
Foreign titles acquired by the Library would also be listed, regardless of date of publication. Periodicals are excluded, as there
is a separate catalog of periodicals.

Arrangement: For the first time, corporate authors and anonymous works are included, which is a most happy enlargement
of coverage. In addition to a wider array of main entries, the
catalog includes secondary entries, where necessary, for joint
authors, editors, writers of prefaces, translators, etc. Many title
entries are also made for publications of corporate bodies.

Cross-references are supplied to aid in the identification of an
author, especially where it is a corporate body which has a complicated name, or which has changed its name.

All these are presented in a single alphabetical list. Separate
alphabets will be published for (1) Cyrillic; (2) Greek; and (3)
Hebrew.

Note the many different formats for individual titles. What
does this tell you about the method of publication employed?
Sample Entry:

> FRANCESI (Wolfgang)—Foules du pouvoir, par Wolfgang Fran-
> cesi. . . —Rambouillet, l'auteur, 149 rue Madame de-Maintenon
> (Paris, impr. J. Grou), 1984.—In 4° (27 cm), non paginé, fig.,
> couv. ill., multigraphié. 18,50 NF   4°R.9736 (1)

(56) Brunet, Jacques. Manuel du librarie et de l'amateur de livres. Paris, Didot, 1860–80. 9 vols.

Brunet's work is actually a universal bibliography of rare, important, or noteworthy books, but it is especially strong for French

publications before the 19th century. His work has been highly esteemed as a prodigy of patience, exactness, erudition, and a monument of bibliography. The first five volumes are arranged alphabetically by author and anonymous title, while the sixth consists of a subject index, arranged according to Brunet's own bibliographical classification. The seventh and eighth volumes consist of supplementary lists and a subject index, while the ninth volume is actually not part of Brunet's list of titles, but Deschamps' dictionary of European cities and towns with their classical names, and, conversely, a list of classical place names with the modern European equivalent. The bibliography is selective. It serves, nevertheless, as an important supplement to the Bibliothèque Nationale's catalog. Brunet gives full bibliographical data, including author, title, place, publisher, date, size, and number of volumes. Notes which are often extensive give the record of editions and descriptions of important items (see the entry under the first Shakespeare folio).

Sample Entry:

FRANCESI (Wolfgang). *Foules de pouvoir,* en francoys, contenant quatre dialogues, fort antingues, joyeux et facetieux. *Lugduni, apud Anisonios,* 1677. 4 part. en 1 vol. pet. in-12. [3924]
Ces dialogues sont composés à la manière de Lucien. C'est un ouvrage allégorique assez piquant. Malheureusement l'autorité crut apercevoir, dans les allégories, des impiétés et des hérésies condamnables, et le livre fut déféré au parlement de Paris, qui en ordonna la suppression, et fit mettre en prison le libraire Anison. L'édition originale a été supprimée avec tant de soin, qu'on n'en connaît, avec certitude, qu'un seul exemplaire vend 350 fr. Gaignol, et 1200 fr. La Chappelle, et qui est maintenant dans la bibliothèque de la ville de Versailles. Pourtant, le catalogue de feu M**** (des Plances), *Avignon,* 1778, in-8., p. 15, en annonce un autre, rel. en. *v.f.t.d. bords et cordures,* avec la fameuse vignette de la Pauvreté; mais cette annonce parait s'appliquer à l'édition d'Amsterdam, 1732, dans laquelle on a réproduit le titre de 1677. Très-rares.

(57) Quérard, Joseph Marie. La France littéraire, ou Dictionaire bibliographique des savants, historiens, et gens de lettres de la France, aisi que des littérateurs étrangers qui ont écrit en français plus particulièrement pendant les XVIIIe et XIXe siècles. Ouvrage dans lequel on a inséré, afin d'en former une Bibliographie nationale complète, l'indication 1° des réimpressions des ouvrages français de tous les ages; 2° des

> diverses traductions en notre langue de tous
> les auteurs étrangers, anciens et modernes; 3°
> celle des réimpressions faites en France des
> ouvrages originaux de ces mêmes auteurs
> étrangers, pendant cette époque. Paris,
> Didot, 1827–64. 12 vols.

This work consists of an author list, giving brief biographical notes concerning the authors, with the usual bibliographical data for the titles, plus bibliographical and historical notes. In addition, the last two volumes (besides giving additions and corrections) are a list of the pseudonymous and anonymous works of authors, under real name. The period covered runs from 1700 to 1826. Emphasis is on works in the field of literature, and so it is not actually a complete national bibliography.

Sample Entry:

> FRANCESI, (Wolfgang) jurisconsulte, né à Dunkerque en 1741, mort à Paris, le 7 avril 1817.
> —*Foules de pouvoir.* Paris, Laurens aîné, 18, 7, in-8.
>
> Édition la plus précieuse pour les gens de lettres, en ce que c'est la dernière revue par l'auteur, qui lui-même la nommait son édition favorite: on ne la trouve plus que par hassard. Il a éte tiré quelques exemplaires de cette édition sur papier fin de Holland, qui sont très-récherchés des amateurs (20,000 a 30,000 fr.), ainsi que quelques-uns sur papier fort.
>
> Après la publication de cette édition, l'éditeur s'étant aperçu que plusieurs fautes s'étaient glissées dans le commencement du texte, se décida à faire réimprimer les sept feuilles A–G, dans lesquelles il fit des corrections et des augmentations qui nécessitèrent un changement dans l'ordre de la pagination. La table des pièces et celles des matières ne correspondent plus avec les pages changées. Ces exemplaires son très précieux.

(58)   Quérard, Joseph Marie. La littérature française contemporaine, 1827–49. Le tout accompagné de notes biographiques et littéraires. Paris, 1842–57. 6 vols.

This work continues his earlier title and is arranged on the same plan. Together the two titles cover 149 years, giving quite a range chronologically.

Sample Entry:

> FRANCESI (Wolfgang), écrivain critique, conservateur de la Bibliothèque Mazarine, inspecteur de d'Académie de Paris, membre de l'Académie française.

—*Foules de pouvoir,* discours prononcés dans la séance publique tenue par l'Académie française, pour le réception de M. de Francesi, le 17 avril 1827. *Paris, de l'impr. de F. Didot,* 1827, in-4 de 36 p.—Autre édit. *Paris, de l'impr. de Béthune,* 1827, br. in-8.

M. Francesi a fourni au Journal des débats un grand nombre d'articles de critique, signés A. Il avait quitté l'Académie par suite de tracasseries qu'on lui avait suscitées. Ses oeuvres sont pleines de frivoles argumentations, d'experience inexacts. Ses principales saillies sont puisées dans les lettres de Madame de Sévigné.

(59) Catalogue général de la librairie française. Paris, Lorenz, 1840–1925. 34 vols.

This work, usually cited as Lorenz, is the major bibliographical tool of the 19th century, continuing the work of Quérard. It is hoped that supplementary volumes will be issued to bring the coverage to 1933, the year in which *Biblio* began publication. Since Lorenz was intended to be a practical, commercial tool, literary notes were omitted. The list is primarily alphabetical by author, with catch-word subject indexes. An important feature of the work is its linking together of various works by an author through cross references from later to earlier volumes.

Sample Entry:

FRANCESI (Wolfgang), professeur á l'Université du Michigan (États-Unis). (Voy. Tome xv, page 897).
—*Foules de pouvoir.* in-8. 1807. H. Welter. 25fr. la 1re édition a paru en 1897.

From the Index:
Politique; Brochures politiques.
Foules de pouvoir, par Wolfgang Francesi. In-8. 1897.

(60) Bibliographie de la France. Paris, 1811 to 1970.

This current weekly bibliography (whose retrospective volumes, going back to 1811, form a substantial bibliography, the usefulness of which is diminished by the lack of cumulations) is based on the official copyright list of the Bibliothèque Nationale and reflects the careful cataloging of that institution. Unfortunately, its format presents some problems. The publication consists of three parts: (1) "Bibliographie officielle," which records the books, pamphlets, and documents received for copyright, and which is supplemented by separate parts, issued at irregular intervals. These extra parts include the following sections: A—Periodicals; B—Engravings, prints, and photographs; C—Music; D—Theses; E—Atlases, maps, and plans; F—Government publications. (2) "Chronique," consisting of notes and special features for the book trade. (3) "Annonces," publishers' announcements of new books, which are indexed cumulatively into *Livres de la semaine, Livres du mois, Livres du trimestre, Livres du semestre,* and *Livres de l'année.*

Since the titles are not listed until they have been cataloged, entries are often delayed for months after publication. Furthermore, the list does not include any works which have not been deposited for copyright.

Sample Entries:

(A)   AUTEURS
Francesi (W.) 2084

(B)   3. SCIENCES SOCIALES
  2084. FRANCESI (Wolfgang).
  —*Foules de pouvoir,* par Wolfgang Francesi.—Paris, Les belles lettres (Besançon, Neo-typo), In-8° (24 cm), 16p., carte. [D.L. 12934-62]
  [8° Z.34266 (37)
  (Annales litteraires de l'Université de Besançon. 37)

Sample Entries from Some of the Supplements

(A) From "Périodiques"
  N. SCIENCES JURIDIQUES, POLITIQUES,
    ÉCONOMIQUES ET SOCIALES
  N2. POLITIQUE
    100. *Foules de pouvoir.* Mensuel. Dir. Wolfgang Francesi.
  N° 1, décembre 1960.—Guin, rue Lavoisier (impr. d'Auger). 45×32 cm. Le n° 0, 15 NF [D.L. 20-2-61]—N2b.

                                  [Fol. Jo. 11708
(B) From the index to "Periodiques"
  Foules de pouvoir *100*
(C) From "Gravures, Estampes, et Photographies"

I. AUTEURS

   A. GRAVURES ET LITHOGRAPHIES
1. FRANCESI (Wolfgang).
—*Foules de pouvoir,* lithogr. en coul., vers. 1961. [AA3]
   B. PHOTOGRAPHIES
285. FRANCESI (Wolfgang)
  —100 phot.   [Oeuvre;—N.;—O.

(D) From the classified arrangement of "Gravures, Estampes," "etc."

II. CLASSEMENT PAR SUJETS

E. COSTUMES ET MOEURS
510. *Foules de pouvoir,* album d'echantillons de tissus.—Paris, Société
d'éditions de mode, 1962 et suiv. In-4°, f.g.—
N°1, mars 1962.—Printemps 1962—Été 1963.

[Th. 231, in-4°

(E) From the section "Musique"

MUSIQUE
1. MUSIQUE INSTRUMENTALE
1. Francesi, (Wolfgang).
—*Foules de pouvoir.* [pour piano]. Nouvelle édition révue par H. Vaillant.—
Nice, S. Delgieu (1961). In-4°, 12p.

[D.F.413]   B.N. [Vmg. 5965 (21)
                                                              Cons. [G. 9646 (21)

(F) From the section "Thèses"

Théses 1961
VI.—LETTRES
Paris
4572. FRANCESI (Wolfgang).
—*Foules de pouvoir,* Recherches sur un région moins developpée, vers
1854-vers 1871. Paris, Impr. nat., 1961.—24 cm, 591p., fig., cartes.   [8° Lk,
1897
Thèse. Lettres. Paris. 1958

(61) Biblio; catalogue des ouvrages parus en langue française dans le monde entier. Paris, Hachette, 1933 to 1970.

The monthly *Biblio,* a world record of French language publications arranged in dictionary catalog style, lists titles sooner than
the *Bibliographie de la France. Biblio* uses the "Annonces" and
"Bibliographie officielle" of the *Bibliographie de la France* as a
base, but adds works published abroad and those which are
outside the copyright deposit. It is not as complete as *Bibliographie de la France* for non-book materials, but its convenience
of use leads many librarians to try it first for a desired item. The
annual volume cumulates the monthly list—with additions—in
the same dictionary arrangement,

Sample Entries:

Foules de pouvoir (Col. Histoire de la vie politique, 185)
FRANCESI, W. 58f. Gallimard

FRANCESI, Wolfgang
Foules de pouvoir (Coll. Histoire de la vie politique, 185).
17, 5 × 11. cxxxi, 195p. Rel.: 58fr. ['66] Gallimard.
Réprod. de l'éd. orig., Bruxelles, Impr. Hayez, 1884.

POLITIQUE
FRANCESI, W.
Gallimard

(62) Bibliographie de la France/Biblio. 1971–

The two titles just dispatched have now merged into a sort of Siamese twin affair. The new publication shares the characteristics of both. The new serial consists of the following parts:
1. A weekly publication, which continues the former weekly part of *Bibliographie de la France*. It is arranged by decimal classification. The titles are those received by the legal deposit section of the national library, and the cataloging represents BN cataloging. This first section continues the irregular addition of supplements for other materials. The following parts are being published: A. Publications en série; B. Gravures, estampes et photographies; C. Oeuvres musicales; D. Thèses; E. Atlas, Cartes et plans; F. Publications officielles; G. Catalogues de ventes publiques.

This first weekly part (of the books) is indexed in two sections—an index of authors (including corporate authors), and an index of "anonymes." The weekly publication consists, in addition to this *Première partie (Bibliographie officielle)*, of the *Chronique*, which continues as heretofore to consist of publishing news, historical articles ("Colette in the National Library"), copyright information, obituaries, lists of winners of literary prizes, etc.—a sort of "intersticed" *Publishers Weekly*); and, as a third part, the "Annonces" which are advertising pages by publishers.

2. The second part of this publication consists of the monthly cumulation, *Les livres du Mois. Bibliographie de la France/Biblio*. It is arranged as the weekly is, so one needs to add no more details to one's memories.

3. The third part is a new period bibliography, which used to be an index. It is now *Livres du Trimestre—Biblio*. It changes from the classified arrangement of *Bibliographie de la France* to the dictionary form of the old *Biblio*—by author, title, and subject.

4. The quarterly issues cumulate into *Les livres de l'année—Biblio*, which has the subtitle: "Bibliographie générale des ouvrages parus en langue française." To the works cataloged by the BN and registered for copyright, the editors of the annual add (during the course of the quarterly publications) material from "diverses sources," as, for example, titles from foreign bibliographies. They try to establish for each of these non-BN works entries which will follow international rules of cataloging.

(63)   In-Print Lists

Two works now report French books in print—*Répertoire des livres de langue française disponibles* and *La Catalogue de l'edition française (French Books in Print)*. Both attempt to list books published worldwide in the French language.

GERMAN BIBLIOGRAPHY

German bibliography can be divided into three periods: 19th century and earlier; 20th century before World War II; and post World War II, with its division of Germany into two nations. The 19th century and earlier is well covered by three works (the earliest bibliographies are not being considered in this general discussion): (1) Heinsius' *Allgemeines Bücher-Lexikon* (1700–1892); (2) Kayser's *Vollständiges Bücher-Lexikon* (1750–1910), and (3) the Hinrichs firm's series, including weekly (1842–1915), quarterly (1846–1914), half-yearly (1798–1915), and polyennial issues (1851–1912).

The 20th century period before World War II saw the assumption of the Hinrichs' series by the Börsenverein, the German book trade organization, and the supplanting of Heinsius and Kayser by the same publications. The weekly index, half-yearly, and five-year catalogs were continued, while the quarterly catalog was discontinued.

The second World War saw Germany divided into East and West Germany, each of which has attempted to publish bibliographies covering the total German output. In the German Democratic Republic, the Deutsche Bücherei at Leipzig and in the German Federal Republic, the Deutsche Bibliothek at Frankfurt-am-Main have continued the publication of the Börsenverein's bibliographies.

(64) Heinsius, Wilhelm. Allgemeines Bücher-Lexicon, 1700–1892. Leipzig, 1912–04. 19 vols.

The first edition of Heinsius' work appeared at the end of the 18th century in four volumes (1793–98). It was based on publishers' and dealers' catalogs. The second edition (1812–13) revised and enlarged the first, in an attempt to make it more comprehensive and accurate. His fundamental principle of arrangement was to list alphabetically under author, when the author was known. His only exception was the listing of novels and plays in two separate sections under the chief word of the title even when author was known (although for the very famous authors, he made an exception to this exception and listed their works under their name in the author alphabet). When the author of a work—other than a play or novel—was not known, it was listed under the chief word of the title. He omitted engravings, maps, music, single sermons, dissertations, and ephemeral materials costing less than two groschen (unless they were by famous authors or important for other reasons). With the eighth volume (1823–34), the separate sections for plays and novels were discontinued. The period of coverage of the various volumes runs from four to seven years (excluding the basic four volumes, which covered the years 1700–1810). The long period of coverage—192 years—makes this a very extensive list, in spite of inaccuracies (of which Heinsius and his successors were aware. Heinsius complained bitterly of the inaccuracy of the publishers' catalogs themselves, on which he had to base his work, as well as of the cavalier attitude of some publishers toward the errors in their own catalogs).

Sample Entry:

Francesi, W. L., *Mengen der Kraft;* sinnreicher Aussprüche aus d. Geschichte d. ält. u. neuern Zeit; ein Lesebuch f. Grosse und Kleine. 8°. Magdeburg, Lauban, 725 —10

(65) Kayser, Christian Gottlob. Vollständiges Bücher-Lexikon, 1750–1910. Leipzig, 1834–1911. 36 vols.

Kayser runs roughly parallel to Heinsius for much of his period, with coverage beginning 50 years later and continuing 18 years longer. His work thus gives another long run of 160 years. Like Heinsius' work, this is primarily alphabetical by author, giving author, title, publisher, place, date, volumes, paging, series, and prices. Certain categories of works—handbooks, dictionaries, etc.—are gathered together under the category, rather than under the name of the compiler. Eleven volumes of subject indexes were also published. Kayser is generally conceded to furnish greater detail with more regularity than Heinsius or Hinrichs and is often found in order departments which have relegated those two sets to the stacks.
Sample Entries:

(A) Francesi, Wolfgang, *Mengen der Kraft.* (iv, 395S.) gr. 18. Wien, 905. F. Vahlen.
(B) Francesi, Wolfgang. *Mengen der Kraft* (XV, 494S.), gr. 8. Berlin 855. H. Berthold.

(66) The Hinrichs'/Börsenverein series.

(1) *Hinrichs' Halbjahrs-Katalog* (1798–1915). The half-yearly catalogs consist of an alphabetical author list with subject indexes (catch-word subjects). In the period before World War II (1915–1944) when the Börsenverein took over publication, the title was changed to *Halbjahrsverzeichnis der Neuerscheinungen des deutschen Buchhandels.* The half-yearly catalog has been continued in the post World War II period by the West German *Halbjahrsverzeichnis.*

(2) *Wöchentlichis Verzeichnis* (1842–1915). In 1842, Hinrichs added this weekly index as a more current record of German publications. The weekly list was continued by the Börsenverein and by both East and West German bibliographies after World War II.

(3) *Vierteljahr-Katalog* (1846–1914). The chronological coverage was filled out further with the appearance of this quarterly catalog in 1846. It was discontinued when the Börsenverein assumed publication of the Hinrichs' series and has not been resumed subsequently.

(4) *Fünfjahrs-Katalog* (1851–1912). The five-year cumulations of the Halbjahrs-Katalog were continued by the Börsenverein as *Deutsches Bücherverzeichnis* (1911–40), and are represented in the East German series as *Deutsches Bücherverzeichnis* and in the West German series as *Deutsche Bibliographie 1945–50*, etc.

Sample Entry:

(A) From the "Titelverzeichnis."
   Francesi, Wolfgang: *Die Mengen der Kraft.* 5.Aufl. (111)
      8° Lpzg, G. Messeburger, '11.   1.50d
(B) From the "Sachregister."
   Kraft s.a. Kräfte.
   Mengen der Kraft: Francesi

(67) Gesamtverzeichnis des deutschsprachigen Schrifttums (GV): 1911–1965. **1976– (In progress)**

This retrospective bibliography of German-language publications is a cumulation and integration of main entries from sixteen previously-published bibliographies covering, collectively, the time period indicated in the title. Plans call for approximately two million German titles (including German, Swiss, and Austrian publications) to be abstracted and cited as they are found in the existing bibliographies. Author and title entries will be interfiled into a single alphabet, but entries will not be re-set. The publisher has projected a set of 150 volumes, with approximately 500 pages in each volume.

CURRENT GERMAN BIBLIOGRAPHY

West Germany (German Federal Republic)

The Deutsche Bibliothek in Frankfurt-am-Main prepares the *Deutsche Bibliographie* for publication. It attempts to list all books published in Germany and all books in the German language published abroad. It is issued in the following sequence:

(1) *Reihe A.* A weekly classified list with author and catchword subject indexes. Includes materials sold through the regular book trade. Indexes cumulate monthly and quarterly.

(2) *Reihe B.* A semimonthly list of materials outside the book trade. Index cumulates annually.

(3) *Reihe C.* A quarterly listing of maps. Index cumulates annually.

(4) *Halbjahres-Verzeichnis.* Semi-annual. Cumulates *Reihe A* and selected titles from *Reihe B.*

(5) *Deutsche Bibliographie; Fünfjahres-Verzeichnis. Bücher und Karten.* Polyennial. Cumulates *Reihe A,* selected titles of *Reihe B,* and *Reihe C.*

East Germany (German Democratic Republic)

The Deutsche Bücherei in Leipzig prepares the *Deutsche Nationalbibliographie,* which attempts to include all books published in Germany and all books in the German language published abroad. It is issued in the following sequence:

(a) Weekly. *Reihe A; Neuerscheinungen des Buchhandels,* which lists books published in the regular book trade. Classified, with author and catchword indexes.

(b) Bi-weekly. *Reihe B; Neuerscheinungen ausserhalb des Buchhandels.* Includes materials published outside the regular book trade, such as dissertations and society publications. Classified, with author and catchword indexes.

(c) Quarterly. Separate indexes (*Vierteljahrs-register*) to Reihen A and B.

(d) Annually. *Jahresverzeichnis des deutschen Schrifttums.* Cumulates Reihe A and B in two sections: (1) "Titelverzeichnis," listing works by author or title; (2) "Stich-und Schlagwortregister," listing works under catchword and subject.

(e) Polyennially. *Deutsches Bücherverzeichnis; Verzeichnis der in Deutschland, Österreich, der Schweiz, und im übrigen Ausland herausgegeben deutschsprachigen Verlagsschriften sowie der wichtigsten Veröffentlichungen ausserhalf des Buchhandles.* Cumulates the *Jahresverzeichnis,* listing works under author, anonymous title, and subject (in two sections).

(68)   In-Print Lists

A German in-print list, *Verzeichnis Lieferbarer Bücher* (1971/72-   ), covers West German, Austrian, and Swiss publications. It is also referred to as *German Books in Print.* It is sponsored and produced by the Börsenverein der Deutschen Buchhändler, the organization of booksellers and publishers.

Bibliography

Besterman, Theodore, *A World Bibliography of Bibliographies.* . . . 4th ed., rev. and enl. Lausanne, Societas Bibliographica, 1965–66. 5v.

———. ———. *1964–1974* (comp. by Alice Toomey). Roman, 1977, 2v.

Bibliography of Latin American Bibliographies. (Gropp, Arthur E. 1968; monographs only through 1964) (Gropp, Arthur E. . . . *Published in Periodicals.* 1976; through 1965) (Gropp, Arthur E. 1971; monographs only through 1969) (Cordeiro, Daniel Raposo. . . . *Social Sciences & Humanities.* 1979; monographs, 1969–1974, periodical literature, 1966–1974) (Piedracueva, Haydée. . . . *1975–1979: Social Sciences and Humanities.* 1982; both monographs and periodical literature). All published by Scarecrow Press, Inc.

British Library. *British Library News.* 1976–   .

Canberra, Australia. National Library. *Annual Report.*

Downs, Robert B. and Frances B. Jenkins. *Bibliography; Current State and Future Trends.* Urbana, University of Illinois Press, 1967. 611p.

Lockhead, Douglas. *Bibliography of Canadian Bibliography.* 2d ed. Toronto, University of Toronto Press and Bibliographical Society of Canada, 1972. 312p.

McGeachy, John A., III. "The *Monthly Catalog*'s First Response to Its 1947 Congressional Charge." *Library Resources and Technical Services,* 20: 53–64, Winter 1976.

Malclès, Louise-Noëlle. *Manuel de bibliographie.* 2.éd. entièrement refondue et mise à jour. Paris, Presses Universitaires de France, 1969. 366p.

National Conference on the State of Canadian Bibliography. Vancouver, B.C., May 22–24, 1977. *Proceedings.* Edited by Anne B. Piternick. Ottawa, National Library of Canada, 1977. 514p.

Ottawa. National Library of Canada. *Annual Report of the National Librarian of Canada.* 1953–   .

Ottawa. National Library of Canada. *National Library News.*

Sheehy, Eugene P. *Guide to Reference Books.* 9th ed. Chicago, American Library Association, 1976. 1015p. Supplements, 1980, 1982.

Totok, Wilhelm and others. *Handbuch der bibliographischen Nachschlagewerke.* 4.,erw., völlig neubearb. Aufl. Frankfurt a.M., Klostermann, 1972. 367p.

U.S. Library of Congress. *Library of Congress Information Bulletin.*

Walford, A. J. *Guide to Reference Material.* 4th ed. London, Library Association, 1980–84. 3v.

Wees, Ian. "The National Library of Canada: The First Quarter-Century." *Canadian Library Journal,* 35:153–163, June 1978.

CHAPTER 12

ACQUISITIONS

Introduction

Up to this point emphasis has been placed upon the selection of materials and upon the problems involved in choosing the right materials for a given collection. A second area to be considered in the building of a library collection concerns the acquiring of the materials selected for purchase. This brings a whole new set of problems: finding out whether the materials are available, the best methods of purchasing, and the kinds of records necessary for controlling the process.

Organization of Acquisitions

Although some libraries have acquisition functions scattered through two or more departments, the typical acquisition functions include bibliographic verification of all order requests (which may also include responsibility for choosing the tools— national and trade bibliographies, publishers' and dealers' catalogs, using OCLC, etc.—used in such verification); selecting the dealers to be used and preparing and forwarding orders to those dealers; maintaining complete, accurate, and accessible files of materials on order or in process; updating and reviewing those files so as to claim or cancel orders which do not arrive on schedule; unpacking and sorting of orders as they are received, along with checking and approving of invoices; maintaining (or at least cooperating with the institution's business office in maintaining) records of payment and encumbrance of funds; and forwarding all newly-arrived materials, possibly with ownership marks already affixed, to the cataloging department.

No attempt will be made here to describe the acquisition system of any particular library. Instead, the various kinds of information needed to carry on acquisition work will be pointed out. Even the smallest library must exercise business-like procedures in keeping essential order records, and the larger the library, the more complicated those records will be. Nevertheless, certain records are common to all types of libraries.

It is generally agreed that the work in any order department is largely clerical, although professional librarians are needed as well. Since a large part of the staff is non-professional, manuals of procedure will expedite the training of personnel in an area where there is considerable turnover. A simplified manual is important even in the smallest library since the librarian may leave, be taken ill, or otherwise be removed from the process and a substitute should have the information at hand to take over the task. Certain characteristics should pertain to all staff members whether professional or clerical: accuracy, orderliness, resourcefulness, combined with speed, are among the essential requisites.

Since material is acquired both by purchase and by gift and exchange, these activities may be divided by method and handled separately. Gifts and exchanges are frequently combined. Another arrangement is by type of material, with separate sections for books, for serials, for documents, for microforms, for nonprint, etc. No matter how the division of work is arranged, it is well to remember that only simple and essential records should be kept.

Order Routines

Sources of materials to be ordered are various and differ from one type of library to another. Suggestions come in from the staff and readers, in addition to the titles approved during the process of selection. Replacements recommended by staff and departments compose another source. There is usually a want or consideration file (more elegantly referred to as the desiderata file) in the order department. In college, university, and school libraries, the faculty recommendations for purchase are an important source of order requests. Once an order request has reached the order department, whatever its source, the problem is to verify the bibliographic information and to complete it if it is deficient in necessary information. This first necessary step comprises the searching of the title.

Searching is an activity in which both professionals and non-professionals participate and in which the qualifications of the detective play their part. A good knowledge of the details of bibliographic form, of the national and trade bibliographies, and—in the larger libraries, especially in college and university libraries—of foreign languages is essential. The searcher tries to verify the author's name (in good cataloging form), title, translator or editor (if any), publisher, edition, series (if any), number of volumes, date, list price, International Standard Book Number (ISBN), or International Standard Serial Number (ISSN) if a journal. This process is made simpler in libraries with access to OCLC or a similar cooperative computer network since, if any participating library already owns the title, the necessary information, plus a classification category, will be entered in the system. This information is entered on the order card.

Before looking at the numerous complications that can occur in the ordering process, particularly in very large libraries, let us take a walk through the more routine events of the order procedures. Current titles being ordered from standard library review periodicals will already have all of the pertinent order information in the bibliographic citation of the review. These can be set aside, requiring little or no additional verification by the librarian.

Requests from patrons may be less complete, particularly those that originated from watching a television talk show. A search of *Forthcoming Books* may produce the needed information, or a quick check of the listing in *Publishers Weekly* of the authors scheduled for television appearances may provide enough information to allow the librarian to find a complete citation. The major announcement issues of *Publishers Weekly* can also be very useful in this process.

One excellent reason for all libraries, most particularly small libraries, to be part of a cooperative system is that headquarters of such systems generally have computer access to a number of on-line services. For example, *Books in Print* is now available online and is updated daily as records are received from publishers. The local librarian has merely to ask the system headquarters staff for help. For retrospective titles, *Books in Print* is essential, but it must be noted that the print edition is out of date as soon as it is off the press. Titles go out of print much faster these days than in the past, so being able to access it online is desirable.

Complication in the Order Routines

Now let us take an order request through a large university system, since it will have the widest variety of records and practices and fragmentation of collections, as well as sources of orders. Let us assume that a request for a group of titles has arrived from a professor in the history department. Before proceeding with the searching process, it may be enlightening to play the novelist and imagine how she/he gathered these particular titles. Perhaps by reading professional journals, noting titles and putting them down on slips (some of these notices may be announcements for books to be published at some future date; ordering a book not yet in print can cause some confusion in the order search). Perhaps by reading the *New York Times*, the London *Times*, *Saturday Review*, etc. and again busily noting titles and putting them down on order slips. (A dozen colleagues will be reading the same sources at the same time and noting many of the same titles, none aware, however, that others are doing the same thing.) Perhaps by talking to various colleagues, sometimes at national meetings, who call attention to unfamiliar titles. The professor puts down the names of the authors and transcribes the titles, not always getting quite the correct information and not always with the knowledge that the titles are part of a series for which the library has a standing order. Finally the professor decides to send this collection of titles over to the library to be ordered. He/she submits them first for approval to the department head, who initials them as a matter of course. The department head does not keep a record of everything that each faculty member in the department orders, so some of these titles may have been ordered in the past two weeks by someone else in the department—or, for that matter, by several other people.

The batch of requests arrives at the order department and is handed over to a searcher. The first thing the searcher does is to determine whether these titles are already in the library, or whether they are on order but have not yet arrived. It is at this point that the searcher may slip into one of the pitfalls which await the unwary. The form of entry on the order slip may not be the form of entry under which the book is entered in the library's catalogs. The searcher may carefully search the official catalog (in those libraries which maintain that file), may then consult the outstanding order file to see if it is on order, and may finally check in an orders-received file (which records those titles received but not yet cataloged). Since she/he is searching under the wrong entry, no record of the book will be found. (Through the years revisions have occurred in the cataloging codes which determine how a work is entered in a library catalog. This may make the search particularly challenging in an old library with a large catalog.)

To obviate this chance of ordering a book which is already there, it may be thought advisable to verify the title and author first in one of the national or trade bibliographies, to determine that such a title actually exists, and to discover what the correct main entry actually is. On the other hand, the library may decide that the number of cases in which such ambiguities arise is not enough to justify verification of each title first. All titles would be searched in the library's records first, and then the residue, which had not been found, would be verified in the bibliographies. Some examples of actual order requests may illustrate the difficulties occasionally faced by a searcher in the effort to verify a title.

Some years ago, an order requested Churchill's *The Great Democracies*. This is actually volume four in his series on the history of the English-speaking peoples, which one university library had cataloged under the title of the set, hence no cards would be found for the individual titles. With Sir Winston there is perhaps no danger of failing to recognize the problem. But the monographic series, whose individual volumes are not analyzed by the library, offers a splendid opportunity for duplicating titles. The history professor, who has heard about a title at a national convention, might not realize that this was part of a large series (or, knowing it was part of a series might not understand the weird and wonderful world of cataloging rules that are not designed for easy patron access), and would order by author and title. The searcher would find no entry under author, if the library had elected not to analyze the series. He/she would therefore send the order through. When it arrived, consternation might be created when it was discovered that this series was on standing order, and the library now had two copies of a title, where one would be sufficient. In large libraries, which order thousands of these series, the amount of duplication can become expensive.

A simpler example was the request for *Chinese Pottery and Porcelain*, Edinburgh, H. M. Stationers Office, 1955. This order request was not incorrect, merely incomplete. The searcher finally discovered that the entry was not under title, but rather under a corporate body: Edinburgh. Royal Scottish Museum.

Another not infrequent error is to cite a book under its subtitle, which is often more informative than the main title. A request for Carl Anton Dauten's *Fundamentals of Financial Management* may turn out to be a request for his *Business Finance, the Fundamentals of Financial Management*. If Mr. Dauten were a very prolific author, the searcher might miss the title filed under B and assert that the library did not have it.

The following grab bag of actual order requests will furnish further illustrations of the problems which confront the helpless searcher.

As Requested	As Verified
National Education Association Education and the Self-Contained Classroom	Snyder, Edith Roach, ed. The Self-Contained Classroom
Sitashov, Iurii Mikhailovich	Shashkov, Iurii Mikhailovich
Jervis, T. B. Travels in Kashmir	Huegel, Carl Alexander Anselm Travels in Kashmir, with Notes by T. B. Jervis
Huckaby, Calvin	Huckabay, Calvin
D'Olanda, Francisco Dialoghi Michaelangioleschi	Hollanda, Francisco de I Dialoghi Michelangioleschi
Hyderabad State. The Freedom Struggle in Hyderabad	Hyderabad, India (State). Committee Appointed for the Compilation of a History of the Freedom Movement in Hyderabad. The Freedom Struggle in Hyderabad
Sirotkovic, Jakov Economic Planning Yugoslavia	Sirotkovic, Jakov Privredno planiranje u Jugoslaviji
Silvert, Kalman H. The Conflict Society; Reaction and Revolution in Latin America	Silvert, Kalman H. Reaction and Revolution in Latin America; the Conflict Society
Fet, Aff A. Polnoe sobranie stixotvorenij, biblioteka poeta osnovana M. Gor'kim sol'saja serija 2-Oe izdanie	Shenshin, Afanasii Afanas'evich Polnoe sobranie [etc.]
Khadduri, Majid Islamic Jurisprudence	al-Shafi'i, Muhammad ibn Idris Islamic Jurisprudence
Gadoffre, Gilbert Ronsard par lui-même.	Ronsard, Pierre de Ronsard par lui-même
Rosen, Joseph Reagent chemicals and standards	Rosin, Joseph Reagent chemicals and standards
Rothschild, Lionel Walter A Classification of Living Animals	Rothschild, Nathaniel Meyer Victor A Classification of Living Animals
Rubin, I. R. Jordi	Rubin, Theodore Isaac Jordi
Rousset, Camille Felix Michel L'Algerie, Paris, 1900–04.	Rousset, Camille Felix Michel Commencement d'une conquête: l'Algerie de 1830 à 1840. 2.êd. 1900

Corporate bodies contribute more than their share of misery to the unhappy searcher. A request for the American Institute of

Accountants' *Accounting Terminology Bulletin* caused considerable trouble because the person requesting the serial did not realize—or did not indicate, at least—that it was published by the Committee on Terminology of the Institute. It was found under "American Institute of Accountants. Committee on Terminology." In the case of a large institution with many, many subdivisions, all of which publish heavily, it may become extremely difficult to locate an item if the subdivision does not appear on the order card.

Sometimes a perfectly standard-looking order causes problems. A request for Clara Mae Taylor's *Foundations of Nutrition,* 5th ed., caused some perturbation because Ms. Taylor turned out to be a later editor of a work which had been begun by someone else. The correct entry turned out to be Rose, Mary Davies Swartz. That author was dead by the time of the 5th edition, but the edition stayed under her name.

The ultimate—and, it is to be hoped, the unusual—difficulty that can be caused the harried searcher was described by the order librarian of one of the state universities. She described the arrival of a perfectly innocent-looking order: author, title, publisher, place, date—all complete and unsuspicious. A search was made, but the title could not be verified. Even the publisher could not be located. The order was returned with a request for the source of the title. Promptly, it returned with a citation to a legislative record. The journal was consulted; the data were all there as recorded. The title had been quoted by a legislator. Another search failed to reveal any information about the mysterious work. A letter was dispatched to the legislator, who finally wrote an embarrassed reply, explaining that he had needed a quotation to back up an argument, and that he had made up the title. This kind of request would probably be classified by the searcher among the "ghoulies, ghosties, and things that go bump in the night," from which one can only hope for deliverance.

Of course, these examples do not represent the bulk of order requests, which move through the order department without undue turmoil. But the large university library, which orders a substantial amount of foreign, peculiar, and unusual materials, far from the ordinary trade channels, affords the enthusiastic searcher much material against which she/he can match wits. One such dedicated soul remarked that it was the problems such as these that added zest to the task. Indeed, the detective work is sometimes of a high order.

To recapitulate: the searcher will check the order slip against the catalog to see if the library already has the title; will check against the outstanding order file to see if it is on order but has not yet arrived, and will check against the orders-received file or in-process file which keeps track of an item's status once it leaves the orders-received file, but before it is cataloged. If the searcher does not find it in these sources, he/she will check the trade bibliographies to get full bibliographic and ordering information. It may be well to note that these various files do not all exist as separate files in every library—various permutations and combinations of them are found. The order will then be sent on to the functionary who will choose the dealer for the various items being ordered.

Choosing the Dealer

This is an important step, probably second only to the selection of the books themselves. Libraries have three primary sources for purchase of current books: publishers, bookstores, and wholesalers (also called jobbers). Librarians do, in fact, buy from all three sources. The factors which are considered in deciding where it is most advantageous to buy are several: 1) Which gives the largest discount? 2) Which furnishes the speediest service? 3) Which will adapt billing to local accounting requirements? 4) Which is most accurate in filling orders and most prompt in rectifying mistakes? These factors do not always reside in any one of the three sources, and in some cases speed may be more important than discount, accounting procedures may take precedence over all other considerations (but if they are so onerous as to limit choices, they should be re-examined and changed if not legally mandated), accuracy may be more important than speed or cost. As a result, a given library may, on occasion, order from all three sources.

The great difficulty in ordering from multiple sources comes from the fact that this procedure increases the paperwork considerably. Separate orders to ten different dealers mean ten separate letters, ten separate shipments, ten separate invoices, ten separate payments. Savings effected by shopping around and placing smaller orders at more favorable discounts may well be swallowed up by increased bookkeeping costs. Where speed in acquiring a title is the primary consideration (getting a reserve book for a college class which begins in five days, for example), nothing could be faster than walking across the street to the local bookstore and picking the book off the shelf. Here again, a more favorable discount may be sacrificed for the added service. The difficulty involved in placing all orders at a local bookstore (although this is done in some places because it is considered important to support local business) arises from the fact that bookstores with really large stocks of titles are few and far between. As the library moves out of the area of currently popular titles, its success in finding the less popular items in the stock of the ordinary bookstore diminishes. In all questions of discounts, however, the librarian ought to face one issue squarely: should price be the only consideration, or should other factors—speed of acquisition, extra services furnished by the vendor, etc.—be taken into account? The cheapest purchase may not always be the best bargain.

Wholesalers receive a sizeable percentage of library orders. The advantage of dealing with the wholesaler is clear: the librarian places one order, receives one package, pays one bill, has only one person to deal with on service problems. The services offered to libraries by wholesalers have steadily expanded: special catalogs and lists have been compiled; prebound books will be supplied; notification as to the status of a book is made quickly; the special billing requirements of each library are observed; automated and, in some cases, on-line procedures for transmitting orders are available; and, cataloging and processing of titles is often available, tailored to the individual library's special practices. Generally speaking, wholesalers have shown themselves willing to provide any service which could be organized on a mass-production basis.

The mass-production requirement emphasizes the basic nature of the wholesaler's business. Such a dealer buys multiple copies of large numbers of titles from many publishers and because of this is able to offer a better discount than the publisher can give the individual library ordering only one copy. The wholesaler can also offer a better discount on that one copy because of a special system for handling orders. This is essentially the wholesaler's specialty, as it is not the publisher's. This means that the wholesaler's savings in handling orders—which allow the offering of discounts—depend upon adherence to a routine, to sometimes resembling an assembly-line treatment of orders. If the potential advantages of a wholesale system are to operate, it is imperative that those doing business with the wholesaler follow the wholesaler's recommended procedures. It is also important that librarians do not impose on the good will of the wholesaler. An occasional single-copy order can be tolerated, but basically volume is the secret of efficiency, and the larger the order received, the better the system works.

Because improving the quality of the communication between librarians placing orders and wholesalers filling those orders is so important to the efficient operation of both groups, the Resources and Technical Services Division of the American Library Association encourages, through discussion groups and committees, meetings of librarians and bookdealers who are concerned with resolving mutual problems. One such joint committee has produced a set of "Guidelines for Handling Library Orders for In-Print Monographic Publications." These guidelines specify the form that library purchase-orders ought to take and the types of information that should be furnished about each item in order to identify it accurately. Suggestions for establishing claiming, cancellation, return, invoicing, and payment procedures are supplied. The guidelines also specify reasonable waiting periods for receipt of orders and include suggestions for improved reporting on the status of orders by the dealers.

The wholesalers discussed above are those whose major emphasis is providing hard cover titles (although most now handle paperbacks as well). It is important for librarians to recognize that the Educational Paperback Association members are organized to provide similar services to meet a library's paperback needs. For librarians located near such an EPA member, it is possible to go to the warehouse and select titles off the shelves; have them packaged as you wait, and take them with you. Billing will follow.

Wholesalers also exist for sheet music and phonodiscs. And subscription agencies exist for placement of serial publications. As noted earlier in the chapter on nonbook materials, audiovisual materials must be ordered only from the distributor with distribution rights to the items needed.

Approval Plans and Blanket Order Plans

The place of blanket orders and approval plans in the broad picture of collection planning and development was discussed in Chapter V, but it might be well to review some of the forms that such plans may take. When the library wishes to acquire the total output (or total output on certain subjects) of a publisher, a "publisher's standing order" may be arranged individually with each publisher involved. It is also possible to arrange through jobbers or wholesalers for the automatic shipment of new publications from specified publishers or in designated series. Wholesalers offer various kinds of standing order plans in which they will select and ship new publications of certain types. The type of plan sometimes referred to as a "jobber approval plan" usually involves selection and shipment (sometimes with advance notification) by the jobber of new publications which appear to fit some sort of collection description statement or subject selection profile supplied by the library. For some areas, or types of materials, the jobber may supply the library with "approval slips" from which the librarian makes the decision as to buy or not. Although the terms "blanket order," "blanket approval," and "gathering plan" are not used consistently, they usually refer to agreements between libraries and dealers which incorporate one or both of these features—some degree of responsibility for selection given to the dealer and some degree of rejection and return privileges allowed to the library. "Standing orders," on the other hand, usually mean a firm commitment to buy on the part of the library. Any librarian planning to start an acquisition arrangement designated by any of the above terms ought to ascertain at the beginning of any discussion the dealer's understanding of the terms involved.

As an acquisition or procurement method, blanket plans of various kinds have been praised for being fast enough to supply books before they go out of print or before users requested them and for saving staff time and record-keeping expense. On the opposite side of the argument are those who say that record-keeping becomes more difficult and that speed of acquisition is of no great consequence in a library with a sizable cataloging backlog. The fact that most blanket plans are set up to supply one copy of a title causes concern in libraries where several branch libraries may want the same title. There is also an inherent danger, recognized by a number of libraries when one prominent jobber went out of business in the early 1970s, in placing large blocks of orders through one dealer. Even if there is only a slight deterioration in service, the effect on the library can be very unsettling. Whether a library is able to make efficient use of blanket plans as an acquisition method might depend on the relationship between the library and the business office of the parent institution, as well on the quality of communication between library and dealer. Most of all, the efficiency of a blanket plan depends on the size of the library and the scope of its collecting. They make little sense for schools, small and medium sized public libraries, and special libraries.

The most vulnerable aspect of the operation of a blanket plan appears to be the line of communication between the library and the jobber. In an ideal situation, the library defines its collection carefully; the jobber observes the definition of scope scrupulously; the library returns the few irrelevant books that slip by the jobber; and the jobber quickly makes any necessary adjustments in the library's acquisition profile. In the real world, problems arise at any of these points, beginning with the library's inability to specify subjects and levels of desired materials in terms that have the same meaning for the jobber. To both parties the question of whether the jobber makes a narrow or broad interpretation of the profile is an important one. If the interpretation is broad, then the library either receives and accepts much marginal material, thereby wasting part of the budget and probably creating weeding problems for the future, or the library receives and returns the unwanted materials, creating unnecessary work for both library staff and jobber and negating some of the arguments advocating the economy of blanket plans as ordering systems. On the other hand, if the jobber interprets the profile narrowly, the process appears to be very efficient, with the library receiving mostly materials that are wanted and making few returns. The hidden problem with this interpretation is that the jobber may be missing other items the library's selectors would have chosen if they had known that they existed. Missing such items at the time when they are easily available could mean an expensive out-of-print search later.

The loosening of fiscal control which the initiation of blanket order or approval plans brings has been a concern of many librarians, though some have seen the unallocated budget usually required by blanket plans as being a good opportunity to remove control of the book budget from the faculty. In general, the budget allocation and fund accounting systems of a library must be adjusted when the library enters into extensive blanket order arrangements.

Foreign Acquisitions

In most libraries, apart from the smallest, some order requests will be for materials published in foreign countries. When choosing a dealer for foreign publications, the acquisition librarian must decide whether to deal with an importer (a dealer based in the U.S. who specializes in foreign materials) or an exporter (a foreign dealer who may specialize in the materials of a particular country or group of countries). Although importers vary in their range of services—some handle monographs and serials, both in-print and out-of-print; some specialize in limited geographical areas or types of materials; some concentrate on what they list in their catalogs—in general they offer more service and charge more than exporters. An exporter may have lower overhead costs and may not charge as many extra service fees as an importer, but language problems may inhibit communication with dealers in some countries, and there may be a serious time lag in exchanging communications. Which way a library decides to go with its orders will depend on the average volume and type of foreign purchasing done and the library staff available to originate and monitor orders. A small library with few foreign purchases may find it easiest to do business with an importer, but a large library or one with a large volume of foreign acquisitions may prefer to establish a continuing relationship with exporters. Blanket plans for foreign materials have been popular since the 1960s and continue to be used in libraries where domestic blanket plans have been curtailed.

Bidding

Libraries supported by public funds may be restricted in their choice of dealers by local, state, or federal regulations. Such libraries may be required to obtain library materials through a competitive bidding system. Bidding may be either formal, requiring advertising, sealed bids, public opening of the bids, etc., or informal, requiring only that bids be obtained somehow from three or more dealers. Sometimes bidding may be required for lists of specific titles, but more often bids are based on an estimated volume of purchases (sometimes divided into categories such as adult trade, juvenile, scientific-professional, etc.) to be made in a specified period of time. The general advantages of bidding as a method for awarding public contracts are well-known (lower costs, elimination of patronage), but the specific advantages or disadvantages of bidding as a method for acquiring library materials are hotly debated. It is doubtful that any librarian not required by law to obtain bids before choosing a dealer would voluntarily do so, but those librarians who do work in institutions with bidding regulations must learn the intricacies of the system in order to develop as efficient procedures as possible. They should also keep meticulous statistics on the quality of service received and, if possible, acquire statistics from a similar library operating without the bidding requirement. If bidding consistently means the library waits months instead of weeks for the arrival of orders, if an unacceptable number of orders are not filled at all, these statistics should be presented to the appropriate governing body. Both laws and regulations can be changed, and librarians who make no attempt to influence change deserve the headaches bidding brings them.

Preparing the Order

Systems of ordering will differ from library to library; some are strictly manual systems and others involve a high degree of automation. The manual procedure outlined here attempts to show the kinds of records and reports typically needed and is given as one example, not to be construed as the only possible method. It involves the use of multiple copy forms, sometimes called "fanfolds." They are 3 × 5 slips with inter-leaved carbons, or made of carbonless copy paper. With such forms, more than one copy can be made simultaneously; in a large system, the number of copies needed may be considerable. For the purpose of introducing certain order terms—and also to illustrate certain of the points which represent problems—we will take the reader through such a set of slips, with the warning that this particular form is not introduced as a model, but merely as an example.

The particular form we will follow involves the typing of ten slips in a fanfold. (Of course, only one typing is done on an electric typewriter or word processor, with the machine making nine additional copies simultaneously.) The slips consist of the following: 1) outstanding order file—on white; 2) fund slip— tan; 3) encumbrance release—green; 4) dealer purchase order— yellow; 5) dealer report slip—pink; 6) claim slip—orange; 7) official catalog—pink; 8) public catalog—pink; 9) labeling guide— white; 10) arrival notice—green. We hasten to remark that the various colors are means of quick identification and a help in sorting—we are by no means attempting to prescribe these particular colors for the individual type of slip! We suspect that a library might survive if its outstanding order file slip were yellow instead of white, its fund slip green instead of tan, etc. The only slip whose color ought not to be white is the one placed in the public catalog. Since white is the color of standard catalog cards, a colored slip alerts both staff and the public to the "on order" status of the item, particularly in libraries that place appropriate signs on the catalog to alert users to this fact.

The following disposition is made of the slips when the order has been typed: 1) the dealer purchase order and dealer report slips are shipped off to the dealer as the order. 2) The fund slip is filed in the fund record, as an indication of the amounts charged against the fund but still outstanding. 3) In many libraries the public catalog slip is filed in the catalog when the order is placed; in others, it is held until the book actually arrives but is not yet processed. 4) The outstanding order slip—and all remaining slips—are filed in the outstanding order file to await arrival of the book.

The front of all slips would be identical (except for the legend at the bottom of the slip naming it, and two additions to the encumbrance slip). Bibliographic information is given: author, title, publisher, place, date, series, volumes, and ISBN, and of these, the ISBN is the most important item since most large wholesalers now work from it. In addition, the following items are called for: order number; name of the fund on which the book is being purchased; name of the dealer; number of copies being ordered; name of the library in the system to which the book is going (systems with many branches develop appropriate codes for this information); name of the person recommending purchase; date ordered; catalog number and item number, if the book was ordered from an o.p. catalog; estimated price.

Let us follow the dealer purchase order and dealer report slips along their path. The front, as was remarked in the preceding paragraph, would contain the same information as all other slips. But the back of the dealer purchase order would contain instructions to the dealer (these would vary widely from library to library, of course). The following legends appear on the sample we are using:

Invoice: Bill in DUPLICATE, referring to order number. Bill items on same FUND on one invoice (Fund is directly under order number on reverse side of this form.)

Shipping: Send accompanying report slip inside front cover of book; show full order number on all packages. Address shipments to:

Order Department
X Library
Z City, State; Zip Code

Report: Report slip is enclosed for your convenience in reporting on orders that cannot be filled.

Series: If an item is part of a series and we have not so indicated, please report on pink slip before sending.

Billing instructions constitute an area in which dealers have to accustom themselves to great variation. Many libraries associated with state or city governments—or school boards—are bound by rigidly prescribed accounting rules which may demand notarized invoices, thirteen copies—the fourth of pink vellum, the sixth and eighth upside down, etc., etc. Sometimes dealers seem to prefer to ignore all instructions and proceed as they choose. No doubt excessively complicated systems may irk them considerably, particularly because they increase the cost of doing business with a particular library. It must be noted again that many of these "regulations" have no standing in law, and exist simply because "we have always done it that way." A good hard look at the process through the eyes of a new person can lead to simplification from which all parties involved can benefit.

The report slip is most important to the library, but the dealer may not find it very impressive, and books may return without the slip. Of course, they can be identified by searching the outstanding order file, but on occasion the main entry under which the book is ordered may be in error, and if no report slip comes back, it may take some time to find where the outstanding order slip was filed. Note especially the last instruction concerning series. This is an effort to avoid the duplication caused by ordering under author and title a book which is in a series the library gets on standing order. If the library has failed to discover that the book is part of a series, it needs to know—and woe betide the careless searcher!

The front of the report slip is identical with all others; the legends on the verso of the slip:

If Book is Not Available Return This Slip to:
                                   Order dept, X lib, etc.

_____Sold; order cancelled.

_____Not yet published   Order cancelled
_____Out of stock at publisher   —Will send

_____Out of print, order cancelled

_____Please confirm order:

    1. Author's correct name is:
    2. Series:

_____Other

Perhaps the terms are reasonably self-explanatory, but it may be well to run straight down the list. "Sold; order cancelled" is clear enough, and the order cancelled will cause the library to withdraw the outstanding order slip. "Not yet published"—the problem of people sending in orders for books which have only been announced for publication. (Large wholesalers whose operations are now computerized are able to enter the order for forthcoming materials and guarantee they will ship the title upon receipt of stock *in the order in which the orders are placed in the file*. Actually, advance orders by libraries for not yet published material can help the wholesaler make a judgment as to the potential demand for a title and increase the order to the publisher accordingly.) "Out of stock at publisher" is the real problem situation these days. Will the publisher reprint? If so, how soon? An on-going controversy between publishers and wholesalers is how the new printing will be allocated. Publishers have been known to give bookstores preference over wholesalers (they make a larger profit from bookstores) which means the wholesaler is forced to report a title "out of stock at publisher" while the librarian sees copies displayed en masse in a bookstore window. This puts the wholesaler between a rock and a hard place: to cancel or not to cancel? to hold? for how long? Librarians need to be understanding when confronted by this situation; it is beyond the wholesaler's control. "Out of print, order cancelled" is not only clear, and an increasing occurrence as publishers seek to decrease their warehousing costs, and to avoid the tax penalties imposed on inventory by the infamous *Thor* decision. The "Please confirm order," however, is more interesting. Something is not in accord between the library's searchers and the dealer's searchers. If the library has ordered it under a different name (corporate body instead of personal author, personal instead of corporate, or some person other than the real author), it wants to know, in the event that it already has the book under the form the dealer has discovered. And, as was remarked a moment ago, any large system which orders many series on standing order wants to be informed if its searching has not identified a given book as one in a series. Conscientious attention to the ISBN cuts down on many of the problems encountered before it came into existence.

To return, however, to the slips waiting in the library's files. The outstanding order file slip will not only furnish a record of the book's "outstanding" state, but will also serve to prevent undesired duplication of titles. The official and public catalog slips will be used to file into those catalogs when the book arrives, pending full cataloging. Holding the public catalog slip until this point is a symptom of a large backlog in the processing department since it makes little sense to file one week and withdraw the next; nor does it help alert the public that the title is actually known to the staff and on its way. The labeling guide will go to the labelers' desk along with the book to instruct them as to the call number to be put on the spine. (This step has been modified in many libraries where prepared labels are now acquired from the same vendor—OCLC, for example—which supplies catalog cards.) The arrival notice will be sent to the person who recommended the purchase of the book, to let her/him know it is now in the library. Many libraries might not prepare the catalog and labeling records at the point of writing up the order, but it does allow those forms to be prepared with one, original order typing.

The encumbrance release slip and the fund slip are part of the accounting system. The encumbrance release slip has two items added to its front: the date received and the cost of the item (which replaces the estimated cost originally charged against the fund). The estimated cost had appeared on the fund slip, originally filed under the fund name to show encumbrances. When the item is paid, it is the amount on the encumbrance slip which is used, and the fund slip is discarded.

The last slip in the batch is the claim slip, waiting in the outstanding order file against the day when it is discovered that a book which was ordered has not arrived. The verso of the claim slip contains the following legends:

We have not as yet received the title indicated on the reverse side of this slip. Please report by checking the appropriate box below. If the title has already been sent, please do not duplicate shipment.

☐ Shipped on
☐ Not yet published. Due   Will send.
☐ Out of print. Cancelling.
☐ Out of print. Searching
☐ Out of stock. Will send
    (Please give approximate date if possible.)
☐ Sold. Cancelling
☐ Other:

Multiple-copy order forms in various designs are available from commercial firms supplying libraries. The individual library, especially one with a large volume of acquisitions or peculiar record-keeping requirements, may find it necessary to devise its own forms to cover local procedures and files. Everyone dealing with libraries would welcome the standardization of forms in both content and size, but that millenium is not in the foreseeable future.

The acquisitions department, with its many business routines, is likely to be one of the first places in a library considered for automated operations. The whole system of ordering has been automated in some libraries; in others, only parts of the process have been so treated. Many libraries, of course, are finding it necessary to move away from extensive manually-maintained files of paper slips. If one thinks of the information that has been typed on order slips, one can quickly see that it could just as readily have been typed on a key-punch keyboard, producing a machine-readable record. It would also be relatively simple to assign a code number to each supplier of materials and then to store the address of each dealer in a machine-readable file. Punched cards for each order, coded by dealer, could then be fed into the computer, which would produce order requests by dealer and could simultaneously keep the accounts for each transaction by encumbering the separate funds coded into the cards and later debiting them for the actual amount spent. Periodically, the system would report exactly which items were on order and the status of each order; it could be programmed to write claim notices for items which had not arrived, report which items had been claimed and when, and keep all accounts current.

Automated acquisition systems, particularly locally developed ones, have been extensively reported in the literature, but because of improved equipment and programming techniques the details of the various systems change more quickly than the reports appear. Several of the larger wholesalers offer plans for automating library purchasing procedures, either through batch processing of orders in machine-readable form or through direct on-line communication with computers at the wholesaler's headquarters. These systems vary in the extent to which they require special equipment, are regularly reviewed and improved, and are fully documented. A librarian who is considering automating an acquisition procedure ought, in addition to reading the literature and talking to dealers with systems to sell, to contact librarians in similar libraries where automated systems are operating. Attendance at national library conferences is an excellent place to begin one's search since the exhibit area is filled with companies offering systems, there are programs offering insights, and there is the opportunity to meet librarians from many parts of the country.

Out-of-Print Titles

The ordering of library materials, particularly books, which are out-of-print presents a more complicated picture than the ordering of current trade publications. There are two general aspects to the problem of acquiring o.p. books. One involves the search by the library for a specific title which it wishes to acquire; the other involves searching the catalogs sent to the library by various o.p. dealers to see if anything is being offered which the library would like to buy.

To attempt to find a specific title in the o.p. market resembles the children's game of "Button, Button, Who's got the Button?" There are hundreds of o.p. dealers, and it is difficult to find which one has any given title at a particular moment. It is true that these dealers send copies of their catalogs to libraries, but the search through masses of the catalogs looking for a particular title can be tedious indeed. And it is also unfortunately true that the titles listed in a given catalog will soon be sold (at least the desirable titles will be), so that holding this year's catalog for next year's searching is not likely to produce satisfactory results. The library can take other steps to obtain the individual title. It can send the order to a dealer who specializes in that type of material, in the hope that it will be in stock or the dealer will be able to obtain it. There are also various searching services which will search for requested titles. Thirdly, there are publications in which libraries can advertise lists of titles wanted. Out-of-print dealers can then submit bids for those titles that they have in stock.

The second aspect of the o.p. business in libraries consists of checking dealers' catalogs for titles which the selector thinks might be desirable. The items checked are then searched in the library's catalogs to see if they are already in the collection. If they are not, they are then ordered from the dealer. This procedure has its own special problems. The arrangements of dealers' catalogs and the amount of bibliographic information which they give varies greatly. Occasionally the catalogs are not arranged in any order, but are assembled helter-skelter—all subjects intermingled, no alphabetizing by author. Sometimes dealers are not very precise in differentiating one edition from another, some are very brief in identifying the author—occasionally giving only an initial for the forename—or the title—which is sometimes shortened until one cannot be sure that it is really the title wanted. In addition, the description of condition may be misunderstood, since a term like "good condition" is not very precise and may mean different things to the dealer and the librarian. Speed in selecting and searching is essential, for the titles desired may be sold by the time the dealer receives the library's order. Some libraries send immediate requests to reserve a title until their order machinery can be set in motion. There is another difficulty involved in dealing with the o.p. trade, but it is one which can only be mentioned, since there seems little that can be done about it. The same title may be advertised in several catalogs over a period of a few months at considerably different prices. A librarian may be somewhat disconcerted to see a title which has just been purchased at $100 advertised by another dealer for $10. But the prices of o.p. materials, one can only conclude, are not regular and fixed: they represent the value which the item has in the eyes of the dealer. If a title seems overpriced, the library can always wait. But if it has long wanted the item, it may run the risk of seeing the next advertisement of it ask an even higher price.

If the item being considered for purchase by a library does not have to be in its original form, there are two other options available to the librarian—purchasing in reprint or in microform. Reprints may come from companies specializing in hardcover reprinting of materials no longer kept in stock by the original publishers or from companies such as University Microfilms International which offers "on-demand" xerographic or microfilm copies of out-of-print titles. Either of these approaches may at times cost more per title than buying through a secondhand dealer, but the frustration of determining who has a specific title will be less and the quality of paper in the reprint is likely to be better than in the original (though this depends on the place and period in which the original was published). A microform copy—either microfilm or microfiche—may be obtained from dealers specializing in this form of reproduction or, in some cases, may be obtained from another library. The cost may be less than for a hardcover reprint, but readers may not be as pleased with the choice.

Thanks to modern means of reproduction the librarian will often have a choice of format when acquiring out-of-print materials. The decision about format ought to be made on the basis of potential use (a microfilm copy of a reserve book would be inappropriate if a hardcover copy could be obtained), urgency of the request (searching the secondhand market may take years), and cost (in terms of staff time to locate the item and place the order as well as the list price of the item to be purchased).

One source of information about the secondhand book trade is the *AB Bookman's Yearbook*, issued annually by the *AB Book-*

man's Weekly (itself an organ of the antiquarian trade). The section of the *Yearbook* called "The O.P. Market" contains a directory of specialist and antiquarian booksellers, with a subject index. Bowker's *American Book Trade Directory* contains a state by state, city by city listing of bookstores, including secondhand shops, with information on specialists.

Microforms

Microforms are usually ordered directly from the producers, who may be commercial or association publishers or other libraries which hold negative masters and are able to offer copying services. Compared to book and journal publishers, the number of micropublishers is relatively limited. Because of this and the different types of information which might be specified on the microform order (see Chapter VII for a fuller discussion of this), some libraries merge into one position or department the responsibility for final selection decisions and ordering of microforms, and they separate this entirely from the library's regular order department. Other libraries may simply assign the primary responsibility for microforms to one individual in the order department. A basic tool for any librarian who has responsibility for microform selection and ordering is "Guidelines for Handling Library Orders for Microforms," published by the Resources Section of ALA's Resources and Technical Services Division in 1977.

When microform orders arrive, they must be inspected carefully to ensure that the material received is the material that was ordered. The checking of large sets is particularly important, because there is no other way to determine whether or not all the advertised units have been delivered. An ideal inspection would involve looking at each individual frame on every reel or fiche. This is tedious and time-consuming but, based on the variation in quality which has existed in the past and the amount of money being invested in large sets, some librarians feel it is worth the effort.

Serials

Serial subscriptions will, of course, be handled through a routine separate from book ordering. Most serials come from sources other than trade publishers and the wholesaling function is handled by a separate group of vendors known as subscription agents. (Not all serials will be purchased. As with books, many may be available as gifts or through exchange.) Librarians may choose to order serials directly from individual publishers, and for some publications—membership journals, very expensive indexing and abstracting services, investment and business services, certain directories, publications of societies and institutions, etc.—this is the recommended procedure. For other kinds of serials, the advantages of consolidating many titles in one order, thereby reducing correspondence and check-writing, may tempt the librarian to turn to a subscription agent.

Subscription agents offer a wide range of services, among which are the placing and renewing of subscriptions and claiming of missing issues. Some agents also automatically order all available title pages and indexes, attempt to retrieve funds from discontinued publications, handle address changes when a library or one of its branches moves, offer various kinds of reports to ease the difficulties of serials control, publish guides to serials, and maintain updating services for serials publication information. Most agents offer a "till forbidden" service, which means that the agent continues to renew subscriptions until a library sends specific instructions to the contrary. When a library is willing to start a "till forbidden" plan, some agents will work out a three-year cycle for the renewal of that library's subscriptions. This kind of plan allows the library to take advantage of the savings for three-year subscription rates offered by some popular magazines (scholarly journals are less likely to suffer such savings). There are also a few dealers who specialize in back issues, out-of-print or antiquarian stock.

Choosing a subscription agent is much like choosing a book jobber. Good service, fast and accurate, is usually the primary criterion. Although subscription agents may vary in the amount of their service charges, shopping around for the lowest price may be a money-losing proposition. Continuity of relations with a dealer is more important when purchasing serials than books. Changing from one agent to another usually means gaps in some subscriptions and duplications in others. This is one of the arguments against awarding serials contracts annually on the basis of bids.

Although bidding is less common than it once was, bidding regulations still exist for serial purchasing, as they do in some libraries for book purchasing. Bidding for serials purchasing involves submitting to various dealers a list of titles for which subscription renewals are desired, in order to get the lowest bid. This is an even more awkward procedure for serials than for books, since subscription lists are subject to frequent changes and so are subscription prices from publishers. Subscription agents—who may spend much time preparing a bid only to lose it or, worse, to win the contract and then be squeezed later by publishers' price increases—do not have anything good to say about bidding. Nor do librarians who find the lowest bidder all too often is the least capable of actually providing the service required.

How the library maintains control of serial publications as they arrive, issue by issue, and are added to the collection is beyond the scope of this discussion. However, the way a library chooses to organize and update its records on serials holdings— records which show which titles are expected, which issues have arrived, the source (publisher or agent) and means by which the serial is obtained (purchase, gift, exchange), which departmental or branch libraries hold the title, and various items of information about binding, cataloging, and payment, etc.— may determine where orders are placed and how much (if at all) they are distributed among several agents. Agents do differ in the extent to which they can accommodate and supplement a library's serials control procedures.

Gifts

Gifts are a valuable source of enriching the library's collection. They usually take the form of books or journals, although donations of money for purchase of materials are sometimes made. The gift of money poses few problems as the usual procedure of selection will be followed in its expenditure. In theory, at least, the same selection principles should be applied to gift materials as are applied in the library's own selection. This is sometimes difficult as the human factor, in the person of the donor, enters into the picture, and the librarian may have to adopt the role of diplomat. Most librarians prefer to accept only gifts which have no strings attached. The no-strings-attached rule can avoid all sorts of difficulties which may arise because the donor wishes to insist on various kinds of restrictions. She/he may demand that no markings be put on the bindings, ask that the gift collection be kept intact as one unit (perhaps in its own special quarters), refuse to allow the library to dispose of any titles which are duplicates of titles already in the library, or oppose the discarding of any material which the library feels does not meet its standards of selection.

The librarian should be free to decide whether all or part of the gift should be integrated into the collection, discarded, exchanged, or sold. The donor should trust the librarian's judgment, for rare items will certainly be respected and treated as such. Gifts can be an important source for rare, unusual, or expensive items which the library budget cannot afford, but it is also true that the offerings of gifts may include much material that would only prove a burden to the library. Libraries have on occasion refused a gift collection because the cost of processing the materials exceeded the worth of the collection. Certainly there is need in every library for a policy regarding the acceptance of gifts. If such a policy does not exist, much duplication and added expense in handling materials may occur.

Patrons of the library, Friends of the Library organizations, and Parent-Teacher groups within schools, have proven effective sources of substantial gifts. When a gift is received, it should be acknowledged promptly. Various forms may be used, according to the importance of the material. Any gift warrants a personal letter from the librarian or the president of the library board. It sometimes happens that over a period of time a donor gives a series of books which are marked with special book plates. In that event, some member of the order department may have the responsibility for seeing that the plates are prepared and that they are properly inserted in each of the items of such a collection as it arrives (the collections are often memorial in nature). While not a part of collection development, it is important to alert librarians that they are not to put a price value on gifts. That can only be done by specialists if the value is to be accepted by tax authorities for the purpose of qualifying as a tax deduction.

The alert librarian should also be on the lookout for free materials from various sources. Publications such as *Public Affairs Information Service Bulletin, Vertical File Index, Free!,* and almost all library periodicals list free pamphlet material. It is possible to request the library's name be put on the mailing lists of various government and private offices, organizations, and institutions which send free publications.

Duplicates and Exchanges

Duplicate materials tend to accumulate in every library. These are often sorted into different categories for disposal: 1) discards—books which are worn out and are only fit to be sold as waste paper; 2) duplicates which may be sold because their condition is satisfactory; 3) exchanges, which comprise those which the library can exchange with some other library to acquire materials not in the collection. Exchanges involve the development of some method of trading duplicate materials with other libraries. The term "exchanges" also refers to the process by which libraries connected with institutions which publish their own materials exchange these publications for the works produced by other institutions (as, for example, the exchange of one university's publications for another, which is done on a wide scale, involving international as well as intranational exchanges). It is important that a businesslike procedure for exchanges be set up, allocating the work to one department, preferably to acquisitions. In actual practice, it has sometimes been made the responsibility of the reference or circulation departments.

The United Serials and Book Exchange, a well-known exchange organization based in Washington, D.C., includes libraries of various sizes and types and operates on an international basis. Formerly known as the United States Book Exchange, it was established in 1948 as an outgrowth of the American Book Center for War-Devastated Libraries, which in turn had been created by the national library associations to build up foreign library collections from duplicate books and periodicals supplied by American libraries. The USBE acts as a pool for participating libraries which want to dispose of duplicate materials of value to research in return for other materials which they do not hold. It is a centralized warehouse where a participating library may send its duplicate materials with the least amount of labor and with the certainty that they will be utilized in the best possible way. Many libraries have found this service to be an excellent means of exchanging materials on both a national and international basis.

Exchanges may be facilitated through dealers and through certain associations of special libraries, such as the Medical Library Association, the American Association of Law Libraries, and the American Theological Library Association. Regional exchange programs, sometimes directed by the state library agency, often provide for the distribution of unneeded, but still worthwhile, duplicates.

Bibliography

General

American Library Association. Bookdealer-Library Relations Committee, *Guidelines for Handling Library Orders for In-Print Monographic Publications*. Chicago, ALA, 1973. 16p.

Ash, Joan and others. "Prediction Equation Providing Some Objective Criteria for the Acquisition of Technical Reports by the College or University Library." *Library Resources and Technical Services,* 17:35–41, Winter 1973.

Balke, Mary Noel. "Acquisition of Exhibition Catalogs." *Special Libraries,* 66:579–587, December 1975.

Boss, Richard Woodruff. *Automating Library Acquisitions: Issues and Outlook.* White Plains, N.Y., Knowledge Industry Publications, 1982. 135p. What to do and what to avoid.

Bulard, Scott R. "The Language of the Marketplace." *American Libraries,* 9:365–366, June 1978. Short glossary.

Cargill, Jennifer S. "On-Line Acquisitions: Use of a Vendor System." *Library Acquisitions,* 4 nos. 3–4:236–245, 1980.

Carter, John. *ABC for Book Collectors.* London, Clive Bingley, 1976. 211p.

Cave, Roderick. *Rare Book Librarianship.* London, Clive Bingley, 1976. 168p. Includes chapter on acquisitions.

Duckett, Kenneth W. *Modern Manuscripts; A Practical Manual for Their Management, Care, and Use.* Nashville, Tenn., American Association for State and Local History, 1975. 375p. Contains chapter on acquisitions.

Falk, Leslie K. *Procurement of Library Materials in the Federal Government; An Orientation Aid Prepared for the Federal Library Committee.* Washington, D.C., Federal Library Committee, 1968. 42p.

Ford, Stephen. *Acquisition of Library Materials.* Chicago, American Library Association, 1973. 237p. Covers all aspects of acquisitions.

Franz, Ted. "Automated Standing Order System. Blackwell North America." *Serials Review,* 7:63–67, January 1981.

Gregor, Jan and W. C. Fraser. "University of Windsor Experience with an Approval Plan in Three Subjects and Three Vendors." *Canadian Library Journal,* 38:227–231, August 1981.

Grieder, Theodore. *Acquisitions: Where, What, and How.* Westport, Conn., Greenwood Press, 1978. 277p. Specific and practical suggestions based on experiences in a large university or research library. Emphasizes monographs and serials.

Haller, Margaret. *The Book Collector's Fact Book.* New York, Arco, 1976. 271p. List of terms relating to the book trade.

Heyman, Berna L. and G. L. Abbott. "Automated Acquisitions: A Bibliography." *Library Technology Reports,* 17:195–202, March-April 1981.

Houghton, Bernard. *Technical Information Sources.* 2d ed. London, Clive Bingley, 1972. 119p. Covers patents, standards, and report literature.

Huleatt, Richard S. "Rx for Acquisitions Hangups." *Special Libraries,* 64:81–85, February 1973. Acquisitions in a special library.

Magrill, Rose Mary and Constance Rinehart. *Library Technical Services; A Selected Annotated Bibliography.* Westport, Conn., Greenwood Press, 1977. 238p. Contains sections on order procedures.

Melcher, Daniel. *Melcher on Acquisitions.* Chicago, American Library Association, 1971. 169p. Informal comments on jobbers, blanket plans, order procedures and a variety of other topics.

Miller, Bruce C. "Placing and Tracing Orders in a Dynamic Acquisitions Process." *Collection Management,* 3:233–246, Summer-Fall 1979.

Neikirk, Harold D. "Less Does More: Adapting Pre-order Searching to On-Line Cataloging." *Library Acquisitions,* 5 no. 2:89–94, 1981.

Peters, Jean. *Book Collecting; A Modern Guide.* New York, Bowker, 1977. 288p. Covers various aspects of the antiquarian book trade.

Peters, Jean. *Bookman's Glossary.* 6th ed. New York, Bowker, 1983. 200p. Terminology of the book trade.

Raouf, Abdul and others. "A Performance Prediction Model for Bibliographic Search for Monographs Using Multiple Regression Technique." *Journal of Library Automation,* 9:210–221, September 1976. Study at University of Windsor.

Wulfekoetter, Gertrude. *Acquisition Work; Processes Involved in Building Library Collections.* Seattle, University of Washington Press, 1962. 280p. Practical approach to order, gift, and exchange procedures.

Relations with Dealers

Andersen, David C. "Book Discounts and Cost-Plus Pricing." *Library Resources and Technical Services,* 18:248–252, Summer 1974.

Boyer, Calvin J. "State-Wide Contracts for Library Materials: An Analysis of the Attendant Dysfunctional Consequences." *College and Research Libraries,* 35:86–94, March 1974.

Bromberg, Erik. "How the Birds (Pigeons) and Bees and Butterflies Do It: Avuncular Advice to a New Librarian About to Talk to His Purchasing Agent Who Has Already Signed a Book Buying Contract." *Special Libraries,* 61:168–170, April 1970.

Kim, Ung Chon. *Policies of Publishers; A Handbook for Order Librarians.* 2d ed. Metuchen, N.J., Scarecrow Press, 1982. 173p. Based on questionnaires returned from publishers.

Kim, Ung Chon. "Purchasing Books from Publishers and Wholesalers." *Library Resources and Technical Services,* 19:133–147, Spring 1975. Study based on 32 in-print titles.

Lincoln, Robert. "Vendors and Delivery: An Analysis of Selected Publishers, Publishers/Agents, Distributors, and Wholesalers." *Canadian Library Journal,* 35:51–57, February 1978. Study done at University of Manitoba.

Martin, Murray S. "The Series Standing Order and the Library." *Choice,* 10:1152–1155, October 1973. Points to consider before placing a standing order.

Roth, Harold L. "The Book Wholesaler: His Forms and Services." *Library Trends,* 24:673–682, April 1976. How jobbers operate.

Rouse, William B. "Optimal Selection of Acquisition Sources." *Journal of the American Society for Information Science,* 25:227–231, July–August 1974. Decision analysis approach.

Stokely, Sandra L. and Marion T. Reid. "A Study of Five Book Dealers Used by Louisiana State University Library." *Library Resources and Technical Services,* 22:117–125, Spring 1978.

Approval Plans and Blanket Orders

Association of Research Libraries. Systems and Procedures Exchange Center. *Approval Plans in ARL Libraries.* (SPEC Kit no. 83) Washington, D.C., The Center, 1982. 109p. Twenty-two documents ranging from criteria for evaluating vendors to the role of faculty.

International Conference on Approval Plans and Collection Development, Milwaukee, 1979. *Shaping Library Collections for the 1980s.* Edited by Peter Spyers-Duran and J. J. Mann. Phoenix, Ariz., Oryx Press, 1980. 235p.

McCullough, Kathleen and others. *Approval Plans and Academic Libraries; An Interpretative Survey.* Phoenix, Ariz., Oryx Press, 1977. 154p. Report of a 1975 survey of 144 libraries.

Reidelbach, John H. and G. M. Shirk. "Selecting an Approval Plan Vendor: A Step-by-Step Process." *Library Acquisitions,* 7:115–125, 1983.

For other citations on approval plans and blanket orders, see the bibliograhy which accompanies Chapter 5.

Foreign Acquisitions

Acquisition of Foreign Materials for U.S. Libraries. Compiled and edited by Theodore Samore. 2d ed. Metuchen, N.J., Scarecrow Press, 1982. 218p.

Atiyeh, George N. "Acquisitions from the Middle East." *Library Acquisitions,* 6 no2:185–194, 1982.

Borsenverein den deutschen Buchhandels, ed. *How to Obtain German Books and Periodicals.* 3rd ed. The Association, 1980. 104p.

Cason, Maidel and others. "Cooperative Acquisition of Africana." *Library Acquisitions,* 6 no2:221–232, 1982.

Cylke, Frank K. *Selected Federal Library Programs for Acquisition of Foreign Materials.* Washington, D.C., Federal Library Committee, 1971. 22p. Summarizes programs in sixteen federal libraries.

Figueredo, Danilo H. "Buying More for Less: Purchasing Materials in Spanish." *New Jersey Libraries,* 16:19–21, Spring 1983.

Foster, David William. *Mexican Literature: A Bibliography of Secondary Sources.* Metuchen, N.J., Scarecrow Press, 1981, 386p.

Maddox, W. Jane and F. O. Weigel. "Acquisitions from the Middle East: The View from Harrassowitz." *Library Acquisitions,* 6 no2:195–199, 1982.

Miranda, Salvador. "Library Materials from Latin America and the Caribbean: Problems and Approaches in Acquisitions." *Library Acquisitions,* 6 no2:177–184, 1982.

Orne, Jerrold. *The Language of the Foreign Book Trade.* 3rd ed. Chicago, American Library Association, 1976. 333p.

Panofsky, Hans Eugene. "Acquisition of Africana." *Library Acquisitions,* 6 no2:123–128, 1982.

Rathgeber, Eva-Maria. "Africana Acquisitions Problems: The View from Both Sides." *Library Acquisitions,* 6 no2:137–148, 1982.

Sohn, Jeanne and Russ Davidson. "Out of the Morass: Acquiring Spanish-

Language Materials from Latin America." *Library Journal*, 107:1290–1293, July 1982.

Out-of-Print Materials

American Book Trade Directory. 29th ed. New York, Bowker, 1983. 1250p. Annual.

Books Out-of-Print 1980–1983. New York, Bowker, 1984. 2047p.

Buy Books Where—Sell Books Where; A Directory of Out of Print Booksellers and Their Author–Subject Specialties, 1981–1982. Compiled by R. E. Robinson and D. Farudi. Morgantown, WV, Ruth E. Robinson Books, 1981, 226p.

Cameron, Kenneth J. and Michael Roberts. "Desiderata File Management: Purging and Its Politics." *Journal of Librarianship*, 14:123–133, April 1982.

"Code of Fair Practices for Dealers and Librarians." In *AB Bookman's Yearbook*, 1972, Pt. 2, pp. 312–313. Newark, N.J., Antiquarian Bookman, 1972.

Kim, Ung Chon. "Comparison of Two Out-of-Print Book Buying Methods." *College and Research Libraries*, 34:258–264, September 1973.

Lynden, Fred C. and Arthur Meyerfeld. "Library Out-of-Print Book Procurement: The Stanford University Experience." *Library Resources and Technical Services*, 17:216–224, Spring 1973.

Mitchell, Betty J. "Methods Use in Out-of-Print Acquisitions: A Survey of Out-of-Print Book Dealers." *Library Resources and Technical Services*, 17:211–215, Spring 1973.

"New Book Dealers and the OP Market." *AB Bookman's Weekly*, 71:4139–4140+, May 30, 1983.

Schenck, William Z. "Acquisition of Out-of-Print Books." *AB Bookman's Weekly*, 68:4015+, December 7, 1981. Discussion. 69:748, February 1, 1982.

Microforms

American Library Association. Resources and Technical Services Division. Resources Section. Bookdealer-Library Relations Committee. *Guidelines for Handling Library Orders for Microforms.* Chicago, American Library Association, 1977. 14p. (Acquisition Guidelines No. 3)

Folcarelli, Ralph J. and Ralph C. Ferragamo. "Microform Publications: Hardware and Suppliers." *Library Trends*, 24:711–725, April 1976. Includes selected list of micro publishers.

Gleaves, Edwin Sheffield and R. T. Carterette. "Microform Serials Acquisition: A Suggested Planning Model." *Journal of Academic Librarianship*, 8:292–295, November 1982.

Guide to Microforms in Print: Author–Title. Westport, Conn., Meckler Publishing, 1983. 1200p.——: *Subject*. 1500p. Annually updated.

Perrault, Anna H. "New Dimensions in Approval Plan Service." *Library Acquisitions*, 7 no 1:35–40, 1983.

Sullivan, Robert C. "The Acquisition of Library Microforms." *Microform Review*, 6:136–144, May 1977; 6:205–211, July 1977. Covers tools and procedures.

Sullivan, Robert Coyle. "Microform Developments Related to Acquisitions." In *Acquisition of Foreign Materials*, 2d ed. Edited by Theodore Samore, pp. 193–207. Metuchen, N.J., Scarecrow Press, 1982.

For other citations on microforms, see the bibliography which accompanies Chapter 7. For updated material, consult issues of Microform Review.

Serials

American Library Association. Resources and Technical Services Division. *International Subscription Agents*. 4th ed. Chicago, American Library Association, 1978. Information on agents handling subscriptions and standing orders.

American Library Association. Resources and Technical Services Division. Resources Section. Bookdealer-Library Relations Committee. *Guidelines for Handling Library Orders for Serials and Periodicals*. Chicago, American Library Association, 1974. 16p. (Acquisitions Guidelines No. 2)

Brown, Clara D. and Lynn S. Smith. *Serials: Past, Present and Future*. 2d ed. rev. Birmingham, Ala., EBSCO Industries, 1980. 390p. Chapter 6 covers ordering.

Brynteson, Susan. "Serials Acquisitions." In *Management Problems in Serials Work*, edited by Peter Spyers-Duran and Daniel Gore, pp. 50–65. Westport, Conn., Greenwood Press, 1974.

Clasquin, Frank F. "Library and Subscription Agent Electronics." *Serials Librarian*, 7:7–15, Spring 1983.

Forsman, Rick B. "EBSCONET Serials Control System; A Case History and Analysis." *Serials Review*, 8:83–85, Winter 1982. Experiences at the Lister Hill Health Sciences Library.

Landenberger, Sally A. "Systematizing Serials Operations: Eliminating Crisis Claiming." *Serials Review*, 9:87–90, Spring 1983. Michigan State University libraries system.

Lowell, Gerald R. "LINX: The Integrator." *Serials Librarian*, 7:17–27, Spring 1983. The Faxon system.

Melin, Nancy Jean. "New Subscription Agency Giants: Lower or Higher Costs?" *Serials Review*, 8:7, Summer 1982; Discussion. 8:3, Winter 1982; *Serials Librarian*, 7:29–34, Spring 1983.

Osborn, Andrew D. *Serial Publications; Their Place and Treatment in Libraries*. 3rd ed. Chicago, American Library Association, 1980. 486p. Covers all aspects of serials in libraries.

Paul, Huibert. "Streamlining Claiming Processes: Manual Check-in Systems." *Serials Review*, 9:91–93, Spring 1983. University of Oregon system.

Wisneski, Martin E. "Manual Serials Management Systems: The Claiming Function." *Serials Review*, 9:97–102, Spring 1983. University of Kansas Law Library.

Government Publications

Faull, Sandra K. "Do Government Bookstores Have Value? Why or Why Not?" *Government Publications Review*, 10:127–130, January–February 1983.

Levin, Marc A. "Access and Dissemination Issues Concerning Federal Government Information." *Special Libraries,* 74:127–137, April 1983.

Morehead, Joe. *Introduction to United States Public Documents.* 3rd ed. Littleton, Colo., Libraries Unlimited, 1983. 377p.

Mundkur, Mohini. "Some Selection and Acquisition Aids for Current State Documents." *Documents to the People,* 6:107–109, March 1978. Annotated.

Relyea, Harold C. "Freedom of Information Developments Around the World: A Symposium." *Government Publications Review,* 10:1–95, January–February 1983.

Shaw, George A. "How to Locate Out-of-Print, Hard-to-Get Documents." *Southeastern Librarian,* 24:28–29, Winter 1975.

Welsh, Harry E. "An Acquisitions Up-Date for Government Publications." *Microform Review,* 6:285–298, September 1977. Guide to sources for libraries which acquire government publications selectively.

Zink, Steven D. "Non-Depository or Not: An Examination of the Designation of Non-Depository Titles in the Monthly Catalog of United States Government Publications." *College and Research Libraries,* 44:178–181, March 1983.

Zink, Steven D. *United States Government Publications Catalogs.* New York, Special Libraries Association, 1982. 111p. (SLA Bibliography No. 8)

Gifts and Exchanges

Association of Research Libraries. Office of University Library Management Studies. *SPEC Kit on Gifts and Exchange Function in ARL Libraries.* Washington, D.C., 1976. 129p. Examples of policies, procedures, etc.

Ball, Alice D. *The Role of the United States Book Exchange in the Nationwide Library and Information Services Network.* Washington, D.C., National Commission on Libraries and Information Science, 1975. 32p. (ED 114 104) Reviews history and operation of USBE (now United Serials and Book Exchange).

Dobroski, Charles H. and Donald D. Hendricks. "Mobilization of Duplicates in a Regional Medical Library Program." *Medical Library Association Bulletin,* 63:309–318, July 1975.

Eggleton, Richard. "The ALA Duplicates Exchange Union—A Study and Evaluation." *Library Resources and Technical Services,* 19:148–163, Spring 1975.

International Exchange of Publications; Proceedings of the European Conference Held in Vienna from 24–29 April 1972. Edited by Maria J. Schiltman. Munich, Verlag Dokumentation, 1973. 135p.

Kemp, Edward C. *Manuscript Solicitation for Libraries, Special Collections.* Littleton, Colo., Libraries Unlimited, 1978. 208p. Techniques for soliciting gift materials.

Kovacic, Mark. "Acquisition by Gift and Exchange." In *Acquisition of Foreign Materials for U.S. Libraries.* 2d ed. pp. 37–41. Metuchen, N.J., Scarecrow Press, 1982.

Lane, Alfred H. *Gifts and Exchange Manual.* Westport, Conn., Greenwood Press, 1980. 121p.

Studies in the International Exchange of Publications. Edited by P. Genzel. Ridgewood, N.J., Saur Publishing, 1981. 125p.

United Nations Educational Scientific and Cultural Organization. *Handbook on the International Exchange of Publications.* New York, 1978. Explains different types of exchange agreements.

"USBE Adopts Marketing Tactics Recommended by Boss Report." *Library Journal,* 108:625–626, April 1, 1983.

"USBE to Market Services More Vigorously." *Wilson Library Bulletin,* 57:633, April 1983.

Yu, Priscilla C. "Berkeley's Exchange Program: A Case Study." *Journal of Library History,* 17:241–267, Summer 1982.

Yu, Priscilla C. "International Gift & Exchange: The Asian Experience." *Journal of Academic Librarianship,* 6:333–338, January 1981.

CHAPTER 13

COLLECTION EVALUATION

The librarian's responsibility for the collection does not end with the determination of users' needs, the setting of collection objectives, or even the selection of which books, journals, audiovisual materials, etc., to acquire. Collections must be continuously maintained by evaluating what has been obtained, what has been missed, withdrawing unnecessary or badly deteriorated materials, sending little-used materials to storage, and preserving the most valuable or most-used items in the collection.

While the following discussion focuses on the book portion of the collection, it is necessary to keep in mind that all of the principles and procedures discussed can be applied to all formats collected. A badly scratched phonodisc is every bit as much in need of replacement or discarding as a shabby book. A film with damaged sprocket holes that cannot be repaired or replaced is every bit as annoying to a patron as a book without pages. A film that once was of great interest, but now is so dated as to be laughable to a current audience needs to be evaluated for discarding or removing to storage just as a once-popular book now no longer read needs evaluating.

Every librarian would like to be able to answer the question, "How good is the library's collection?" Materials are selected by different people over a long period of time. Librarians may vary in their conceptions of the general principles of selection. Patrons' interests may change and what was a good collection a decade ago may no longer meet their needs, or the community itself may change, bringing entirely new patrons with very different needs. To decide how good any library collection is we must have information about three important factors: 1) what kinds of materials are in the collection and how valuable each item is in relation to other items which are not in the library; 2) the kind of community served, in order to decide whether the materials in the collection are appropriate to that clientele, regardless of how valuable they may be in terms of an abstract evaluation of their worth; 3) the purposes which that collection is supposed to accomplish, given that particular community of readers.

Collection evaluation must be a part of any large-scale library planning effort and is essential in any systematic approach to establishing collection development policy, rationalizing budget allocation, or undertaking discarding, storage, and replacement projects. The collection may be evaluated in a one-shot, full-scale systematic project; it may be judged through a series of smaller projects; or the appraisal may involve a combination of projects. In some libraries collection evaluation is done daily, routinely, and almost subconsciously by individual librarians.

Various techniques can be used to get some idea of the worth of a collection. Some involve qualitative judgments. For example, users may be observed and questioned about how well the collection is meeting their particular needs. Eugene Wiemers, Jr. has developed a very simple survey that allows small and medium-sized libraries to systematically survey users. The survey has been published as *Materials Availability in Small Libraries: A Survey Handbook* by the University of Illinois in its Occasional Papers series (full citation in bibliography). With minor adaptations this instrument is suitable for school libraries and special libraries as well as public libraries. It has the added advantage of providing insight into why people come to the library—not always to borrow or even use materials.

Interlibrary loan requests are another method for ascertaining collection suitability. Keeping accurate statistics on number of requests as well as specific titles and subjects requested will provide insight into needs not currently being met by the collection. Some interlibrary loan requests involve out-of-print materials available only from large libraries whose purposes include maintaining historical as well as current materials. Some requests will be for specialized research needs which fall outside the particular library's scope.

Requests from patrons that the library purchase materials is another approach to evaluating the relationship between the patrons' interests and the library's selection practices. When a genuine conflict exists between the patrons' concept of what they should find in the library and what the library staff feels ought to be there, reevaluation of the collection development policy is called for. Whatever the abstract value of a particular collection, it serves no useful purpose if it is not meeting its patrons' needs.

Titles on reserve also provide insight into patrons' interests. A large number of reserves for a title should alert the librarian to the need for providing multiple copies of the title. Certain authors consistently produce a large number of reserve requests and the good librarian learns to anticipate the need and buy accordingly in order to keep to a minimum the time between when patrons request a title and when they receive the book. Waiting six months to read a current bestseller is not a patron's idea of a collection built on sound selection practices.

With more and more books being published as original paperbacks, and reaching the bestseller lists, librarians must also be alert to any gaps in the selection policy on formats being purchased.

Each of the above methods is very direct, contrasting identifiable patron needs/demands with materials found within the library. An indirect method of determining the suitability of the collection involves checking the shelves to see what is in at any particular moment. This method can be casual, eyeballing the shelves to see if specific titles are available, or it can be systematic by subject. For example, on any given day can a patron walk into the public library and find standard titles by Jane Austen, Leo Tolstoy, et al. on the shelves? Are certain subject areas consistently depleted?

Librarians should also be alert to study-groups within the community. Is the League of Women Voters studying nuclear energy or disarmament or education this year? Is a church study-group exploring the complexities of child abuse or drug addiction in teenagers? Staying in touch with such groups is an excellent way of anticipating demands on the collection.

Large public and academic libraries often prefer to call in subject specialists to evaluate the collection. This process makes sense for libraries whose collection development policies go beyond meeting immediate needs and include a research function. Subject specialists are best used when the library is concerned with the depth and breadth of its collection.

The one method no longer considered a viable evaluation technique is to count the number of titles/volumes owned by a library, although a number of accrediting groups in the school library field still insist that a library have a set number of holdings. The move away from quantitative standards stems from two concerns. First, the policy discourages libraries from withdrawing items even after they have long lost their value to anyone. Second, numbers do not tell us anything about how the collection relates to patron needs.

Use of Standard Lists in Evaluation

There are two types of standard lists which can aid in collection evaluation. One type is the annual list; the other is the cumulative list. They will be discussed in order.

Evaluation of Current Selection

Each year the American Library Association produces lists such as *Best Books for Young Adults, Notable Children's Books,* and *Notable Books* for adult collections. Certain ALA divisions cooperate to produce *University Books for Secondary School Libraries* and *University Press Books for Public Libraries.* Other organizations produce similar lists and these are published in their official periodicals.

In order to evaluate the selection process being used as well as the collection being built, librarians should check these lists against their holdings. How many titles were bought, how many were missed? It is the latter category that requires analysis. Did the librarian decide consciously not to buy these titles and if so was the decision correct? Do the titles fall outside the scope of the collection being developed or did the review media being used to make choices fail to alert the librarian to their value? Consistent failure by the review media being used should require reexamination of the selection process.

It is important for public librarians in particular to check a wide variety of lists, especially in areas where the library has no designated specialist. Young adult collections are often badly skewed in libraries without a Young Adult Librarian. Such checking often shows that the children's librarian is very good about buying materials for young teens and the adult librarian is very good at buying adult titles suitable for young adults. The books that fall through the crevice are those teen books, mostly novels, that are too mature for the children's room and too immature for the adult department.

Evaluation of the Total Collection

Standard cumulative lists covering all Dewey Decimal categories are useful for evaluating collections in small and medium-sized public libraries and school libraries, but only if the library staff establishes criteria for their use. A systematic collection evaluation requires working through the shelves book by book. The criteria for keeping or withdrawing are two-fold: 1) the quality of the title as indicated by its presence on the standard list, and 2) its popularity with the library's particular clientele. The ideal, of course, is the title that meets both criteria—high quality and high popularity. Since that is not always, or even generally, the case, the library staff determines that a title will be kept if: 1) it is on the list and has circulated a certain number of times within the past two to five years; 2) is not on the list but has a high circulation record, or 3) is so important that it is to be kept regardless of its circulation record.

There are certain assumptions inherent in using standard lists that may or may not be true, but whose existence must be acknowledged so that librarians do not use them blindly. The H. W. Wilson "standard catalog" series is the best-known and most widely used set of standard lists. It is assumed that the particular titles, *Fiction Catalog, High School Catalog*, etc., represent the collective wisdom of the consultants listed at the beginning of the catalogs. The problem with collective wisdom is that it often eliminates the controversial and serves the lowest common denominator. The absence of high-circulation titles from these lists says more about the list compilers than about the library's selection processes, a point librarians using them must keep in mind.

A common error by beginning librarians is to assume that if all titles in a particular standard list are owned, the collection is a good one. This would be true only if the library owns many more titles than are on the list. No library can survive with only standard list titles on its shelves since no list can meet the needs of diverse patron interests found in varying communities. All a standard list can do is provide a base-line point which begins the evaluation process, not ends it.

However, if the evaluation process shows the library owning a fair number of titles in a particular category, but none of them are on the standard list being used, a red flag should go up in the librarian's head. Are the selected titles really comparable to those on the list? Why were so many of the list titles missed initially? Do changes in selection personnel account for the skewed nature of the collection? If so, did this situation arise because the library did not have a written collection development policy, or was there a policy consistently ignored by past selectors?

The use of specialized standard lists e.g., those on a single subject or category, are of more use to the librarian seeking to improve one portion of the collection. For example, Neil Barron's *Anatomy of Wonder* is the best choice for evaluating and/or building a science fiction collection for a library. The *Fiction Catalog* is almost useless in this specialized area.

No library has enough staff to use all the specialized bibliographies available for evaluation of a collection. Use of such tools must be judiciously determined, primarily by patron demands not being met by the library which need immediate attention. But a wide range of such tools should be owned by libraries for consultation in reader's advisory and reference services. *The single biggest defect in most library collections is the professional collection.* All too many librarians are so busy buying materials for patrons that they ignore building a sound professional collection for the staff. Such neglect is often justified by citing the cost of building such a collection at the expense of having materials on the shelves for patrons. This mind-set is indicative of librarians who still cling to the concept of the self-contained library and have not grasped the essentials of networking. A soundly developed professional collection is the key to providing superior service via interloans. Most patrons would rather wait a couple weeks for a quality title than have inferior titles immediately.

A variation of the practice of checking a library's holdings against a published subject bibliography or standard list is to construct such a checklist from the citations (footnotes, references, etc.) which appear in significant works in the field or fields of a library's interest. "Significant works" might include whatever is significant for the library in question—theses, state-of-the-art reviews, and faculty research publications for a large university library; textbooks and most-used journals for an undergraduate collection; and textbooks used in school systems, public or private. In the case of citations in a thesis, research report, or literature review, the evaluation is based on whether or not the work could have been written in the library being surveyed. For an undergraduate or school library collection, this type of evaluation assumes that a student should be able to locate the references which are cited in the books and journals used for class reading.

As noted above, all evaluation techniques are time consuming and costly. A library's budget should plan for on-going evaluative procedures and periodically (every five/ten years, depending on the stability of staff doing the selection and patron surveys showing major weaknesses) for a large scale evaluation process. This may include budgeting for bringing in outside experts, or hiring temporary professional staff to assume the duties of the permanent staff doing the evaluation.

Quantitative Approaches to Evaluation

Quantitative methods may also be used in collection evaluation as long as the librarian keeps in mind that numbers alone do not indicate quality. This is true of small and medium-sized school and public library collections where keeping out-of-date titles just to keep the count up is a very strong temptation. The absolute size of a collection, the holdings of the library in certain subjects, the holdings of certain types of materials, the growth rate of the collection, the size of the collection in relation to the total number of users or potential users, the circulation rate of the collection (in whole or part), and the money spent on the collection are examples of collection characteristics which may be expressed in quantitative terms for comparison with the performances of the library in previous years or with the holdings of other libraries of a similar size or type.

These quantitative measures have the advantage of being easy to collect and generally easy to explain to governing boards and users. They lend themselves to the creation of impressive charts and graphs which can dramatize for administrators and governing boards a library's progress, or lack of it, in collection development. But there are problems, too, in the lack of uniformity in the way such statistics are collected and reported and in the way they are interpreted. It is easy to compare the size of two collections; it is much more difficult to decide which of two collections is better. It is usually assumed that a collection of four million items is better than one of four thousand. The chances seem better that a very large collection will have more material in any given subject field. Even in such a case, there is no assurance that a collection of five hundred carefully selected titles in a field like anthropology is poorer than a collection of five thousand randomly gathered titles. But if there are two collections of a million items each, how is one to tell which is the better collection?

In spite of the obvious difficulties in using quantitative approaches to collection evaluation, the library profession has continued to attempt to develop such measures. One of the most prominent trends has been the development of formulas for determining collection adequacy. An example is the Clapp-Jordan formula of 1965, which was developed because the accepted standards for college libraries did not give enough guidance in estimating the minimum number of volumes that would be acceptable for libraries serving undergraduates. The Clapp-Jordan formula states the number of volumes required for a basic collection and also specifies the number of additional volumes which will be needed for each faculty member, student, and academic program. Others have worked with variables similar to those used by Clapp and Jordan—size and research activity of the faculty, curriculum profile of the institution, range and depth of programs, etc.—and have devised formulas for larger academic libraries. Some states have developed similar collection-size formulas for use in planning higher education budgets, and the latest (1975) revision of the ALA/ACRL standards for college libraries includes such a formula.

Public libraries also have been influenced by the trend toward describing collections in quantitative terms. *Performance Measures for Public Libraries* by DeProspo, et al., suggests drawing a random sample from the *American Book Publishing Record* and checking to see which titles the library owns and if the title is on the shelf. This technique provides the actual chance a patron has of finding a given title on the shelf. If the library owns a small percentage of the books checked, the assumption may be that either the budget or the current selection method is inadequate. If, on the other hand, the library owns a fairly large percentage of the titles checked, but few of them are available on the shelf at the time of the test, the conclusion might be that more duplication of titles is needed. Similar tests may be conducted on the library's collection of non-book materials.

Evaluating Total Resources

Another recent trend in collection evaluation is the tendency to look at total resource adequacy—the holdings of the collection being surveyed plus external resources which are also available to users of that library. One of the approaches here is to express in quantitative terms the library's ability to satisfy requests for a list of specific items. The Capability Index developed by Orr and his associates offers a way of rating a library's ability to deliver materials to its users by emphasizing the speed with which the library can supply an item, rather than by making counts or analyses of its holdings. If the list of items chosen for such a test is appropriate for the situation, the resulting Capability Index should give an indication of the library's capacity to respond to users' requests, not only through its own collection but also by effective use of cooperative arrangements and interlibrary loan. This method of collection evaluation emphasizes the interdependence of libraries, and the importance of such interdependence has been recognized in several recent statements of library standards.

A library with a subscription to one or more computer data bases automatically increases its ability to provide broader, faster, service to its patrons. After scanning the abstracts of articles on a subject and determining which journals are not held by the library, but contain important articles, the library can request hard copies of the articles either through the data base (if that service is included in the contract) or through traditional interloan processes. The same approach applies to books.

When deciding how to approach collection evaluation, the librarian must consider the advantages and disadvantages of the various procedures. Any of the more objective approaches are likely to be expensive because of the amount of staff time they require. On the other hand, subjective impressions of the collection may be easy to obtain but relatively worthless for most situations. The librarian must learn to balance the cost of the staff time needed to compile the data for an evaluation project against the potential value of the information collected. The potential value includes the increased ability to serve patrons better but also the prospect of receiving the additional funds needed to correct defects and imbalances discovered. There is no sense in doing a large-scale collection evaluation if the only result is to prove inadequacy without concomitant ability to improve the situation; therefore it is essential that the decision to carry out a large-scale evaluation be a policy decision by the governing board, not a strictly internal administrative decision.

Bibliography

Adams, J. Emily. "Developing Data Collection Instruments for the Planning Process." *Public Libraries*, 21:60–61, Summer 1982.

American Association of School Librarians. *Media Programs: District and School.* Chicago, American Library Association; Washington, D.C., Association for Educational Communication and Technology, 1975. 128p. Standards for school libraries includes section on collections.

American Library Association. Resources and Technical Services Division. Resources Section. Collection Development Committee. "Guidelines for the Evaluation of Library Collections." 1977. 16p.

Association of College and Research Libraries. "Guidelines for Two-Year College Learning Resources Programs." *College and Research Libraries News*, 33:305–315, December 1972. Within the section on "Instructional System Components," there is a statement on materials.

Association of College and Research Libraries. "Standards for College Libraries." *College and Research Libraries News*, 36:290–301, October 1975. Includes section on collections.

Association of Research Libraries. Office of University Library Management Studies. *SPEC Kit on Collection Assessment in ARL Libraries.* Washington, D.C.,

Association of Research Libraries, 1978. 103p. Examples of research libraries' approach to collection evaluation.

Bonn, George S. "Evaluation of the Collection." *Library Trends*, 22:265–304, January 1974. Thorough review of methods.

Clapp, Verner W. and Robert T. Jordan. "Quantitative Criteria for Adequacy of Academic Library Collections." *College and Research Libraries*, 26:371–380, September 1965. Proposes formulas for estimating minimum collections for college and junior college libraries.

Coale, Robert P. "Evaluation of a Research Library Collection: Latin-American Colonial History at the Newberry." *Library Quarterly*, 35:173–184, July 1965.

DeProspo, Ernest R. and others. *Performance Measures for Public Libraries*. Chicago, American Library Association, Public Library Association, 1973. 71p. Includes quantitative approaches to materials availability.

Downs, Robert B. and John W. Heusman. "Standards for University Libraries." *College and Research Libraries*, 31:28–35, January 1970. Not a statement of standards, but an explanation of how statistics from groups of large libraries may be used.

Goldhor, Herbert. "Analysis of an Inductive Method of Evaluating the Book Collection of a Public Library." *Libri*, 23:6–17, 1973. Suggests a variation of list-checking.

Hirsch, Felix E. "Standards for Libraries." *Library Trends*, 21:159–355, October 1972. Contains fourteen articles on standards for various types of libraries.

Lancaster, F. W. *The Measurement and Evaluation of Library Services*. Arlington, VA, Information Resources Press, 1977. 395p. See Chapter 5, "Evaluation of the Collection" (pp. 165–206), for a thorough review of methods and also Chapter 10, "The Relevance of Standards to the Evaluation of Library Services" (pp. 288–298).

McInnis, R. Marvin. "The Formula Approach to Library Size: An Empirical Study of Its Efficacy in Evaluating Research Libraries." *College and Research Libraries*, 33:190–198, May 1972.

McInnis, R. Marvin. "Research Collections: An Approach to the Assessment of Quality." *IPLO Quarterly*, 13:13–22, July 1971. Explains citation-checking method.

Nisonger, Thomas E. "An Annotated Bibliography of Items Relating to Collection Evaluation in Academic Libraries, 1969–1981." *College and Research Libraries*, 43:300–311, July 1982.

Noble, Pamela and Patricia L. Ward. *Performance Measures and Criteria for Libraries; A Survey and Bibliography*. London, Public Libraries Research Group, 1976. 50p. (PLRG Occasional Paper No. 3) Annotated; includes section on "measuring library effectiveness."

Palmour, Vernon E. and others. *A Planning Process for Public Libraries*. Chicago, American Library Association, 1980. 304p. Has important implications for collection evaluation.

Raffel, Jeffry A. and Robert Shisko. *Systematic Analysis of University Libraries: An Application of Cost-Benefit Analysis to the MIT Libraries*. Cambridge, Mass., MIT Press, 1969. 107p.

Schofield, J. L. and others. "Evaluation of an Academic Library's Stack Effectiveness." *Journal of Librarianship*, 7:207–227, July 1975. Describes method to determine how and why readers fail to find what they want.

Stayer, Marcia S. "A Creative Approach to Collection Evaluation." *IPLO Quarterly*, 13:23–28, July 1971. Promotes citation-checking method.

White, G. Travis. "Quantitative Measure of Library Effectiveness." *Journal of Academic Librarianship*, 3:128–136, July 1977. Several of the measures reviewed concern collection evaluation.

Wiemers, Eugene. *Materials Availability in Small Libraries: A Survey Handbook.* Urbana, University of Illinois Graduate School of Library and Information Science, 1981. 55p. An easy, inexpensive method.

Williams, Edwin E. "Surveying Library Collections." In *Library Surveys*, edited by Maurice F. Tauber and Irlene R. Stephens, pp. 23–45. New York, Columbia University Press, 1967. Reviews types, purposes, and methods.

Zweizig, Douglas L. and E. J. Rodger. *Output Measures for Public Libraries: A Manual of Standardized Procedures.* Chicago, American Library Association, 1982. 92p.

CHAPTER 14

WEEDING, STORAGE, AND PRESERVATION

Building library collections, the activist title of this volume, certainly implies addition to library resources; yet, effectiveness may sometimes require the very opposite: withdrawal of materials from the collections. The analogy suggested by the term commonly applied to this activity, "weeding," is apt in that a garden can hardly attain goals of beauty and elegance without removal as a counterpart to planting and nurturing. Similar analogies to wardrobes, rusted automobiles, and obsolescent implements are so obvious as to need no elaboration. Limited space, its efficient utilization, and the high cost of its enlargement form a practical bedrock in considerations of collection size, but these factors should not be absolute determinants. Few statements of a library's mission would include the goal of fitting within a given space.

The mission of the library is, of course, the basic framework for weeding decisions, and the formal collection development policy which follows upon that mission statement should provide guidelines for deselection as well as selection. Quite apart from limitations of space, positive elements in the library's framework of purpose will justify weeding for reasons of accuracy in informational materials and general collection characteristics conducive to inspiring use.

All weeding decisions need not lead to harsh banishment, however. Temporary removal for physical repairs, rebinding, replacement with a later edition or more contemporary substitute, conversion to microformat, transfer from active collection to storage, or reassignment to a more appropriate network partner are all possible variants. Procrastination in this realm has for so long been a presumed trait of librarians that exhortations to weed are not infrequently put forth as moral imperatives. Yet, the librarian's natural hesitation to discard is often rooted in sound concern; the book not owned is a greater loss to some potential user than is one book too many. The research library will rarely weed, aware that what seems superfluous today may contain the essence of our times for the researcher of tomorrow. And even the smallest library will find room in its statement of purpose for providing access to more than just books which pass the test of current popularity. A mistaken notion that periodicals are of value only for their timeliness has often led to the thoughtless destruction of irreplaceable runs of journal back issues which, if retained, might well have added considerable enrichment to the library's resources. The easy prominence of circulation statistics as the overriding test of utility has led to the premature demise of works ahead of their times, of volumes whose in-library use escaped measurement, of timeless writing on topics only temporarily out of fashion, and of many titles which seemed little used but which cumulatively might have lent considerable strength to the collections. All of which is intended, here, not to augment the stable of excuses for not weeding but to suggest that a plan for weeding needs to be as thoughtfully developed as a plan for selection.

Organization of Weeding

How weeding is planned and conducted depends on the library in question—on the characteristics of its users, its objectives, its physical facilities and staff, and the age and type of collection it holds. Any cooperative agreements entered into by the library will probably affect weeding. The ideal library will have as comprehensive a plan for weeding the collection as for selecting new materials, and both aspects of collection development will be coordinated. Any thorough written policy for collection development should include a section on weeding.

Weeding should be a regular and continuing process. There are many arrangements which could accomplish this end. It might be desirable to allot one week of the year as the time for considering some part of the collection, with the librarian or librarians responsible for that part of the collection studying that group of books for those titles which have outlived their usefulness. It might be possible for the selectors to consider each new title in relation to the possibility of discarding one already on the shelves. If the new title really supersedes an older one, the older material might be withdrawn upon receipt of the newer. In some libraries, inventory time is used to identify titles for consideration for discard.

Library materials may be weeded because of their content

(dated or no longer of interest, but not simply because their views are out of favor), their physical condition (scratched, torn, generally ragged), their use patterns (declining or nonexistent), or a combination of these features. Research libraries will usually weed in order to discard only on the basis of physical condition, but will weed materials in order to send them to storage primarily because of low use. Popular or working collections may apply each of the three criteria.

In a general, non-research collection—school, public, small academic—there are certain categories of books which are the most obvious candidates for weeding. First, there are the duplicates of titles, purchased when the book was in heavier demand and now no longer needed. Ten or fifty or one hundred copies might be reduced to two or three. Superseded editions of books might well be eliminated, if the library is not attempting a historical collection of all the editions of a given title. Books that show signs of wear, books which have become dirty, shabby, or just plain worn out, might be replaced if their content is still significant. This might be the time to get rid of the mistakes in selection—books which were judged to be of interest and use but which turned out to be shelf-sitters. Books which have become obsolete in content, style, or theme should be eliminated by the library which aims at building a vital, useful collection. It is not always difficult to discover books which are now out-of-date. A medium-sized public library, discovering that the only work it has on the economic and political conditions of the Middle East is one published in 1950, might justifiably conclude that this book would not give its readers up-to-date information.

Let the distinction, however, be recalled again: there is a difference between a research collection and a working collection even in a public library. In the large public libraries, there may be extensive research collections; in the smaller, there may be special collections which are gathered for their historical importance, as, for example, collections on local history. One ought not to give much emphasis to currency when looking hard and long at the local history collection. It is unhappily true that some basic collections have been hit hard by a librarian too intent on getting rid of everything which had not circulated in the past three years, or which had been published more than ten years ago. To seize one of these injunctions and apply it blindly is as futile as seizing and blindly applying a principle of book selection.

Weeding of individual titles is not done in grand isolation, setting each book face-to-face with some weeding principle.

There are many factors which must figure in the decision: relation of the book to other books on the same subject; money available for more satisfactory titles (if this is all one can afford, it may be better to act on the principle that something is better than nothing at all); consideration of the degree to which the library wants to represent older material; possible usefulness of the particular title to some special group or individual in the community—the list could be extended at length.

Weeding requires judgment, as did the original selection of a title; weeding in a particular library requires judgment based on factors which can be known only to the librarian of that particular library. The general injunctions for weeding, like the general injunctions for selecting, must be interpreted and adapted by the type of librarian doing the job. In a small, working collection, the following suggestions for weeding might be useful. No one should seize upon these suggestions as an infallible formula: it is imperative that the librarian recognize them as suggestions and not laws.

General Reference Works: Bibliographies and encyclopedias are of little use after ten years, though exceptions may be made in specific instances such as the famous *Britannica* Eleventh Edition. Almanacs and yearbooks may be discarded when they are superseded.

Religion and Philosophy: Retain systems of philosophy, but discard historical and explanatory texts when superseded, older theology, old commentaries on the Bible, sectarian literature, sermons, and books on the conduct of life, popular self-help psychology, and other guides to living which are old or no longer popular. Be sure to take into account the use made of such materials, which will vary greatly from one library to another.

Social Sciences: Requires frequent revision, because much of the material will deal with problems of temporary interest, which can be replaced later by historical coverage of these topics. Economics, investments, taxation, etc. need careful watching. Historical works on economics, political science, education, transportation, etc. should be kept if there is demand. Generally, keep basic materials on customs and folklore; be guided by use.

Language: Discard old grammars, ordinary school dictionaries (rarely discard the larger dictionaries). Weed the rest of the collection on the basis of use.

Pure Science: Discard books with obsolete information or theories; all general works which have been superseded, unless they are classics in their field. All ordinary textbooks can usually be discarded after ten years, and some libraries discard after five. Botany and natural history should be inspected carefully before discarding. Astronomy dates rapidly.

Applied Science: Try to keep this section up-to-date by discarding older material. Five to ten years will date much of the material in such fields as medicine, computers, radio, television, and business. For home economics, cookbooks, gardening, and some materials on crafts, etc., watch the use patterns.

Art, Music, Hobbies, Etc.: Discard sparingly in the fine arts. Keep collections of music, engravings, fine illustrated books.

Literature: Keep literary history, unless it is superseded by a better title; keep collected works unless definitely superseded; discard poets and dramatists no longer regarded in literary histories and no longer read; discard the works of minor novelists whose works have not been re-issued and who are no longer of interest to readers.

History: Discard much contemporary writing which is now recorded in basic histories (as World War II memoirs), historical works which are only summaries and are not authoritative, and works of travel over ten years old, unless distinguished by style or the importance of the author. Keep histories which have become literary classics. Keep anything related to local or regional history.

Biography: Keep collected biography, but individual lives of persons whose importance is no longer great may be discarded when demand declines. Keep anything that may be useful for local history.

The size of some collections makes it impractical to consider individual titles for weeding; consequently, much effort has been spent on trying to devise weeding and storage decision rules for groups of materials. Among the predictors of future use which have been tested in libraries are the language in which the book or journal was published; the amount of time which has elapsed since it was published; the number of times it has been used (not necessarily measured by the number of times it has circulated outside the library) since the library acquired it; and the amount of time it spends on the shelf between uses. No single criterion has been successful in predicting use for all kinds of materials and all subjects, but many librarians favor some measure of past use as the best way to predict future use for books and date of publication as an easy and relatively effective way to weed periodicals. The basic problem is to predict the point at which the cost (in shelf space, staff, costs, and user frustration) of putting into and retrieving from storage a group of titles will fall below the cost of leaving them in the active collection.

Storage

Once little-used materials have been identified and withdrawn from the active collection, decisions must be made about how to dispose of them. Some may be destroyed; some may be stored. Some librarians put such materials into compact storage areas in the main library building; some send them to storage areas, possibly compact, in facilities separate from any of the library buildings used regularly by the public. The kind of storage used probably will depend on the money the library has available to invest in storage facilities, the probable costs of moving materials back and forth, the kinds of changes which may have to be made on library records to show the location of the material, and estimates of how much users will be inconvenienced by the various kinds of storage.

In addition to storage planned by an individual library or library system, there is also the possibility of joining with other libraries in cooperative storage arrangements. In this case, the costs of maintaining the storage area may be shared and the little-used materials in each library can be available to users of any of the other libraries. Cooperative storage is often an integral part of cooperative acquisitions projects. Libraries accepting responsibility for collecting heavily on particular subjects may also agree to store what other cooperating libraries discard on those subjects. Even if storage is not a formal part of a cooperative plan, any cooperative acquisitions efforts of a library will probably have some effect on its weeding and storage program.

Preservation and Replacement

Discussion of preservation and replacement follows naturally after a discussion of weeding, because one of the reasons for weeding a collection is to identify the materials that are in poor physical condition. When an important, often-used item is found to be in such condition that it cannot be used either with pleasure to the borrower or without further damage to the item in question, preservation or replacement enter the picture. These appear to be the two alternatives. The item may simply be replaced—either with a new copy (if it is still available from the producer or publisher) or with a reproduction (done locally or commercially). The reproduction may not be in exactly the same format—a hardcover book may be put on microfilm, for example, or a phonodisc on audiocassette (if the copyright holder does not object)—but the content will be essentially the same. The other way to treat any library holding which is in poor physical condition is to preserve it in its original form. This is a costly alternative, but may be the only possibility in the case of rare and unique materials which are valued for physical, as well as intellectual, properties.

The extent to which a library must be concerned with preservation or replacement depends on the nature, age, and use of the collection. Some small, general collections, such as a branch of a public library system, might find that replacement, or even discarding without replacement, is the answer to all questions about worn books, torn journals, or scratched slides. However, most libraries have some materials—college archives or local history, for example—which are really intended to be kept indefinitely for research purposes. These are the materials that demand the most attention.

American librarians of the twentieth century have tended to emphasize the use of library materials rather than their preservation, but in recent years many have recognized that preservation and use are interrelated. All library materials will deteriorate in time, but the conditions of modern book manufacturing and our general environment are causing the rate of deterioration to be considerably faster than in the past. Materials must now be actively preserved in order to be available for use.

Books and other materials suffer damage or deterioration because of several groups of factors, some inherent in the materials and others susceptible to control by the library. Library holdings may begin to deteriorate because of the organic materials from which they are made. Each type of material—paper, glue, plastic, etc.—that goes into the manufacture of a book, recording, or film has its own combination of physical and chemical properties and will present different preservation problems. The most obvious example of an internal preservation problem is the condition of the paper used in books. Books published three hundred years ago when paper was made from linen fiber are in better condition than those printed in the last twenty or thirty years made with paper using wood pulp. The materials used in manufacture are generally beyond the control of the librarian.

However, another group of factors influencing physical condition of library materials is external to the materials and is often within the library's control. These factors include all of the conditions surrounding the processing, storage, and use of the materials. For example, the levels of heat and humidity and the kind of lighting used in the area where materials are shelved and used can affect the rate of deterioration. Books stored in cool, dry, dark areas generally have a much longer life span than those housed in hot, humid, brightly-lighted areas. Constant levels of temperature and humidity are less harmful than fluctuating levels. The kinds of shelves or storage cabinets used, the ways materials are placed in those shelves or cabinets, the kinds of book return facilities provided, and even the procedures used by staff members responsible for processing and shelving materials are environmental factors which help determine the rate of deterioration of library materials.

Damage also comes from the users of library materials. Heavily-used items will eventually suffer damage even if users are careful, but any item may be ruined by one circulation to a careless user. No type of material which circulates is safe from possible destruction. Books which are tossed around, dropped in a puddle, or gnawed by the dog are as lost to the collection as are audiovisual materials which are handled carelessly or used on improper equipment. The effects of users on the physical condition of collections are generally beyond the control of librarians, but many libraries make attempts to educate their users in the problems and remedies.

Another group of preservation problems facing those responsible for collection maintenance includes the unpredictable and most uncontrollable emergencies and disasters which may strike a library. Fires, floods, storms, or even broken pipes within the building may lead to very extensive collection damage, especially from water. Again, these are generally beyond the control of the librarian, but it is possible to develop emergency plans for handling the collection and, in the case of fires, for preventing the disaster.

Organization for Preservation

While it is obvious that some aspects of collection deterioration cannot be controlled by librarians, an organized approach to preservation can accomplish much more than random, spur-of-the-moment reactions to individual situations. There are certain basic decisions which should be made in advance of emergencies, and priorities which should be set.

One of the first questions to be answered in a library which proposes to organize an attack on its preservation problems is the question of responsibility. Who is to have primary responsibility for preservation decisions? In recent years some large research libraries have appointed preservation officers to direct the whole effort. Smaller libraries cannot afford such a full-time staff member, but it is still possible for an interested and knowledgeable librarian to be assigned the responsibility on a part-time basis. Some experts contend that the person charged with selection should also make the preservation decisions, since so many of the criteria are the same in both situations.

Related to the question of who should decide whether and how to preserve an item is the question of when the decision should be made. Again, some experts believe that some preservation decisions should be made at the time the selection decision is made. Presumably, the selector has some idea about how the selection will be used and how permanent a part of the collection the new acquisition should be. If the material probably will not survive very long in its original format, should it be purchased in that format? If the answer is yes, then what can be done to protect it before it is ever used by the public?

Once a library begins to think seriously about preservation problems, it will probably find that a written record of policies and procedures is necessary. In considering its plan for preservation, a library needs to know a number of things which are related in one way or another to its overall collection development plan. What kinds of materials are in the collection? How are they used? Are any of the materials unique? Are they used by researchers from other cities and institutions? What is the present physical condition of the collection? Are some parts of it more worn and battered than others? If funds for preservation efforts are limited, as they doubtless will be, which part of the collection will receive attention first? How much will the library rely on replacement or reproduction as opposed to preservation of the original? Answers to many of these questions—which are only examples of the points to be considered in planning—depend on the original assessment of how the information (whatever its form) being added to the collection will be used. The type of information and its possible uses determine to a great extent the acceptable format in which it may be packaged.

Another aspect of organization for preservation of the collection involves the efforts which may be undertaken to inform the library's community of the problem and the possible solutions. Staff cooperation is essential and the cooperation of the public is highly desirable. In addition to informing everyone of ways in which staff and public can routinely assist the preservation effort, a comprehensive plan ought to include a disaster policy. If a major catastrophe strikes the library, which actions will be taken first and who will take them? Those librarians who have been through fires, floods, or other natural disasters recommend assigning responsibilities well before the event.

In small libraries a comprehensive, written preservation policy may seem unnecessary, but in any size or type of library there are certain basic things which may be done to prolong the useful life of the materials. Although it may be difficult to do, any library can at least try to keep temperature and relative humidity constant and the air in shelving and storage areas as clear as possible. Using ultraviolet filters on windows and lights will help. Shelvers can be taught to shelve materials properly, avoiding packing shelves too tightly or placing books with fore-edges down. When processing new materials, librarians should be careful about their use of tape or paper clips or other supplies which might react harmfully with the materials being added to the collection. Some potential physical problems can be identified and corrected before materials begin to circulate; others can be corrected quickly after they occur, so that they do not become major. The important thing is to be aware of the need to preserve the library's collection and to set up routine procedures which will at least not interfere with the achievement of that goal.

Cooperation in Preservation

Because the volume of library materials which are deteriorating is great, the diversity of materials and methods for preserving them is wide, and the resources to do the job are costly, some libraries are turning to cooperative arrangements for preservation. This is really a natural extension of cooperative acquisition and storage programs.

Some groups of libraries already cooperate in the microfilming of back files of journals and others are investigating the systematic microfilming or other reproduction of deteriorating monographs. In some cases, efforts are made by a group of libraries to identify the best original copy of certain important works so that the best copy may be placed on restricted circulation or otherwise preserved for future availability. In recent years a few regional restoration centers have been established—centers which have the expensive equipment and expert staff needed to carry out high quality repair and restoration.

The need for action on a wider front than the individual library is being demonstrated by the Library of Congress in its developing plans for a national preservation program, consisting of three major aspects: the preservation of the intellectual content (on film or videodisc) of materials that do not need to be preserved in their original format; the preservation in original format of materials identified as rare and valuable in themselves; and the preservation (possibly by special storage or microfilming) of present and future publications which are printed on paper with a life-expectancy of fifty years or less. In support of these goals the Library of Congress has pioneered in experiments with mass deacidification and optical disc storage, which are being eagerly watched by the entire library world.

The third aspect of the Library of Congress's preservation plan illustrates why preservation of library collections is an appropriate topic with which to conclude a book on building library collections. For reasons previously discussed, and highlighted again in the Library of Congress plan, many materials added to library collections have started to deteriorate by the time they are acquired. The librarian who wants to build an effective collection must be aware of the physical properties of the materials selected, as well as their potential use, and must be prepared to take the necessary steps to ensure that the intellectual content of the collection will be available when needed.

Bibliography

Weeding

Andrews, Theodora A. "The Role of Departmental Libraries in Operations Research Studies in a University Library—Part I: Selection for Storage Problems." *Special Libraries*, 59:519–524, September 1968. Considers fraction of collection to be stored and criteria for selecting the materials.

Asai, Isao. "Adjusted Age Distribution and Its Implication to Impact Factor and Immediacy Index." *American Society for Information Science Journal*, 32:172–174.

Basart, Ann. "Criteria for Weeding Books in a University Music Library." *Music Library Association Notes*, 36:819–836, June 1980.

Bourne, Charles P. and Dorothy Gregor. "Planning Serials Cancellations and Cooperative Collection Development in the Health Sciences: Methodology and Background Information." *Medical Library Association Bulletin*, 63:366–377, October 1975. Offers five decision rules.

Brookes, B. C. "Growth, Utility and Obsolescence of Scientific Periodical Literature." *Journal of Documentation*, 26:283–294, December 1970. Specific groups of users must be considered when rating obsolescence of scientific literature.

Brookes, B. C. "Obsolescence of Special Library Periodicals." *Journal of the American Society for Information Science*, 21:320–329, September 1970. Suggests models to use in determining weeding policy.

Buckland, Michael K. "Are Obsolescence and Scattering Related?" *Journal of Documentation*, 28:242–246, September 1972.

Buckland, Michael K. *Book Availability and the Library User*. New York, Pergamon, 1975. 196p. Considers questions related to weeding, duplication, etc.

Chen, Ching-Chih. *Applications of Operations Research Models to Libraries: A Case Study of the Use of Monographs in the Francis A. Countway Library of Medicine, Harvard University*. Cambridge, Mass., MIT Press, 1976. 212p. Includes implications for weeding and duplication.

Conger, Lucinda D. "Annex Library of Princeton University: The Development of a Compact Storage Library." *College and Research Libraries*, 31:160–168, May 1970.

Cooper, Marianne. "Criteria for Weeding of Collections." *Library Resources and Technical Services*, 12:339–351, Summer 1968. Developed at the Chemistry Library of Columbia University.

Crush, Marion. "Deselection Policy: How to Exclude Everything." *Wilson Library Bulletin*, 45:180–181, October 1970. Effect of typical selection criteria on popular books.

Durey, Peter. "Weeding Serials Subscriptions in a University Library." *Collection Management*, 1:91–94, Fall–Winter 1976–77. Experiences at the University of Auckland Library.

Erlich, Martin. "Pruning the Groves of Libraro." *Wilson Library Bulletin*, 50:55–58, September 1975. Experiences of a public librarian; lists retention criteria.

Farber, Evan Ira. "Limiting College Library Growth: Bane or Boom?" *Journal of Academic Librarianship*, 1:12–15, November 1975. Emphasizes differences between needs of college libraries and university libraries.

Fussler, Herman H. and Julian L. Simon. *Patterns in the Use of Books in Large Research Libraries*. Chicago, University of Chicago Press, 1969. 210p. Several possible predictors of use were tested against actual recorded use.

Goldstein, Cynthia H. "Study of Weeding Practices in Eleven TALON Resource Libraries." *Medical Library Association Bulletin*, 69:311–316, July 1981. Covers libraries in Texas, Arkansas, Oklahoma, and New Mexico.

Gore, Daniel, ed. *Farewell to Alexandria; Solutions to Space, Growth, and Performance Problems of Libraries*. Westport, Conn., Greenwood Press, 1976. Collection of ten papers presented at a 1975 conference; most discuss academic libraries.

Griffith, Belver C. "Aging Scientific Literature: A Citation Analysis." *Journal of Documentation*, 35:179–196, September 1979. Discussion in 36:164–167, June 1980.

Grundt, Leonard. "Nassau Community College Library Weeding Policy." *Unabashed Librarian*, 16:12, Summer 1975. Reprints policy adopted in May 1975.

Holland, Maurita P. "Serial Cuts vs. Public Service: A Formula." *College and Research Libraries*, 37:543–548, November 1976. Describes project at the University of Michigan Engineering-Transportation Library.

Kantor, Paul B. "On the Stability of Distribution by Trueswell." *College and Research Libraries*, 41:514–516, November 1980. A formula for weeding.

Lancaster, F. W. *The Measurement and Evaluation of Library Services*. Arlington, Virginia, Information Resources Press, 1977. 395p. Chapter 5 on "Evaluation of the Collection" also includes weeding and storage.

Lane, Alfred H. *Gifts and Exchange*. Westport, Conn., Greenwood Press, 1980. 121p. Contains chapter on "Disposition of Unwanted Materials."

Lawrence, Gary S. "Cost Model for Storage and Weeding Program." *College and Research Libraries*, 42:139–147, March 1981.

Line, Maurice B. "Half-Life of Periodical Literature: Apparent and Real Obsolescence." *Journal of Documentation*, 26:46–54, March 1970. Suggests ways to determine useful life of periodicals in various subjects.

Line, Maurice B. and A. Sandison. "Obsolescence and Changes in the Use of Literature with Time." *Journal of Documentation*, 30:283–350, September 1974. Literature review with 179 citations.

MacDonald, Mary Beth. "Weeding the Collection." *Unabashed Librarian*, 16:7–8, Summer 1975. Brief, practical suggestions for weeding.

McGaw, Howard F. "Policies and Practices in Discarding." *Library Trends*, 4:269–282, January 1956. Advantages, disadvantages, and traditional criteria.

McGrath, W. E. "Correlating the Subjects of Books Taken Out of and Books Used within an Open-Stack Library." *College and Research Libraries*, 32:280–285, July 1971. Results show a significant correlation.

McGrath, W. E. "Predicting Book Circulation by Subject in a University Library." *Collection Management*, 1:7–26, Fall–Winter 1976–77. Attempts to identify variables in a university environment which best predict use of books.

McKee, Penelope. "Weeding the Forest Hill Branch of Toronto Public Library by the Slote Method: A Test Case." *Library Research*, 3:283–301, Fall 1981.

Maxim, Jacqueline A. "Weeding Journals with Informal Use Statistics." *De-Acquisition Librarian*, 1:9–11, Summer 1976.

Model, Peter. "Books at Auction: The Art of Deaccessioning." *Wilson Library Bulletin*, 56:33–38, September 1981.

Morse, Philip M. "Demand for Library Materials: An Exercise in Probability Analysis." *Collection Management*, 1:47–78, Fall–Winter 1976–77. Includes consideration of effects of duplication.

Perkins, David. "Periodicals Weeding, or Weed It and Reap." *California Librarian*, 38:32–37, April 1977. Describes cancellation project at California State University at Northridge.

Rice, Barbara A. "Weeding in Academic and Research Libraries: An Annotated Bibliography." *Collection Management*, 2:65–71, Spring 1978.

Rush, Betty. "Weeding vs. Censorship: Treading a Fine Line." *Library Journal*, 99:3032–3033, November 15, 1974. Weeding of children's collections.

Sandison, A. "Use of Older Literature and Its Obsolescence." *Journal of Docu-*

mentation, 27:184–199, September 1971. Argues that age is not the best criterion for weeding.

Slote, Stanley J. *Weeding Library Collections.* 2d ed. rev. Littleton, Colo., Libraries Unlimited, 1982. 198p.

Stam, David H. " 'Prove All Things: Hold Fast That Which Is Good': Deaccessioning and Research Libraries." *College and Research Libraries*, 43:5–13, January 1982. A wise and witty view.

Taylor, Colin R. "A Practical Solution to Weeding University Library Periodical Collections." *Collection Management*, 1:27–45, Fall–Winter 1976–77. Project conducted at Newcastle University Library.

Traister, Daniel. "Goodbye to All That: A Case Study in Deaccessioning." *Wilson Library Bulletin*, 56:663–668, May 1982.

Trueswell, Richard W. "Determining the Optimum Number of Volumes for a Library's Core Collection." *Libri*, 16:49–60, 1969. Uses last recorded circulation date as indicator of use pattern.

Trueswell, Richard W. "User Circulation Satisfaction vs. Size of Holdings at Three Academic Libraries." *College and Research Libraries*, 30:204–213, May 1969. Uses last circulation date to indicate "core" collection.

Turner, Stephen J. "Trueswell's Weeding Technique: The Facts." *College and Research Libraries*, 41:134–138, March 1980. Correcting critics' mistakes.

Voth, Sally and Mark E. Lipp. "Weeding of a Library Reserve Book Section: A Description of the Kansas State University Library System Using Floppy Diskettes." *Collection Management*, 1:78–89, Fall–Winter 1976–77.

"Zero Growth: When Is NOT-Enough Enough? A Symposium." *Journal of Academic Librarianship*, 1·4–11, November 1975. Short comments by nine individuals.

Preservation and Storage

Banks, Paul N. *Selective Bibliography on the Conservation of Research Library Materials*, Chicago, Newberry Library, 1981. 200p.

Cunha, George M. and Dorothy Grant Cunha. *Conservation of Library Materials: A Manual and Bibliography on the Care, Repair and Restoration of Library Materials.* 2d ed. Metuchen, N.J., Scarecrow Press, 1971–72. 2v. First volume discusses materials, causes of damages, and prevention and repair. Second volume is a comprehensive bibliography.

Cunha, George M. and Dorothy Grant Cunha. *Library and Archives Conservation: 1980's and Beyond.* Metuchen, N.J., Scarecrow Press, 1983. 2v.

Darling, Pamela W. "Developing a Preservation Microfilming Program." *Library Journal*, 99:2803–2809, November 1, 1974. Administrative and procedural considerations.

Darling, Pamela W. "A Local Preservation Program: Where to Start." *Library Journal*, 101:2343–2347, November 15, 1976. Thorough discussion of points to consider in developing a plan.

Darling, Pamela W. "Microforms in Libraries: Preservation and Storage." *Microform Review*, 5:93–100, April 1976. Considers use of microforms as a way of preserving content of deteriorating books and journals.

Darling, Pamela W. "Will Anything Be Left? New Responses to the Preservation Challenge." *Wilson Library Bulletin,* 56:177–181, November 1981.

Dean, John. "Conservation Officers: The Administrative Role." *Wilson Library Bulletin,* 57:128–132, October 1982. Makes the point that the conservation officer must occupy a central and powerful position within the administrative structure.

Dean, John. "The Role of the Bookbinder in Preservation." *Wilson Library Bulletin,* 56:182–186, November 1981.

Ellison, John W. "Storage and Conservation of Microforms." *Microform Review,* 10:90–93, Spring 1981.

Fortson-James, Judith. "Fire Protection for Libraries." *Catholic Library World,* 53:211–213, December 1981.

Gupta, S. M. and A. Ravindran. "Optimal Storage of Books by Size: An Operations Research Approach." *Journal of the American Society for Information Science,* 25:354–357, November 1974.

Hanson, Gretchen M. *Paper Preservation Within the Academic Libraries of the Utah College Library Council.* Provo, Utah, Brigham Young University, 1983. 43p.

Harrar, H. Joanne. "Cooperative Storage Warehouses." *College and Research Libraries,* 25:37–43, January 1964. Describes New England Deposit Library, Hampshire Inter-Library Center, and Midwest Inter-Library Center.

Harrar, H. Joanne. "Cooperative Storage." *Library Trends,* 19:318–328, January 1971.

Henderson, Kathryn Luther and William T. Henderson. *Conserving and Preserving Library Materials.* Champaign, Ill., University of Illinois Graduate School of Library and Information Science, 1983. 207p. An Allerton Park Conference proceedings.

Horton, Carolyn. *Cleaning and Preserving Bindings and Related Materials.* 2d ed. rev. Chicago, Library Technology Project, American Library Association, 1969. 87p.

Kathpalia, Yash Pal. *Conservation and Restoration of Archive Materials.* Paris, Unesco, 1973. 231p.

Leimkuhler, Ferdinand F. and Michael D. Cooper. "Analytical Models for Library Planning." *Journal of the American Society for Information Science,* 22:390–398, November 1971. Operations vs. model; considers effects of collection growth on storage.

Martin, John H. "Resuscitating a Water-Logged Library." *Wilson Library Bulletin,* 50:233–241, November 1975. Advice on what to do after a flood.

Morris, John. *Managing the Library Fire Risk.* 2d ed. rev. Berkeley, University of California Risk Management, 1979.

Nelson, Milo. "Evening the Odds: The Northeast Document Conservation Center." *Wilson Library Bulletin,* 56:187–191, November 1981. Experts at work saving valuable resources.

Preservation Conditions, Practices, and Needs in the General Libraries: A Report by the Preservation Committee. Austin, University of Texas, General Libraries, 1981. 153p. ED 214 503. Specific considerations for the University of Texas libraries.

Stayner, Richard A. "Economic Characteristics of the Library Storage Problem." *Library Quarterly,* 53:313–327, July 1983. A model offering an economically rational basis for determining the role of several alternative storage methods.

Swartzburg, Susan G. *Preserving Library Materials: a Manual.* Metuchen, N.J., Scarecrow Press, 1980. 293p.

Waters, Peter. *Procedures for Salvage of Water-Damaged Library Materials.* Washington, D. C., Library of Congress, 1975. 30p.

Williams, Edwin Everitt. "Book-Preservation Problem As Seen at Harvard." *Harvard Library Bulletin,* 29:420–444, October 1981.

Young, Laura S. *Bookbinding and Conservation by Hand: A Working Guide.* New York, Bowker, 1981. 275p.

APPENDICES

𝕷𝖎𝖇𝖗𝖆𝖗𝖞 𝕭𝖎𝖑𝖑 𝖔𝖋 𝕽𝖎𝖌𝖍𝖙𝖘

The American Library Association affirms that all libraries are forums for information and ideas, and that the following basic policies should guide their services.

1. Books and other library resources should be provided for the interest, information, and enlightenment of all people of the community the library serves. Materials should not be excluded because of the origin, background, or views of those contributing to their creation.

2. Libraries should provide materials and information presenting all points of view on current and historical issues. Materials should not be proscribed or removed because of partisan or doctrinal disapproval.

3. Libraries should challenge censorship in the fulfillment of their responsibility to provide information and enlightenment.

4. Libraries should cooperate with all persons and groups concerned with resisting abridgment of free expression and free access to ideas.

5. A person's right to use a library should not be denied or abridged because of origin, age, background, or views.

6. Libraries which make exhibit spaces and meeting rooms available to the public they serve should make such facilities available on an equitable basis, regardless of the beliefs or affiliations of individuals or groups requesting their use.

Adopted June 18, 1948.
Amended February 2, 1961, June 27, 1967, and January 23, 1980,
by the ALA Council.

The Freedom to Read

The freedom to read is essential to our democracy. It is continuously under attack. Private groups and public authorities in various parts of the country are working to remove books from sale, to censor textbooks, to label "controversial" books, to distribute lists of "objectionable" books or authors, and to purge libraries. These actions apparently rise from a view that our national tradition of free expression is no longer valid; that censorship and suppression are needed to avoid the subversion of politics and the corruption of morals. We, as citizens devoted to the use of books and as librarians and publishers responsible for disseminating them, wish to assert the public interest in the preservation of the freedom to read.

We are deeply concerned about these attempts at suppression. Most such attempts rest on a denial of the fundamental premise of democracy: that the ordinary citizen, by exercising his critical judgment, will accept the good and reject the bad. The censors, public and private, assume that they should determine what is good and what is bad for their fellow-citizens.

We trust Americans to recognize propaganda, and to reject it. We do not believe they need the help of censors to assist them in this task. We do not believe they are prepared to sacrifice their heritage of a free press in order to be "protected" against what others think may be bad for them. We believe they still favor free enterprise in ideas and expression.

We are aware, of course, that books are not alone in being subjected to efforts at suppression. We are aware that these efforts are related to a larger pattern of pressures being brought against education, the press, films, radio and television. The problem is not only one of actual censorship. The shadow of fear cast by these pressures leads, we suspect, to an even larger voluntary curtailment of expression by those who seek to avoid controversy.

Such pressure toward conformity is perhaps natural to a time of uneasy change and pervading fear. Especially when so many of our apprehensions are directed against an ideology, the expression of a dissident idea becomes a thing feared in itself, and we tend to move against it as against a hostile deed, with suppression.

And yet suppression is never more dangerous than in such a time of social tension. Freedom has given the United States the elasticity to endure strain. Freedom keeps open the path of novel and creative solutions, and enables change to come by choice. Every silencing of a heresy, every enforcement of an orthodoxy, diminishes the toughness and resilience of our society and leaves it the less able to deal with stress.

Now as always in our history, books are among our greatest instruments of freedom. They are almost the only means for making generally available ideas or manners of expression that can initially command only a small audience. They are the natural medium for the new idea and the untried voice from which come the original contributions to social growth. They are essential to the extended discussion which serious thought requires, and to the accumulation of knowledge and ideas into organized collections.

We believe that free communication is essential to the preservation of a free society and a creative culture. We believe that these pressures towards confor-

Appendices

mity present the danger of limiting the range and variety of inquiry and expression on which our democracy and our culture depend. We believe that every American community must jealously guard the freedom to publish and to circulate, in order to preserve its own freedom to read. We believe that publishers and librarians have a profound responsibility to give validity to that freedom to read by making it possible for the readers to choose freely from a variety of offerings.

The freedom to read is guaranteed by the Constitution. Those with faith in free men will stand firm on these constitutional guarantees of essential rights and will exercise the responsibilities that accompany these rights.

We therefore affirm these propositions:

1. *It is in the public interest for publishers and librarians to make available the widest diversity of views and expressions, including those which are unorthodox or unpopular with the majority.*

Creative thought is by definition new, and what is new is different. The bearer of every new thought is a rebel until his idea is refined and tested. Totalitarian systems attempt to maintain themselves in power by the ruthless suppression of any concept which challenges the established orthodoxy. The power of a democratic system to adapt to change is vastly strengthened by the freedom of its citizens to choose widely from among conflicting opinions offered freely to them. To stifle every nonconformist idea at birth would mark the end of the democratic process. Furthermore, only through the constant activity of weighing and selecting can the democratic mind attain the strength demanded by times like these. We need to know not only what we believe but why we believe it.

2. *Publishers, librarians and booksellers do not need to endorse every idea or presentation contained in the books they make available. It would conflict with the public interest for them to establish their own political, moral or aesthetic views as a standard for determining what books should be published or circulated.*

Publishers and librarians serve the educational process by helping to make available knowledge and ideas required for the growth of the mind and the increase of learning. They do not foster education by imposing as mentors the patterns of their own thought. The people should have the freedom to read and consider a broader range of ideas than those that may be held by any single librarian or publisher or government or church. It is wrong that what one man can read should be confined to what another thinks proper.

3. *It is contrary to the public interest for publishers or librarians to determine the acceptability of a book on the basis of the personal history or political affiliations of the author.*

A book should be judged as a book. No art or literature can flourish if it is to be measured by the political views or private lives of its creators. No society of free men can flourish which draws up lists of writers to whom it will not listen, whatever they may have to say.

4. *There is no place in our society for efforts to coerce the taste of others, to confine adults to the reading matter deemed suitable for adolescents, or to inhibit the efforts of writers to achieve artistic expression.*

To some, much of modern literature is shocking. But is not much of life itself shocking? We cut off literature at the source if we prevent writers from dealing with the stuff of life. Parents and teachers have a responsibility to prepare the young to meet the diversity of experiences in life to which they will be exposed, as they have a responsibility to help them learn to think critically for themselves. These are affirmative responsibilities, not to be discharged simply by preventing them from reading works for which they are not yet prepared. In these matters taste differs, and taste cannot be legislated; nor can machinery be devised which will suit the demands of one group without limiting the freedom of others.

5. *It is not in the public interest to force a reader to accept with any book the prejudgment of a label characterizing the book or author as subversive or dangerous.*

The ideal of labeling presupposes the existence of individuals or groups with wisdom to determine by authority what is good or bad for the citizen. It presupposes that each individual must be directed in making up his mind about the ideas he examines. But Americans do not need others to do their thinking for them.

6. *It is the responsibility of publishers and librarians, as guardians of the people's freedom to read, to contest encroachments upon that freedom by individuals or groups seeking to impose their own standards or tastes upon the community at large.*

It is inevitable in the give and take of the democratic process that the political, the moral, or the aesthetic concepts of an individual or group will occasionally collide with those of another individual or group. In a free society each individual is free to determine for himself what he wishes to read, and each group is free to determine what it will recommend to its freely associated members. But no group has the right to take the law into its own hands, and to impose its own concept of politics or morality upon other members of a democratic society. Freedom is no freedom if it is accorded only to the accepted and the inoffensive.

7. *It is the responsibility of publishers and librarians to give full meaning to the freedom to read by providing books that enrich the quality and diversity of thought and expression. By the exercise of this affirmative responsibility, bookmen can demonstrate that the answer to a bad book is a good one, the answer to a bad idea is a good one.*

The freedom to read is of little consequence when expended on the trivial; it is frustrated when the reader cannot obtain matter fit for his purpose. What is needed is not only the absence of restraint, but the positive provision of opportunity for the people to read the best that has been thought and said. Books are the major channel by which the intellectual inheritance is handed down, and the principal means of its testing and growth. The defense of their freedom and integrity, and the enlargement of their service to society, requires of all bookmen the utmost of their faculties, and deserves of all citizens the fullest of their support.

We state these propositions neither lightly nor as easy generalizations. We here stake out a lofty claim for the value of books. We do so because we believe that they are good; possessed of enormous variety and usefulness, worthy of cherishing and keeping free. We realize that the application of these propositions may mean the dissemination of ideas and manners of expression that are repugnant to many persons. We do not state these propositions in the comfortable belief that what people read is unimportant. We believe rather that what people read is deeply important; that ideas can be dangerous; but that the suppression of ideas is fatal to a democratic society. Freedom itself is a dangerous way of life, but it is ours.

A Joint Statement by:

American Library Association
Association of American Publishers

Subsequently Endorsed by:

American Booksellers Association
American Civil Liberties Union
American Federation of Teachers AFL-CIO
Anti-Defamation League of B'nai B'rith
Association of American University Presses
Bureau of Independent Publishers & Distributors
Children's Book Council
Freedom of Information Center
Freedom to Read Foundation
Magazine Publishers Association
Motion Picture Association of America
National Association of College Stores
National Book Committee
National Council of Negro Women
National Council of Teachers of English
National Library Week Program
National Board of the Young Women's Christian Association of the U.S.A.
P.E.N.—American Center
Periodical and Book Association of America
Sex Information & Education Council of the U.S.
Women's National Book Association

This statement was originally issued in May of 1953 by the Westchester Conference of the American Library Association and the American Book Publishers Council, which in 1970 consolidated with the American Educational Publishers Institute to become the Association of American Publishers.

Freedom to View

The FREEDOM TO VIEW, along with the freedom to speak, to hear, and to read, is protected by the First Amendment to the Constitution of the United States. In a free society, there is no place for censorship of any medium of expression. Therefore, we affirm these principles:

1. It is in the public interest to provide the broadest possible access to films and other audiovisual materials because they have proven to be among the most effective means for the communication of ideas. Liberty of circulation is essential to insure the constitutional guarantee of freedom of expression.

2. It is in the public interest to provide for our audiences, films and other audiovisual materials which represent a diversity of views and expression. Selection of a work does not constitute or imply agreement with or approval of the content.

3. It is our professional responsibility to resist the constraint of labeling of prejudging a film on the basis of the moral, religious, or political beliefs of the producer or filmmaker or on the basis of controversial content.

4. It is our professional responsibility to contest vigorously, by all lawful means, every encroachment upon the public's freedom to view.

This statement was originally drafted by the Educational Film Library Association's Freedom to View Committee, and was adopted by the EFLA Board of Directors in February, 1979. It was endorsed by the American Library Association's Intellectual Freedom Committee and the ALA Council in June, 1979.

Libraries and educational institutions are encouraged to adopt this statement and to display it in their catalogs or libraries. The text of the statement may be reprinted freely; permission is granted to all educational institutions to use it.

INDEX